CHILTON'S
REPAIR & TUNE-UP GUIDE

MUSTANG COUGAR 1965-73

Covers all Mustang and Cougar models

SO-AQM-914

President, Chilton Enterprises	David S. Loewith
Senior Vice President	Ronald A. Hoxter
Publisher and Editor-In-Chief	Kerry A. Freeman, S.A.E.
Managing Editors	Peter M. Conti, Jr. □ W. Calvin Settle, Jr., S.A.E.
Assistant Managing Editor	Nick D'Andrea
Senior Editors	Debra Gaffney □ Ken Grabowski, A.S.E., S.A.E.
	Michael L. Grady □ Richard J. Rivele, S.A.E.
	Richard T. Smith □ Jim Taylor
	Ron Webb
Director of Manufacturing	Mike D'Imperio
Editor	Ron Webb

CHILTON BOOK COMPANY

*ONE OF THE DIVERSIFIED PUBLISHING COMPANIES,
A PART OF CAPITAL CITIES/ABC, INC.*

SAFETY NOTICE

Proper service and repair procedures are vital to the safe, reliable operation of all motor vehicles, as well as the personal safety of those performing repairs. This book outlines procedures for servicing and repairing vehicles using safe, effective methods. The procedures contain many NOTES, CAUTIONS and WARNINGS which should be followed along with standard safety procedures to eliminate the possibility of personal injury or improper service which could damage the vehicle or compromise its safety.

It is important to note that repair procedures and techniques, tools and parts for servicing motor vehicles, as well as the skill and experience of the individual performing the work vary widely. It is not possible to anticipate all of the conceivable ways or conditions under which vehicles may be serviced, or to provide cautions as to all of the possible hazards that may result. Standard and accepted safety precautions and equipment should be used when handling toxic or flammable fluids, and safety goggles or other protection should be used during cutting, grinding, chiseling, prying, or any other process that can cause material removal or projectiles.

Some procedures require the use of tools specially designed for a specific purpose. Before substituting another tool or procedure, you must be completely satisfied that neither your personal safety, nor the performance of the vehicle will be endangered.

Although information in this guide is based on industry sources and is as complete as possible at the time of publication, the possibility exists that the manufacturer made later changes which could not be included here. While striving for total accuracy, Chilton Book Company cannot assume responsibility for any errors, changes, or omissions that may occur in the compilation of this data.

PART NUMBERS

Part numbers listed in this reference are not recommendations by Chilton for any product by brand name. They are references that can be used with interchange manuals and aftermarket supplier catalogs to locate each brand supplier's discrete part number.

ACKNOWLEDGMENTS

The Chilton Book Company expresses its appreciation to the FORD MOTOR COMPANY for the technical information and pictures contained within this manual. Also, special thanks to Mr. Paul L. Sabold of NORRISTOWN FORD, INC., whose time and efforts as mechanic-advisor have helped to assure the technical accuracy and clarity of the information herein.

Manufactured in the United States of America
Sixteenth Printing, April 1994

Chilton's Repair & Tune-Up Guide: Mustang and Cougar 1965-73
ISBN 0-8019-7405-4 pbk.
Library of Congress Catalog Card No. 76-9506

CONTENTS

Quick Reference Specifications For Your Vehicle

Fill in this chart with the most commonly used specifications for your vehicle. Specifications can be found in Chapters 1 through 3 or on the tune-up decal under the hood of the vehicle.

 Tune-Up

Firing Order_____

Spark Plugs:

    Type_____

    Gap (in.)_____

Point Gap (in.)_____

Dwell Angle (°)_____

Ignition Timing (°)_____

    Vacuum (Connected/Disconnected)_____

Valve Clearance (in.)

    Intake_____   Exhaust_____

Capacities

Engine Oil (qts)

    With Filter Change_____

    Without Filter Change_____

Cooling System (qts)_____

Manual Transmission (pts)_____

    Type_____

Automatic Transmission (pts)_____

    Type_____

Front Differential (pts)_____

    Type_____

Rear Differential (pts)_____

    Type_____

Transfer Case (pts)_____

    Type_____

FREQUENTLY REPLACED PARTS

Use these spaces to record the part numbers of frequently replaced parts.

PCV VALVE

Manufacturer_____

Part No._____

OIL FILTER

Manufacturer_____

Part No._____

AIR FILTER

Manufacturer_____

Part No._____

General Information and Maintenance

HOW TO USE THIS BOOK

This book has been written to aid the car owner perform maintenance, tune-ups and repairs on his automobile. It is intended for both the novice and for those more familiar with auto repairs. Since this book contains information on both very simple and more involved operations, the user will not outgrow the book as he masters simple repairs and is ready to progress to more difficult operations.

Several things were assumed of you while the repair procedures were being written. They are mentioned here so that you will be aware of them. It was assumed that you own, or are willing to purchase, a basic set of hand tools and equipment. A skeletal listing of tools and equipment has been drawn up for you.

For many repair operations, the factory has suggested a special tool to perform the repairs. If it was at all possible, a conventional tool was substituted for the special tool in these cases. However, there are some operations which cannot be done without the use of these tools. To perform these jobs correctly, it will be necessary to order the tool through your local Ford dealer's parts department or procure through a tool supply dealer.

Two basic rules of automobile mechanics deserve mentioning here. Whenever the left-side of the car is referred to, it is meant to specify the driver's side. Likewise, the right-side of the car means the passenger's side. Also, most screws, nuts, and bolts are removed by turning counterclockwise and tightened by turning clockwise.

Before performing any repairs, read the entire section of the book that deals with that job. In many places a description of the system is provided. By reading this first, and then reading the entire repair procedure, you will understand the function of the system you will be working on and what will be involved in the repair operation, prior to starting the job. This will enable you to avoid problems and also to help you learn about your car while you are working on it.

While every effort was made to make the book as simple, yet as detailed as possible, there is no substitute for personal experience. You can gain the confidence and feel for mechanical things needed to make auto repairs only by doing them yourself. If you take your time and concentrate on what you are doing, you will be amazed at how fast you can learn.

TOOLS AND EQUIPMENT

Now that you have purchased this book and committed yourself to maintaining your car, a small set of basic tools and equipment will prove handy. The first group of items should be adequate for most maintenance and light repair procedures:

• Sliding T-bar handle or ratchet wrench;
• ⅜ in. drive socket wrench set (with breaker bar) (metric);
• Universal adapter for socket wrench set;
• Flat blade and phillips head screwdrivers;
• Pliers;
• Adjustable wrench;
• Locking pliers;
• Open-end wrench set (metric);
• Feeler gauge set;
• Oil filter strap wrench;
• Brake adjusting spoon;
• Drift pin;
• Torque wrench;
• Hammer.

Along with the above mentioned tools, the following equipment should be on hand;

• Scissors jack or hydraulic jack of sufficient capacity;
• Jackstands of sufficient capacity;
• Wheel blocks;
• Grease gun (hand-operated type);
• Drip pan (low and wide);
• Drop light;
• Tire pressure gauge;
• Penetrating oil (spray lubricant);
• Waterless hand cleaner.

In this age of emission controls and high priced gasoline, it is important to keep your car in proper tune. The following items, though they will represent an investment equal or greater to that of the first group, will tell you everything you might need to know about a car's state of tune:

• 12-volt test light;
• Compression gauge;
• Manifold vacuum gauge;
• Power timing light;
• Dwell-tachometer.

IDENTIFICATION

Vehicle

On the rear edge of the left door of all cars is a plate (or decal) stating the vehicle serial number and other coded information about the original equipment. The accompanying illustrations and charts show what this plate or decal looks like, and provide translations for the drive train coding.

Engines, Transmissions, and Differentials

Before 1968, all engines used in the cars bore the serial number on the top surface of

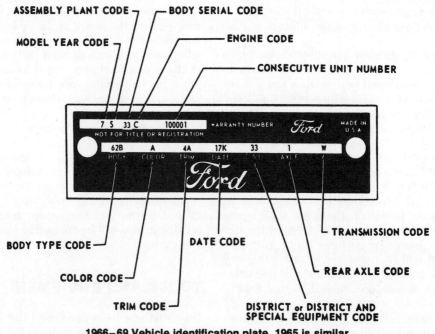

1966–69 Vehicle identification plate, 1965 is similar

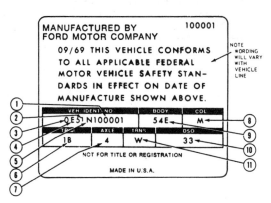

1. Consecutive unit no.
2. Body serial code
3. Model year code
4. Assembly plant code
5. Engine code
6. Trim code
7. Rear axle code
8. Color code
9. Body type code
10. District spec equip code
11. Transmission code

1970–73 Vehicle identification plate

the engine block, near the crankcase breather pipe, at the front left side of the engine. From 1968 to the present, this serial number has appeared on a tag which is usually mounted under the coil.

Standard placement for the identification on the transmission has usually been on a small plate which is riveted to the case, on the right side near the front.

Differentials have an identification tag which is affixed to the unit by one of the carrier retaining bolts.

TIRE PRESSURES

Recommended maximum tire pressures can usually be found on the side wall of the tire itself. Further information may be obtained from your owner's manual.

ROUTINE MAINTENANCE AND LUBRICATION

Manual Transmission Oil Check

The recommended maintenance interval for checking the lubricant level in manual transmissions is every six months or 6,000 miles (8 months or 8,000 miles—1973). The procedure for checking the level of lubricant is as follows:

Engine Codes

Model	1965	1966	1967	1968	1969	1970	1971	1972	1973
6 cylinder									
170 cu in.	U								
200 cu in.	T	T	T	T	T	T			
250 cu in.					L	L	L	L	L
V8									
260	F								
289 2V	C	C	C	C					
289 4V	A	A	A						
289 High-Performance	K	K	K						
302 2V					F	F	F	F	F
302 4V				J					
302 4V Boss					G	G			
351 2V ①					H	H	H	H	
351 4V ②					M	M	M	M	M
351 4V Boss ②							R		
351 4V CJ or GT ②							Q		
351 4V HO ②								R	Q
390 2V					Y				
390 4V			S	S	S				
427 4V				W					
428 4V				P					
428 4V CJ					Q	Q			
428 4V JCJ ③					R	R			
429 4V Boss					Z	Z			
429 4V SCJ							J		

①Cleveland or Windsor-Refer to chapter 3 for description of differences.
②Cleveland only.
③Ram Air.

Transmission Codes

Model	1965	1966	1967	1968	1969	1970	1971	1972–73
Manual Three-Speed	1	1	1	1	1	1	1	1
Manual Four-Speed	5	5	5	5	5	5	5	5
Manual Close-Ratio Four-Speed					6	6	6	E
C4 Automatic	6	6	W	W	W	W	W	W
FMX Automatic					X	X	X	X
C6 Automatic			U	U	U	U	U	U

Rear Axle Ratio Codes

Ratio: Regular Axle	Ratio: Locking Axle	1965	1966	1967	1968	1969	1970	1971	1972	1973
2.35						F				
2.50					O					
2.75				8	1	2	2	2	2	2
2.79					2	3	3	3	3	3
2.80		6	6	6	3	4	4	4	4	
2.83		2	2	2	4	5	5			
3.00		1	1	1	5	6	6	6	6	6
3.07							B	B		
3.08						C	C			
3.10						7				
3.20		3	3	3	6		8			
3.25		4	4	4	7	9	9	9	9	9
3.50		5	5	5	8	A	A	A	A	A
4.11		9	9	9						
	2.75				H	A	K	K	K	K
	2.79				B					L
	2.80	F	F	F	C	M	M	M	M	
	2.83	B	B	B	D					
	3.00	A	A	A	E	O				O
	3.08					U				
	3.20	C	C	C	F					
	3.25	D	D	D	G	R	R	R	R	R
	3.50	E	E	E	H	S	S	S	S	S
	3.91					V	V	V	V	
	4.11	I	I	I				Y		
	4.30					W	W			

1. Make sure that the vehicle is standing level.

2. Clean the area around the filler plug, and remove the plug from the side of the case.

3. If lubricant does not flow from the filler hole, fill the transmission case with the specified lubricant until it is level with the bottom of the filler hole.

4. Install the filler plug.

Automatic Transmission Fluid Check

Ford recommends that the automatic transmission fluid level be checked every six months or 6,000 miles (8 months or 8,000 miles—1973). The procedure for checking the fluid level is as follows.

1. Make sure that the vehicle is standing level. Firmly apply the parking brake.

2. Run the engine at idle until the fluid reaches normal operating temperature.

3. On a vehicle equipped with a vacuum brake release, disconnect the release line and plug the end of the line. If vacuum release line is not disconnected, the parking brake will not hold the car in any drive position.

4. Shift the selector lever through all positions, and place it in Park. Apply the service brake as an extra precaution while running the selector lever through the quadrant positions.

Maintenance Schedule

	1965	1966	1967	1968	1969	1970	1971	1972	1973
ENGINE									
Change engine oil and filter ①	6	6	6	6	6	6	6	6	4
Check engine oil level				at every fuel stop					
Adjust carburetor—idle speed and mixture, and fast (cold) idle				as required					
Adjust power steering idle compensator (6 cylinder)				as required					
Adjust accelerator pump lever				seasonal					
Clean carburetor air cleaner and filter (Paper type only) ①	6	6	6	—	—	—	—	—	—
Replace carburetor air cleaner filter	12	12	36	12	12	12	12	12	12
Clean crankcase oil filler breather cap ①	6	6	6	6	6	6	6	6	12
Check engine accessory drive belts				as required					
Replace pcv system valve and clean passages ①	12	12	12	12	12	12	12	12	12
Check ignition timing	12	12	12	12	12	12	12	12	12
Check spark plugs and points	6	6	6	12	12	12	12	12	12
Replace fuel system filter	36	36	36	12	12	12	12	12	12
Replace engine coolant	24	24	24	24	24	24	24	24	24
Check engine coolant level				as required					
Check engine accessory drive belts				as required					
Replace thermactor air pump filter	—	12	12	12	12	12	—	—	—
Clean and inspect distributor cap and rotor	12	12	12	12	12	12	12	12	12
Inspect cooling system hoses for deterioration, leaks, and loose hose clamps	12	12	12	12	12	12	12	12	12
Check exhaust control valve for free operation	—	—	6	6	6	—	—	—	8
Inspect thermactor exhaust emission system hoses and replace if necessary	—	12	12	12	12	12	—	—	—
Check power steering and brake master cylinder fluid level	6	6	6	6	6	6	6	6	4
Check battery fluid level	6	6	6	6	6	6	6	6	6
Check choke external linkage	12	12	12	12	12	12	12	12	12
Inspect fuel lines and filter for leaks	12	12	12	12	12	12	12	12	12
Inspect ignition wiring	12	12	12	12	12	12	12	12	12
Torque intake manifold bolts (8 cyl)	—	—	—	12	12	12	12	12	24
Adjust valves (mechanical type)	12	12	12	—	12	12	12	—	—
Replace breather element in air cleaner (351) ①	—	—	—	—	—	24	6	6	—
Replace spark delay valve	—	—	—	—	—	12	12	12	12
Replace fuel evaporative emission control valve	—	—	—	—	—	12	12	12	12
Check for correct spark control system advance, and retard vacuum cut-in speed, and function of thermal switch. Adjust or repair	—	—	—	—	—	12	12	12	12
Check functioning of air intake temperature control system	—	—	—	12	12	12	12	12	12
Replace evaporative emission control canister and purge hose	—	—	—	—	—	24	24	24	24
Check EGR system	—	—	—	—	—	—	—	—	12
TRANSMISSION									
Adjust automatic transmission bands									
289 Hi-P only front	6	6	6	—	—	—	—	—	—
rear	12	12	12	—	—	—	—	—	—
427 only (front and rear)	—	—	—	6②	—	—	—	—	—
All others front	36	36	36	36	12	12	6	12	
rear	as required ②			36②	12②	6②	6	12	
Check fluid level (manual and auto)	6	6	6	6	6	6	6	6	8

Maintenance Schedule (cont.)

Chassis	*1965*	*1966*	*1967*	*1968*	*1969*	*1970*	*1971*	*1972*	*1973*
CHASSIS									
Lubricate:									
Front ball joints	36	36	36	36	36	36	36	36	36
Power steering actuator valve and ball stud	36	36	36	36	36	36	36	36	36
Steering arm stops	—	—	6	6	6	6	12	12	12
Universal joints	36	36	—	—	—	—	—	—	—
Lube automatic trans linkages					as required				
Check:									
Steering linkage for play	12	12	12	12	12	12	12	12	12
Steering gear preload	as required		—	—	—	—	—	—	—
Power steering reservoir fluid level	6	6	6	6	6	6	6	6	4
Brake master cylinder fluid level	6	6	6	6	6	6	6	6	8
Brake lines and linings	30	30	30	30	30	30	30	30	24
Parking brake (adjust if necessary)					as required				
Tire pressure					as required				8
Front wheel alignment					as required				
Rear axle fluid	6	6	6	6	6	6	6	6	
Battery fluid level					as required				
Air conditioning system				at beginning of season or every 12 months					
Check clutch linkage adjustment		as required			6	6	6	6	12
Inspect, clean, and repack wheel bearings	30	30	30	30	30	30	30	30	24
Rotate tires					as required				
BODY									
Lubricate:									
Door striker pins		as required		—	—	—	—	—	—
Door hinge pivots		as required		6	6	6	6	6	8
Door lock cylinders	6	6	6	6	6	6	6	6	8
Hood and trunk hinges		as required		6	6	6	6	6	8
Hood latch and safety latch		as required		6	6	6	6	6	8
Trunk latch		as required		6	6	6	6	6	8
Trunk lock cylinder	6	6	6	6	6	6	6	6	8
Seat tracks					as required				
Check:									
Headlamp alignment					as required				
Convertible top operation					as required				
Clean body and door drain holes					as required				
Replace wiper blades					as required				

① More frequent service intervals will be required if the vehicle is operated in extremely dusty or low-temperature areas, or for extended periods of idling. This also applies if car is used to tow a trailer or is operated exclusively for short runs which do not permit the engine to reach its normal operating temperature.

② C-6 Automatic Transmissions (all automatics used in engines of 390 CID or more) do not have rear bands.

NOTE: *Maintenance schedule in months or miles, whichever occurs first.*

5. Clean all dirt from the transmission dipstick cap before removing the dipstick from the filler tube.

6. Pull the dipstick out of the filler tube, wipe it clean, and push it all the way back in. Make sure it is properly seated.

7. Pull the dipstick out of the tube again and check the fluid level. Fluid level should be above the "add" mark. When necessary, add enough fluid through the filler tube to bring the transmission fluid level between the "add" and "full" marks on the dipstick. Do not overfill the transmission. Use only fluid meeting Ford specifications. Install the dipstick, making sure it is properly seated on the tube.

8. On vehicles so equipped, connect the vacuum brake release line and test for proper operation.

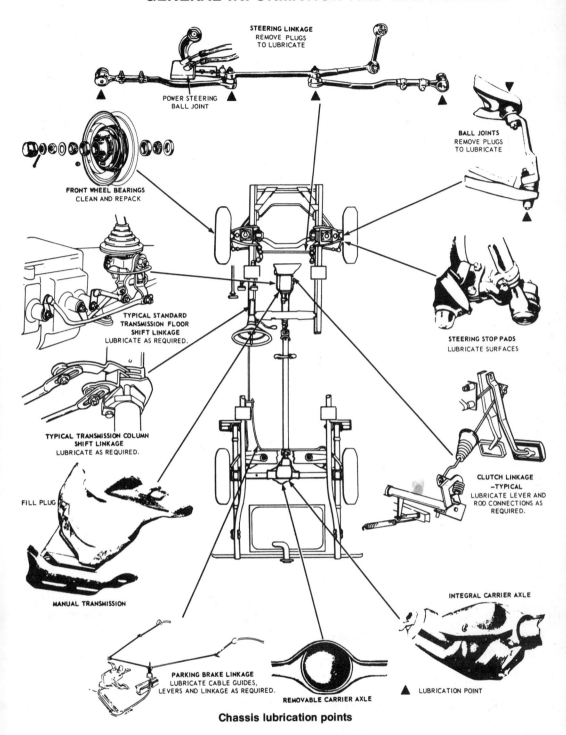

Chassis lubrication points

Transmission Linkage Lubrication

At the recommended intervals in the maintenance schedule, the transmission linkage should be lubricated.

Manual Shift Control and Linkage

Clean and lubricate the shift linkage, trunnions, and external shift mechanism (floor-shift models only) with lithium-based chassis and ball joint grease. When encountering hard shifting efforts, apply a few drops of 10W motor oil to the shift arm pivot points.

Automatic Kick-down Linkage

Lubricate all pivot points in the kick-down linkage with chassis and ball joint grease.

Front Wheel Bearing Cleaning and Repacking

The procedure for this maintenance operation is discussed in chapter nine.

Brake System Maintenance

All maintenance procedures for the brake systems are discussed in Chapter nine.

Steering Linkage Lubrication

Prior to removing the plugs for lubrication, wipe all accumulated dirt or foreign material from around the lubrication plugs. If the vehicle has been sitting out in a temperature below 20 degrees Fahrenheit (20° F) for any length of time, park it in a heated garage for 30 minutes or until the tie rod ends will accept lubrication.

Remove the plugs, install grease fittings in the tie-rod ends, and apply suitable chassis grease to each steering linkage fitting with a pressure gun.

Steering Arm Stop Lubrication

The maintenance schedule specifies the proper interval for lubricating the steering arm stops. The stops are located on the inside of the steering arm and the upturned end of the front suspension strut where it is attached to the lower control arm. Clean all friction points and apply ball joint and chassis grease.

Front Suspension Ball Joint Lubrication

At the recommended intervals in the maintenance schedule, the front suspension upper and lower ball joints must be lubricated. The plugs are located on the top of the upper ball joint and on the underside of the lower ball joint. Prior to removing the plugs for lubrication, wipe all accumulated dirt or other foreign material from around the lubrication plugs. If the vehicle has been sitting out in a temperature below 20° F for any length of time, park it in a heated garage for 30 minutes or until the joints will accept the lubricant.

Remove the plugs and install grease fittings. Using a hand-operated, low-pressure grease gun loaded with suitable ball joint lubricant, force the lubricant into the joint until the joint boot can be seen or felt to swell. At this point, the boot is full. Any further lubrication will destroy the weather-tight seal. Remove the grease fittings and install the plugs.

Power Steering Actuator Valve Ball Stud Lubrication

The power steering actuator valve ball stud must be lubricated every 36 months or 36,000 miles. Wipe the area around the grease fitting or plug to remove all dirt or foreign material. On models without a grease fitting, remove the plug and install a fitting. Apply ball joint or multipurpose chassis lubricant to the fitting with a low-pressure grease gun. When the boot seal is seen or felt to bulge with lubricant, cease application. Any further lubrication will destroy the weather-tight seal. Remove the grease fitting and install a plug.

Power Steering Idle Compensator Adjustment

The procedure for this adjustment is explained in Chapter Eight.

Steering Linkage Play Check

Every 12 months or 12,000 miles, the tie-rod ends should be checked for looseness. In addition, the front suspension ball joints, ball joint mountings, brake caliper attaching bolts, and all steering gear mountings and linkage connections should be checked for looseness. Torque all loose nuts and bolts to specifications. Make sure all cotter pins are properly installed. Looseness of steering components can adversely affect wheel alignment and can be a major cause of steering wander and loss of vehicle control.

Body Lubrication

Lubricate the following body parts at the intervals recommended in the maintenance schedule.

After lubricating the above body parts, operate them several times to work the lubricant in and avoid binding.

Part	Lubricant
Door latch striker pins	Stick wax
Door hinges, hinge pivots, checks	Polyethylene grease
Door lock cylinders	Silicone or graphite lock lubricant
Hood and trunk hinges	Polyethylene grease
Hood latch and safety catch	Polyethylene grease
Trunk latch	Polyethylene grease
Trunk lock cylinders	Silicone or graphite lock lubricant
Glove box door latch	Silicone lubricant

Tire Rotation

The accompanying illustration of the order of tire rotation is self-explanatory. Rotation of the tires as required by wear patterns will greatly increase the serviceable life of a set of tires. In addition to periodic rotation, tires should be kept balanced and properly inflated to obtain full mileage.

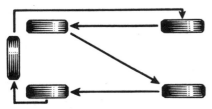

Tire rotation diagram

Body and Door Drain Hole Cleaning

The drain holes in the doors, rocker panels, and quarter panels should be checked occasionally to ensure that they are free from obstruction. To remove obstructions that might prevent water drainage, use a small screwdriver or awl. Visually check the dust valves for proper draining and sealing operation.

Windshield Wiper Blade Replacement

Depending on the type of weather, amount of use, or chemical reaction from road salts or tars, the recommended replacement interval for wiper blades will vary. After making sure that the windshield glass surface is free of all oil, tree sap, or other foreign substance that cannot be easily wiped off, check the wiper pattern for streaking. If the blades are cracked or the pattern is streaked or uneven, replace the blades.

Convertible Top Operation Check

If convertible top operation becomes slow or sluggish, check the fluid level in the hydraulic reservoir behind the rear seat. Fluid level should be maintained ¼ in. from the filler opening. Top up with automatic transmission fluid. The procedure for checking the fluid level is as follows:

1. Remove the rear seat and raise the top.
2. Pace absorbent cloths below the filler plug.
3. Remove the filler plug and check the fluid level. It should be level with the bottom edge of the hole.
4. If the fluid level is low, check the system for leaks. Top up as necessary.

Master Cylinder Fluid Level Check

The recommended maintenance interval for checking the fluid level in the master cylinder is six months or 6,000 miles. On 1965–1966 models, unscrew the filler cap and diaphragm which seals the master cylinder. Fill the reservoir to ⅜ in. from the top and install the filler cap, making sure that the diaphragm is properly seated in the cap. On 1967 and later models with dual master cylinders, push the retaining clip to one side and remove the filler cap and diaphragm. Fill the reservoir to ¼ in. from the top and install the cap and diaphragm. If factory-recommended, high-temperature, heavy duty brake fluid is not available, top up with fluid of SAE 70 R3 quality or better, for both drum and disc brake applications.

Rear Axle Fluid Level Check

The fluid level in the rear axle should be checked at six-month or 6,000 mile intervals. It is unnecessary to periodically drain the fluid. The factory fill should remain in the housing for the life of a vehicle, except when repairs are made. When adding to or replacing rear axle fluid, use SAE 80 hypoid gear lubricant for winter applications (−25° F), and SAE 90 hypoid gear lubricant for regular use. Limited-slip differential models require special fluid and locking differential additive. On all 1965–69 models, the fluid level should be maintained at the bottom of the filler plug hole. Starting in 1970, all models with integral carrier axles having 7¼, 8, and 6¾ in. ring gear diameters are full when the fluid level is ¼ in. below the filler hole. All other 1970 and 1971 vehicles should be filled to the filler hole. Any 1972–73 models not having 6¾ in. ring gear integral axle carriers are filled to ⅜ in. below the bottom edge of the filler plug hole. To check the fluid level in the axle, bend a clean, straight piece of wire to a 90° angle and insert the bent end of the wire in the axle while resting it on the lower edge of the filler hole. When checking fluid level, the axle must be at normal curb attitude.

Power Steering Reservoir Fluid Level Check

The level of the fluid in the power steering reservoir should be checked every six months or 6,000 miles (4 months or 4,000 miles—1973). Run the engine until the fluid is at normal operating temperature. Turn the steering wheel from lock to lock several times, and turn off the engine. On 1965–1966 models, the reservoir must be filled to the bottom of the filler neck. On 1967 and later models, a dipstick is affixed to the reservoir cap. The level must show on the cross hatching between the bottom of the dipstick and the "full" mark. To top up the reservoir, use automatic transmission fluid.
NOTE: *Do not overfill.*

Clutch Pedal Free-Play Adjustment

Refer to chapter six for this maintenance operation.

Accessory Drive Belt Check

Drive belts should be properly adjusted at all times. Loose belts cause improper operation of the water pump, fan, and generator or alternator. A belt that is too tight places a severe strain on the water pump and generator or alternator bearings. Replace any belt that is glazed, worn, or stretched so that it cannot be tightened sufficiently. On vehicles with matched belts, replace both belts. New belts are to be adjusted to the tension of 140 pounds (lbs). Any belt that has been operating for a minimum of 10 minutes is considered a used belt. Used belts are to be ad-

justed to a tension of 110 lbs. After installing a new belt, run the engine for 10 minutes and reset the tension to used belt specifications.

Alternator (Generator) Drive Belt Adjustment

1. Position a ruler perpencidular to the drive belt, and stationary in relation to the water pump. Test the tightness of the belt by pressing it firmly with your thumb. The deflection should not exceed ¼ in.
2. If the deflection is in excess of ¼ in., loosen the alternator (generator) mounting bolts and the adjusting arm bolt.
3. Move the alternator (generator) away from the engine to obtain correct belt tension. When using a metal pry bar to obtain correct tension, be sure to apply pressure on the alternator (generator) front only. Positioning such a device against the rear end housing will damage the unit.
4. When the belt feels adequately tight, tighten the adjusting arm bolt only. Retest the deflection of the belt. If tension is incorrect, loosen the adjusting bolts and make the appropriate corrections. Retighten the adjusting bolts and test again.
5. When belt is properly tightened, secure the mounting bolts.

Power Steering Drive Belt Adjustment

1. Same as alternator (generator) adjustment.
2. If the deflection is in excess of ¼ in., loosen the adjusting and mounting bolts on the front face of the pump cover plate (hub side) and the one nut at the rear.
3. On six-cylinder engines, fix a $^9/_{16}$ in. open-end wrench on the projecting ½ in. boss and pry upward to correct the tension. To adjust the belt on V8 engines, loosen the mounting bolt in the adjusting slot and loosen the nut directly above the slot. Place a suitable pry bar between the cast boss on the mounting bracket and the cast boss on the pump cover plate, and pry upward to correct tension. Do not pry against the pump reservoir as it can be deformed and cause a leak.
4. Tighten the adjusting bolts and test the deflection of the belt. If the deflection is not in excess of ¼ in., secure the mounting bolts.

Coolant Level Check

The coolant level in the radiator should be checked at least once a month. On a vertical-

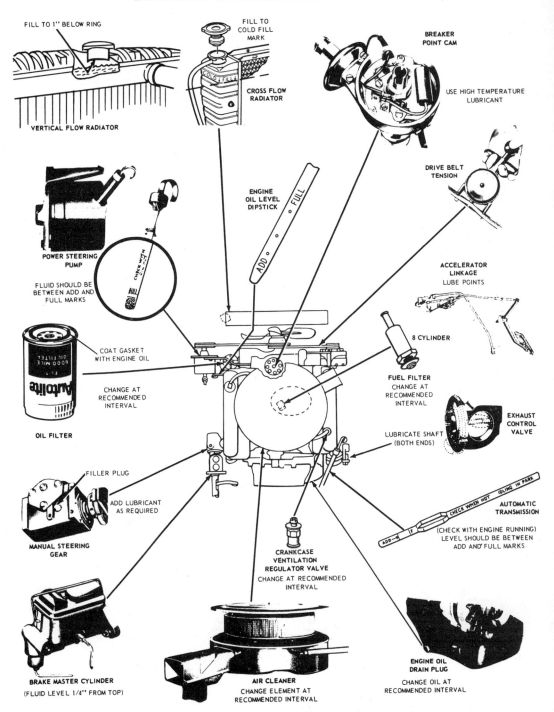

FILL TO 1" BELOW RING

VERTICAL FLOW RADIATOR

FILL TO COLD FILL MARK

CROSS FLOW RADIATOR

BREAKER POINT CAM

USE HIGH TEMPERATURE LUBRICANT

DRIVE BELT TENSION

ENGINE OIL LEVEL DIPSTICK

FULL
ADD

POWER STEERING PUMP

FLUID SHOULD BE BETWEEN ADD AND FULL MARKS

CHECK WITH DIPSTICK

FULL

ACCELERATOR LINKAGE LUBE POINTS

8 CYLINDER

COAT GASKET WITH ENGINE OIL

CHANGE AT RECOMMENDED INTERVAL

FUEL FILTER CHANGE AT RECOMMENDED INTERVAL

EXHAUST CONTROL VALVE

OIL FILTER

LUBRICATE SHAFT (BOTH ENDS)

FILLER PLUG

ADD LUBRICANT AS REQUIRED

MANUAL STEERING GEAR

IDLING IN PARK

CHECK WHEN HOT

AUTOMATIC TRANSMISSION

ADD — IF

(CHECK WITH ENGINE RUNNING) LEVEL SHOULD BE BETWEEN ADD AND FULL MARKS

CRANKCASE VENTILATION REGULATOR VALVE CHANGE AT RECOMMENDED INTERVAL

BRAKE MASTER CYLINDER (FLUID LEVEL 1/4" FROM TOP)

AIR CLEANER CHANGE ELEMENT AT RECOMMENDED INTERVAL

ENGINE OIL DRAIN PLUG CHANGE OIL AT RECOMMENDED INTERVAL

V8 Engine lubrication service points

flow radiator, the level of the coolant must be 1 in. below the radiator cap seat. The cross-flow radiator is at proper level when the coolant level is 2 in. below the cap seat at the cold fill mark. Both types of radiator should only be checked when the engine is cold and not running. If it is imperative that the level of a hot engine must be checked, muffle the radiator cap with a thick cloth and turn it slowly counterclockwise until the pressure starts to escape. After the pressure has completely dissipated, finish removing the cap. Some 1972 and later vehicles are equipped with a constant full coolant recovery system.

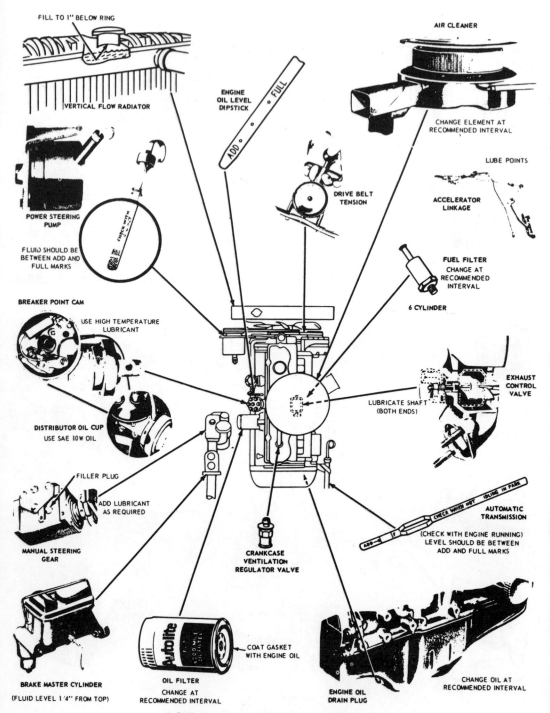

FILL TO 1" BELOW RING

AIR CLEANER

VERTICAL FLOW RADIATOR

ENGINE
OIL LEVEL
DIPSTICK

FULL

ADD

CHANGE ELEMENT AT
RECOMMENDED INTERVAL

LUBE POINTS

POWER STEERING
PUMP

DRIVE BELT
TENSION

ACCELERATOR
LINKAGE

FLUID SHOULD BE
BETWEEN ADD AND
FULL MARKS

CHECK WITH
FULL

FUEL FILTER
CHANGE AT
RECOMMENDED
INTERVAL

6 CYLINDER

BREAKER POINT CAM

USE HIGH TEMPERATURE
LUBRICANT

EXHAUST
CONTROL
VALVE

LUBRICATE SHAFT
(BOTH ENDS)

DISTRIBUTOR OIL CUP
USE SAE 10W OIL

FILLER PLUG

ADD LUBRICANT
AS REQUIRED

CHECK WHEN HOT   IDLING IN PARK

AUTOMATIC
TRANSMISSION

ADD

(CHECK WITH ENGINE RUNNING)
LEVEL SHOULD BE BETWEEN
ADD AND FULL MARKS

MANUAL STEERING
GEAR

CRANKCASE
VENTILATION
REGULATOR VALVE

COAT GASKET
WITH ENGINE OIL

CHANGE OIL AT
RECOMMENDED INTERVAL

BRAKE MASTER CYLINDER

(FLUID LEVEL 1/4" FROM TOP)

OIL FILTER
CHANGE AT
RECOMMENDED INTERVAL

ENGINE OIL
DRAIN PLUG

6 Cylinder engine lubrication service points

On these models there is a plastic recovery tank adjacent to the radiator. When adding coolant to a constant full system, add only to the plastic tank and not to the radiator.

When adding coolant between changes, use a mixture of permanent antifreeze and water that keeps the freeze protection at an adequate level for the temperatures that may occur in the area. A minimum freeze protection level should be maintained to at least 0°F to prevent boiling and corrosion. Do not mix brands or types of antifreeze.

Radiator and Hose Inspection

If coolant level is constantly low, there is a possibility that the cooling system is leaking. Check the radiator core and tanks for seepage at the seams. Inspect all radiator and heater hoses for evidence of heat cracking or leaking. Replace any hose in questionable condition. Check for proper installation of hoses in supporting brackets. Make sure there are no bends or kinks in hoses at fittings.

Coolant Replacement

Ford recommends that the coolant be drained, flushed, and replaced every two years or 24,000 miles. To drain the system, open the drain cock at the bottom of the radiator and remove the cylinder block drain plugs. On six-cylinder models, the drain plug is located at the right rear of the block near the starter. On V8 models, there are two drain plugs, one on each side of the block.

To remove rust, sludge, and other foreign material from the cooling system, a cooling system cleanser should be used. In severe cases of rust or sludge deposits, it will be necessary to use the pressure flushing method. A reversed-direction water flow will loosen sediment more quickly than a steady flow in the normal direction of coolant flow. Before pressurizing the system, make sure that the cylinder head bolts are tightened to specifications to prevent possible water leakage into the cylinders.

NOTE: *Always remove the thermostat prior to pressure-flushing.*

To fill the cooling system, close the radiator drain cock. Install the cylinder block drain plugs. Disconnect the heater outlet hose at the water pump to relase trapped air in the system. When the coolant begins to escape, connect the hose. After operating the vehicle at 2,000 revolutions per minute (rpm) for approximately 20 minutes, the level of coolant may drop, due to the displacement of entrapped air in the system. Refill to proper level.

The antifreeze used should be of the ethylene glycol, permanent type. Mixture strength must provide minimum protection to 0°F. To avoid possible overheating in hot weather, do not use mixtures with more than 50 percent antifreeze except in areas anticipating −35° temperatures. When running a minimum solution of antifreeze to water, it is good practice to add rust inhibitor to the cooling system.

NOTE: *The hose connecting the heater valve to the intake manifold must be replaced each time the coolant is replaced.*

Breather Element Cleaning

The crankcase oil filler breather cap should be removed and cleaned every six months or 6,000 miles. After removing the cap, wash it in a low-volatility, petroleum-based solvent (e.g., kerosene). Probe the breather holes to assure removal of any accumulated deposits. Shake the cap dry and install it. With the advent of the closed crankcase ventilation system in 1968, the filler cap must be disconnected from the connecting hose to the air cleaner before cleaning.

NOTE: *Do not dry with compressed air as filter element damage may result.*

Integral Fuel Pump and Filter (Replaceable Element Type)

Prior to 1966, the fuel pump was equipped with an integral fuel filter, featuring a replaceable element. It is recommended that this filter element be replaced every 36 months or 36,000 miles, or in the event that the filter becomes clogged. It is important to use the proper filter element for your fuel pump and to observe the instructions for positioning the element within the fuel pump unit. These instructions will be printed on the replacement element.

Inline Fuel Filter (Non-Replaceable Element Type)

The fuel filters on all engines since 1966 are of one-piece construction and cannot be cleaned. The filter is located inline at the carburetor inlet. The interval for replacing the single-unit filter is specified in the maintenance schedule. The procedure for replacing the fuel filter is as follows:

1. Remove the air cleaner.
2. Loosen the clamps securing the fuel inlet hose to the fuel filter.
3. Unscrew the fuel filter from the carburetor and discard the gasket, if so equipped. Disconnect the fuel filter from the inlet hose and discard the retaining clamps.
4. Install a new clamp on the inlet hose and reconnect the hose to the new filter. Screw the new filter into the carburetor inlet port and tighten.

5. Position the fuel line hose clamps and crimp the clamps securely.

6. Start the engine and check for fuel leaks.

7. Install the air cleaner.

Changing Oil and Filter

When adding to oil, or changing the oil or filter, at other than an authorized dealer, it is imperative that oil or filters of equal quality to original equipment be used. Use of inferior oil or filters may establish the basis for denying warranty coverage of any engine part damaged as a result. Generally speaking, heavy-duty detergent oil of the MS rating meets warranty requirements. A new set of oil designations are slowly being phased into use by the American Petroleum Institute. Oil of the SE designation is comparable to MS under the old system.

Oil of the MS and SE variety performs a multitude of functions, in addition to its basic lubricating properties. Through a balanced formula of metallic detergents and polymeric dispersants, the oil prevents high- and low-temperature deposits and keeps dirt particles and sludge in suspension. Acids, particularly sulphuric acid, and other by-products of combustion are neutralized by the oil. These acids, if permitted to concentrate, may cause rust and corrosion in the engine.

It is important to choose an oil of the proper viscosity for climatic and operational conditions. The SAE viscosity rating is printed on the top of the oil container. For winter operation, a "W" is added after the SAE rating to indicate the oil's suitability for cold temperatures. The oil viscosity-temperature range chart is useful in selecting the proper grade.

Ford recommends that the oil and filter be changed every six months or 6,000 miles (4 months or 4,000 miles—1973). However, certain operating conditions may warrant more frequent changes. If the vehicle is used for short trips, the presence of water and low-temperature deposits may make it necessary to change the oil more frequently. If the vehicle is used in stop-and-go city traffic, corrosive acids and high-temperature deposits may necessitate shorter oil changing intervals. The shorter intervals are applicable for industrial or rural areas where high concentrations of dust in the atmosphere contaminate the oil.

Oil Viscosity Selection Chart

	Anticipated Temperature Range	SAE Viscosity
Multi-grade	below 32° F	5W-30 ①
	−10° to 90° F	10W-30
	above −9° F	10W-40
	above 10° F	20W-40
Single grade	−10° to 32° F	10W
	10° to 60° F	20W-20
	32° to 90° F	30
	above 60° F	40

① When sustained high-speed driving is anticipated, use the next higher grade.

The procedure for changing the oil and filter is as follows:

Removal

1. Raise the car, taking proper safety precautions.

2. Remove the oil pan drain plug, allowing the engine oil to drain into a container.

3. Place a drip pan under the filter.

4. Turn the filter counterclockwise with a strap wrench, if necessary, and remove it from the engine.

Installation

1. Clean the gasket surface at the adaptor.

2. Coat the filter gasket with light engine oil. Hand-turn the filter clockwise until the filter gasket contacts the sealing surface. Then hand-turn the filter one-half turn clockwise.

3. Remove drip pan with the old oil. If the oil pan drain plug gasket is defective, replace and tighten the plug to 15–20 foot pounds (ft. lbs.) of torque. Lower the car.

4. Fill the crankcase to the proper level on the dipstick with the recommended grade of oil.

5. Start the engine and operate it at fast idle. Check for oil leaks. Recheck the oil level.

Air Filter Cleaning

On 1967 and earlier models, the air cleaner assembly should be cleaned and inspected every six months or 6,000 miles. In order to clean the filter, the wing nut retaining the air cleaner assembly to the carburetor must be removed. On vehicles equipped with closed crankcase ventilation systems, the hose at the vent filter must be disconnected. Remove the air cleaner cover and filter element. Hold the element in a vertical position and tap it lightly against a smooth horizontal surface to shake the dust and dirt out. Direct clean, compressed air through the element in the opposite direction of normal air flow. Clean the inside of the filter housing with a solvent-dampened rag. Inspect the filter by placing a light bulb in its center, and check for cracks and remaining dirt. Install the air cleaner body on top of the carburetor so that the word "front" faces the front of the car. Place the filter in the cleaner housing and place the cleaner cover on top. Connect the air duct to the air cleaner and tighten the retaining wing nuts. On vehicles with closed crankcase ventilation, connect the vent hose to the vent filter and tighten the hose retaining clamp.

Air Filter Replacement

The interval for replacing the air filter varies with the model year, engine, and type of element. Refer to the maintenance schedule for the proper interval. The procedure for removing the old filter and installing the new one is the same procedure as for cleaning. When installing the new filter, be sure that the word "top" faces up.

Positive Crankcase Ventilation Inspection and Service

Open System with Serviceable Ventilation Valve

1. Remove the air cleaner.
2. Pull the PCV valve out of the grommet on the valve cover.
3. Remove the crankcase ventilating hose and clamp from the carburetor fitting, using a pair of hose-clamp pliers.
4. Remove the other end of the hose and clamp from the PCV fitting, using the hose-clamp pliers.
5. On six-cylinder models, remove the fitting from the carburetor. On V8 models, remove the 90° elbow from the PCV valve.

VALVE DISASSEMBLY

1. Using a snap-ring retainer tool, remove the retaining ring from the end of the PCV valve assembly.
2. Remove the retaining washer, valve, and spring.

CLEANING AND INSPECTION

1. Soak all metal fittings and PCV valve parts in carburetor solvent.
2. Remove all emission deposits by probing all fitting passages and valve orifices with an appropriate diameter drill or wire.
3. Wash all metal parts in clean solvent and dry them with compressed air.
4. Soak the rubber ventilation hose in a low-volatility petroleum-base solvent.
5. Clean the rubber ventilation hose by passing a cloth through the hose with a wire or rod.
6. Rewash the hose in clean carburetor solvent and dry with compressed air.
7. Wash the oil filler cap in clean carburetor solvent. Shake the cap dry.
8. Clean out the fitting at the carburetor with a 5/16 in. diameter drill.
9. Inspect all parts for damage, wear, or deterioration. Replace if necessary.

ASSEMBLY

1. Place the spring in the valve body.
2. Position the valve in the valve body with the pointed end toward the hose connection.
3. Place the retaining washer in position.
4. Install the retaining ring on the end of the PCV valve assembly.

INSTALLATION

1. On six-cylinder models, install the fitting on the carburetor. On V8 models, attach the 90° elbow to the PCV valve.
2. Using a pair of hose-clamp pliers, install the hose and clamp on the PCV valve.
3. Attach the hose and clamp to the carburetor fitting.
4. Insert the PCV valve into the rubber grommet on the valve cover.
5. Install the air cleaner.

Open System (Non-Serviceable Ventilation Valve)

All 1965, 1966, and 1967 models sold outside California are equipped with positive crankcase ventilation systems with non-serviceable ventilation valves. These positive crankcase ventilation systems are of the open type, drawing ventilating air through the oil breather filler camp and discharging the crankcase vapors into the intake manifold. The ventilation valve is a single unit and cannot be cleaned. Therefore, it is imperative that the valve be replaced every 12 months or 12,000 miles, whichever occurs first. The procedure for removal, cleaning and inspection, and installation of the open system with the non-serviceable ventilation valve is the same as that of the serviceable valve system, except that all references to disassembly, cleaning, and assembly of the PCV valve should be deleted.

Closed System (Non-Serviceable Ventilation Valve)

Starting in 1965, California has required that all new cars sold in that state be equipped with closed crankcase ventilation systems. Federal law requires the closed system on all 1968 and later models. The closed ventilation system features a sealed breather cap which is connected to the air cleaner by a rubber hose. Thus, the crankcase receives air from the air cleaner, making the entire system sealed from the atmosphere. The recycling of the crankcase vapors places a severe load on the PCV valve, hoses, and fittings, making the 12 month, 12,000 mile service interval mandatory. The procedure for cleaning the closed PCV system is as follows:

REMOVAL

1. Remove the oil filler cap and its connecting hose to the air cleaner.
2. Remove the air cleaner (and duct and valve assembly if so equipped).
3. Remove the hose from the ventilator valve in the valve cover. Remove the oil separator from the valve cover, if so equipped. Remove the other end of the hose from the intake manifold, or carburetor spacer connection, if so equipped. On models with a "T" fitting or hot idle compensator, disconnect it from the hose assembly.
4. Pull the ventilator valve from the grommet in the valve cover. Discard the ventilator valve assembly. Do not clean this valve.

Exhaust Gas Recirculation System Service

All 1973 models are equipped with an exhaust gas recirculation (EGR) system to control oxides of nitrogen. Because the system channels exhaust gases through narrow passages into the induction system, deposits build up quickly in the system, eventually blocking the exhaust gas recirculation flow. Therefore, to keep the car's emission levels up to federal standards, it is necessary to service the system at the recommended intervals. EGR service consists of cleaning or replacing the EGR valve, and cleaning all of the exhaust gas channels.

EGR Valve Cleaning

Remove the EGR valve for cleaning. Do not strike or pry on the valve diaphragm housing or supports, as this may damage the valve operating mechanism and/or change the valve calibration. Check orifice hole in the EGR valve body for deposits. A small hand drill of no more than 0.060 in. diameter may be used to clean the hole if plugged. Extreme care must be taken to avoid enlarging the hole or damaging the surface of the orifice plate.

EGR Passage Cleaning

Remove the carburetor and carburetor spacer on engines so equipped. Clean the supply tube with a small power-driven rotary type wire brush or blast cleaning equipment. Clean the exhaust gas passages in the spacer using a suitable wire brush and/or scraper. The machined holes in the spacer can be cleaned by using a suitable round wire brush. Hard encrusted material should be probed loose first, then brushed out.

Battery Electrolyte Level Check

The fluid level in the battery cells should be checked monthly, and more frequently during hot, dry weather. To top up the battery, ordinary tap water may be used except in areas known to have a high mineral or alkali content in the water. In these areas, distilled water must be used. The fluid level should meet the ring at the bottom of the filler well.

In cold weather, the battery's state of charge should be checked with the fluid level. If water is added during freezing weather, drive for several miles afterward to mix the water and battery electrolyte.

JACKING, HOISTING, AND TOWING PROCEDURES

Jack up the car at the front under the spring seat of the lower control arm. Jack up the car at the rear axle housing, close to the differential case.

For twin post lifts, the front adaptors must be carefully placed, and must be large enough to cover the entire spring seat area. Rear adaptors or forks must be placed under the axle not more than 1 in. outboard from the welds near the differential housing.

For frame contact lifts, place the adaptors as shown in the diagram. Be sure that the pads cover at least 12 sq in. of area.

It is not necessary to raise the rear wheels in order to tow cars with automatic transmissions, but it is essential to make sure that the transmission is in Neutral.

Models with automatic transmissions cannot be push-started. To push-start a car with a manual transmission, always push the car from behind. Attempting to tow the car to start it creates the danger of the towed vehicle accelerating into the tow vehicle.

FRONT RAIL TYPE, FORK LIFT
OR FLOOR JACK CONTACT AREA

FRONT FRAME CONTACT AREA

REAR FRAME CONTACT AREA

REAR RAIL TYPE, FORK LIFT OR
FLOOR JACK CONTACT AREA

Front and rear hoisting points

Capacities

Year	Model	Engine Crankcase Add 1 Qt. for New Filter	Transmissions Pts. to Refill after Draining			Drive Axle (pts)	Gasoline Tank (gal)	Cooling System	
			Manual		Auto-matic			(qt) with Heater	with A/C
			3 Spd	4 Spd					
1965	6—170	3½	2½	4½	15	2½	16	9½	—
	6—200	3½	2½	4½	15	2½	16	9½	—
	8—260	4	3½	4	17	4½	16	15	—
	8—289	4	3½	3½	17	4½	16	15	—
	8—289 HP	4	None	3½	17	5	16	15	—
1966	6—200	3.5	2	4.5	15	2.5	16	9.5	10.5
	8—289	4	3.5	3.5	17	4.5 ③	16	15	15.5
1967	6—200	3.5	2	—	15	2.5	16	9.5	9.5
	8—289	4	3.5	4	17	4	17	15	15
	8—390	4	3.5	4	26	5	16	20.5	20.5
1968	6—200	3.5	3.5	—	16	2.5	16	9.5	9.5
	8—289, 302	4	3.5	4	18	4	16	15	15
	8—390, 427, 428	4	3.5	4	26	5	16	20.5	20.5
1969	6—200	3.5	3.5	—	16	4	20	9	9
	6—250	3.5	3.5	—	18	4	20	10	10
	8—302, 351	4	3.5	4	18 ⑥	4 ⑦	20	13.5	15
	8—390, 428	4	—	4	26	5	20	14.5	16
	8—429 BOSS	8	—	4	25½	5	20	19.6	—
1970	6—200	3.5	3.5	—	16	2.25	22	9	9
	6—250	3.5	3.5	—	18	4	22	10	10
	8—302	4	3.5	4	18	4	22	13.5	15
	8—351	4	3.5	4	22	5	22	14.5	16
	8—428	4	—	4	26	5	22	19.5	19.5
	8—429 BOSS	8	—	4	25½	5	20	19.6	—

Capacities (cont.)

Year	Model	Engine Crankcase Add 1 Qt. for New Filter	Transmissions Pts. to Refill after Draining			Drive Axle (pts)	Gasoline Tank (gal)	Cooling System	
			Manual		Auto-matic			(qt) with Heater	with A/C
			3 Spd	4 Spd					
1971	6—250	3.5	3.5	—	18	4	20	11	11
	8—302	4	3.5	—	18	4	20	15	15.5
	8—351	4	3.5	4	22	5	20	15.5	16
	8—429	6 ⑨	—	4	26	5	20	19.5	19.5
1972–73	6—250	3.5	3.5	—	18	4	19.5	11	11
	8—302	4	3.5	—	18	4	19.5	15	15.5
	8—351	4	3.5	4	22 ⑫	5	19.5	16	16

① Not used
② Not used
③ 5 pts with high performance engine
④ Not used
⑤ Not used
⑥ 22 pts with 351 engine
⑦ 5 pts with 351 engine
⑧ Not used
⑨ 429 4 bbl—4 qts
    428, 429, CJ, SCJ—6 qts
    add 1 qt if equipped with oil cooler
⑩ Not used
⑪ Not used
⑫ Less 1 pt with 4 bbl
— Not applicable

Tune-Up and Performance Maintenance

TUNE-UP PROCEDURES

The tune-up is a routine maintenance operation which incorporates a series of specific procedures essential for the efficient and economical operation—as well as the long life—of your car's engine. The interval between tune-ups is a variable factor which depends upon the way in which you drive your car, the conditions under which you drive it (weather, road type, etc.), and the type of engine with which your car is equipped. It is generally correct to say that no engine should be driven more than 12,000 miles between tune-ups. In the case of cars which have been driven extremely hard, or under severe weather conditions, the tune-ups should be performed at closer intervals. Needless to say, high-performance engines require more frequent tuning than other engines, regardless of weather or road conditions.

The replaceable parts involved in a tune-up are: spark plugs, breaker points, condenser, distributor cap, rotor, spark plug wires, and the ignition coil high-tension wire. In addition to these parts and adjustments involved in installing them, there are several adjustments of other parts involved in completing the job. These include carburetor idle speed and fuel/air mixture, valve lash, ignition timing, and dwell angle.

Spark Plugs

REMOVAL

All Models (Except 390 and Larger V8s with Thermactor Controls and Air Conditioning)

1. If the spark plug wires are not numbered as to their cylinder, place a piece of masking tape on each wire and number it.

2. Grasp each wire by its rubber boot on the end and remove it from the spark plug. If the wire sticks to the plug, a slight clockwise turn should help to loosen it. Do not attempt to remove the wires from the spark plugs by pulling on the wires themselves, as this will damage the wires.

3. Using a $^{13}/_{16}$ in. spark plug socket, loosen each plug by making several counterclockwise turns. If your car is equipped with a 351 Cleveland engine, Boss 302, Boss 429, or 429 SCJ, a $^5/_8$ in. spark plug socket should be substituted for the $^{13}/_{16}$ in. size.

4. Using compressed air (if available), blow the area around each spark plug clean. If no compressed air is available, wipe these areas clean with a rag. Make sure that no foreign matter enters the cylinders through the spark plug holes.

5. Remove the spark plugs from the engine.

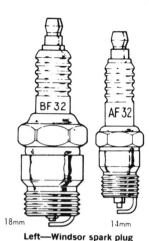

BF 32   AF 32

18mm   14mm

Left—Windsor spark plug
Right—Cleveland spark plug

351 V8 Spark plug applications

390 and Larger V8s with Thermactor Controls and Air Conditioning

NOTE: *It is advisable to have the following group of tools in order to remove the difficult-to-reach spark plugs of the above-mentioned engines:*
1. Swivel ratchet handle
2. Flexible spark plug wrench of the proper size for the spark plugs in your engine.
1. Remove the carburetor air cleaner assembly and the braces which connect the spring towers to the cowl.
2. Disconnect the ignition wires from the distributor cap.
3. Remove the rocker arm covers, carburetor choke tube, and vacuum hoses.
4. Disconnect the ignition wires from the spark plugs.
5. If compressed air is available, blow the dirt from around the spark plugs. If no compressed air is available, wipe the areas around the spark plugs with a rag.
6. Using the recommended tools, remove the spark plugs from the engine, making sure that dirt does not enter the spark plug holes.

INSPECTION

Compare the condition of all spark plugs (to pictures on the "Tune-Up" tip insert). If you wish to reuse the plugs, wipe off the porcelain insulator on each plug and check for cracks or breaks. Check the electrodes for excessive wear. If one spark plug is damaged, it is advisable to replace the entire set.

If all plugs appear to be usable, have them cleaned on a plug cleaning machine, which can be found in most service stations. An alternative to this is to remove all deposits on the electrode end of the plug with a stiff wire brush.

On both new and used plugs, it is essential to check the gap before installing the plug in the engine. The ground electrode and the specified size wire gauge must pass through the opening with a slight drag, which should be uniform for all spark plugs to be used in your engine.

On used spark plugs, uneven wear of the center or ground electrode must be corrected by leveling off the unevenly worn electrode with a file.

If the air gap between the two electrodes is not correct, the ground electrode must be opened or closed with the proper tool in order to bring it to correct specifications.

INSTALLATION

All Models (Except 390 and Larger V8s with Thermactor Controls and Air Conditioning)

1. Insert the plugs into their holes, and hand-tighten them, taking care not to cross-thread the plugs.
2. Using the spark plug socket on a torque wrench, torque the plugs to the proper specifications. (See the table in the general tune-up information.)
3. Install the spark plug wires, each on its respective plug. Make sure that the wires are firmly installed on the plugs. Check the firing order illustrations for the proper positioning of the wires.

390 and Larger V8s with Thermactor Controls and Air Conditioning

1. Insert and tighten the spark plugs, using the same combination of tools as used during removal.
2. Install the ignition wires to the spark plugs. Make sure that they are installed firmly and in their proper positions. Refer if necessary to the firing order illustrations.
3. Thoroughly clean the gasket surfaces on the rocker arm covers and the cylinder heads.
4. Position new rocker arm cover gaskets, install the rocker arm covers, tighten the bolts, and torque them. Torque for all engines, except Boss 429 and 429 SCJ, is 3–5 ft. lbs. Torque for the 429 SCJ is 2½–4 ft. lbs. For the Boss 429, proper torque is 12–15 ft. lbs.

Tune-Up Specifications

When analyzing compression test results, look for uniformity among cylinders rather than specific pressures.

Year	Engine No. Cyl Displacement (cu in.)	hp	Spark Plugs Type §	Gap (in.)	Distributor Point Dwell* (deg)	Point Gap (in.)	Ignition Timing ▲ (deg) ● Man Trans ■	Auto Trans	Intake Valve Opens ■(deg) ●	Fuel Pump Pressure (psi)	Idle Speed ●(rpm)▲ Man Trans	Auto Trans
1965	6—170	105	BF-82	0.034	38	0.025	8B	12B	13B	4½	500	485
	6—200	120	BF-82	0.034	38	0.025	8B	12B	6B	4½	500	485
	8—260	164	BF-42	0.034	27	0.015	4B	4B	21B	5	575	500
	8—289	200, 225	BF-42	0.034	27	0.015	8B	8B	20B	5	575	500
	8—289 H.P.	271	BF-32	0.034	27	0.020	10B	—	46B	5	750	—
1966	6—200	120	BF-82	0.034	39	0.025	6B (TDC)	12B (TDC)	7	4½	600(650)	525②(575)
	8—289	200	BF-42	0.034	29	0.017	6B (TDC)	6B (TDC)	16	4½–5½	600(635)	500
	8—289	225	BF-42	0.034	29	0.017	6B (TDC)	6B (TDC)	16	4½–5½	600(635)	500
	8—289 H.P.	271	BF-32	0.034	31	0.020	12B	—	46	4½–5½	775	—
1967	6—200	120	BF-82	0.034	39	0.025	6B (5B)	12B (5B)	7(9)	4½–5½	575(700)	550②
	8—289	200	BF-42	0.034	29	0.017	6B (5B)	6B (5B)	15	4½–5½	575(625)	475(550)

Engine	HP	Plug	Gap	Dwell	Point Gap	Timing	Timing		Pressure	Idle	Idle
8—289	225	BF-42	0.034	29	0.017	6B (5B)	6B (5B)	16	4½–5½	600(625)	525(500)
8—289 H.P.	271	BF-32	0.034	32	0.020	12B	12B	46	4½–5½	750	650
8—390	320	BF-32	0.034	29	0.017	12B (6B)	12B (6B)	18	4½–5½	600(625)	575(550)
1968											
6—200	115	BF-82	0.034	38	0.027	6B	6B	9	4–6	700	550 ②
8—289	195	BF-42	0.034	27	0.021	6B	6B	15	4–6	700	550
8—302	230	BF-32	0.034	29 (27)①	0.017 (0.021)①	6B	6B	15	4–6	625	550 ②
8—390	265	BF-32	0.034	29 (27)①	0.017 (0.021)①	6B	6B	13	4½–6	625	550
8—390 GT	325	BF-32	0.034	29	0.016	6B	6B	18	4½–6	700	550
8—427	390	BF-32	0.034	29	0.017	—	6B	18	4½–6	—	600
8—428	335	BF-32	0.034	29	0.017	6B	—	18 4½–6		—	600
1969											
6—200	115	BF-32	0.034	38	0.027	6B	6B	9	4½–5½	750	550 ③
6—250	155	BF-82	0.034	38	0.025	6B	6B	10	4½–5½	700 [700/500]	550 [550/450]
8—302	220	BF-42	0.034	29 ③	0.021 ④	6B	6B	16	4½–5½	650	550 ③
8—302	290	BF-32	0.035	32	0.020	16B	—	40	4½–5½	800/500	—
8—351	250	BF-42	0.034	29	0.017	6B	6B	11	4½–5½	650	550
8—351	290	BF-32	0.034	29	0.017	6B	6B	11	4½–5½	675	575

Tune-Up Specifications (cont.)

When analyzing compression test results, look for uniformity among cylinders rather than specific pressures.

Year	Engine No. Cyl Displacement (cu in.)	hp	Spark Plugs Type §	Gap (in.)	Distributor Point Dwell* (deg)	Point Gap (in.)	Ignition Timing ▲(deg)● Man Trans ■	Auto Trans	Intake Valve Opens ■(deg)●	Fuel Pump Pressure (psi)	Idle Speed ●(rpm)▲ Man Trans	Auto Trans
	8—390	320	BF-42	0.034	29③	0.017③	6B	6B	16	4½—5½	700	550
	8—428	335	BF-32	0.034	27⑥	0.021④	6B	6B	18	4½—5½	700	650
	8—429 BOSS	375	AF-32	0.035	30	0.020	10B	10B	40B	6—8	700/500	700/500
1970	6—200	120	BF-82	0.035	38	0.027	6B	6B	9	4—6	750⑦	550⑤
	6—250	155	BF-82	0.035	38	0.025	6B	6B	10	4—6	750/500	600/500
	8—302	210	BF-42	0.035	27	0.021	6B	6B	16	4—6	800/500	600/500
	8—302	290	AF-32	0.035	32	0.020	16B	—	40	4½—6½	800/500	—
	8—351 C	250	AF-42	0.035	27	0.021	6B	6B	12	5—7	700/500	600
	8—351 W	250	BF-42	0.035	27	0.021	10B	10B	11	5—7	700/500	575 [600/500]
	8—351 C	300	BF-32	0.035	27	0.021	6B	6B	16	5—6	800/500	600 [600/500]
	8—248	335	BF-32	0.035	32	0.020	6B	6B	18	4½—6½	725	675 [675/500]
	8—429	BOSS	AF-32	0.035	27/29	0.021/0.017	10B	10B	16	6½—8½	650/500	700/500

Year	Engine		Spark Plug	Gap								
1971	6—250	145	BRF-82	0.034	36	0.027/0.025	6B	6B	10	4–6	750	600
	8—302	210	BRF-42	0.034	27	0.021	6B	6B	16	4–6	800/500	575 [600/500]
	8—351 C	240	ARF-42	0.034	27	0.021	6B	6B	12	5–7	700/500	600
	8—351 W	240	BRF-42	0.034	27	0.021	6B	6B	12	5–7	700/500	575 [600/500]
	8—351 CJ	280	ARF-42	0.034	27	0.021	6B	6B	18	5–7	800/500	600
	8—351	BOSS	ARF-32	0.034	27/29	0.021/0.017	6B	6B	18	4½–5½	800	590
	8—249	SCJ	ARF-42	0.034	28	0.020	10B	10B	40½	4½–6½	650/500	700/500
1972	6—250	95	BRF-82	0.034	37	0.027	6B	6B	10 (16)	4½–6½	750/500	600/500
	8—302	140	BRF-42	0.034	28	0.017	6B	6B	16	5½–6½	800/500	575 [600/500]
	8—351 C	165	ARF-42	0.034	28	0.017	6B	6B	12	5½–6½	750/500	575/500 ⑩
	8—351 W	165	BRF-42	0.034	28	0.017	—	6B	12	5½–6½	—	575 [600/500]
	8—351 CJ	266	ARF-42	0.034	28	0.017 ⑩	16B	16B	14	5½–6½	1000/500	750/500
	8—351 HO	N.A.	ARF-42	0.034	28	0.020	10B	—	17½	5½–6½	1000/500	—
1973	6—250	99	BRF-82	0.034	37	0.027/0.025	6B	6B	16	4½–6½	750/500	600/500

Tune-Up Specifications (cont.)

When analyzing compression test results, look for uniformity among cylinders rather than specific pressures.

Year	Engine No. Cyl Displacement (cu in.)	hp	Spark Plugs Type §	Gap (in.)	Distributor Point Dwell* (deg)	Point Gap (in.)	Ignition Timing ▲ (deg) ● Man Trans ■	Auto Trans	Intake Valve Opens ■(deg) ●	Fuel Pump Pressure (psi)	Idle Speed ●(rpm) ▲ Man Trans	Auto Trans
	8—302	140	BRF-42	0.034	28	0.017	6B	6B	16	5½–6½	800/500	575 [600/500]
	8—351	165	BRF-42	0.034	28	0.017	—	6B	12	5½–6½	—	575 [600/500]
	8—351 CJ	266	ARF-42	0.034	28 ⑬	0.017 ⑦	16B	16B	14	5½–6½	1000/500	800/500

* Where two figures are separated by a slash, the first figure is for engines equipped with dual diaphragm distributors and the second figure is for engines equipped with single diaphragm distributors.

▲ See text for procedure

● Figures in parentheses apply to California engines. Figures in brackets are for solenoid equipped vehicles only. In all cases where two figures are separated by a slash, the first is for idle speed with solenoid energized and automatic transmission in Drive, while the second is for idle speed with solenoid disconnected and automatic transmission in Neutral.

■ All figures are in degrees Before Top Dead Center

§ All spark plug listings are Autolite original equipment numbers

① Figure in parentheses applies to thermactor
② A/C off
③ Figure is 27 degrees for automatic transmission
④ Figure is 0.017 for automatic transmission

⑤ Figure is 0.021 for automatic transmission
⑥ Figure is 29 degrees for automatic transmission
⑦ For air conditioned vehicles, adjust idle speed to 800 rpm with A/C on
⑧ Not used
⑨ Figure is 625/500 for California engines
⑩ Figure is 0.020 for manual transmission
⑪ Not used
⑫ Figure is 800/500 for California engines
⑬ Figure is 32°–35° on manual transmission model with dual point distributor with both point sets combined
⑭ Figure is 0.020 for manual transmission with dual point distributor

B Before Top Dead Center
C Cleveland
CJ Cobra Jet
HO High Output
N.A. Not available
SCJ Super Cobra Jet
W Windsor
— Not applicable

5. Connect and/or install:

    A. Choke heat tube

    B. Vacuum hoses and emission system hoses

    C. Spark plug wires to the distributor cap, referring to the firing order diagrams to make sure that the wires are properly positioned.

    D. Spring tower-to-cowl braces

    E. Carburetor air cleaner and vacuum hose-to-heat stove fitting

FIRING ORDER

To avoid confusion, replace spark plug wires one at a time.

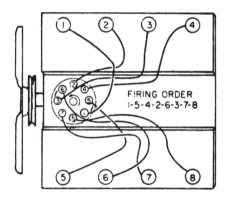

FIRING ORDER
1-5-4-2-6-3-7-8

All V8 except 351

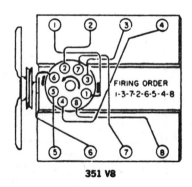

FIRING ORDER
1-3-7-2-6-5-4-8

351 V8

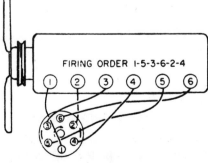

FIRING ORDER 1-5-3-6-2-4

All 6 cyl.

Distributor Breaker Points and Condenser

It is important to remember that for purposes of replacement, the breaker points and the condenser should be treated as a unit. One should never be replaced without replacing the other.

There are two ways to check the breaker point gap: with a feeler gauge or with a dwell meter. Both methods serve the purpose of adjusting the amount of time (in degrees of distributor rotation) that the points will remain open. If you adjust the points with a feeler gauge, you are setting the maximum distance which the points will open when the rubbing block, which is affixed to the point assembly, is on the highest point of a distributor cam lobe. When you perform the same point adjustment with a dwell meter, you are measuring the number of degrees (of distributor cam rotation) during which the points will remain closed before they start to open as a high point of the distributor cam approaches the rubbing block on the point assembly. Either/both method of point gap adjustment may be employed during a tune-up, but the dwell meter adjustment is the more precise and should be used last as the final adjustment of point gap.

A final rule governing the adjustment of point gap is that whenever point gap is adjusted, ignition timing must also be checked and adjusted accordingly.

DISTRIBUTOR TUNE-UP PROCEDURES

1. Disconnect the high-tension wire from the coil and unsnap the distributor cap retaining clips.

2. Remove the distributor cap from the distributor with its wires still in place. Turn it so that you can examine the inside of the cap. Check carefully for cracks. Examine the metal strikers. If they are excessively worn or burned, or if the cap is at all cracked, it should be replaced. If you are replacing the distributor cap, leave the wires in place on the old cap until you have the new cap in hand, and ready to install. Transfer the wires one at a time, to avoid installing them on the wrong fittings. Position the distributor cap out of the way of the distributor.

3. Remove the rotor from the distributor

shaft by pulling it straight up. Examine its condition. If the rotor is cracked or the metallic tip is excessively burned, it should be replaced.

4. Remove the metal point shield, if your car is so equipped.

5. Place a screwdriver against the breaker points and pry them open. Examine the condition of the contact points. If they are excessively worn, burned, or pitted, they should be replaced.

6. If the points are in good condition and not in need of replacement, proceed to the breaker point adjustment section which follows the breaker point replacement procedure.

7. Disconnect the primary lead and the condenser wires from the breaker point assembly. On centrifugal advance distributors, remove the jumper strap also.

8. Remove the breaker point assembly and condenser retaining screws. Lift the breaker point assembly and the condenser from the distributor.

9. Lightly lubricate the distributor cam with heat-resistant lubricant.

10. Place the new breaker point assembly and condenser in position within the distributor, and install but do not tighten the screws.

11. On Loadomatic distributors (pre-1968 six-cylinder engines), position the ground wire under the breaker point assembly screw, and connect the primary and condenser wires to the breaker point assembly. On all V8 engines, except those equipped with a centrifugal advance distributor, place the ground wire under the breaker point assembly screw farthest from the breaker point contacts. On six-cylinder engines from 1968 to the present, this ground wire should be placed under the condenser retaining screw.

12. If the two contact points of the breaker point assembly are not parallel, bend the stationary contact slightly to correct. Bend only the bracket portion of the assembly, do not damage the contact surface.

13. Turn the engine until the rubbing block on the point assembly is resting on the high point of a distributor cam lobe. Using the proper thickness gauge for the point gap specifications of your car, adjust the point gap, and tighten the retaining screw.

14. Check the gap with a feeler gauge, in order to make sure that it was not altered by the tightening of the retaining screws.

15. Connect the primary and condenser

wires to the breaker point assembly in the same order in which they were removed. If your distributor is equipped with the metal point shield, the wires should be positioned at right angles to each other, or at 180° to each other. The purpose of this placement is to avoid the possibility of wire terminals contacting the metal point shield, thus creating a short circuit and a resultant no-start situation.

16. Install the metal point shield if your distributor is so equipped.

17. Push the rotor onto the distributor shaft, after aligning the tab inside the rotor with the notch on the shaft. Make sure that the rotor is fully seated on the shaft.

18. Align the tab inside the base of the distributor cap with the notch on the rim of the distributor body. Install the cap on the distributor, making certain that it is fully seated. Snap the distributor cap retaining clamps into place on either side of the cap.

19. Install the coil high-tension wire at the coil.

20. If you are checking your breaker point adjustment with a dwell meter, read carefully all instructions included with your dwell meter and connect the dwell meter accordingly.

21. Start the engine.

CAUTION: *When working on a vehicle whose engine is running, make certain that your work area is well ventilated, the transmission is in Neutral, and the parking brake is firmly applied. Always keep hands, clothing, and tools well clear of the engine fan.*

22. Observe the reading on the dwell meter. If the reading is within the specified range, stop the engine and disconnect the meter.

23. If the reading is above the specified range (in number of degrees) the breaker point gap is too small. If the reading is below the specified range, the breaker point gap is too large. In either case, stop the engine. Remove the distributor cap, rotor, and point shield (if so equipped), and adjust the points accordingly. Reassemble the distributor, start the engine, and take another reading on the meter. Repeat the process if necessary.

Ignition Timing Adjustment

1. Locate the timing marks and pointer on the lower engine pulley and engine front cover (see illustrations).

Timing Marks

1968–1973 6 Cylinder

1965–1967 260 and 289 V8

1967 390 V8

1968–1973 302 V8

2. Clean the timing marks and pointer.

3. Mark the proper timing mark (see "Tune-Up Specifications" for the correct timing for your engine) and the pointer with white chalk or day-glo paint. Attach a tachometer to the engine.

4. Attach a timing light according to the manufacturer's instructions.

5. Disconnect any and all vacuum lines from the distributor, and plug the vacuum line(s) with the end of a pencil, a golf tee, or any other suitable object.

6. Check to make sure that the timing light wires are well clear of the fan assembly. Start the engine.

NOTE: *Follow the precautions discussed earlier for working on an automobile with the engine running.*

7. If the recommended engine idle speed is in excess of 500 rpm, set the idle at 500 rpm for purposes of setting the ignition timing. If the recommended idle is below 500 rpm, do not alter it. Refer to chapter four for idle speed setting procedures. In all cases, references in this procedure are for idle speeds with the engine at its full operating temperature.

8. Aim the timing light at the timing mark and pointer on the front of the engine. If the marks which you made on the pointer and timing mark align when the timing light flashes, set the idle to its proper specification, remove the timing light and tachometer, and connect the vacuum lines at the distributor. If the marks do not align when the light flashes, continue with the procedures for ignition timing adjustment.

9. Stop the engine with the timing light

still connected. Loosen the distributor hold-down clamp slightly.

10. Start the engine again, and observe the timing mark and pointer with the timing light. Timing may be advanced by turning the distributor of a six-cylinder engine counterclockwise. On V8 engines, the timing is advanced by turning the distributor clockwise. When the proper timing has been attained (when the paint marks on the pointer and the timing mark align), stop the engine. Tighten the distributor hold-down clamp. Restart the engine and check the timing to make sure that it was not altered while you tightened the hold-down clamp.

11. On all engines, except pre-1968 six-cylinder models, the centrifugal advance must be checked for proper operation. Start the engine and accelerate it to approximately 2,000 rpm. Properly aim your timing light at the mark and pointer. If the ignition timing advances, the centrifugal advance mechanism is functioning properly. Note the engine speed when the advance begins, and the amount of advance which is attained. Stop the engine.

12. On all engines except pre-1968 high-performance engines equipped with centrifugal advance distributors, connect the vacuum line at the outer side of the diaphragm. Start the engine and accelerate it to approximately 2,000 rpm. Note the speed when the advance begins and the amount of advance attained. On pre-1968 six-cylinder engines, any advance indicates that the vacuum advance is in proper working order. On all others equipped with vacuum advance, the timing should now advance sooner and farther than before the vacuum lines were connected. If this occurs, the vacuum advance is working properly. Stop the engine.

13. On dual-diaphragm distributors, check the vacuum retard operation by connecting the intake manifold vacuum line to the inner side of the diaphragm. Start the engine and adjust the carburetor to its normal idle speed. The initial timing should retard to approximately top dead center (TDC) if the initial ignition timing is correct. On some engines, the timing may retard as far as six degrees after top dead center (ATDC).

14. If the vaccum advance (or vacuum retard, in the case of dual-diaphragm distributors) is not functioning properly, it will be necessary to remove the distributor from the engine and have it tested on a distributor testing machine. Refer to chapter three for

distributor removal procedures. If either diaphragm is leaking or cannot be calibrated to specifications, it will be necessary to replace the diaphragm unit.

15. If all vacuum advance and retard units are found to be in proper working order, remove all testing equipment from the engine.

Valve Lash Adjustment

V8s with Mechanical Lifters (Except Boss 429)

1. Run the engine until it is at full operating temperature.

2. Stop the engine. Remove the rocker covers.

3. Check the "Valve Clearance Specifications" chart for the proper clearance for your engine.

4. Start the engine. Insert a step type feeler gauge (go and no-go) of the specified thickness between the rocker arm and the top of the valve. Adjustment is accomplished by loosening the jam nut (or locking nut)—the top nut on the rocker arm stud—and moving the adjusting nut (the lower nut) up or down as needed. When the proper adjustment has been attained, tighten the jam nut against the adjusting nut while holding the adjusting nut in position with a separate wrench. Check the clearance to make sure that the tightening of the jam nut against the adjusting nut did not alter the proper adjustment of the valve clearance.

5. When all valves have been adjusted in this manner, stop the engine and reinstall the rocker covers.

Boss 429

The valve lash on this engine should be adjusted only when the engine is cold. Refer if necessary to the firing order diagram found earlier in this chapter.

1. Remove the valve rocker arm covers.

2. Rotate the crankshaft damper until the number 1 (no. 1) piston is at TDC at the end of the compression stroke. This position can be determined by observing the distributor rotor. When it is at the no. 1 firing position with the breaker points just starting to open, the engine is in the proper position for the adjustment of the valves in the no. 1 cylinder.

3. On the no. 1 intake and exhaust valves only, torque the rocker shaft to cylinder head retaining nuts to 12–15 ft. lbs.

4. Adjust the clearance between the

rocker arm and the top of the valves on the no. 1 cylinder only, using a feeler gauge of the specified thickness. Adjustment is made by loosening the locking nut, turning the adjusting screw to obtain the desired clearance, and tightening the locking nut while holding the adjusting screw in position with the screwdriver. Check the clearance to make sure that it was not altered during the tightening of the adjusting nut.

5. Rotate the crankshaft 90° in order to position the no. 5 piston at TDC, checking the position of the distributor rotor as in the adjustment of the valves for no. 1 cylinder. Repeat steps three and four.

6. Follow this procedure throughout the entire firing order (1-5-4-2-6-3-7-8), until all valves have been adjusted.

7. Install the valve rocker arm covers.

Carburetor

Carburetor adjustments are the final step in any thorough tune-up.

Complete information on all stock carburetors is provided in chapter four. Refer to that section after all other tune-up procedures have been completed.

Valve Clearance Specifications
V8 Engines, Mechanical Lifters

Year	Displacement (cu in.)	Tappet (Hot) Clearance (in.)	
		Intake	Exhaust
1965	289 High Performance	0.018	0.018
1966	289 High Performance	0.018	0.018
1967	289 High Performance	0.019	0.021
1969 1970 302 BOSS		0.025	0.025
1969 1970 429 BOSS		0.013 (Cold)	0.013 (Cold)
1971	351 BOSS	0.025	0.025
1971	429 SCJ	0.019	0.019
1972	351 HO	0.025	0.025

Engine and Engine Rebuilding

3

ENGINE ELECTRICAL

Distributor

There have been three different types of distributor used on Mustangs. From 1965 to 1967, the six-cylinder engines were equipped with Loadomatic vacuum advance units. During this same period, certain high-performance V8 engines used a centrifugal advance distributor, which is most readily identifiable by the absence of a vacuum control line. All engines from .1968 to the present, as well as those V8 engines prior to 1968 (other than the types with centrifugal advance distributors) have been equipped with dual advance distributors.

Loadomatic Vacuum Advance Distributor

Ignition timing changes are entirely satisfied by the action of the breaker plate. The position of the plate is controlled by a vacuum-actuated diaphragm working against the tension of two accurately calibrated breaker plate springs. The diaphragm moves the breaker plate counterclockwise to advance the spark. The springs tend to counteract this movement to return timing to a retarded position. Cam and rotor rotation are clockwise as viewed from the top.

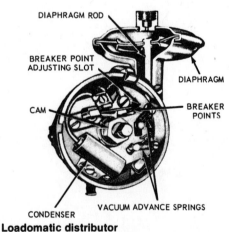

Loadomatic distributor

Centrifugal Advance Distributor

A purely mechanical unit, this distributor contains two centrifugal weights which cause the cam to move ahead with respect to the distributor driveshaft. The rate of advance is controlled by two calibrated springs which act against the centrifugal force of the two weights. The unit is also equipped with a governor to regulate the amount of advance possible.

Dual Advance Distributor

The dual advance distributor has two independently operated spark-timing control systems. A governor type and a vacuum type control are used on each distributor of standard production engines. Centrifugal weights cause the cam to advance or rotate ahead, relative to the distributor shaft.

The vacuum control mechanism operates through a spring-loaded diaphragm and movable breaker plate, about the same as the vacuum advance distributor.

Distributor Modulator

Many post-1970 Ford engines are equipped with a distributor modulator system to reduce engine emissions. It consists of four major components: a speed sensor, a thermal switch, an electronic control amplifier, and a three-way solenoid valve.

DISTRIBUTOR REMOVAL

1. Unfasten and remove the distributor cap. Disconnect the primary wire at the coil and the vacuum control line(s) at the distributor.

2. Scribe a mark on the distributor body, to show the position of the rotor, and another mark on the distributor body and the block to show the position of the distributor in the block. Do not disturb the engine until after you have completely reinstalled the distributor, as this will defeat the purpose of the marks that you have just made. The marks are for the purpose of eliminating the need to retime the engine upon completion of the distributor work.

3. Remove the screw, lockwasher, and hold-down clamp. Pull the distributor out of the block.

DISTRIBUTOR INSTALLATION

1. Line up the rotor slightly to the left of the mark that you made to indicate its position.

2. Insert the distributor into the block, aligning the marks that you made on the distributor body and the block. Push the distributor firmly into the block. As it descends into the installed position, the rotor lines up with the mark that you made to indicate its position.

3. Install, but do not tighten, the hold-down clamp, lockwasher, and screw.

4. If the engine has not been disturbed, there should be no need for retiming. Install and fasten the distributor cap, connect the distributor primary wire at the coil, and connect the vacuum control line at the distributor. After checking your marks on the block

and the distributor housing for precise alignment, tighten the screw which secures the distributor holddown clamp.

5. If timing is necessary, refer to the "Tune-Up and Troubleshooting" chapter for instructions.

Charging System

All models are equipped with alternating current (AC) generators (alternators). unlike the direct current (DC) generators used in many older cars, there are several precautions which must be strictly observed in order to avoid damaging the unit. They are as follow:

1. Reversing the battery connections will result in damage to the one-way electrical valves (rectifiers).

2. Booster batteries should be connected from negative to negative, and positive to positive.

3. Never use a fast charger as a booster to start cars with AC circuits.

4. When servicing the battery with a fast charger, always disconnect the car battery cables.

5. Never attempt to polarize an AC generator.

6. Avoid long soldering times when replacing diodes or transistors. Prolonged heat is damaging to AC generators.

7. Do not use test lamps of more than 12 volts (V) for checking diode continuity.

8. Do not short across or ground any of the terminals on the AC generator.

9. The polarity of the battery, generator, and regulator must be matched and considered before making any electrical connections within the system.

10. Never operate the AC generator on an open circuit. Make sure that all connections within the circuit are clean and tight.

11. Disconnect the battery terminals when performing any service on the electrical system. This will eliminate the possibility of accidental reversal of polarity.

12. Disconnect the battery ground cable if arc welding is to be done on any part of the car.

ALTERNATOR REMOVAL

1. Disconnect the battery ground cable.

2. Loosen the alternator mounting bolts, remove the adjustment arm-to-alternator attaching bolt and remove the alternator drive belt from the alternator.

Alternator terminal locations

3. Remove the alternator mounting bolt and spacer, and lift the alternator from the engine.

4. With the alternator removed from its installed position, remove the electrical connectors. On units with integral regulators mounted on the back of the alternator housing, depress the sides of the retainer clip and remove the wire from the regulator.

ALTERNATOR INSTALLATION

Reverse the removal procedures.

BELT TENSION ADJUSTMENT

1. Loosen the alternator adjusting arm bolt and the mounting bolts.

2. Properly position the belt on its pulley(s).

3. Pull the alternator away from the engine so that the belt tightens. If you are using a pry bar, be sure that you position it only against the front end housing of the alterna-

tor. Positioning such a device against the rear end housing will damage the alternator.

4. When the belt feels adequately tight, tighten the adjusting arm bolt only. Test the tightness of the belt by pressing it firmly with your thumb. The deflection should not exceed ¼ in. If further adjustment is required, loosen the adjusting arm bolt and make the correction. Tighten the adjusting arm bolt and test the belt tension again.

5. If the belt is properly tightened, secure the mounting bolts.

FUSE LINK REPLACEMENT

1. Disconnect the negative battery cable.

2. Disconnect the eyelet end of the fuse link from the starter relay.

3. Cut the other end of the fuse link from the wiring harness at the splice.

4. Connect the eyelet end of a new fuse link to the starter relay.

NOTE: *Use only an original equipment fuse link. Under no conditions should standard wire be submitted.*

5. Splice the open end of the new fuse link into the wiring harness.

6. Solder the splice with rosin core solder and wrap the splice with electrical tape. This splice must be soldered.

7. Connect the negative battery cable.

8. Start the engine, to make sure that the new connections complete the circuit.

VOLTAGE REGULATOR REMOVAL AND INSTALLATION

1. Remove the battery ground cable. On models with the regulator mounted behind

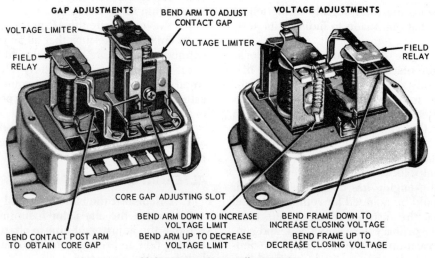

Voltage regulator adjustments

the battery, it is necessary to remove the battery hold-down and to move the battery.

2. Remove the regulator mounting screws.

3. Disconnect the regulator from the wiring harness.

4. Connect the new regulator to the wiring harness.

5. Mount the regulator to the regulator mounting plate. The radio suppression condenser mounts under one mounting screw, the ground lead under the other mounting screw. Tighten the mounting screws.

6. If the battery was moved to gain access to the regulator, position the battery and install the hold-down. Connect the battery ground cable and test the system for proper voltage regulation.

MECHANICAL REGULATOR ADJUSTMENTS

Erratic operation of the regulator, indicated by erratic movement of the voltmeter pointer during a voltage limiter test, may be caused by dirty or pitted regulator contacts. Vehicle ammeter pointer waver at certain critical engine speeds and electrical loads, is normal. Use a very fine abrasive paper such as silicon carbide, 400 grade, to clean the field relay and the voltage limiter contacts. Wear off the sharp edges of the abrasive by rubbing it against another piece of abrasive paper. Fold the abrasive paper over and pull the paper through the contacts to clean them. Keep all oil or grease from contacting the points. Do not use compressed air to clean the regulator. When adjusting the gap spacing use only hospital-clean feeler gauges.

Gap Adjustment

VOLTAGE LIMITER

The difference between the upper stage and lower stage regulation (0.3 V), is determined by the voltage limiter contact and core gaps. Make the gap adjustment with the regulator removed from the car. Bend the lower contact bracket to obtain a 0.017–0.022 in. gap at the lower contacts with the upper contacts closed. Maintain the contacts in alignment.

Adjust the core gap with the upper contacts closed. Loosen the center lockscrew ¼ turn. Use a screwdriver blade in the adjustment slot under the lockscrew. Adjust the core gap for a 0.049–0.056 in. clearance between the armature and the core at the edge of the core closest to the contact points.

Tighten the lockscrew and recheck the core gap.

FIELD RELAY

Place a 0.010–0.018 in. feeler gauge on top of the coil core closest to the contact points. Hold the armature down on the gauge. Do not push down on the contact spring arm. Bend the contact post arm until the bottom contact just touches the upper contact.

VOLTAGE LIMITER ADJUSTMENT

Final adjustment of the regulator must be made with the regulator at normal operating temperature.

The field relay closing voltage is adjusted by bending the relay frame. To increase the closing voltage, bend the armature frame down. To decrease the closing voltage, bend the frame up.

The voltage limiter is adjusted by bending the voltage limiter spring arm. To increase the voltage setting, bend the adjusting arm downward. To decrease the voltage setting, bend the adjusting arm upward.

Before setting the voltage and before making a final voltage test, the alternator speed must be reduced to zero and the ignition switch opened momentarily, to cycle the regulator.

On some cars the location of the regulator may prevent adjustment on the car. Remove the regulator to an alternator-regulator test stand if adjustment is necessary.

TRANSISTORIZED REGULATOR ADJUSTMENTS

Voltage Limiter Adjustment

The only adjustment on the transistorized alternator regulator is the voltage limiter adjustment.

Adjustment of the transistor voltage limiter must be made with the regulator at normal operating temperature. Remove the regulator mounting screws and remove the bottom cover from the regulator. The voltage setting may be moved up or down by adjusting the 40 ohm adjustable resistor.

Starter

Your car is equipped with a four-brush, series-parallel wound starter unit. The circuit is completed by means of a relay-control switch which is part of the ignition switch.

Alternator and Regulator Specifications

Year	Alternator Part No. or Manufacturer	Field Current @12 V	Output (amps)	Regulator Part No. or Manufacturer	Field Relay Air Gap (in.)	Field Relay Point Gap (in.)	Field Relay Volts to Close	Regulator Air Gap (in.)	Regulator Point Gap (in.)	Volts @75°
1965–69	Autolite	2.8–3.3	38	Autolite	—	—	2.5	0.049–0.056	0.017–0.022	13.8–14.4
	Autolite	2.9–3.1	42	Autolite	0.012–0.022	0.015–0.022	2.5	0.049–0.056	0.017–0.022	13.8–14.4
	Autolite	2.9	45	Autolite	0.015	—	2.5–4	0.052	0.019	13.8–14.6
	Autolite	2.9	55	Autolite	0.015	—	2.5–4	0.052	0.019	13.8–14.6
	Leece-Neville	2.9	53	Leece-Neville	0.012	0.025	7	0.047	0.019	14.1–14.9
1970	Autolite Purple	2.4	38	Autolite	—	—	2–4.2	—	—	13.5–15.3
	Autolite Orange	2.9	42	Autolite	—	—	2–4.2	—	—	13.5–15.3
	Autolite Red	2.9	55	Autolite	—	—	2–4.2	—	—	13.5–15.3
	Autolite Green	2.9	61	Autolite	—	—	2–4.2	—	—	13.5–15.3
	Autolite Black	2.9	65	Autolite	—	—	2–4.2	—	—	13.5–15.3
1971	Autolite Purple	2.4	38	Autolite	—	—	2.5–4	—	—	13.5–15.3
	Autolite Orange	2.9	42	Autolite	—	—	2.5–4	—	—	13.5–15.3
	Autolite Red	2.9	55	Autolite	—	—	2.5–4	—	—	13.5–15.3
	Autolite Green	2.9	61	Autolite	—	—	2.5–4	—	—	13.5–15.3
	Autolite Black	2.9	65	Autolite	—	—	2.5–4	—	—	13.5–15.3
1972–73	Motorcraft Purple	2.4	38	Motorcraft	—	—	2.5–4	—	—	13.5–15.4
	Motorcraft Orange	2.9	42	Motorcraft	—	—	2.5–4	—	—	13.5–15.4

Alternator and Regulator Specifications (cont.)

	Alternator			Regulator	Field Relay			Regulator		
Year	Part No. or Manufacturer	Field Current @12 V	Output (amps)	Part No. or Manufacturer	Air Gap (in.)	Point Gap (in.)	Volts to Close	Air Gap (in.)	Point Gap (in.)	Volts @75°
	Motorcraft Red	2.9	55	Motorcraft	—	—	2.5–4	—	—	13.5–15.4
	Motorcraft Green	2.9	61	Motorcraft	—	—	2.5–4	—	—	13.5–15.4
	Motorcraft Black	2.9	65	Motorcraft	—	—	2.5–4	—	—	13.5–15.4

—Not Applicable

Battery and Starter Specifications

		Battery			Starter	Lock Test			No-Load Test			Brush
Year	Engine Displacement (cu in.)	Ampere Hour Capacity	Volts	Terminal Grounded	Amps	Volts	Torque (ft. lbs.)	Amps	Volts	RPM	Spring Tension (oz)
1965	6	40	12	Neg.	540	4.2	14.0	50	12	9,500	45
	8	55	12	Neg.	670	6.0	15.5	70	12	9,500	45
1966	6	45	12	Neg.	460	5	9	70	12	9,500	40
	8	55	12	Neg.	670	5	15.5	70	12	9,500	40
	Option	70	12	Neg.	670	5	15.5	70	12	9,500	40
	Option	80	12	Neg.	670	5	—	70	12	9,500	40
1966 73	6—170	45	12	Neg.	460	5	9	50	12	9,500	40
	6—200	45	12	Neg.	670	5	15.5	70	12	9,500	40
	8—exc. below	55	12	Neg.	460 ①	5	9 ②	70	12	9,500	40
	8—351 4-BBL	70	12	Neg.	460 ①	5	9 ②	70	12	9,500	40
	8—428, 429	80	12	Neg.	460 ①	5	9 ②	70	12	9,500	40

① in. diameter starter—670
② 4½ in. diameter starter—15.5

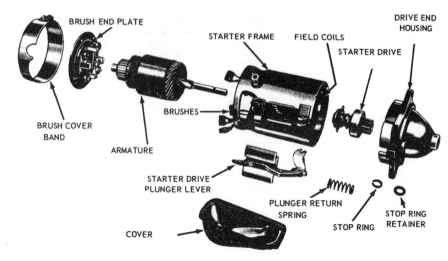

Starter disassembled

REMOVAL

1. On cars with V8s, disconnect the battery negative terminal and raise the vehicle.

2. Disconnect the starter cable at the starter terminal.

3. Remove the flywheel housing-to-starter retaining screws. On all cars, these are ½ in. hex-head bolts.

4. Remove the starter assembly and the rubber dust ring (if so equipped).

INSTALLATION

1. Position the rubber dust ring on the flywheel housing.

2. Position the starter assembly to the flywheel housing and start the mounting bolts.

3. Secure the mounting bolts by alternately step-tightening them while holding the starter firmly against its mounting surface.

4. Torque the mounting bolts. If your car is equipped with three bolts of 5/18 in. diameter, the torque should be 12–15 ft. lbs. If it has two bolts of ⅜ in. diameter, 15–20 ft. lbs. is recommended.

STARTER DRIVE REPLACEMENT

1. Loosen and remove the brush cover band and the starter drive lunger lever cover.

2. Loosen the thru-bolts enough to facilitate the removal of the drive end housing and the starter drive plunger lever return spring.

3. Some drive end housings are equipped with needle bearings. If yours is so equipped, and you are not replacing the bearings, insert a dummy shaft through the housing in order to prevent the loss of any of the bearing needles.

4. Remove the pivot pin which retains the starter drive plunger lever. Remove the lever.

5. Remove the drive gear stop-ring retainer and the stop-ring from the end of the armature shaft. Remove the drive gear assembly.

6. Apply a thin coating of Lubriplate or a similar product on the armature shaft splines. Install the drive gear assembly on the armature shaft and install a new stopring.

7. Position the starter gear plunger lever on the starter frame and install the pivot pin. Make sure that the plunger lever properly engages the starter drive assembly.

8. Install a new stop-ring retainer. Remove the dummy shaft from the drive end housing and lightly grease the needle bearing. Position the starter drive plunger lever return spring and the drive end housing to the starter frame.

9. Tighten and torque the thru-bolts. Recommended torque is 55–75 in. lbs.

10. Position the starter drive plunger lever cover and the brush cover band, with its gasket, on the starter. Tighten the brush cover band retaining screw.

Battery

REMOVAL AND INSTALLATION

1. Disconnect both battery cables at the battery. Negative cable first.

2. Unfasten and remove the battery hold-down.

3. Attach a battery carrier to both terminals and lift the battery from beneath the hood, being careful not to tilt the battery so as to leak fluid.

4. Reverse the procedure to install a battery. Connect the ground cable first.

ENGINE MECHANICAL

Three different six-cylinder engines have been offered: the 170, the 200, and the 250 cu in. engines. These engines are all of the same family; the only great difference among them is their bore and stroke. One distinguishing characteristic is the fact that the intake manifold is cast as an integral part of the cylinder head.

Optional V8 engines have been quite numerous and, like the family of six-cylinder engines, there is a great amount of similarity among them.

The most widely used are the 260, 289, and 302 cu in. V8 engines. These are remarkably compact engines with stud-mounted rockers and wedge-shaped combustion chambers. The 260 V8 was dropped from production in 1965, and the 289 saw its last use in 1968.

In 1969, Ford Motor Company introduced a longer-stroke, higher-block version of the 302 engine. This is the 351 Windsor engine and features the wedge-shaped combustion chambers and stud-mounted rockers of the small block engine in a new intermediate-sized block.

Also in 1969, Ford Motor Company added the 351 Cleveland engine. This engine has the same bore and stroke as the Windsor unit, but that is where the similarity ends. It has different-sized main bearings, larger valves, smaller spark plug holes, and semi-hemispherical combustion chambers. It is used concurrently with the Windsor engine in all models. Although the Windsor engine is fitted only with a two-barrel carburetor, the Cleveland engine is used with either two or four-barrel carburetion.

Starting in 1967, the 390 cu in. V8 became available. The following year saw the availability of still other large-block V8s, the 427 and the 428 Cobra Jet.

To qualify for Trans-American sedan racing, Ford built a small number of cars in 1969–70, equipped with a special Boss 302

V8. This is essentially a 302 cu in. engine of the 260–289 family, topped by cylinder heads from the 351 Cleveland engine.

The Boss 302 V8 was eliminated from production in 1971 and it was replaced by a high-performance version of the 351 Cleveland engine. It is designated as the Boss 351 engine.

In 1969 and 1970, Ford released a small number of cars powered by the Boss 429 engine. This unique engine features modified hemispherical combustion chambers, very large valves and ports, valve seats which are canted in two planes, rockers with individual rocker shafts, and O-rings and chevron seals in place of head gaskets. The heads are of aluminum, the valves require special seals, the main bearings have four-bolt main caps, and the spark plugs pass through the rocker covers. In many ways, this highly individual engine requires special procedures for maintenance and repair.

The last of the big-block models is the 429 Super Cobra Jet engine, which was offered only in 1971. Outstanding features of this engine include the use of special rods, forged pistons, big valve heads, four-bolt main caps, small 14 (mm) spark plugs, solid lifters, and a 6,000 rpm governor.

For 1972, only a 250 cu in. six-cylinder or 302 or 351 cu in. V8 engines were available.

In mid-1972, Ford re-entered the performance car category with the introduction of the 351 HO (for High Output) engine. Basically the Boss 351 engine, this new offering was modified to meet emission control standards in all fifty states. Changes have included reducing the compression ratio to 8.8:1 and changing to a drastically refined camshaft, despite the retention of mechanical lifters. The car in which this engine is featured is equipped in the same manner as the 1971 Boss, although it no longer carries the Boss name.

For 1973 there are four engines available: the 250 cu in. one-barrel, six-cylinder; the 302 cu in. two-barrel, V8; and two 351 cu in. V8s, one with a two-barrel carburetor and the CJ model with a four-barrel carburetor.

Engine Removal

1. Scribe the hood hinge outline on the underhood, disconnect the hood, and remove it.

2. Drain the entire cooling system and

General Engine Specifications

	Displacement (cu in.)	Carburetion	BHP ■ @ (rpm)	Torque ■ @ (rpm)	Bore x Stroke (in.)	Comp. Ratio	Oil Pressure (lbs./sq in.)
1965	6—170	1 bbl	105@4400	158@2400	3.500x2.940	9.1:1	35–60
	6—200	1 bbl	120@4400	185@2400	3.680x3.126	9.2:1	35–60
	8—260	2 bbl	164@4400	258@2200	3.800x2.870	8.8:1	35–60
	8—289	2 bbl	200@4400	282@2400	4.000x2.870	9.3:1	35–60
	8—289	4 bbl	225@4800	305@3200	4.000x2.870	10.0:1	35–60
	8—289 H.P.	4 bbl	271@6000	312@3400	4.000x2.870	10.5:1	35–55
1966	6—200	1 bbl	120@4400	190@2400	3.680x3.126	9.2:1	35–55
	8—289	2 bbl	200@4400	282@2400	4.000x2.870	9.3:1	35–55
	8—289	4 bbl	225@4800	305@3200	4.000x2.870	9.8:1	35–55
	8—289 H.P.	4 bbl	271@6000	312@3400	4.000x2.870	10.0:1	35–55
1967	6—200	1 bbl	120@4400	190@2400	3.680x3.130	9.2:1	35–55
	6—289	2 bbl	200@4400	282@2400	4.000x2.870	9.3:1	35–55
	8—289	4 bbl	225@4800	305@3200	4.000x2.870	9.8:1	35–55
	8—289 H.P.	4 bbl	271@6000	312@3400	4.000x2.870	10.0:1	35–55
	8—390	4 bbl	320@3600	427@3200	4.050x3.784	10.5:1	35–65
1968	6—200	1 bbl	115@3800	190@2200	3.680x3.130	8.8:1	35–60
	8—289	2 bbl	195@4600	288@2600	4.000x2.870	8.7:1	35–60
	8—302	4 bbl	230@4800	310@2800	4.000x3.000	10.0:1	35–60
	8—390	2 bbl	265@4400	390@2600	4.050x3.784	9.5:1	35–60
	8—390 GT	4 bbl	325@4800	427@3200	4.050x3.784	10.5:1	35–60
	8—427	4 bbl	390@5600	460@3200	4.236x3.781	10.9:1	35–60
	8—428 CJ	4 bbl	335@5400	440@3400	4.130x3.984	10.6:1	35–60
1969	6—200	1 bbl	120@4400	190@2400	3.680x3.130	8.1:1	35–60
	6—250	1 bbl	155@4000	240@1600	3.682x3.910	9.0:1	35–60
	8—302	2 bbl	210@4400	295@2400	4.000x3.000	9.5:1	35–60

General Engine Specifications (cont.)

	Displacement (cu in.)	Carburetion	BHP ■ @ (rpm)	Torque ■ @ (rpm)	Bore x Stroke (in.)	Comp. Ratio	Oil Pressure (lbs./sq in.)
	8—302 BOSS	4 bbl	290@5800	290@4300	4.000x3.000	10.5:1	35–60
	8—351	2 bbl	250@4600	355@2600	4.000x3.000	9.5:1	35–60
	8—351 C	4 bbl	290@4800	385@3200	4.000x3.000	10.7:1	35–60
	8—390	4 bbl	320@4600	427@3200	4.050x3.784	10.5:1	35–60
	8—428 CJ	4 bbl	335@5200	440@3400	4.130x3.984	10.6:1	35–60
	8—429 BOSS	4 bbl	375@5200	450@3400	4.360x3.590	10.5:1	45–60
1970	6—200	1 bbl	120@4400	190@2400	3.680x3.130	8.7:1	35–60
	6—250	1 bbl	155@4400	240@1600	3.682x3.910	9.0:1	35–60
	8—302	2 bbl	210@4400	295@2400	4.000x3.000	9.5:1	35–60
	8—302 BOSS	4 bbl	290@5800	290@4300	4.000x3.000	10.5:1	35–60
	8—351	4 bbl	250@4600	355@2600	4.000x3.500	9.5:1	35–60
	8—351 C	4 bbl	300@5400	380@3400	4.000x3.500	11.4:1	35–60
	8—428 CJ	4 bbl	335@5200	440@3400	4.130x3.984	10.6:1	35–60
	8—429 BOSS	4 bbl	375@5200	450@3400	4.362x3.590	10.5:1	45–60
1971	6—250	1 bbl	145@4000	232@1600	3.682x3.910	9.0:1	35–60
	8—302	2 bbl	210@4600	296@2600	4.000x3.000	9.0:1	35–60
	8—351	2 bbl	240@4600	355@2600	4.000x3.500	9.5:1	35–60
	8—351 BOSS	4 bbl	330@5800	380@3400	4.000x3.500	11.0:1	35–60
	8—351 CJ	4 bbl	280@5800	345@3800	4.000x3.500	9.0:1	35–60
	8—351 C	4 bbl	285@5400	370@3400	4.000x3.500	10.7:1	35–60
	8—429 SCJ	4 bbl	375@5600	450@3400	4.362x3.590	11.3:1	35–75
1972– 73	6—250	1 bbl	99@3600	184@1600	3.680x3.910	8.0:1	35–60
	8—302	2 bbl	141@4000	242@2000	4.000x3.000	8.5:1	35–60

General Engine Specifications (cont.)

Displacement (cu in.)	Carburetion	BHP ■ @ (rpm)	Torque ■ @ (rpm)	Bore x Stroke (in.)	Comp. Ratio	Oil Pressure (lbs./sq in.)
8—351	2 bbl	164 @ 4000	276 @ 2000	4.000 x 3.500	8.6 : 1	35—85
8—351 HO	4 bbl	266 @ 5400	301 @ 3600	4.000 x 3.500	8.6 : 1	35–85
8—351 CJ ①	4 bbl	248 @ 5400	290 @ 3800	4.000 x 3.500	8.0 : 1	35–85

■ 1972 horsepower and torque are SAE net figures. They are measured at the rear of the transmission with all accessories installed and operating. Since the figures vary when a given engine is installed in different models, some are representative rather than exact.
① 1973—CJ replaced HO as optional 4 bbl engine.

crankcase. Remove the evaporative emissions and EGR system lines.

3. Remove the air cleaner and disconnect the battery at the cylinder head. On cars with automatic transmissions, disconnect the oil cooler lines at the radiator.

4. Remove the upper and lower radiator hoses and the radiator. If the car is equipped with air conditioning, unbolt the compressor and position the compressor out of way with the refrigerant lines intact. Unbolt and lay the refrigerant radiator forward without disconnecting the refrigerant lines. On some 428 CJ engines and all 429 Super CJ, Boss 302, and Boss 429 engines, disconnect the inlet and outlet lines from the engine oil cooler, remove the hold-down bracket, and remove the cooler.

5. Remove the fan, fan belt, and upper pulley.

6. Disconnect the heater hoses at the water pump and the carburetor spacer.

7. Disconnect the generator wires at the generator, the starter cable at the starter, the accelerator rod at the carburetor, and, on the six-cylinder engine, the choke control cable at the carburetor.

8. Disconnect the fuel tank line at the fuel pump and plug the line.

9. Disconnect the coil primary wire at the coil. Disconnect the wires at the oil pressure and water temperature sending units.

10. Remove the starter and dust seal.

11. On a car equipped with a manual transmission, remove the clutch retracting spring. Disconnect the clutch equalizer shaft and arm bracket at the underbody rail and remove the arm bracket and equalizer shaft.

12. Raise the car. Remove the flywheel or converter housing upper retaining bolts through the access holes in the floor pan.

13. Disconnect the exhaust pipe or pipes at the exhaust manifold. Disconnect the right and left motor mounts at the underbody bracket. Remove the flywheel or converter housing cover.

14. On a car with manual shift, remove the flywheel housing lower retaining bolts.

15. On a car with an automatic transmission, disconnect the throttle valve vacuum line at the intake manifold and the converter from the flywheel. Remove the converter housing lower retaining bolts. On a car with power steering, disconnect the power steering pump from the cylinder head. Move the drive belt and wire the steering pump out of the way.

16. Lower the car. Support the transmission and flywheel or converter housing with a jack.

17. Attach an engine lifting hook. Lift the engine up and out of the compartment and onto an adequate workstand.

Engine Installation

1. Place a new gasket over the studs of the exhaust manifold(s).

2. Attach an engine sling and lifting device. Lift the engine from the workstand.

3. Lower the engine into the engine compartment. Be sure the exhaust manifold(s) is in proper alignment with the muffler inlet pipe(s), and the dowels in the block engage the holes in the flywheel housing.

Torque Specifications
(ft. lbs.)

Year	Displacement (cu in.)	Cylinder Head Bolts *	Rod Bearing Bolts	Main Bearing Bolts	Crankshaft Pulley Bolts	Flywheel-to-Crankshaft Bolt	Manifold Bolts	
							Intake	Exhaust
1965	6—170, 200	70–75	19–24	60–70	85–100	75–85	None	13–18
	8—260, 289	65–70	19–24	60–70	70–90	75–85	12–15	15–20
	8—289 H.P.	65–70	40–45	60–70	70–90	75–85	12–15	15–20
1966–68	6—200	70–75	19–24	60–70	85–100	75–85	None	13–18
	8—260, 289, 302	65–70	19–24 ①	60–70	70–90	75–85	20–22	15–20
	8—390, 428	80–90	40–45	95–105	70–90	75–85	32–35	18–24
	8—427	100–110	53–58	95–105	70–90	75–85	32–35 ·	18–24
1969	6—200	70–75	19–24	60–70	85–100	75–85	—	13–18
	8—302	65–72	19–24	60–70	70–90	75–85	23–25	12–16
	8—351 W	95–100	40–45	95–105	70–90	75–85	23–25	18–24
	8—390	80–90	40–45	95–105	70–90	75–85	32–35	18–24
	8—428	80–90	53–58	95–105	70–90	75–85	32–35	18–24
1970–73	6—200	70–75	19–24 ③	60–70	85–100	75–85	—	13–18
	8—302	65–72	19–24 ④	60–70 ⑤	70–90	75–85	23–25	12–16
	8—351	95–100 ②	40–45 ⑦	95–105 ⑧	70–90	75–85	23–25 (5/16) 28–32 (3/8) 6–9 (1/4)	12–22
	8—428	80–90	53–58	95–105	70–90	75–85	32–35	18–24
	8—429	130–140	40–45	95–105 ⑥	70–90	75–85	25–30	28–33
	8—429 Boss	90–95	85–90	70–80	70–90	75–85	25–30	28–33

① 289 High perf. 40–45
② 351 BOSS and HO three steps—40, 80, 120 ft. lbs.
③ 250—21–26
④ 302 BOSS—40–45
⑤ 302 BOSS—outer bolts 35–40
⑥ 7/16 in. bolts—70–80
⑦ 351 BOSS and HO—43–48 ft. lbs.
⑧ 3/8 in. bolts—34–45 ft. lbs.
*Tighten cylinder head bolts in three steps

Valve Specifications

Year	Model	Seat Angle (deg)	Face Angle (deg)	Valve Spring Pressure (lbs. @in.)	Valve Spring Installed Height (in.)	Stem Guide Clearance (in.)		Stem Diameter (in.)	
						Intake	Exhaust	Intake	Exhaust
1965	6—200	45	44	142–158 @1.222	$1^9/_{16}$– $1^{39}/_{64}$	0.0008–0.0025	0.0018–0.0035	0.3100– 0.3107	0.3090– 0.3097
	6—170	45	44	112–122 @1.222	$1^9/_{16}$– $1^{39}/_{64}$	0.0008–0.0025	0.0018–0.0035	0.3100– 0.3107	0.3090– 0.3097
	8—289	45	44	161–178 @1.380	$1^3/_4$– $1^{25}/_{32}$	0.0010–0.0027	0.0020–0.0037	0.3416– 0.3423	0.3406– 0.3413
	8—260	45	44	161–177 @1.390	$1^3/_4$– $1^{25}/_{32}$	0.0008–0.0025	0.0018–0.0035	0.3100– 0.3107	0.3090– 0.3097
1966	6—200	45	44	150@1.22	$1^{19}/_{32}$	0.0008–0.0025	0.0010–0.0027	0.3104	0.3102
	8—289	45	44	169@1.39	$1^{25}/_{32}$	0.0010–0.0027	0.0020–0.0037	0.3420	0.3410
	8—289 ①	45	44	247@1.31	$1^{25}/_{32}$	0.0010–0.0027	0.0020–0.0037	0.3420	0.3410
1967	6—200	45	44	150@1.22	$1^{19}/_{32}$	0.0008–0.0025	0.0010–0.0027	0.3104	0.3102
	8—289	45	44	180@1.23	$1^{21}/_{32}$	0.0010–0.0027	0.0010–0.0027	0.3420	0.3420
	8—289 ①	45	44	247@1.31	$1^{25}/_{32}$	0.0010–0.0027	0.0010–0.0027	0.3420	0.3420
	8—390	45	44	220@1.38	$1^{13}/_{16}$	0.0010–0.0024	0.0010–0.0024	0.3715	0.3715
1968	6—200	45	44	150@1.22	$1^{19}/_{32}$	0.0008–0.0025	0.0010–0.0027	0.3104	0.3102
	8—289, 302	45	44	180@1.23	$1^{21}/_{32}$	0.0010–0.0027	0.0015–0.0032	0.3420	0.3415
	8—390	45	44	220@1.38	$1^{13}/_{16}$	0.0010–0.0024	0.0015–0.0032	0.3715	0.3710
	8—390 ②	45	44	268@1.31	$1^{13}/_{16}$	0.0010–0.0024	0.0015–0.0032	0.3715	0.3710
	8—427	③	④	268@1.31	$1^{13}/_{16}$	0.0010–0.0024	0.0020–0.0034	0.3715	0.3705
1969	6—200	45	44	150@1.22	$1^{19}/_{32}$	0.0008–0.0025	0.0010–0.0027	0.3104	0.3102
	6—250	45	44	150@1.22	$1^{19}/_{32}$	0.0008–0.0025	0.0010–0.0027	0.3104	0.3102
	8—302	45	44	180@1.23	$1^{21}/_{32}$	0.0010–0.0027	0.0015–0.0032	0.3420	0.3415
	8—351	45	44	215@1.34	$1^{25}/_{32}$	0.0010–0.0027	0.0015–0.0032	0.3420	0.3415
	8—390	45	44	220@1.38	$1^{13}/_{16}$	0.0010–0.0027	0.0015–0.0032	0.3715	0.3710
	8—428	③	④	268@1.31	$1^{13}/_{16}$	0.0010–0.0027	0.0015–0.0032	0.3715	0.3710
1970	6—200	45	44	150@1.22	$1^{19}/_{32}$	0.0008–0.0025	0.0010–0.0027	0.3104	0.3102
	6—250	45	44	150@1.22	$1^{19}/_{32}$	0.0008–0.0025	0.0010–0.0027	0.3104	0.3102
	8—302	45	44	180@1.23	$1^{21}/_{32}$	0.0010–0.0027	0.0010–0.0027	0.3420	0.3415
	8—302 ⑤	45	44	315@1.31	$1^{13}/_{16}$	0.0010–0.0027	0.0015–0.0032	0.3420	0.3415

Valve Specifications (cont.)

Year	Model	Seat Angle (deg)	Face Angle (deg)	Valve Spring Pressure (lbs. @in.)	Valve Spring Installed Height (in.)	Stem Guide Clearance (in.)		Stem Diameter (in.)	
						Intake	Exhaust	Intake	Exhaust
	8—351 ⑥	45	44	215@1.34	1^{25}/$_{32}$	0.0010−0.0027	0.0010−0.0027	0.3420	0.3415
	8—351 ⑦	45	44	209@1.42	1^{13}/$_{16}$	0.0010−0.0027	0.0015−0.0032	0.3420	0.3415
	8—351 ⑧	45	44	285@1.31	1^{13}/$_{16}$	0.0010−0.0027	0.0015−0.0032	0.3420	0.3415
	8—428	③	④	265@1.31	1^{13}/$_{16}$	0.0015−0.0032	0.0015−0.0032	0.3715	0.3710
	8—429 ⑤	③	④	315@1.31	1^{13}/$_{16}$	0.0010−0.0024	0.0020−0.0034	0.3715	0.3705
1971	6—250	45	44	150@1.22	1^{19}/$_{32}$	0.0008−0.0025	0.0010−0.0027	0.3104	0.3102
	8—302	45	44	180@1.23	1^{21}/$_{32}$	0.0010−0.0027	0.0015−0.0032	0.3420	0.3415
	8—351 ⑥	45	44	215@1.34	1^{25}/$_{32}$	0.0010−0.0027	0.0015−0.0032	0.3420	0.3415
	8—351 ⑦	45	44	210@1.42	1^{13}/$_{16}$	0.0010−0.0027	0.0015−0.0032	0.3420	0.3415
	8—351 ⑧	45	44	285@1.31	1^{13}/$_{16}$	0.0010−0.0027	0.0015−0.0032	0.3420	0.3415
	8—429	45	45	229@1.33	1^{13}/$_{16}$	0.0010−0.0027	0.0010−0.0027	0.3420	0.3420
1972	6—250	45	44	150@1.22	1^{19}/$_{32}$	0.0008−0.0025	0.0010−0.0027	0.3104	0.3102
	8—302	45	44	200@1.23	1^{11}/$_{16}$	0.0010−0.0027	8.0015−0.0032	0.3420	0.3415
	8—351 ⑥	45	44	200@1.34	1^{25}/$_{32}$	0.0010−0.0027	0.0015−0.0032	0.3420	0.3415
	8—351 ⑦	45	44	210@1.42	1^{13}/$_{16}$	0.0010−0.0027	0.0015−0.0032	0.3420	0.3415
	8—351 ⑧	45	44	285@1.23	1^{13}/$_{16}$	0.0010−0.0027	0.0015−0.0032	0.3420	0.3415
	8—351 ⑤	45	44	315@1.23	1^{13}/$_{16}$	0.0010−0.0027	0.0015−0.0032	0.3420	0.3415
1973	6—250	45	46	150@1.22	1^{19}/$_{32}$	0.0008−0.0025	0.0010−0.0027	0.3104	0.3102
	8—302	45	46	200@1.22	1^{9}/$_{16}$	0.0010−0.0027	0.0015−0.0032	0.3420	0.3415
	8—351 ⑥	45	46	200@1.34	1^{25}/$_{32}$	0.0010−0.0027	0.0015−0.0027	0.3420	0.3415
	8—351 ⑧	45	46	282@1.32	1^{13}/$_{16}$	0.0010−0.0027	0.0015−0.0032	0.3420	0.3415

① Hi-Performance
② GT
③ Intake valve seat angle 30°
　 Exhaust valve seat angle 45°
④ Intake valve face angle 29°
　 Exhaust valve face angle 44°
⑤ Boss
⑥ Windsor heads
⑦ Cleveland 2 bbl
⑧ Cleveland 4 bbl
⑨ Cobra Jet

Piston Specifications
(in.)

Engine	Coded Red	Coded Blue	0.003 Oversize	Piston-to-Cylinder Bore Clearance	Piston Pin Bore Diameter
6—170	3.4982–3.4987	3.4993–3.4999	3.5001–3.5005	0.0014–0.0020	0.9122–0.9125
6—200	3.6778–3.6784	3.6790–3.6796	3.6802–3.6808	0.0014–0.0020	0.9122–0.9125
6—250	3.6778–3.6784	3.6790–3.6796	3.6802–3.6808	0.0014–0.0020	0.9122–0.9125
V8—260	3.7976–3.7982	3.7988–3.7994	—	0.0021–0.0039	0.9124–0.9127
V8—289	3.9984–3.9990	3.9996–4.0002	4.0008–4.0014	0.0018–0.0026	0.9123–0.9126
V8—289HP	3.9978–3.9984	3.9990–3.9996	4.0002–4.0008	0.0030–0.0038	0.9123–0.9126
V8—302	3.9984–3.9990	3.9996–4.0002	4.0008–4.0014	0.0018–0.0026	0.9123–0.9126
V8—302 Boss	3.9968–3.9974	3.9980–3.9986	3.9992–3.9998	0.0034–0.0042	0.9122–0.9125
V8—351W	3.9980–3.9986	3.9992–3.9998	4.0004–4.0010	0.0018–0.0026	0.9123–0.9126
V8—351C	3.9982–3.9988	3.9994–4.0000	4.0006–4.0012	0.0014–0.0022	0.9122–0.9125
V8—390	4.0484–4.0490	4.0496–4.0502	4.0508–4.0514	0.0015–0.0023	0.9752–0.9755
V8—427	4.2298–4.2299	4.2305–4.2311	4.2317–4.2323	0.0030–0.0038	0.9752–0.9755
V8—428	4.1284–4.1290	4.1296–4.1302	4.1308–4.1314	0.0015–0.0023	0.9752–0.9755
V8—429 SCJ and Boss	4.3569–4.3575	4.3581–4.3587	4.3593–4.3599	0.0030–0.0038	1.0402–1.0405

Groove Widths—Upper Compression Ring—0.080–0.081 (All Cars).
Lower Compression Ring—427—0.096–0.096, All others 0.080–0.081.
Oil Ring—0.080–0.081 (All Engines).

Piston Ring Specifications
(in.)

Engine (cylinders) —cu in.)	Compression Ring Width		Ring Side Clearance			Ring Gap Width		
	Top	Bottom	Top	Bottom	Oil Ring	Top	Bottom	Oil Ring
6—170	0.0774–0.0781	0.0770–0.0780	0.0019–0.0036	0.0020–0.0040	Snug	0.010–0.020	0.010–0.020	0.015–0.055
6—200	0.0774–0.0781	0.0770–0.0780	0.0019–0.0036	0.0020–0.0040	Snug	0.010–0.020	0.010–0.020	0.015–0.055
6—250	0.077–0.078	0.077–0.078	0.002–0.004	0.002–0.004	Snug	0.010–0.020	0.010–0.020	0.015–0.055
V8—260	0.0774–0.0781	0.0930–0.0940	0.0019–0.0036	0.001–0.004	Snug	0.010–0.032	0.010–0.032	0.015–0.067
V8—289	0.0774–0.0781	0.0770–0.0780	0.0019–0.0036	0.002–0.004	Snug	0.010–0.020	0.010–0.020	0.015–0.055
V8—302	0.077–0.078	0.077–0.078	0.002–0.004	0.002–0.004	Snug	0.010–0.020	0.010–0.020	0.015–0.069
V8—302 Boss	0.077–0.078	0.077–0.078	0.002–0.004	0.002–0.004	Snug	0.010–0.020	0.010–0.020	0.015–0.069
V8—351W	0.077–0.078	0.077–0.078	0.002–0.004	0.002–0.004	Snug	0.010–0.020	0.010–0.020	0.015–0.069
V8—351C	0.077–0.078	0.077–0.078	0.002–0.004	0.002–0.004	Snug	0.010–0.020	0.010–0.020	0.015–0.069
V8—390	0.077–0.078	0.093–0.094	0.002–0.004	0.002–0.004	Snug	—	—	0.015–0.055
V8—427	0.0774–0.0781	0.0930–0.0940	0.0024–0.0041	0.0020–0.0040	Snug	0.010–0.031	0.010–0.020	0.015–0.066
V8—428	0.077–0.078	0.077–0.078	0.002–0.004	0.002–0.004	Snug	0.010–0.020	0.010–0.020	0.015–0.035
V8—429	0.077–0.078	0.077–0.078	0.002–0.004	0.002–0.004	Snug	0.010–0.020	0.010–0.020	0.010–0.035

Crankshaft Bearing Journal Specifications

Year	Model	Main Bearing Journals (in.)				Connecting Rod Bearing Journals (in.)		
		Journal Diameter	Oil Clearance	Shaft End-Play	Thrust on No.	Journal Diameter	Oil Clearance	Side Clearance
1965–73	6 Cyl—170	2.2482–2.2490	0.0005–0.0022	0.004–0.008	3	2.1232–2.1240	0.0008–0.0024	0.003–0.010
	6 Cyl—200	2.2482–2.2490	0.0005–0.0022	0.004–0.008	5	2.1232–2.1240	0.0008–0.0024	0.003–0.010
	6 Cyl—250	2.3982–2.3990	0.0005–0.0022	0.004–0.008	5	2.1232–2.1240	0.0008–0.0024	0.003–0.010
	V8—302, 289	2.2482–2.2490	0.0005–0.0024 ⑤	0.004–0.008	3	2.1228–2.1236 ①	0.0008–0.0026 ②	0.010–0.020
	V8—351W	2.2994–3.0002	0.0013–0.0030	0.004–0.008	3	2.3103–2.3111	0.0008–0.0026	0.010–0.020
	V8—351C	2.7484–2.7492	0.0009–0.0026	0.004–0.010	3	2.3103–2.3111	0.0008–0.0026	0.010–0.020
	V8—390	2.7484–2.7492	0.0008–0.0020	0.004–0.010	3	2.4380–2.4388	0.0008–0.0030	0.010–0.020
	V8—427	2.7484–2.7492	0.0010–0.0031	0.004–0.010	3	2.4380–2.4388	0.0013–0.0032	0.010–0.020
	V8—428	2.7484–2.7492	0.0010–0.0020	0.004–0.010	3	2.4380–2.4388	0.0010–0.0030	0.010–0.020
	V8—429	2.9994–3.0002	0.0005–0.0025 ③	0.004–0.008	3	2.4992–2.5000	0.0008–0.0028 ④	0.010–0.020

①—Boss 302—2.1222–2.1230.
②—Boss 302—0.0015–0.0025.
③—Boss 429—0.0010–0.0025.
④—Boss 429—0.0015–0.0025.
⑤—302—0.001–0.0018 No. 1 bearing only.

On a car with an automatic transmission, start the converter pilot into the crankshaft.

On a car with a manual transmission, start the transmission main drive gear into the clutch disc. If the engine hangs up after the shaft enters, rotate the crankshaft slowly (with the transmission in gear) until the shaft and clutch disc splines mesh.

4. Install the flywheel or converter housing upper bolts.

5. Install engine support insulator-to-bracket retaining nuts. Disconnect the engine lifting sling and remove the lifting brackets.

6. Raise the front of the car. Connect the exhaust line(s) and tighten the attachments.

7. Position the dust seal and install the starter.

8. On cars with manual transmissions, install the remaining flywheel housing-to-engine bolts. Connect the clutch release rod. Position the clutch equalizer bar and bracket and install the retaining bolts. Install the clutch pedal retracting spring.

9. On cars with automatic transmission, remove the retainer holding the converter in the housing. Attach the converter to the flywheel. Install the converter housing inspection cover and the remaining converter housing retaining bolts.

10. Remove the support from the transmission and lower the car.

11. Connect the engine groups strap and the coil primary wire.

12. Connect the water temperature gauge wire and the heater hose at the coolant outlet housing. Connect the accelerator rod at the bellcrank.

13. On cars with automatic transmissions connect the throttle valve vacuum line.

14. On cars with power steering, install the drive belt and power steering pump bracket. Install the bracket retaining bolts. Adjust the drive belt to the proper tension.

15. Remove the plug from the fuel tank line. Connect the flexible fuel line and the oil pressure sending-unit wire.

16. Install the pulley, belt, spacer, and fan. Adjust belt tension.

17. Tighten the generator adjusting bolts. Connect the generator wires and the battery ground cable.

18. Install the radiator. Connect the radiator hoses. On air-conditioned cars, install the compressor and refrigerant radiator. On some 428 CJ engines, and all 429 Super CJ, Boss 302, and Boss 429 engines, install the engine oil cooler and hold-down bracket, and connect the inlet and outlet lines.

19. On cars with automatic transmissions connect the oil cooler lines.

20. Install the oil filter. Connect the heater hose at the water pump, after bleeding the system. Install evaporative emissions and EGR lines.

21. Bring the crankcase to level with the correct grade of oil. Run the engine at fast idle and check for leaks. Install the air cleaner and make the final engine adjustments.

22. Install and adjust the hood.

23. Road-test the car.

Cylinder Head
REMOVAL, 6 CYLINDER

1. Drain the cooling system, remove the air cleaner, and disconnect the battery cable at the cylinder head.

2. Disconnect the exhaust pipe at the manifold end, spring the exhaust pipe down, and remove the flange gasket.

3. Disconnect the fuel and vacuum lines from the carburetor. Disconnect the intake manifold line at the intake manifold.

4. Disconnect the accelerator and retracting spring at the carburetor. Disconnect the manually operated choke cable (if so equipped).

5. Disconnect the carburetor spacer outlet line at the spacer. Disconnect the radiator upper hose and the heater hose at the water outlet elbow. Disconnect the radiator lower hose and the heater hose at the water pump.

6. Disconnect the distributor vacuum control line at the distributor. Disconnect the gas filter line on the inlet side of the filter and the vacuum line at the fuel pump. Remove these lines as an assembly, then remove the windshield wiper line at the vacuum pump, (if so equipped).

7. Disconnect the spark plug wires and remove the plugs.

8. Remove the rocker arm cover.

9. Back off all of the tappet adjusting screws to relieve the tension from the rocker shaft. Loosen the rocker arm shaft attaching bolts and remove the rocker arm and shaft assembly. Remove the valve pushrods, in order, and keep them that way. Disconnect the EGR tube from the exhaust manifold.

10. Remove one cylinder head bolt from each end of the head (at opposite corners) and install cylinder head guide studs. Remove the remaining cylinder head bolts and lift off the cylinder head.

To help in removal and installation of cylinder head, two 6 in. $\times 7/16$—14 bolts with the heads cut off and the head end slightly tapered and slotted for installation and removal, with screwdriver, will reduce the possibility of damage during head replacement. These guide studs make a hand tool during head removal and gasket and head replacement.

INSTALLATION, 6 CYLINDER

1. Clean the cylinder head and block surfaces. Be sure of flatness and no surface damage.

2. Apply cylinder head gasket sealer to both sides of the new gasket and slide the gasket down over the two guide studs in the cylinder block.

NOTE: *Apply gasket sealer only to the steel shim head gaskets. Steel-asbestos composite head gaskets are to be installed without any sealer.*

3. Carefully lower the cylinder head over the guide studs. Place the exhaust pipe flange on the manifold studs (new gasket).

4. Coat the threads of the end bolts for the right side of the cylinder head with a small amount of water-resistant sealer. Install, but do not tighten, two head bolts at opposite ends to hold the head gasket in

Head bolt torque sequences—6 cylinder

place. Remove the guide studs and install the remaining bolts.

5. Cylinder head torquing should proceed in three steps and in prescribed order. Tighten to 55 ft. lbs, then give them a second tightening to 65 ft. lbs. The final step is to 75 ft. lbs, at which they should remain undisturbed.

6. Lubricate both ends of the pushrods and install them in their original locations.

7. Apply a petroleum jelly-type lubricant to the rocker arm pads and the valve stem tips, and position the rocker arm shaft assembly on the head. Be sure the oil holes in the shaft are in a down position.

8. Tighten all the rocker shaft retaining bolts to 30–35 ft. lbs. and do a preliminary valve adjustment (make sure there are no tight valve adjustments). Refer to the procedures for "Preliminary Valve Lash Adjustment" at the end of the "Cylinder Head" section of this chapter.

9. Hook up the exhaust pipe.

10. Reconnect the heater and radiator hoses.

11. Reposition the distributor vacuum line, the carburetor gas line, and the intake manifold vacuum line on the engine. Hook them up to their respective connections and reconnect the battery cable to the cylinder head.

12. Connect the accelerator rod and retracting spring. Connect the choke control cable and adjust the choke.

13. Reconnect the vacuum line at the distributor. Connect the fuel inlet line at the fuel filter and the intake manifold vacuum pump. Connect the windshield wiper vacuum line to the other side of the vacuum pump.

14. Lightly lubricate the spark plug threads, install them and torque them to 25 ft. lbs. Connect the spark plug wires and be sure the wires are all the way down in their sockets. Reconnect the EGR tube.

15. Fill the cooling system and bleed it. Run the engine for about ½ hour at a fast idle to stabilize all engine part temperatures.

16. Adjust the engine idle speed and idle fuel-air adjustment.

17. Reset the valve tappet adjustment to 0.016 in. for a hot adjustment of both intake and exhaust valves, on those engines not using hydraulic lifters.

18. Coat one side of a new rocker cover gasket with oil-resistant sealer. Lay the treated side of the gasket on the cover and install the cover. Be sure the gasket seals evenly all around the cylinder head.

REMOVAL, 260, 289 (ALL) 302 (EXCEPT BOSS), 351 W, 429 SCJ

1. Drain the cooling system.

2. Remove the intake manifold and the carburetor as an assembly, following the intake manifold removal procedures.

3. Disconnect the spark plug wires, marking them as to placement. Position them out of the way of the cylinder head. Remove the spark plugs.

4. Disconnect the resonator or muffler inlet pipe(s) at the exhaust manifold(s).

5. Disconnect the battery ground cable at the cylinder head (if applicable).

6. Remove the rocker arm covers.

7. On cars with air conditioning, remove the mounting bolts and the drive belt, and position the compressor out of the way of the cylinder head. Remove the compressor upper mounting bracket from the cylinder head.

CAUTION: *If the compressor refrigerant lines do not have enough slack to permit repositioning of the compressor without first disconnecting the refrigerant lines, the air conditioning system will have to be evacuated by a trained air conditioning serviceman. Under no circumstances should an untrained person attempt to disconnect the air conditioning refrigeration lines.*

8. If the left cylinder head is to be removed from a car equipped with power steering, remove the steering pump and bracket, remove the drive belt, and wire or tie the pump out of the way, but in such a way as to prevent the loss of its fluid.

9. If the right head is to be removed, remove the alternator mounting bracket bolt and spacer, the ignition coil, and the air cleaner inlet duct from the right cylinder head.

10. If the left cylinder head is to be removed from a car equipped with a Thermactor exhaust emission control system, disconnect the hose from the air manifold on the left cylinder head.

11. If the right cylinder head is to be removed from a car equipped with a Thermactor exhaust emission control system, remove the Thermactor air pump and its mounting bracket. Disconnect the hose from the air manifold on the right cylinder head.

12. Loosen the rocker arm stud nuts enough to rotate the rocker arms to the side, in order to facilitate the removal of the pushrods. Remove the pushrods in sequence, in order that they may be installed in their original positions.

13. Remove the cylinder head retaining bolts, noting their positions. On the 351 W engine, it is first necessary to remove the exhaust manifold from the cylinder head. Lift the cylinder head off the block.

14. Remove and discard the old cylinder head gasket.

INSTALLATION, 260, 289 (ALL), 302 (EXCEPT BOSS), 351 W, AND 429 SCJ

1. Clean all surfaces where gaskets are to be installed. These include the cylinder head, intake manifold, valve rocker arm cover, and cylinder block surfaces. On 351 W engines—which have had the exhaust manifold removed to facilitate removal of the head from the block—the cylinder head exhaust manifold gasket surface should also be cleaned.

2. If the head was removed to replace the head gasket, check the flatness of the cylinder head and engine block gasket surfaces. The method for this checking is explained in the "Engine Rebuilding" section under "Cylinder Head Reconditioning."

3. On 351 W engines, from which the exhaust manifold has been removed, coat cylinder head and the exhaust manifold gasket areas with a film of graphite grease.

4. Position the new cylinder head gasket over the cylinder dowels on the block. Coat the head bolts with water-resistant sealer.

5. Position a new gasket(s) on the muffler inlet pipe(s).

6. Position the cylinder head to the block and install the retaining bolts, each in its original position. Remember that on the 429 cu in. engine, the longer bolts belong in the lower row of bolt holes. On all engines except the 351 W, from which the exhaust manifold has been removed to facilitate the removal of the head, it is important to make sure that the exhaust manifold studs are guided properly into position on the resonator or muffler inlet pipe when positioning the head.

7. Step-torque all the cylinder head retaining bolts in their proper sequence. On the 260, 289, 302, and 351 W engines, the bolts should be torqued first to 50 ft. lbs., then 60 ft. lbs., and finally to the torque specification found in the torque specification table. On the 429 SCJ engine, the bolts should be torqued first to 75 ft. lbs., then 105 ft. lbs., and finally to the specification listed in the table.

8. On 351 W engines, install a new exhaust manifold gasket, and position the exhaust manifold(s), making sure that the exhaust manifold studs are fitted properly into the resonator or muffler inlet pipe connection(s). Torque the exhaust manifold bolts to specifications.

9. Tighten the nuts on exhaust manifold studs, and torque them to 18 ft. lbs.

10. Clean and inspect the pushrods one at a time. Clean the oil passage within each pushrod with a suitable solvent and blow the passage out with compressed air. Check the ends of the pushrods for nicks, grooves, roughness, or excessive wear. Visually inspect the pushrods for straightness, and re-

260, 289, 302, and 351 Head bolt tightening sequence

place any bent ones. Do not attempt to straighten pushrods.

11. Install the pushrods in their original positions. Apply Lubriplate or a similar product to the valve stem tips and to the pushrod guides in the cylinder head.

12. Apply Lubriplate or a similar product to the fulcrum seats and sockets. Turn the rocker arms to their proper position and tighten the stud nuts enough to hold the rocker arms in position. Make sure that the lower ends of the pushrods have remained properly seated in the valve lifters.

13. Perform a preliminary valve adjustment, as described at the end of the "cylinder Head" section of this chapter.

14. Apply a coat of oil-resistant sealer to the upper side of a new valve cover gasket. Position the gasket on the valve cover with the cemented side of the gasket facing the valve cover.

15. Install the valve cover(s). Tighten and torque the bolts. Torque for all except the 429 SCJ is 3–5 ft. lbs. The 429 SCJ requires 2½–4 ft. lbs.

16. Install the intake manifold and carburetor, following the procedure under "Intake Manifold Installation."

17. Refer to steps 6–11 (inclusive) of the "Cylinder Head Removal" procedure, and reverse the procedures.

18. Refer to the "Belt Tension Adjustment" procedure at the end of the "Engine Electrical" section, and adjust all drive belts which were removed.

19. Refill the cooling system.

20. Connect the battery ground cable at the cylinder head (if applicable).

21. Install the spark plugs and connect the spark plug wires to them.

22. Start the engine and check for leaks.

23. With the engine running, check and adjust the carburetor idle speed and mixture as explained in chapter four.

24. With the engine running, listen for abnormal valve noises or irregular idle, and correct them.

25. Road-test the vehicle.

REMOVAL, BOSS 302, BOSS 351, AND 351 C

1. Drain the cooling system.

2. Remove the intake manifold and the carburetor as an assembly, following the procedures under "Intake Manifold Removal."

3. Disconnect the resonator(s) or muffler inlet pipes at the exhaust manifold.

4. Disconnect the spark plug wires, labeling them as to placement. Position or tie them out of the way of the cylinder head. Remove the spark plugs, noting their positions if they are to be reinstalled.

5. Follow steps 7–11 (inclusive) under "Cylinder Head Removal," 260, 289, etc.

6. On Boss 302, remove the ignition coil.

7. Remove the attaching bolts and the rocker arm cover(s).

8. On 351 C engines, remove the ground wire at the back of the cylinder head.

9. Loosen the rocker arm stud nuts enough to rotate the rocker arms to the side, in order to facilitate the removal of the pushrods. Remove the pushrods in sequence, in order that they may be installed in their original positions.

10. Remove the cylinder head attaching bolts and lift the cylinder heads from the block. Note the positions of the attaching bolts, in order that they may be installed in their original positions.

11. Remove and discard the head gasket(s).

INSTALLATION, BOSS 302, BOSS 351, AND 351 C

1. Follow steps 1, 2, 4, 5, and 6 of the "Cylinder Head Installation" procedures for 260, 289, etc., engines.

2. Step-torque all cylinder head retaining bolts in sequence, first to 50 ft. lbs., then to 60 ft. lbs., and finally to the specifications listed for each individual engine in the "Torque Specifications" table.

3. Clean the pushrods in a suitable solvent, blow the oil passages clean with compressed air, and roll the pushrods across a flat surface to test them for straightness. Replace any bent pushrods. Under no circumstances should you attempt to straighten bent pushrods.

4. Follow steps 11–14 (inclusive) of the "Cylinder Head Installation" procedure for 260, 289, etc., engines.

5. Install the valve rocker arm covers, insert the retaining bolts, tighten them, and torque them to 3–5 ft. lbs.

6. Install and tighten nuts on the exhaust manifold studs, and torque them to 18–24 ft. lbs.

7. Install the intake manifold and carburetor assembly, following the procedure under "Intake Manifold Installation."

8. On the Boss 302, install the ignition coil.

9. Refer to steps 7–11 (inclusive) under "Cylinder Head Removal," for 260, 289, etc., engines. Reverse all procedures which are applicable to your engine.

10. Refer to the "Belt Tension Adjustment" procedure at the end of the "Engine Electrical System" section of this chapter and adjust all drive belts which were removed.

11. On 351 C engines, connect the ground wire at the back of the cylinder head.

12. Install the spark plugs and connect the spark plug wires in their proper positions.

13. Refill the cooling system.

14. Start the engine and check for leaks. Check and adjust the carburetor idle speed and mixture as explained in chapter two. Listen for abnormal valve noises and/or rough idle, and correct these problems.

15. Road-test the vehicle.

REMOVAL, 390, 427, AND 428

1. Drain the cooling system.

2. On Thermactor-equipped engines, disconnect the air lines and hoses as necessary.

3. Remove the intake manifold, crankcase ventilation components, carburetor, and thermostat housing as an assembly, following the procedures under "Intake Manifold Removal."

4. On 390 and 428 cu in. engines, disconnect the exhaust manifold(s) at the muffler inlet pipe(s), allowing the exhaust manifold to remain attached to the cylinder head. On 427 cu in. engines, disconnect the exhaust manifold(s) from the cylinder head(s), allowing them to remain affixed to the muffler inlet pipe(s). On these engines, wire the exhaust assembly to the frame in a position which allows ample access to the cylinder head(s).

5. If the left cylinder head is to be removed, remove the ignition coil, and the engine identification tag.

6. Refer to steps 7–9 (inclusive) of the "Cylinder Head Removal" procedure for 260, 289, etc., engines and follow the procedures applicable to your engine.

7. Disconnect the spark plug wires, noting their positions. Remove the spark plugs.

8. Remove the cylinder head bolts, noting their positions.

9. Lift the cylinder head off the block. Do not pry it off. Remove and discard the old cylinder head gasket.

INSTALLATION, 390, 427, AND 428

1. Thoroughly clean all surfaces where new gaskets are to be installed.

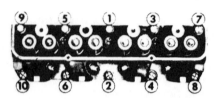

Cylinder head bolt torquing sequence, 390, 427, and 428

2. If the head was removed for the purpose of replacing the head gasket, check the flatness of the cylinder head and engine block gasket surfaces. The method for this checking is explained in the "Engine Rebuilding" section under "Cylinder Head Reconditioning."

3. On 427 cu in. engines—which have had the exhaust manifold(s) removed from the cylinder head(s)—coat the cylinder head and the exhaust manifold gasket areas with a thin film of graphite grease.

4. On the 427 cu in. engine only, apply cylinder head gasket sealer to both sides of a new gasket. Do not apply any sealer to the gaskets for 390 or 428 cu in. engines, as these engines use a specially treated composition gasket.

5. Guided by the word "front" on the upper side of the gasket, install the new cylinder head gasket(s) over the cylinder head dowels, which are located in the block.

6. Place a new gasket(s) on the muffler inlet pipe(s) on 390 and 428 cu in. engines.

7. Place the cylinder head on the engine. On 390 and 428 cu in. engines, guide the exhaust manifold studs into position on the muffler inlet pipe(s).

8. Install the cylinder bolts in their original positions. Tighten and step-torque them in sequence. On 390 and 428 cu in. engines, torque the bolts first to 70 ft. lbs., then to 80 ft. lbs., and finally to the figure recommended under "Torque Specifications." The same procedure applies to the 427 cu in. engine, except that preliminary torquing should be first to 90 ft. lbs., then to 100 ft. lbs., and then to specifications.

9. On 427 cu in. engines, install a new exhaust manifold gasket, and position the exhaust manifold(s), taking care to properly guide the studs into the muffler inlet pipe connection(s). Install the exhaust manifold retaining bolts and torque them to the figure given in the "Torque Specifications" table.

10. Install the intake manifold assembly, using the procedure under "Intake Manifold Assembly."

11. Install the ignition coil and the engine identification tag.

12. Install the spark plugs, and connect the spark plug wires in their proper positions.

13. Refer to steps 7–9 (inclusive) of the "Cylinder Head Removal" procedure for 260; 289, etc., engines and reverse the procedures applicable to your car.

14. On Thermactor-equipped cars, connect any air lines and hoses which were disconnected during removal of the cylinder head.

15. Fill the cooling system.

16. Start the engine, check for leaks, adjust the carburetor idle speed and mixture, and listen for noisy valves and/or rough idle.

17. Road-test the vehicle.

REMOVAL, BOSS 429

1. Drain the cooling system.

2. Disconnect the battery.

3. Remove the cap which connects the crankcase ventilation hose (PCV) to the left rocker cover.

4. Remove the air cleaner.

5. If removing the left head, remove the crankcase ventilation hose.

6. Remove each spark plug wire from its retaining bracket.

7. Disconnect the wires from the spark plugs by twisting and pulling on the molded dust caps.

8. If removing the left head, disconnect the brake master cylinder from the booster and move it to one side to provide clearance.

9. Remove the rocker cover attaching bolts and nuts, noting their placement.

10. Lift the rocker covers from the heads.

11. Thoroughly clean all gasket material from the rocker covers and the heads.

12. Remove the intake manifold assembly, following the procedure under "Intake Manifold Removal."

13. Back off all rocker arm adjusting screws.

14. Remove all rocker shaft attaching nuts from the rocker shafts. Note that the Boss 429 engine is equipped with a separate rocker shaft for each rocker.

15. Remove the rocker arms, shafts, and pedestals in sequence, in order that they may be installed in their original positions.

16. Remove the pushrods from the cylinder head in sequence, in order that they may be installed in their original positions.

17. Disconnect the air hose from the Thermactor check valve on the head which is being removed.

19. Remove the 10 cylinder head bolts, noting their placement.

20. Locate the lifting eye at each end of the cylinder head, near the top. Connect a lifting sling to the eyes, attach the sling to a hoist, and lift the head from the engine block.

21. Remove all rubber and steel gaskets from the block and head.

22. Clean the cylinder head and block mating surfaces thoroughly.

INSTALLATION, BOSS 429

1. Wipe the head and block mating surfaces with chlorathane.

2. Coat the upper end of the cylinder head and block with silicone rubber primer (Dow Corning A-4094 or an equivalent). Coat the gasket counter bores with quick-drying adhesive sealer to prevent the dropping of gaskets during the installation of the head.

3. Position four combustion chamber gaskets in counter bores with the tabs seated down. Locate the tabs by rotating the gasket between the finger and thumb to feel the tabs.

4. Press four ¼ in. ID gaskets into the cylinder head counter bores with the stepped side facing up.

5. Press the seventeen ½ in. ID gaskets into the cylinder head counter bores with the stepped side facing up.

6. Apply a continuous strip of sealant along the top edge of the cylinder head.

7. Install a guide pin at each end of the cylinder block.

8. Lower the cylinder head into place over the guide pins. Take care not to drop any gaskets.

9. Install but do not tighten the eight attaching bolts and flat washers.

11. Torque the attaching bolts in sequence to 55–60 ft. lbs. Then torque to 75–80 ft. lbs. Finally torque to 90–95 ft. lbs.

12. Connect the Thermactor air hose to the check valve.

13. Place a new gasket on the muffler inlet pipe, and connect the pipe to the exhaust manifold. Install nuts on the studs and torque them to 18–24 ft. lbs.

14. Lubricate both ends of the pushrods and install them.

15. Lubricate the rocker arms and shafts with engine oil and install them with loos-

ened adjusting screws. Do not torque the shafts down at this time.

16. Rotate the crankshaft damper until no 1. piston is at TDC at the end of the compression stroke.

17. Install the distributor in the cylinder block with the rotor at no. 1 firing position and the points just beginning to open. Install the hold-down clamp and bolt.

18. Torque the rocker shaft nuts on no. 1 cylinder intake and exhaust to 12–15 ft. lbs. If the engine is equipped with a solid lifter camshaft, adjust the valve clearance to specification (cold) using a feeler gauge or valve gapper between the rocker arm and the valve stem tip. Refer to the Specification Chart in Chapter 2. Torque the adjusting screws in place. If the engine is equipped with an hydraulic lifter camshaft, loosen the locknut and turn in the adjusting screw on no. 1 cylinder intake and exhaust rocker until all clearance is removed. Rotate the pushrod with fingers while tightening the adjusting screw to determine the point when clearance is removed. Tighten the adjusting screws $1/16$ turn further. Hold the adjusting screws in place and torque the locknuts to 20–30 ft. lbs.

19. Rotate the crankshaft 90° to position no. 5 piston at TDC and repeat step 18 for no. 5 intake and exhaust rockers.

20. Rotate the crankshaft 90° and repeat the procedure in Step 18 for each cylinder in firing order (1-5-4-2-6-3-7-8).

21. Remove the distirbutor.

22. Coat one side of the new rocker cover gasket with oil-resistant sealer and lay the cemented side in place on the cover.

23. Install the cover. Make sure the gasket seats evenly all around the cover.

24. Tighten the cover attaching bolts evenly and alternately in two steps. Then torque the cover bolts to 12–15 ft. lbs. Wait two minutes and retorque them to 12–15 ft. lbs.

25. Install the intake manifold, following the procedures under "Intake Manifold Installation."

26. Connect each spark plug wire to its respective plug. Insert plug wires into the brackets on the valve cover.

27. Install the cap and crankcase ventilation hose (PCV) on valve cover.

28. If installing the left head, install the master cylinder on the booster.

29. Install the air cleaner and connect the battery.

30. Fill the cooling system.

31. Start the vehicle, visually check for leaks, adjust the carburetor idle speed and mixture, and listen for rough idle and/or noisy valves.

32. Road-test the vehicle.

OVERHAUL

Procedures for the overhaul of cylinder heads are explained in the "Engine Rebuilding" section, found at the end of this chapter.

Rocker Shafts

All six-cylinder engines have been equipped with shaft-mounted rocker arm assemblies. The only V8 engines to include this type of valve assembly, however, are the 390, 427, and 428 cu in. engines.

Removal and installation procedures for the six-cylinder rocker shaft assemblies are included under the cylinder head removal and installation procedures for those engines. For the V8 engines, the rocker shaft removal and installation procedures are explained under the intake manifold removal and installation procedures for those engines.

In all cases, the correct torque sequence for the rocker shaft retaining bolts is from the front to the rear of the engine.

Preliminary Valve Adjustment

With the exception of certain high-performance V8 engines (289 High-Performance, Boss 302, Boss 429, Boss 351, 429 SCJ, and 351 HO of 1972) all engines used have been equipped with hydraulic valve lifters operate with zero clearance in the valve train and, because of this, the rocker arms are nonadjustable. The only means by which valve system clearances can be altered is by installing 0.060 in. over or undersize pushrods; but, because of the hydraulic lifter's natural ability to compensate for slack in the valve train, all components of the valve system should be checked for wear if there is excessive play in the system.

When a valve in the engine is in the closed position, the valve lifter is resting on the base circle of the camshaft lobe and the pushrod is in its lowest position. To remove this additional clearance from the valve train, the valve lifter expands to maintain zero clearance in the valve system. When a rocker arm is loosened or removed from the engine, the proper valve setting is obtained by tightening the rocker arm to a specified limit. But with the lifter fully expanded, if the camshaft lobe is on a high point it will require excessive torque to compress the lifter and obtain the proper setting. Because of this, when any component of the valve system has been removed, a preliminary valve adjustment procedure must be followed to ensure that when the rocker arm is reinstalled on the engine and tightened, the camshaft lobe for that cylinder is in the low position.

6 Cylinder

1. Crank the engine until the TDC mark on the crankshaft damper is aligned with timing pointer on the cylinder front cover.

2. Scribe a mark on the damper at this point.

3. Scribe two more marks on the damper, each equally spaced from the first mark (see illustration).

3. Scribe two more marks on the damper, each equally spaced from the first mark (see illustration).

4. With the engine on TDC of the compression stroke, (mark A aligned with the pointer) back off the rocker arm adjusting nut until there is end-play in the pushrod. Tighten the adjusting nut until all clearance is removed, then tighten the adjusting nut one additional turn on 1969 and later models and ¾ of a turn on all 1965–68 cars. To de-

termine when all clearance is removed from the rocker arm, turn the pushrod with the fingers. When the pushrod can no longer be turned, all clearance has been removed.

5. Repeat this procedure for each valve, turning the crankshaft ⅓ turn to the next mark each time and following the engine firing order of 1-5-3-6-2-4.

260, 289, and 1968–69 302 V8

NOTE: *This procedure for the 289 and early 302 V8 engines is designed for engines in which the rocker arm mounting studs do not incorporate a positive stop shoulder on the mounting stud. These engines were originally equipped with this kind of stud. However, due to production differences, it is possible some 289 or early 302 engines may be encountered that are equipped with positive stop rocker arm mounting studs. Before following this procedure, verify that the rocker arm mounting studs do not incorporate a positive stop shoulder. On studs without a positive stop, the shank portion of the stud that is exposed just above the cylinder head is the same diameter as the threaded portion, at the top of the stud is of greater diameter than the threaded portion, this identifies it as a positive stop rocker arm stud and the procedure for the 351 engine should be followed.*

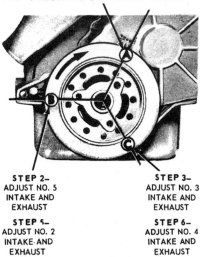

STEP 1–SET NO. 1 PISTON ON T.D.C. AT END OF COMPRESSION STROKE ADJUST NO. 1 INTAKE AND EXHAUST

STEP 4–ADJUST NO. 6 INTAKE AND EXHAUST

STEP 2–
ADJUST NO. 5
INTAKE AND
EXHAUST

STEP 3–
ADJUST NO. 3
INTAKE AND
EXHAUST

STEP 5–
ADJUST NO. 2
INTAKE AND
EXHAUST

STEP 6–
ADJUST NO. 4
INTAKE AND
EXHAUST

Position of crankshaft for valve adjustment—6 cylinder

STEP 1–SET NO.1 PISTON ON T.D.C. AT END OF COMPRESSION STROKE –ADJUST NO.1 INTAKE AND EXHAUST

STEP 5–ADJUST NO.6 INTAKE AND EXHAUST

STEP 2–ADJUST NO.5 INTAKE AND EXHAUST

STEP 6–ADJUST NO.3 INTAKE AND EXHAUST

STEP 4–ADJUST NO.2 INTAKE AND EXHAUST

STEP 8–ADJUST NO.8 INTAKE AND EXHAUST

STEP 3–ADJUST NO.4 INTAKE AND EXHAUST

STEP 7–ADJUST NO.7 INTAKE AND EXHAUST

Postion of crankshaft for valve adjustment—260 and 289 V8

1. Crank the engine until no. 1 cylinder is at TDC of the compression stroke and the timing pointer is aligned with the mark on the crankshaft damper.

2. Scribe a mark on the damper at this point.

3. Scribe three more marks on the damper, dividing the damper into quarters (see illustration).

4. With mark A aligned with the timing pointer, adjust the valves on no. 1 cylinder by backing off the adjusting nut until the pushrod has free-play in it. Then, tighten the nut until there is no free-play in the rocker arm. This can be determined by turning the pushrod while tightening the nut; when the pushrod can no longer be turned, all clearance has been removed. After the clearance has been removed, tighten the nut an additional ¼ of a turn.

5. Repeat this procedure for each valve, turning the crankshaft ¼ turn to the next mark each time and following the engine firing order of 1-5-4-2-6-3-7-8.

351 and 1970–72 302V8

1. Crank the engine until no. 1 cylinder is at TDC of the compression stroke and the timing pointer is aligned with the mark on the crankshaft damper.

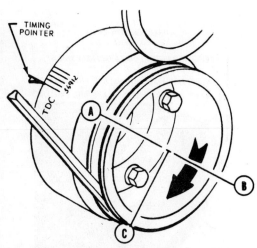

With No. 1 at TDC at end of compression stroke make a chalk mark at points B and C approximately 90 degrees apart.

POSITION A – No. 1 at TDC at end of compression stroke.
POSITION B – Rotate the crankshaft 180 degrees (one half revolution) clockwise from POSITION A.
POSITION C – Rotate the crankshaft 270 degrees (three quarter revolution) clockwise from POSITION B.

Position of crankshaft for valve adjustment—302 and 351 V8

2. Scribe a mark on the damper at this point.

3. Scribe two additional marks on the damper (see illustration).

4. With the timing pointer aligned with mark A on the damper, tighten the following valves to the specified torque:
  - *302:* no. 1, 7, and 8 Intake; no. 1, 5, and 4 Exhaust
  - *351:* no. 1, 4, and 8 Intake; no. 1, 3, and 7 Exhaust

5. Rotate the crankshaft 180° to point B and tighten the following valves:
  - *302:* no. 5 and 4 Intake; no. 2 and 6 Exhaust.
  - *351:* no. 3 and 7 Intake; no. 2 and 6 Exhaust.

6. Rotate the crankshaft 279° to point C and tighten the following valves:
  - *302:* no. 2, 3, and 6 Intake; no. 7, 3, and 8 Exhaust
  - *351:* no. 2, 5, and 6 Intake; no. 4, 5, and 8 Exhaust.

7. Rocker arm tighten specifications are: 302 and 351 W—tighten nut until it contacts the rocker shoulder, then torque to 18–20 ft. lbs.; 351 C—tighten bolt to 18–25 ft. lbs.; 429—tighten nut until it contacts rocker shoulder, then torque to 18–22 ft. lbs.

390, 427, and 428

1. Position the left rocker arm and oil deflector assembly on the head, making sure the oversize bolt is installed in the second rocker arm stand from the front of the engine.

2. Install each rocker arm stand attaching bolt finger-tight, then, working from the front of the engine back, tighten each bolt two turns at a time until the rocker arm is mounted on the head.

3. Torque the bolts to 40–45 ft. lbs.

4. Position the right rocker arm and oil deflector assembly on the head, making sure the oversize bolt is installed in the third rocker arm stand from the front of the engine.

5. Repeat steps two and three on the right side, this time working from the rear of the engine forward.

V8 Engines with Mechanical Lifters

NOTE: *In all cases, the preliminary valve adjustment must be done with the tappet on the low radius of the camshaft lobe.*

1. Before turning the engine, make sure

that the distributor is properly installed and accurately timed.

2. Locate the TDC mark on the crankshaft damper and make a chalk mark at that location.

3. Make three more chalk marks on the crankshaft damper—one every 90° of crankshaft rotation—so that the marks divide the damper into four equal segments.

4. Position the crankshaft at the TDC position as marked. Check the distributor rotor to make sure that it is in the no. 1 firing position.

5. Install and secure the pushrods and rocker arms for the no. 1 cylinder, using the thickness gauge recommended for the final adjustment. Tighten the locking nut while holding the adjusting nut (or screw) in position. If the final adjustment for your engine is a cold adjustment, check the clearance with the feeler gauge to make certain that it was not altered while tightening the locking nut.

6. Rotate the crankshaft 90° forward. Check the firing order diagram and the position of the rotor to make sure that the engine is at TDC for the second cylinder in the firing order. Repeat step five for that cylinder.

7. Repeat steps five and six until all valves have been adjusted.

8. If your engine calls for a cold tappet clearance adjustment, install the rocker covers. If it requires a hot adjustment, bring the engine to its full operating temperature and check the clearances with the engine running. Make all necessary adjustments to the clearances, stop the engine, and install the rocker covers.

Intake Manifold

REMOVAL AND INSTALLATION

6 Cylinder

All six-cylinder engines used feature an intake manifold which is an integral part of the cylinder head and, therefore, cannot be removed.

260, 289 (all), 302 (except Boss), 351 W, 390, 427, 428 (all), and 429 SCJ

1. Drain the cooling system.

2. Disconnect the upper radiator hose from the thermostat housing and the bypass hose from the manifold.

3. Remove the air cleaner and ducts.

4. Remove the distributor cap and wires from the engine. Mark the position of the dis-

tributor rotor in relationship to the intake manifold, remove the primary wire from the coil, then remove the distributor hold-down bolt and the distributor.

5. Remove all vacuum lines from the intake manifold and remove the temperature sending unit wire.

6. Disconnect the fuel line and any vacuum lines from the carburetor.

7. Remove all carburetor linkage and kick-down linkage that attaches to the intake manifold.

8. On 390, 427, and 428 engines, remove the valve covers, the rocker arm assemblies, and the pushrods. The rocker arms should be removed by backing off each of the four bolts two turns in sequence from front to back. Keep the pushrods in order so that they can be installed in their original position.

9. Remove the manifold attaching bolts and remove the manifold. If it is necessary to pry the manifold to loosen it from the engine, use care not to damage any gasket sealing surfaces.

10. Clean all gasket surfaces and firmly cement new gaskets in place. The gaskets should be securely locked in place before attempting to install the manifold.

11. Reverse the above procedures to reinstall. On 390, 427, and 428 engines, refer to the procedures for "Preliminary Valve Lash Adjustment," found at the end of the "Cylinder Head," section.

12. Torque to intake manifold bolts in sequence, and to the specifications listed in the "Torque Specifications" chart.

Boss 302, Boss 351, and 351 C

1. Drain the cooling system and remove the air cleaner. On the Boss 302 engine, disconnect the Thermactor air hose from the check valve at the rear of the intake manifold and loosen the hose clamp at the hose bracket. Remove the air hose and Thermactor air bypass valve from the bracket and position it out of the way.

2. Disconnect the accelerator linkage and accelerator downshift linkage, if so equipped, and position it out of the way. On the Boss 302, disconnect the choke cable from the carburetor.

3. Disconnect the high-tension lead and wires from the coil. Disconnect the engine wire loom and move it out of the way.

4. Disconnect the spark plug wires from the spark plugs by grasping, twisting, and

Intake Manifold Torque Sequences

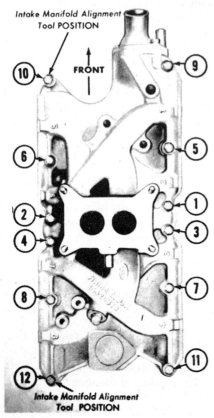

260 and 289

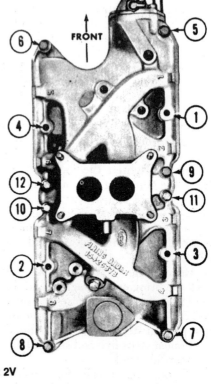

302 2V

pulling, molded cap only. Remove the distributor cap and wire assembly.

5. Remove the carburetor fuel inlet line.

6. Disconnect the distributor vacuum hoses from the distributor. Remove the hold-down bolt and the distributor.

7. Disconnect the radiator upper hose from the coolant outlet housing and disconnect the temperature sender wire.

8. Loosen the clamp on the water pump

bypass hose at the coolant outlet housing and slide the hose off the outlet housing.

9. Disconnect the crankcase vent hose (PCV) at the rocker cover.

10. If the vehicle is air-conditioned, remove the compressor-to-intake manifold brackets.

11. Remove the intake manifold and carburetor as an assembly. Discard all used gaskets and clean all mating surfaces.

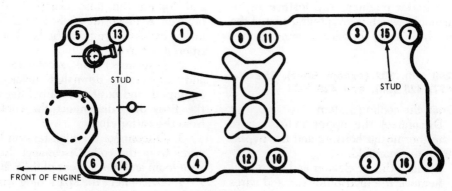

351 W

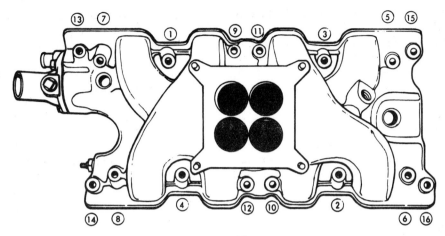

Boss 302

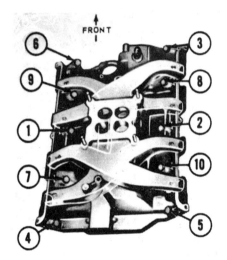

390, 427, and 428

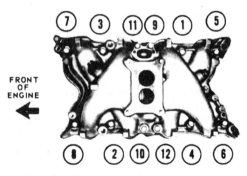

351 Cleveland

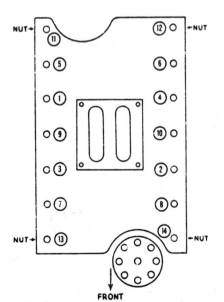

Boss 429

12. Reverse the procedure for installation.

13. Torque the intake manifold retaining bolts in sequence to the specifications listed in the "Torque Specifications" table.

Boss 429

1. Disconnect the battery.

2. Drain the cooling system.

3. Disconnect the heater hose from the manifold.

4. Disconnect the positive crankcase ventilation (PCV) hose from the righthand rocker cover. Disconnect and tag all vacuum lines from the rear of the intake manifold.

5. Twist and pull the molded spark plug wire cap from each plug. Remove the plug wires from the brackets on the rocker covers.

6. Disconnect the high-tension lead from the coil and remove the distributor cap and wires from the distributor as an assembly.

7. Disconnect the accelerator linkage from the carburetor. Remove the bolts that attach the accelerator linkage bellcrank. Disconnect the linkage spring and position the linkage to one side.

8. Disconnect all distributor vacuum lines from the carburetor and vacuum control valves, and tag them.

9. Disconnect the carburetor fuel line.

10. Disconnect the wiring harness from the coil battery terminal, temperature sender unit, oil pressure sending unit, and other connections, as necessary. Disengage the wiring harness from the retaining clips at the left rocker cover bolts. Move the harness out of the way.

11. Disconnect the Thermactor air bypass valve from the mounting bracket and place it to one side.

12. Remove the coil and bracket assembly.

13. Disconnect the manifold heat inlet and outlet tubes from the rear of the manifold and from the exhaust pipe.

14. Remove the distributor from the engine.

15. Remove the intake manifold attaching bolts.

16. Remove the manifold and carburetor as an assembly. Discard used gaskets.

17. To install the intake manifold, reverse the above procedure—the manifold should be torqued in place as shown in the illustration.

Exhaust Manifold

REMOVAL AND INSTALLATION

6 Cylinder

1. Remove the air cleaner and heat duct body.

2. Disconnect the muffler inlet pipe and remove the choke hot air tube from the manifold.

3. Bend the exhaust manifold attaching bolt locktabs back, then remove the bolts and the manifold.

4. Clean all manifold mating surfaces and place a new gasket on the muffler inlet pipe.

5. Reinstall the manifold by reversing the above procedure, torque the attaching bolts in sequence from the centermost bolt outward.

All V8 except 428 CJ, 428 SCJ, and Boss 429

1. On the right exhaust manifold, remove the air cleaner, automatic choke heat tube, and air cleaner heat ducts.

2. Disconnect the exhaust manifold(s) from the muffler inlet pipe(s).

3. Remove the manifold attaching bolts and remove the manifold(s).

4. Reverse the above procedure to reinstall, using new inlet pipe gaskets.

5. Torque the exhaust manifold retaining bolts to specifications (see "Torque Specifications" table).

NOTE: *To remove the left side exhaust manifold from a car equipped with a 351 C engine, it is necessary to remove the oil filter and the transmission selector crossshaft or clutch linkage and equalizer shaft bracket, depending on the transmission-type.*

428 CJ and 428 SCJ

This procedure is for removing both manifolds. If only one manifold is to be removed, do not remove any equipment located on or near the opposite side of the engine.

1. Remove the air cleaner, heat tubes, choke, and vacuum lines from the manifold.

2. Remove the air cleaner heat tube mounting studs and the three forward attaching bolts from the right-side manifold.

3. Raise the car on a hoist and remove the idler arm bracket from the frame.

4. Disconnect the starter cable and remove the starter motor.

5. Remove the remaining right-side manifold attaching bolts.

6. Disconnect all exhaust system hangers and lower the exhaust system.

7. Remove the inlet pipes from the manifolds.

8. On vehicles with a manual transmission, remove the clutch linkage and equalizer bracket from the engine.

9. Disconnect the pitman arm from the steering sector shaft and, on vehicles with power steering, remove the steering control valve bracket from the frame.

10. Lower the car, disconnect the steering shaft flex joint, and unbolt and remove the steering gear box assembly from the frame.

11. Raise the car again and disconnect and remove both motor mounts and the rear crossmember support attaching bolts.

12. Position a jack under the engine and, using a piece of wood under the oil pan, raise the engine slightly.

13. Remove the remaining manifold attaching bolts and remove the manifolds.

14. Clean all gasket surfaces and, using new inlet pipe gaskets, reverse above procedure to reinstall the manifolds.

15. Torque the exhaust manifold retaining bolts to specifications.

Boss 429

1. Remove the battery ground cable.
2. Remove the valve covers.
3. Disconnect the Thermactor air manifolds from the check valves.
4. Remove the air manifolds from the exhaust manifolds.
5. With the car on a hoist, remove the eight exhaust manifold attaching bolts and disconnect the muffler inlet pipes.
6. Disconnect the clutch linkage and equalizer bracket from the engine.
7. Work the manifolds rearward and remove them through the engine compartment.
8. Clean all gasket surfaces and install new gaskets on the muffler inlet pipes.
9. Reinstall the manifold, working them into position from under the vehicle.
10. Tighten and torque the manifold retaining bolts, working from the middle of the manifold toward the ends.

Timing Cover and Chain
REMOVAL AND INSTALLATION

6 Cylinder
REMOVAL

1. Drain the cooling system and crankcase.
2. Disconnect the upper radiator hose from the intake manifold and the lower hose from the water pump. On cars with an automatic transmission, disconnect the cooler lines from the radiator.
3. Remove the radiator, fan and pulley, and engine drive belts. On models with air conditioning, remove the condenser retaining bolts and move the condenser forward. *Do not disconnect the refrigerant lines.*
4. On 170 and 200 cu in. engines, remove the cylinder front cover retaining bolts and front oil pan bolts and gently pry the cover away from the block. On 250 engines, it is necessary to remove the oil pan cover before removing the front cover.
5. Remove the crankshaft pulley bolt and use a puller to remove the vibration damper.
6. With a socket wrench of the proper size on the crankshaft pulley bolt, gently rotate the crankshaft in a clockwise direction until all slack is removed from the left side of the timing chain. Scribe a mark on the engine block parallel to the present position of the left side of the chain. Next, turn the crank-

TIMING MARKS

Aligning timing marks—6 cylinder

shaft in a counterclockwise direction to remove all the slack from the right side of the chain. Force the left side of the chain outward with the fingers and measure the distance between the reference point and the present position of the chain. If the distance exceeds ½ in., replace the chain and sprockets.

7. Crank the engine until the timing marks are aligned as shown in the illustration. Remove the bolt, slide the sprocket and chain forward, and remove them as an assembly.

INSTALLATION

1. Position the sprockets and chain on the engine, making sure that the timing marks are aligned.
2. Reinstall the front cover, applying oil resistant sealer to the new gasket.
NOTE: *On 170 and 200 engines, trim away the exposed portion of the old oil pan gasket flush with the front of the engine block. Cut and position the required portion of a new gasket to the oil pan, applying sealer to both sides of it.*
3. On 250 engines, reinstall the oil pan.
4. Install the fan, pulley and belts. Adjust the belt tension.
5. Install the radiator, connect the radiator hoses and transmission cooling lines. If equipped with air conditioning, install the condenser.
6. Fill the crankcase and cooling system. Start the engine and check for leaks.

All V8
REMOVAL

1. Drain the cooling system, remove the air cleaner, and disconnect the battery.
2. Disconnect the radiator hoses and remove the radiator.
3. Disconnect the heater hose at the

TIMING MARKS

Aligning timing marks on V8

water pump. Slide the water pump bypass hose clamp toward the pump.

4. Loosen the generator mounting bolts at the generator. Remove the generator support bolt at the water pump. Remove the Thermactor pump from 428 CJ, 429 Super CJ, Boss 302, and Boss 429 engines.

5. Remove the fan, spacer, pulley, and drive belt.

6. Remove the pulley from the crankshaft pully adapter. Remove the cap screw and washer from the front end of the crankshaft. Remove the crankshaft pulley adapter with a puller.

7. Disconnect fuel pump outlet line at the pump. Remove fuel pump retaining bolts and lay the pump to the side.

8. Remove the front cover attaching bolts. On the 351 C engine, it is necessary to remove the oil pan before the front cover can be removed.

9. Remove the crankshaft oil slinger if so equipped.

10. Check the timing chain deflection, using the procedure outlined in step six of the six-cylinder cover and chain removal.

11. Crank the engine until the sprocket timing marks are aligned as shown in valve timing illustration.

12. Remove the crankshaft sprocket cap

screw, washers, and fuel pump eccentric. Slide both sprockets and chain forward and off as an assembly.

INSTALLATION

1. Position the sprockets and chain on the camshaft and crankshaft with both timing marks on a certerline. Install the fuel pump eccentric, washers and sprocket attaching bolt. Torque the sprocket attaching bolt to 30–35 ft. lbs.

2. Install the crankshaft front oil slinger.

3. Clean the front cover and mating surfaces of the old gasket material.

4. Coat a new cover gasket with sealer and position it on the block.

NOTE: *On all except 351 C engines, trim away the exposed portion of the oil pan gasket flush with the cylinder block. Cut and position the required portion of a new gasket to the oil pan, applying sealer to both sides of it. On 351 C engines, after installing the cylinder front cover, install the oil pan using a new gasket.*

5. Install front cover, using a crank-shaft-to-cover alignment tool. Torque the attaching bolts to 12–15 ft. lbs.

6. Install fuel pump, torque the attaching bolts to 23–28 ft. lbs., connect the fuel pump outlet tube.

7. Install the crankshaft pulley adapter and torque the attaching bolt to 70–90 ft. lbs. Install the crankshaft pulley.

8. Install the water pump pulley, drive belt, spacer, and fan.

9. Install the generator support bolt at the water pump. Tighten the generator mounting bolts. Adjust the drive belt tension. Install the Thermactor pump if so equipped.

10. Install the radiator and connect all coolant and heater hoses. Connect the battery cables.

11. Refill and bleed the cooling system.

12. Start the engine and operate at fast idle to reach operating temperature.

13. Check for leaks, install the air cleaner. Adjust the ignition timing and make all final adjustments.

TIMING GEAR COVER OIL SEAL REPLACEMENT

All Engines

It is a recommended practice to replace the cover seal any time the front cover is removed.

1. With the cover removed from the car, drive the old seal from the rear of cover with a pin-punch. Clean out the recess in the cover.

2 Coat the new seal with grease and drive it into the cover until it is full y seated. Check the seal after installation to be sure the spring is properly positioned in the seal.

Camshaft

REMOVAL AND INSTALLATION

6-Cylinder Engine

1. Remove the cylinder head as directed in that section.

2. Remove the cylinder front cover, timing chain and sprockets as outlined in the preceding section.

3. Disconnect and remove the grille. Remove the gravel deflector.

4. Using a magnet, remove the valve lifters and keep them in order so that they can be installed in their original positions.

5. Remove the camshaft thrust plate and remove the camshaft by pulling it from the front of the engine. Use care not to damage the camshaft lobes or journals while removing the cam from the engine.

6. Before installing the camshaft, coat the lobes with Lubriplate and coat the journals and all valve parts with heavy oil.

7. Reverse the above procedure for installation following the recommended torque settings and tightening sequences.

All V8s

1. Remove the intake manifold as outlined previously.

2. Remove the cylinder front cover, tim-

ing chain and sprockets as directed previously.

3. Remove the grille and, on models with air conditioning, remove the condenser retaining bolts and move it out of the way. *Do not disconnect the refrigerant lines.*

4. Remove the rocker arm covers.

5. On 390, 427, and 428 engines it is necessary to remove the rocker arm shafts to remove the intake manifold. On all other engines with individually mounted rocker arms, loosen the rocker arm fulcrum bolts and rotate the rocker arms to the side.

6. Remove the pushrods and lifters and keep them in order so that they can be installed in their original positions.

7. Remove the camshaft thrust plate and washer if so equipped. Remove the camshaft from the front of the engine. Use care not to damage the camshaft lobes or journals while removing the cam from the engine.

8. Before installing the camshaft, coat the lobes with Lubriplate and coat the journals and valve parts with heavy oil.

9. Reverse the above procedure for installation.

NOTE: *On engines with individually mounted rocker arms, it is necessary to perform a preliminary valve adjustment before starting the engine.*

Pistons and Connecting Rod

REMOVAL AND INSTALLATION

All Engines

REMOVAL

1. Drain the crankcase and remove the oil pan. Remove the oil baffle tray if so equipped.

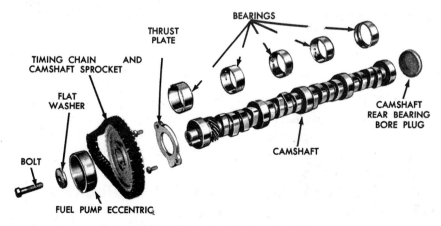

Camshaft and related parts—V8

2. Drain the cooling system and remove the cylinder head or heads.

3. Remove any ridge and/or deposits from the upper end of the cylinder bores with a ridge reamer.

4. Check the rods and pistons for identificaton numbers and, if necessary, number them.

5. Remove the connecting rod cap nuts and caps. Push the rods away from the crankshaft and install the caps and nuts loosely to their respective rods.

6. Push the piston and rod assemblies up and out of the cylinders.

INSTALLATION

1. Lightly coat the pistons, rings, and cylinder walls with light engine oil.

2. With the bearing caps removed, install pieces of protective rubber hose on the bearing cap bolts.

3. Install each piston in its respective bore, using thread guards on each assembly. Guide the rod bearing into place on the crankcase journal.

4. Remove the thread guards from connecting rods and install the lower half of the bearing and cap. Check clearances.

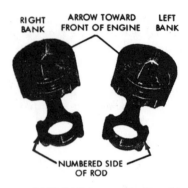

302 Boss and 351-C Piston and rod position

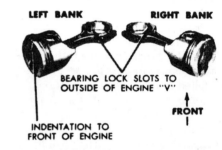

390, 427, and 428 V8 Piston and rod position

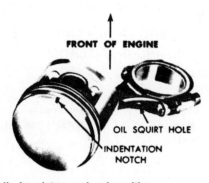

6 Cylinder piston and rod position

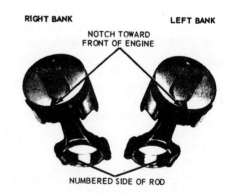

429 SCJ and Boss 429 Piston and rod position

260, 289, 302, 351-W V8 Piston and rod position

5. Install the oil pan.
6. Install the cylinder head.
7. Refill the crankcase and cooling system.
8. Start the engine, bring it to operating temperature, and check for leaks.

ENGINE LUBRICATION

All engines are equipped with full-flow type oil filters to condition the oil before it reaches the main bearings. The filter is equipped with an internal, relief, bypass valve as a safety precaution.

Under normal driving conditions, the engine oil and oil filter should be changed at 6,000 mile (4,000—1973) intervals. However, adverse driving conditions, dusty operation, snort trips, winter driving, etc., may justify the change at much shorter intervals.

Oil Pan

On certain engine-chassis combinations, interference will be encountered between the oil pan and oil pump while attempting to remove the oil pan. If this occurs, lower the oil pan and reach inside it and remove the two bolts retaining the oil pump and pick-up tube to the engine block. Lower the pump and pick-up tube assembly into the pan and remove it with the pan.

REMOVAL AND INSTALLATION

6-Cylinder 1965–1970

1. Drain the crankcase, and remove the dip-stick and flywheel inspection plate.
2. Disconnect the stabilizer bar and pull it downward out of the way.
3. Remove one bolt, loosen the other and swing no. 2 crossmember out of the way.
4. Remove the oil pan. Reverse the procedure for installation.

260, 289 (all), 302 (1969–1970) Boss 302, and 351 W

1. Remove the oil level dipstick. Drain the oil pan.
2. Disconnect the stabilizer bar from the lower control arms and pull the ends down.
3. Remove the oil pan attaching bolts and position the pan on the front cross-member.
4. Remove the one oil inlet tube bolt and loosen the other to position the tube out of the way to remove the pan.
5. Turn the crankshaft as required for clearance to remove the pan.
6. Install in the reverse from above.

351 C

1. Remove the dipstick, raise the vehicle, and drain the crankcase.
2. Disconnect the starter cable and remove the starter.
3. Remove the stabilizer bar.
4. Remove the two bolts retaining no. 2 crossmember and remove the crossmember.

5. Remove the pan bolts, turn the crankshaft for maximum clearance, and remove the pan. Reverse the procedure for installation.

390, 427, 428 (all), and Boss 429

1. Raise the car and place safety stands in position. Drain the oil from the crankcase.
2. Disconnect the stabilizer bar links and pull the ends down. On models equipped with a fan shroud, remove the shroud from the radiator and position it rearward over the fan.
3. Remove the nuts and lockwashers from the engine front support insulator-to-intermediate support bracket.
4. Install a block of wood on the jack and position the jack under the leading edge of the pan.
5. Raise the engine approximately 1¼ in. and insert a 1 in. block between the insulators and the crossmember. Remove the floor jack.
6. Remove the oil pan attaching screws and lower the pan-to-frame crossmember.
7. Turn the crankshaft to obtain clearance between the crankshaft counterweight and the rear of the pan.
8. Remove the oil pump attaching bolts.
9. Position the tube and screen out of the way and remove the pan.
10. Install in reverse of above.
NOTE: *From 1971 on, the no. 2 crossmember is welded to the frame. Previously, this crossmember was bolted into place. This change has resulted in revised oil pan removal procedures for all engines from 1971 to the present.*

250 cu in. 6 Cylinder, 1971–73

REMOVAL

1. Drain the cooling system.
2. Disconnect the radiator upper and lower hoses. If the car is equipped with an automatic transmission, dissconect the fluid cooler inlet and outlet lines from the radiator.
3. On a crossflow radiator, remove the radiator upper support retaining bolts and the upper support(s). Remove the radiator. If equipped with a down-flow radiator, remove the radiator attaching bolts from the radiator side supports and remove the radiator.

On a vehicle equipped with an air conditioner, remove the bolts retaining the radiator shroud to the radiator. Remove the radiator upper or side retaining bolts. Remove the upper support retaining bolts, if so equipped. Remove the radiator. Lift the radiator shroud from the engine compartment.

4. Raise the vehicle and drain the crankcase.

5. Remove the sway bar retaining nuts and bolts. Allow the sway bar to hang in place.

6. Remove both front engine supports through the bolts and nuts.

7. Raise the engine. Place blocks (2 in. long) between the engine supports and the chassis brackets.

8. Remove the starter motor retaining bolts and place the starter motor out of the way on the steering linkage.

9. Remove the oil pan retaining bolts, lower the oil pan, and remove the oil pump pick-up tube and screen assembly.

10. Position the oil cooler lines up and out of the way.

11. Push the oil pan forward over the front crossmember and into the radiator area to allow the oil pan to clear the crossmember and be removed from the bottom.

INSTALLATION

1. Clean the gasket surfaces of the block and oil pan. Coat the block and oil pan gasket surfaces with oil-resistant sealer. Position the oil pan gasket and seals to the block.

2. Reversing the removal procedure, position the oil pan to the engine. Install the oil pump pick-up tube and screen assembly.

3. Install the oil pan retaining bolts and torque them to 7–9 ft lbs.

4. Install the starter.

5. Raise the engine, remove the blocks, and lower the engine to the chassis. Install the engine support bolts and nuts and torque them to 20–30 ft. lbs.

6. Reposition the sway bar, install the nuts and bolts, and torque them to 6–12 ft. lbs.

7. Lower the vehicle and install the radiator.

8. Fill the crankcase and the cooling system.

9. Start the engine and check for leaks.

302 and 351 (ALL;, 1971–73
REMOVAL

1. Remove the oil level dipstick. Remove the bolts attaching the fan shroud to the radiator. Position the shroud over the fan.

2. Raise the vehicle.

3. Drain the crankcase.

4. Remove the stabilizer bar from the chassis.

5. Remove the engine front support thru-bolts.

6. Raise the engine and place wood blocks between the engine front supports and the chassis brackets.

7. If equipped with an automatic transmission, disconnect the oil cooler lines at the radiator.

8. Remove the oil pan retaining bolts and lower the oil pan onto the crossmember.

9. Remove oil pump pick-up tube and screen from the oil pump. Rotate the crankshaft for clearance and remove the oil pan.

INSTALLATION

1. Clean the gasket surfaces of the block and oil pan. The oil pan has a two-piece gasket.

2. Clean the oil pump pick-up tube and screen.

3. Coat the block surface and the oil pan gasket with sealer. Position the oil pan gaskets on the cylinder block.

4. Position the oil pan front seal on the cylinder front cover. Be sure the tabs on the seal are over the oil pan gasket.

5. Position the oil pan rear seal on the rear main bearing cap. Be sure the tabs on the seal are over the oil pan gasket.

6. Position the oil pan on the crossmember. Install a new gasket on the oil pump and install the oil pump pick-up tube.

7. Position the oil pan against the block and install a bolt, finger-tight, on each side of the block. Install the remaining bolts. Tighten the bolts from the center outward in each direction to 9–11 ft. lbs.

8. If equipped with an automatic transmission, connect the oil cooler lines at the radiator.

9. Raise the engine and remove the wood blocks from between the engine supports and the chassis brackets. Lower the engine and install the engine support thru-bolts. Tighten the bolts to 20–30 ft. lbs.

10. Install the stabilizer bar to the chassis.

11. Lower the vehicle.

12. Install the fan shroud.

13. Install the oil level dipstick. Fill the crankcase with the proper grade and quantity of engine oil. Start the engine and check for oil leaks.

429 SCJ
REMOVAL

1. Remove the fan shroud attaching bolts and position the fan shroud over the fan.

2. Remove the air cleaner assembly and the right-hand rocker cover emission hose.

3. Raise the vehicle and drain the crankcase.

4. Remove both engine front support thru-bolts.

5. Remove the sway bar attaching bolts from the chassis and lower the bar for clearance.

6. Raise the engine and place 1½ in. spacers between the engine support insulators and chassis brackets.

7. Remove the oil pan attaching bolts and the oil pan.

8. Remove the oil pump pick-up tube and screen assembly.

INSTALLATION

1. Clean the oil pan and cylinder block gasket surfaces. Clean and install the pick-up tube and screen assembly.

2. Position the oil pan gaskets and seals to the cylinder block.

3. Replace the oil pan and attaching bolts. Torque the bolts to 7–9 ft. lbs.

4. Raise the engine and remove the spacers.

5. Install the engine support thru-bolts. Torque to 20–30 ft. lbs.

6. Install the sway bar. Torque bolts to 6–12 ft. lbs.

7. Lower the vehicle.

8. Install the fan shroud.

9. Install the air cleaner and right-hand rocker cover emission hose.

10. Fill the crankcase. Start the engine and check for leaks.

Rear Main Oil Seal
REPLACEMENT
390, 427, 428, All Engines From 1970–1972

1. Remove the oil pan and, if required, the oil pump.

2. Loosen all main bearing caps allowing the crankshaft to lower slightly.

NOTE: *The crankshaft should not be allowed to drop more than 1/32 in.*

3. Remove the rear main bearing cap and remove the seal from the cap and block.

4. Carefully clean the seal grooves in the cap and block with solvent.

5. Soak the new seal halves in clean engine oil.

6. Install the upper half of the seal in the block with the undercut side of the seal toward the front of the engine. Slide the seal

around the crankshaft journal until ⅜ in. protrudes beyond the base of the block.

7. Repeat, the above procedure on the lower seal, allowing an equal length of the seal to protrude beyond the opposite end of the bearing cap.

8. Install the rear bearing cap and torque all main bearings to specifications. Apply sealer only to the rear of the seals.

9. Dip the bearing cap side seals in oil, then immediately install them. Do not use any sealer on the side seals. Tap the seals into place and do not clip the protruding ends.

10. Install the oil pump and pan. Fill the crankcase with oil, start engine check for leaks.

All Other Engines

The manufacturer recommends the removal of the engine and the crankshaft to replace the seals. An aftermarket tool is available to replace some of these seals with the engine in the car.

Oil Cooler

Four high-performance engines (Boss 302, 428 SCJ, 429 SCJ and Boss 429) have been equipped with engine oil coolers. Removal and installation procedures for all four are as follows:

REMOVAL

1. Disconnect the inlet and outlet lines from the oil cooler and drain them into a container.

2. Remove the hold-down bracket from on top of the cooler.

3. Lift the cooler from the lower mount.

INSTALLATION

1. Position the oil cooler on the lower mount.

2. Install the upper hold-down bracket.

3. Connect the inlet and outlet lines.

4. Fill the crankcase to the proper level with the specified oil.

5. Start the engine and check for oil leaks.

Oil Pump
REMOVAL
6 Cylinder

1. Remove the oil pan.

2. Remove the oil pump inlet tube and screen assembly.

3. Remove the oil pump attaching bolts

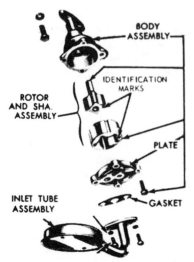

Oil pump assembly—6 cylinder shown generally typical of all engines

and the oil pump gasket and intermediate shaft.

260, 289, 302, 351 W, and Boss 302

1. Remove the oil pan.
2. Remove the oil pump pick-up tube and screen from the oil pump.
NOTE: *It is not necessary to remove the oil baffle tray on Boss 302 engines to do this job.*
3. Remove the oil pump attaching bolts and the oil pump, gasket, and intermediate driveshaft.

351 C

1. Remove the oil pan.
2. Remove the oil pump attaching bolts and the oil pump with the pick-up tube and screen, gasket, and intermediate shaft.

390, 427, and 428

1. Remove the oil pan.
2. Remove the oil pump attaching screws, the oil pump, and the intermediate driveshaft.
3. Remove the inlet tube and screen assembly from the oil pump. Discard the gasket.

429 SCJ and Boss 429

1. Remove the oil pan.
2. Remove the oil pump mounting bolts and then remove the oil pump from the cylinder block.

INSTALLATION
All Engines

1. Prime the oil pump by filling the inlet on outlet ports with engine oil and rotating the shaft of the pump to distribute it.
2. Position the intermediate driveshaft into the distributor socket.
3. Position a new gasket on the pump body and insert the intermediate driveshaft into the pump body.
4. Install the pump and intermediate shaft as an assembly.
NOTE: *Do not force pump if it does not seat readily. The driveshaft may be misaligned with the distributor shaft. To align, rotate the intermediate driveshaft into a new position.*
5. Install and torque the oil pump attaching screws to 12–15 ft. lbs. on six-cylinder engines, 20–25 ft. lbs. on V8s.
6. Install the oil pan.

ENGINE COOLING

Both six-cylinder and V8 engines employ cooling systems that are basically similar.

In the six-cylinder engine, coolant flows from the cylinder head, past the thermostat (if it is open), and into the radiator upper tank. In the V8 engine, coolant from each cylinder head flows through water passages in the intake manifold, then past the thermostat (if it is open), and into the radiator upper tank.

The standard thermostat operating temperature is 185°–192°F. However, a low reading thermostat of 157°–162°F is available for use with non-permanent antifreeze solutions.

A single water pump assembly is used. The pump has a sealed bearing integral with the water pump shaft. The bearing requires no lubrication. There is a bleed hole in the water pump housing. This is not a lubrication hole.

Radiator
REMOVAL

1. Drain the cooling system.
2. Disconnect the upper and lower hoses at the radiator.
3. On cars with automatic transmissions, disconnect the oil cooler lines at the radiator.
4. On vehicles equipped with a fan

shroud, remove the shroud retaining screws and position the shroud out of the way.

5. Remove the radiator attaching bolts and lift out the radiator.

INSTALLATION

1. If a new radiator is to be installed, transfer the petcock from the old radiator to the new one. On cars equipped with automatic transmissions, transfer the oil cooler line fittings from the old radiator to the new one.

2. Position the radiator and install, but do not tighten, the radiator support bolts. On cars equipped with automatic transmissions, connect the oil cooler lines. Then tighten the radiator support bolts.

3. On vehicles equipped with a fan shroud, reinstall the shroud.

4. Connect the radiator hoses. Close the radiator petcock. Then fill and bleed the cooling system.

5. Start the engine and bring it to operating temperature. Check for leaks.

6. On cars equipped with automatic transmissions, check the cooler lines for leaks and interference. Check the transmission fluid level.

Water Pump

REMOVAL AND INSTALLATION

1. Drain the cooling system.

2. On the 351 C, disconnect the negative battery cable.

3. On cars with power steering, remove the drive belt. On models with 390, 427, or 428 engines, remove the power steering mounting retaining screws and remove the pump and bracket as an assembly and position it out of the way.

4. If the vehicle is equipped with air conditioning, remove the idler pulley bracket and the air conditioner drive belt.

5. On engines with Thermactor controls, remove the belt; on 1968 models, remove the pump.

6. Disconnect the lower radiator hose and heater hose from the water pump.

7. On cars equipped with a fan shroud, remove the retaining screws and position the shroud rearward.

8. Remove the fan and spacer from the engine, and if the car is equipped with a fan shroud, remove the fan and shroud from the engine as an assembly.

9. Loosen the alternator mounting bolts,

remove the alternator belt, and remove the alternator adjusting arm bracket from the water pump.

10. Loosen the bypass hose at the water pump.

11. Remove the water pump retaining screws and the pump from the engine.

12. Clean any gasket material from the pump mounting surface and, on the 429 V8, remove the water pump backing plate and replace the gasket.

NOTE: *The 250 CI six-cylinder engines originally used a one-piece gasket for the cylinder front cover and water pump. Trim away the old gasket at the edge of the cylinder cover and replace with service gasket.*

13. Remove the heater hose fitting from the old pump and install it on the new pump.

14. Coat both sides of the new gasket with a water-resistant sealer, then reinstall the pump reversing the above procedure.

Thermostat

REMOVAL

1. Drain the radiator so that the coolant level is below the thermostat.

2. Remove the coolant outlet housing retaining bolts. Pull the elbow away from the cylinder head or manifold sufficiently to provide access to the thermostat. Remove the thermostat and gasket.

INSTALLATION

Check the thermostat before installing it, following the thermostat test.

1. Clean the coolant outlet housing and cylinder head or manifold gasket surfaces.

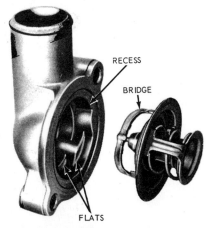

Thermostat and housing

Coat a new gasket with water resistant sealer. Position the gasket on the cylinder head opening. The gasket must be positioned on the cylinder head or the intake manifold, before the thermostat is installed. To prevent the incorrect installation of the thermostat, the water outlet casting on all engines contains a locking recess into which the thermostat is turned and locked. Install the thermostat with the bridge section in the outlet casting. Turn the thermostat clockwise to lock it in position on the flats cast into the outlet elbow.

2. Position the coolant outlet elbow against the cylinder head, or the intake manifold. Install and torque the retaining bolts to specifications.

3. Fill the cooling system with the recommended permanent antifreeze and water mixture. If equipped with a cross-flow radiator, follow the special instructions regarding checking the coolant level. Check for leaks and the proper coolant level after the engine has reached the normal operating temperatures.

TEST

It is good practice to test new thermostats before installing them in the engine.

Remove the thermostat and immerse it in boiling water. Replace the thermostat if it does not open more than ¼ in.

If the problem being investigated is insufficient heat, the thermostat should be checked for leakage. This may be done by holding the thermostat up to the lighted background. Light leakage around the thermostat valve (thermostat at room temperature) indicates that the thermostat is unacceptable and should be replaced. It is possible, on some thermostats, that a slight leakage of light at one or two locations on the perimeter of the valve may be detected. This should be considered normal.

Special Filling Instructions for Crossflow Radiators

Coolant level cannot be accurately checked while the engine is running, due to the construction of this radiator. Check the level while the engine is cold and fill only to the left side tank about 2 in. below the fill cap seat.

ENGINE REBUILDING

Most procedures involved in rebuilding an engine are fairly standard, regardless of the type of engine involved. This section is a guide to accepted rebuilding procedures. Examples of standard rebuilding practices are illustrated and should be used along with specific details concerning your particular engine, found earlier in this chapter.

The procedures given here are those used by any competent rebuilder. Obviously some of the procedures cannot be performed by the do-it-yourself mechanic, but are provided so that you will be familiar with the services that should be offered by rebuilding or machine shops. As an example, in most instances, it is more profitable for the home mechanic to remove the cylinder heads, buy the necessary parts (new valves, seals, keepers, keys, etc.) and deliver these to a machine shop for the necessary work. In this way you will save the money to remove and install the cylinder head and the mark-up on parts.

On the other hand, most of the work involved in rebuilding the lower end is well within the scope of the do-it-yourself mechanic. Only work such as hot-tanking, actually boring the block or Magnafluxing (invisible crack detection) need be sent to a machine shop.

Tools

The tools required for basic engine rebuilding should, with a few exceptions, be those included in a mechanic's tool kit. An accurate torque wrench, and a dial indicator (reading in thousandths) mounted on a universal base should be available. Special tools, where required, are available from the major tool suppliers. The services of a competent automotive machine shop must also be readily available.

Precautions

Aluminum has become increasingly popular for use in engines, due to its low weight and excellent heat transfer characteristics. The following precautions must be observed when handling aluminum (or any other) engine parts:

—Never hot-tank aluminum parts.

—Remove all aluminum parts (identification tags, etc.) from engine parts before hot-tanking (otherwise they will be removed during the process).

—Always coat threads lightly with engine oil or anti-seize compounds before installation, to prevent seizure.

—Never over-torque bolts or spark plugs in aluminum threads. Should stripping occur, threads can be restored using any of a number of thread repair kits available (see next section).

Inspection Techniques

Magnaflux and Zyglo are inspection techniques used to locate material flaws, such as stress cracks. Magnaflux is a magnetic process, applicable only to ferrous materials. The Zyglo process coats the matrial with a fluorescent dye penetrant, and any material may be tested using Zyglo. Specific checks of suspected surface cracks may be made at lower cost and more readily using spot check dye. The dye is sprayed onto the suspected area, wiped off, and the area is then sprayed with a developer. Cracks then will show up brightly.

Overhaul

The section is divided into two parts. The first, Cylinder Head Reconditioning, assumes that the cylinder head is removed from the engine, all manifolds are removed, and the cylinder head is on a workbench. The camshaft should be removed from overhead cam cylinder heads. The second section, Cylinder Block Reconditioning, covers the block, pistons, connecting rods and crankshaft. It is assumed that the engine is mounted on a work stand, and the cylinder head and all accessories are removed.

Procedures are identified as follows:

Unmarked—Basic procedures that must be performed in order to successfully complete the rebuilding process.

Starred (*)—Procedures that should be performed to ensure maximum performance and engine life.

Double starred (**)—Procedures that may be performed to increase engine performance and reliability.

When assembling the engine, any parts that will be in frictional contact must be pre-lubricated, to provide protection on initial start-up. Any product specifically formulated for this purpose may be used. NOTE: *Do not use engine oil. Where semi-permanent* (locked but removable) installation of bolts or nuts is desired, threads should be cleaned and located with **Loctite** ® or a similar product (non-hardening).

Repairing Damaged Threads

Several methods of repairing damaged threads are available. Heli-Coil® (shown here), Keenserts® and Microdot® are among the most widely used. All involve basically the same principle—drilling out stripped threads, tapping the hole and installing a pre-wound insert—making welding, plugging and oversize fasteners unnecessary.

Two types of thread repair inserts are usually supplied—a standard type for most Inch Coarse, Inch Fine, Metric Coarse and Metric Fine thread sizes and a spark plug type to fit most spark plug port sizes. Consult the individual manufacturer's catalog to determine exact applications. Typical thread repair kits will contain a selection of pre-wound threaded inserts, a tap (corresponding to the outside diameter threads of the insert) and an installation tool. Spark plug inserts usually differ because they require a tap equipped with pilot threads and a combined reamer/tap section. Most manufacturers also supply blister-packed thread repair inserts separately in addition to a master kit containing a variety of taps and inserts plus installation tools.

Before effecting a repair to a threaded hole, remove any snapped, broken or damaged bolts or studs. Penetrating oil can be used to free frozen threads; the offending item can be removed with locking pliers or with a screw or stud extractor. After the hole is clear, the thread can be repaired, as follows:

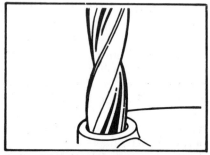

Drill out the damaged threads with specified drill. Drill completely through the hole or to the bottom of a blind hole

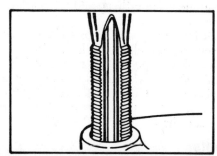

With the tap supplied, tap the hole to receive the thread insert. Keep the tap well oiled and back it out frequently to avoid clogging the threads

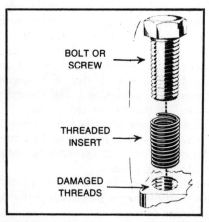

BOLT OR SCREW

THREADED INSERT

DAMAGED THREADS

Damaged bolt holes can be repaired with thread repair inserts

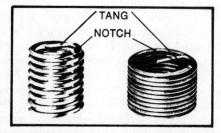

TANG

NOTCH

Standard thread repair insert (left) and spark plug thread insert (right)

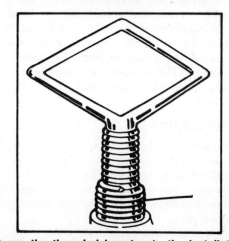

Screw the threaded insert onto the installation tool until the tang engages the slot. Screw the insert into the tapped hole until it is ¼–½ turn below the top surface. After installation break off the tang with a hammer and punch

Standard Torque Specifications and Fastener Markings

The Newton-metre has been designated the world standard for measuring torque and will gradually replace the foot-pound and kilogram-meter. In the absence of specific torques, the following chart can be used as a guide to the maximum safe torque of a particular size/grade of fastener.

- There is no torque difference for fine or coarse threads.
- Torque values are based on clean, dry threads. Reduce the value by 10% if threads are oiled prior to assembly.
- The torque required for aluminum components or fasteners is considerably less.

U. S. BOLTS

SAE Grade Number	1 or 2			5			6 or 7		

Bolt Markings

Manufacturer's marks may vary—number of lines always 2 less than the grade number.

Usage	Frequent			Frequent			Infrequent		
Bolt Size (inches)—(Thread)	Maximum Torque			Maximum Torque			Maximum Torque		
	Ft-Lb	kgm	Nm	Ft-Lb	kgm	Nm	Ft-Lb	kgm	Nm
¼—20	5	0.7	6.8	8	1.1	10.8	10	1.4	13.5
—28	6	0.8	8.1	10	1.4	13.6			
⁵⁄₁₆—18	11	1.5	14.9	17	2.3	23.0	19	2.6	25.8
—24	13	1.8	17.6	19	2.6	25.7			
⅜—16	18	2.5	24.4	31	4.3	42.0	34	4.7	46.0
—24	20	2.75	27.1	35	4.8	47.5			
⁷⁄₁₆—14	28	3.8	37.0	49	6.8	66.4	55	7.6	74.5
—20	30	4.2	40.7	55	7.6	74.5			
½—13	39	5.4	52.8	75	10.4	101.7	85	11.75	115.2
—20	41	5.7	55.6	85	11.7	115.2			
⁹⁄₁₆—12	51	7.0	69.2	110	15.2	149.1	120	16.6	162.7
—18	55	7.6	74.5	120	16.6	162.7			
⅝—11	83	11.5	112.5	150	20.7	203.3	167	23.0	226.5
—18	95	13.1	128.8	170	23.5	230.5			
¾—10	105	14.5	142.3	270	37.3	366.0	280	38.7	379.6
—16	115	15.9	155.9	295	40.8	400.0			
⅞— 9	160	22.1	216.9	395	54.6	535.5	440	60.9	596.5
—14	175	24.2	237.2	435	60.1	589.7			
1— 8	236	32.5	318.6	590	81.6	799.9	660	91.3	894.8
—14	250	34.6	338.9	660	91.3	849.8			

METRIC BOLTS

NOTE: *Metric bolts are marked with a number indicating the rela-tive strength of the bolt. These numbers have nothing to do with size.*

Description	Torque ft-lbs (Nm)			
Thread size x pitch (mm)	Head mark—4		Head mark—7	
6 x 1.0	2.2–2.9	(3.0–3.9)	3.6–5.8	(4.9–7.8)
8 x 1.25	5.8–8.7	(7.9–12)	9.4–14	(13–19)
10 x 1.25	12–17	(16–23)	20–29	(27–39)
12 x 1.25	21–32	(29–43)	35–53	(47–72)
14 x 1.5	35–52	(48–70)	57–85	(77–110)
16 x 1.5	51–77	(67–100)	90–120	(130–160)
18 x 1.5	74–110	(100–150)	130–170	(180–230)
20 x 1.5	110–140	(150–190)	190–240	(160–320)
22 x 1.5	150–190	(200–260)	250–320	(340–430)
24 x 1.5	190–240	(260–320)	310–410	(420–550)

NOTE: *This engine rebuilding section is a guide to accepted rebuilding procedures. Typical examples of standard rebuilding procedures are illustrated. Use these procedures along with the detailed instructions earlier in this chapter, concerning your particular engine.*

Cylinder Head Reconditioning

Procedure	Method
Remove the cylinder head:	See the engine service procedures earlier in this chapter for details concerning specific engines.
Identify the valves:	Invert the cylinder head, and number the valve faces front to rear, using a permanent felt-tip marker.
Remove the rocker arms (OHV engines only):	Remove the rocker arms with shaft(s) or balls and nuts. Wire the sets of rockers, balls and nuts together, and identify according to the corresponding valve.
Remove the camshaft (OHC engines only):	See the engine service procedures earlier in this chapter for details concerning specific engines.
Remove the valves and springs:	Using an appropriate valve spring compressor (depending on the configuration of the cylinder head), compress the valve springs. Lift out the keepers with needlenose pliers, release the compressor, and remove the valve, spring, and spring retainer. See the engine service procedures earlier in this chapter for details concerning specific engines.

Cylinder Head Reconditioning

Procedure	Method

Check the valve stem-to-guide clearance:

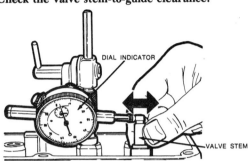

DIAL INDICATOR

VALVE STEM

Check the valve stem-to-guide clearance

Clean the valve stem with lacquer thinner or a similar solvent to remove all gum and varnish. Clean the valve guides using solvent and an expanding wire-type valve guide cleaner. Mount a dial indicator so that the stem is at 90° to the valve stem, as close to the valve guide as possible. Move the valve off its seat, and measure the valve guide-to-stem clearance by rocking the stem back and forth to actuate the dial indicator. Measure the valve stems using a micrometer, and compare to specifications, to determine whether stem or guide wear is responsible for excessive clearance.
NOTE: *Consult the Specifications tables earlier in this chapter.*

De-carbon the cylinder head and valves:

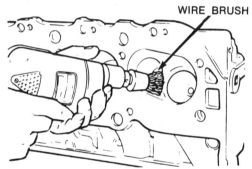

WIRE BRUSH

Remove the carbon from the cylinder head with a wire brush and electric drill

Chip carbon away from the valve heads, combustion chambers, and ports, using a chisel made of hardwood. Remove the remaining deposits with a stiff wire brush.
NOTE: *Be sure that the deposits are actually removed, rather than burnished.*

Hot-tank the cylinder head (cast iron heads only):
CAUTION: *Do not hot-tank aluminum parts.*

Have the cylinder head hot-tanked to remove grease, corrosion, and scale from the water passages.
NOTE: *In the case of overhead cam cylinder heads, consult the operator to determine whether the camshaft bearings will be damaged by the caustic solution.*

Degrease the remaining cylinder head parts:

Clean the remaining cylinder head parts in an engine cleaning solvent. Do not remove the protective coating from the springs.

Check the cylinder head for warpage:

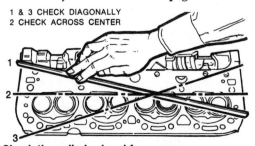

1 & 3 CHECK DIAGONALLY
2 CHECK ACROSS CENTER

Check the cylinder head for warpage

Place a straight-edge across the gasket surface of the cylinder head. Using feeler gauges, determine the clearance at the center of the straight-edge. If warpage exceeds .003″ in a 6″ span, or .006″ over the total length, the cylinder head must be resurfaced.
NOTE: *If warpage exceeds the manufacturer's maximum tolerance for material removal, the cylinder head must be replaced.* When milling the cylinder heads of V-type engines, the intake manifold mounting position is altered, and must be corrected by milling the manifold flange a proportionate amount.

Cylinder Head Reconditioning

Procedure	Method
*Knurl the valve guides:	*Valve guides which are not excessively worn or distorted may, in some cases, be knurled rather than replaced. Knurling is a process in which metal is displaced and raised, thereby reducing clearance. Knurling also provides excellent oil control. The possibility of knurling rather than replacing valve guides should be discussed with a machinist.

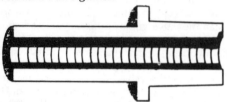

Cut-away view of a knurled valve guide

Replace the valve guides:
NOTE: *Valve guides should only be replaced if damaged or if an oversize valve stem is not available.*

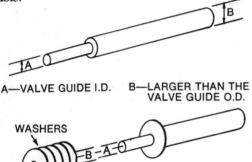

A—VALVE GUIDE I.D.   B—LARGER THAN THE VALVE GUIDE O.D.

WASHERS

A—VALVE GUIDE I.D.   B—LARGER THAN THE VALVE GUIDE O.D.

Valve guide installation tool using washers for installation

See the engine service procedures earlier in this chapter for details concerning specific engines. Depending on the type of cylinder head, valve guides may be pressed, hammered, or shrunk in. In cases where the guides are shrunk into the head, replacement should be left to an equipped machine shop. In other cases, the guides are replaced using a stepped drift (see illustration). Determine the height above the boss that the guide must extend, and obtain a stack of washers, their I.D. similar to the guide's O.D., of that height. Place the stack of washers on the guide, and insert the guide into the boss.
NOTE: *Valve guides are often tapered or beveled for installation.* Using the stepped installation tool (see illustration), press or tap the guides into position. Ream the guides according to the size of the valve stem.

Replace valve seat inserts:

Replacement of valve seat inserts which are worn beyond resurfacing or broken, if feasible, must be done by a machine shop.

Resurface (grind) the valve face:

Using a valve grinder, resurface the valves according to specifications given earlier in this chapter.
CAUTION: *Valve face angle is not always identical to valve seat angle.* A minimum margin of

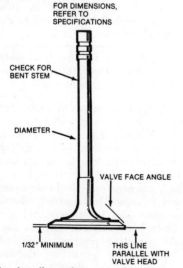

FOR DIMENSIONS, REFER TO SPECIFICATIONS

CHECK FOR BENT STEM

DIAMETER

VALVE FACE ANGLE

1/32" MINIMUM   THIS LINE PARALLEL WITH VALVE HEAD

Critical valve dimensions

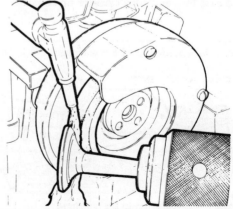

Valve grinding by machine

Cylinder Head Reconditioning

Procedure	Method

Procedure / *Method*

$^1/_{32}"$ should remain after grinding the valve. The valve stem top should also be squared and resurfaced, by placing the stem in the V-block of the grinder, and turning it while pressing lightly against the grinding wheel.

NOTE: *Do not grind sodium filled exhaust valves on a machine. These should be hand lapped.*

Resurface the valve seats using reamers or grinder:

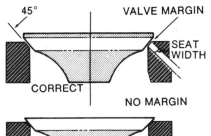

Valve seat width and centering

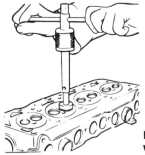

Reaming the valve seat with a hand reamer

Select a reamer of the correct seat angle, slightly larger than the diameter of the valve seat, and assemble it with a pilot of the correct size. Install the pilot into the valve guide, and using steady pressure, turn the reamer clockwise.

CAUTION: *Do not turn the reamer counterclockwise.* Remove only as much material as necessary to clean the seat. Check the concentricity of the seat (following). If the dye method is not used, coat the valve face with Prussian blue dye, install and rotate it on the valve seat. Using the dye marked area as a centering guide, center and narrow the valve seat to specifications with correction cutters.

NOTE: *When no specifications are available, minimum seat width for exhaust valves should be $^5/_{64}"$, intake valves $^1/_{16}"$.*

After making correction cuts, check the position of the valve seat on the valve face using Prussian blue dye.

To resurface the seat with a power grinder, select a pilot of the correct size and coarse stone of the proper angle. Lubricate the pilot and move the stone on and off the valve seat at 2 cycles per second, until all flaws are gone. Finish the seat with a fine stone. If necessary the seat can be corrected or narrowed using correction stones.

Check the valve seat concentricity:

Coat the valve face with Prussian blue dye, install the valve, and rotate it on the valve seat. If the entire seat becomes coated, and the valve is known to be concentric, the seat is concentric.

*Install the dial gauge pilot into the guide, and rest of the arm on the valve seat. Zero the gauge, and rotate the arm around the seat. Run-out should not exceed .002".

Check the valve seat concentricity with a dial gauge

Cylinder Head Reconditioning

Procedure	Method
*Lap the valves: NOTE: *Valve lapping is done to ensure efficient sealing of resurfaced valves and seats.*	*Invert the cylinder head, lightly lubricate the valve stems, and install the valves in the head as numbered. Coat valve seats with fine grinding compound, and attach the lapping tool suction cup to a valve head. NOTE: *Moisten the suction cup.* Rotate the tool between the palms, changing position and lifting the tool often to prevent grooving. Lap the valve until a smooth, polished seat is evident. Remove the valve and tool, and rinse away all traces of grinding compound.

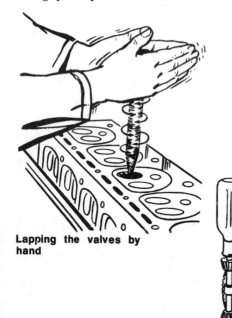

Lapping the valves by hand

Home-made valve lapping tool

HAND DRILL

ROD

SUCTION CUP

	**Fasten a suction cup to a piece of drill rod, and mount the rod in a hand drill. Proceed as above, using the hand drill as a lapping tool. CAUTION: *Due to the higher speeds involved when using the hand drill, care must be exercised to avoid grooving the seat.* Lift the tool and change direction of rotation often.

Check the valve springs:	Place the spring on a flat surface next to a square. Measure the height of the spring, and rotate it against the edge of the square to measure distortion. If spring height varies (by comparison) by more than $1/16''$ or if distortion exceeds $1/16''$, replace the spring.

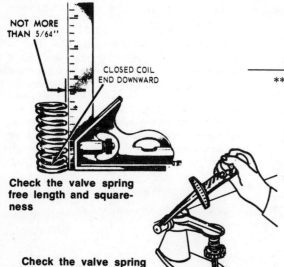

NOT MORE THAN 5/64"

CLOSED COIL END DOWNWARD

Check the valve spring free length and squareness

Check the valve spring test pressure

	**In addition to evaluating the spring as above, test the spring pressure at the installed and compressed (installed height minus valve lift) height using a valve spring tester. Springs used on small displacement engines (up to 3 liters) should be ∓ 1 lb of all other springs in either position. A tolerance of ∓ 5 lbs is permissible on larger engines.

Cylinder Head Reconditioning

Procedure	Method

*Install valve stem seals:

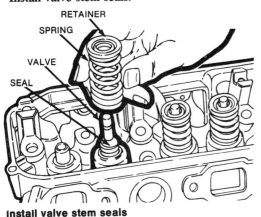

RETAINER

SPRING

VALVE

SEAL

Install valve stem seals

* Due to the pressure differential that exists at the ends of the intake valve guides (atmospheric pressure above, manifold vacuum below), oil is drawn through the valve guides into the intake port. This has been alleviated somewhat since the addition of positive crankcase ventilation, which lowers the pressure above the guides. Several types of valve stem seals are available to rocker arms and balls, and install them on the the stem and guide boss, while others require that the boss be machined. Recently, Teflon guide seals have become popular. Consult a parts supplier or machinist concerning availability and suggested usages.

NOTE: *When installing seals, ensure that a small amount of oil is able to pass the seal to lubricate the valve guides; otherwise, excessive wear may result.*

Install the valves:

See the engine service procedures earlier in this chapter for details concerning specific engines.

Lubricate the valve stems, and install the valves in the cylinder head as numbered. Lubricate and position the seals (if used) and the valve springs. Install the spring retainers, compress the springs, and insert the keys using needle-nose pliers or a tool designed for this purpose.

NOTE: *Retain the keys with wheel bearing grease during installation.*

Check valve spring installed height:

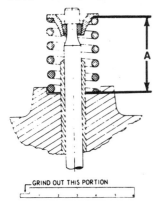

A

GRIND OUT THIS PORTION

Measure the valve spring installed height (A) with a modified steel rule

Valve spring installed height (A)

Measure the distance between the spring pad and the lower edge of the spring retainer, and compare to specifications. If the installed height is incorrect, add shim washers between the spring pad and the spring.

CAUTION: *Use only washers designed for this purpose.*

Install the camshaft (OHC engines only) and check end-play:

See the engine service procedures earlier in this chapter for details concerning specific engines.

Cylinder Head Reconditioning

Procedure	Method

Inspect the rocker arms, balls, studs, and nuts (OHV engines only):

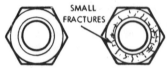

Stress cracks in the rocker nuts

Visually inspect the rocker arms, balls, studs, and nuts for cracks, galling, burning, scoring, or wear. If all parts are intact, liberally lubricate the rocker arms and balls, and install them on the cylinder head. If wear is noted on a rocker arm at the point of valve contact, grind it smooth and square, removing as little material as possible. Replace the rocker arm if excessively worn. If a rocker stud shows signs of wear, it must be replaced (see below). If a rocker nut shows stress cracks, replace it. If an exhaust ball is galled or burned, substitute the intake ball from the same cylinder (if it is intact), and install a new intake ball.

NOTE: *Avoid using new rocker balls on exhaust valves.*

Replacing rocker studs (OHV engines only):

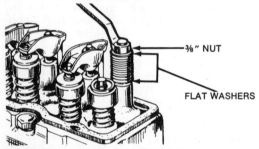

Extracting a pressed-in rocker stud

In order to remove a threaded stud, lock two nuts on the stud, and unscrew the stud using the lower nut. Coat the lower threads of the new stud with Loctite, and install.

Two alternative methods are available for replacing pressed in studs. Remove the damaged stud using a stack of washers and a nut (see illustration). In the first, the boss is reamed .005–.006″ oversize, and an oversize stud pressed in. Control the stud extension over the boss using washers, in the same manner as valve guides. Before installing the stud, coat it with white lead and grease. To retain the stud more positively drill a hole through the stud and boss, and install a roll pin. In the second method, the boss is tapped, and a threaded stud installed.

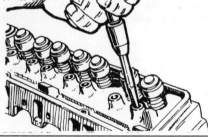

Ream the stud bore for oversize rocker studs

Inspect the rocker shaft(s) and rocker arms (OHV engines only)

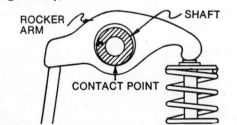

Check the rocker arm-to-rocker shaft contact area

Remove rocker arms, springs and washers from rocker shaft.

NOTE: *Lay out parts in the order as they are removed.* Inspect rocker arms for pitting or wear on the valve contact point, or excessive bushing wear. Bushings need only be replaced if wear is excessive, because the rocker arm normally contacts the shaft at one point only. Grind the valve contact point of rocker arm smooth if necessary, removing as little material as possible. If excessive material must be removed to smooth and square the arm, it should be replaced. Clean out all oil holes and passages in rocker shaft. If shaft is grooved or worn, replace it. Lubricate and assemble the rocker shaft.

Cylinder Head Reconditioning

Procedure	Method
Inspect the pushrods (OHV engines only):	Remove the pushrods, and, if hollow, clean out the oil passages using fine wire. Roll each pushrod over a piece of clean glass. If a distinct clicking sound is heard as the pushrod rolls, the rod is bent, and must be replaced.
	*The length of all pushrods must be equal. Measure the length of the pushrods, compare to specifications, and replace as necessary.
Inspect the valve lifters (OHV engines only): 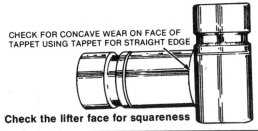 CHECK FOR CONCAVE WEAR ON FACE OF TAPPET USING TAPPET FOR STRAIGHT EDGE **Check the lifter face for squareness**	Remove lifters from their bores, and remove gum and varnish, using solvent. Clean walls of lifter bores. Check lifters for concave wear as illustrated. If face is worn concave, replace lifter, and carefully inspect the camshaft. Lightly lubricate lifter and insert it into its bore. If play is excessive, an oversize lifter must be installed (where possible). Consult a machinist concerning feasibility. If play is satisfactory, remove, lubricate, and reinstall the lifter.
*Testing hydraulic lifter leak down (OHV engines only):	Submerge lifter in a container of kerosene. Chuck a used pushrod or its equivalent into a drill press. Position container of kerosene so pushrod acts on the lifter plunger. Pump lifter with the drill press, until resistance increases. Pump several more times to bleed any air out of lifter. Apply very firm, constant pressure to the lifter, and observe rate at which fluid bleeds out of lifter. If the fluid bleeds very quickly (less than 15 seconds), lifter is defective. If the time exceeds 60 seconds, lifter is sticking. In either case, recondition or replace lifter. If lifter is operating properly (leak down time 15–60 seconds), lubricate and install it.

Cylinder Block Reconditioning

Procedure	Method
Checking the main bearing clearance: 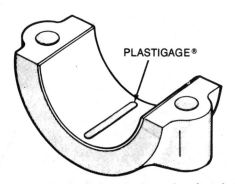 PLASTIGAGE® **Plastigage® installed on the lower bearing shell**	Invert engine, and remove cap from the bearing to be checked. Using a clean, dry rag, thoroughly clean all oil from crankshaft journal and bearing insert. NOTE: *Plastigage® is soluble in oil; therefore, oil on the journal or bearing could result in erroneous readings.* Place a piece of Plastigage along the full length of journal, reinstall cap, and torque to specifications. NOTE: *Specifications are given in the engine specifications earlier in this chapter.* Remove bearing cap, and determine bearing clearance by comparing width of Plastigage to the scale on Plastigage envelope. Journal taper is determined by comparing width of the Plastigage strip near its ends. Rotate crankshaft 90° and retest, to determine journal eccentricity. NOTE: *Do not rotate crankshaft with Plastigage*

Cylinder Block Reconditioning

Procedure	Method

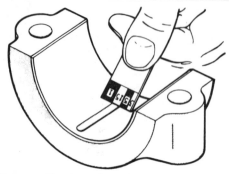

Measure Plastigage® to determine main bearing clearance

installed. If bearing insert and journal appear intact, and are within tolerances, no further main bearing service is required. If bearing or journal appear defective, cause of failure should be determined before replacement.

* Remove crankshaft from block (see below). Measure the main bearing journals at each end tiwce (90° apart) using a micrometer, to determine diameter, journal taper and eccentricity. If journals are within tolerances, reinstall bearing caps at their specified torque. Using a telescope gauge and micrometer, measure bearing I.D. parallel to piston axis and at 30° on each side of piston axis. Subtract journal O.D. from bearing I.D. to determine oil clearance. If crankshaft journals appear defective, or do not meet tolerances, there is no need to measure bearings; for the crankshaft will require grinding and/or undersize bearings will be required. If bearing appears defective, cause for failure should be determined prior to replacement.

Check the connecting rod bearing clearance:

Connecting rod bearing clearance is checked in the same manner as main bearing clearance, using Plastigage. Before removing the crankshaft, connecting rod side clearance also should be measured and recorded.

* Checking connecting rod bearing clearance, using a micrometer, is identical to checking main bearing clearance. If no other service is required, the piston and rod assemblies need not be removed.

Remove the crankshaft:

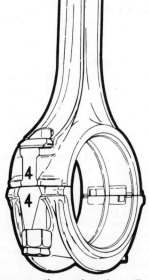

Match the connecting rod to the cylinder with a number stamp

Using a punch, mark the corresponding main bearing caps and saddles according to position (i.e., one punch on the front main cap and saddle, two on the second, three on the third, etc.). Using number stamps, identify the corresponding connecting rods and caps, according to cylinder (if no numbers are present). Remove the main and connecting rod caps, and place sleeves of plastic tubing or vacuum hose over the connecting rod bolts, to protect the journals as the crankshaft is removed. Lift the crankshaft out of the block.

Match the connecting rod and cap with scribe marks

Cylinder Block Reconditioning

Procedure	Method
Remove the ridge from the top of the cylinder: 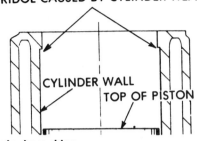 RIDGE CAUSED BY CYLINDER WEAR / CYLINDER WALL / TOP OF PISTON **Cylinder bore ridge**	In order to facilitate removal of the piston and connecting rod, the ridge at the top of the cylinder (unworn area; see illustration) must be removed. Place the piston at the bottom of the bore, and cover it with a rag. Cut the ridge away using a ridge reamer, exercising extreme care to avoid cutting too deeply. Remove the rag, and remove cuttings that remain on the piston. **CAUTION:** *If the ridge is not removed, and new rings are installed, damage to rings will result.*
Remove the piston and connecting rod: 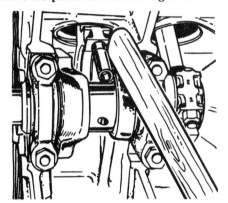 **Push the piston out with a hammer handle**	Invert the engine, and push the pistons and connecting rods out of the cylinders. If necessary, tap the connecting rod boss with a wooden hammer handle, to force the piston out. **CAUTION:** *Do not attempt to force the piston past the cylinder ridge* (see above).
Service the crankshaft:	Ensure that all oil holes and passages in the crankshaft are open and free of sludge. If necessary, have the crankshaft ground to the largest possible undersize.
	** Have the crankshaft Magnafluxed, to locate stress cracks. Consult a machinist concerning additional service procedures, such as surface hardening (e.g., nitriding, Tuftriding) to improve wear characteristics, cross drilling and chamfering the oil holes to improve lubrication, and balancing.
Removing freeze plugs:	Drill a small hole in the middle of the freeze plugs. Thread a large sheet metal screw into the hole and remove the plug with a slide hammer.
Remove the oil gallery plugs:	Threaded plugs should be removed using an appropriate (usually square) wrench. To remove soft, pressed in plugs, drill a hole in the plug, and thread in a sheet metal screw. Pull the plug out by the screw using pliers.
Hot-tank the block: **NOTE:** *Do not hot-tank aluminum parts.*	Have the block hot-tanked to remove grease, corrosion, and scale from the water jackets. **NOTE:** *Consult the operator to determine whether the camshaft bearings will be damaged during the hot-tank process.*

Cylinder Block Reconditioning

Procedure	Method

Check the block for cracks:	Visually inspect the block for cracks or chips. The most common locations are as follows:
	    Adjacent to freeze plugs.
	    Between the cylinders and water jackets.
	    Adjacent to the main bearing saddles.
	    At the extreme bottom of the cylinders.
	Check only suspected cracks using spot check dye (see introduction). If a crack is located, consult a machinist concerning possible repairs.

	** Magnaflux the block to locate hidden cracks. If cracks are located, consult a machinist about feasibility of repair.
Install the oil gallery plugs and freeze plugs:	Coat freeze plugs with sealer and tap into position using a piece of pipe, slightly smaller than the plug, as a driver. To ensure retention, stake the edges of the plugs. Coat threaded oil gallery plugs with sealer and install. Drive replacement soft plugs into block using a large drift as driver.
	* Rather than reinstalling lead plugs, drill and tap the holes, and install threaded plugs.
Check the bore diameter and surface: 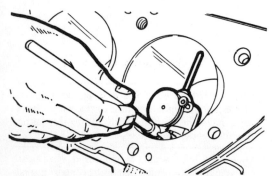 Measure the cylinder bore with a dial gauge	Visually inspect the cylinder bores for roughness, scoring, or scuffing. If evident, the cylinder bore must be bored or honed oversize to eliminate imperfections, and the smallest possible oversize piston used. The new pistons should be given to the machinist with the block, so that the cylinders can be bored or honed exactly to the piston size (plus clearance). If no flaws are evident, measure the bore diameter using a telescope gauge and micrometer, or dial gauge, parallel and perpendicular to the engine centerline, at the top (below the ridge) and bottom of the bore. Subtract the bottom measurements from the top to determine taper, and the parallel to the centerline measurements from the perpendicular measurements to determine eccentricity. If the measurements are not within specifications, the cylinder must be bored or honed, and an oversize piston installed. If the measurements are within specifications the cylinder may be used as is, with only finish honing (see below).

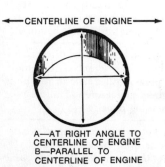

A—AT RIGHT ANGLE TO CENTERLINE OF ENGINE
B—PARALLEL TO CENTERLINE OF ENGINE

Cylinder bore measuring points

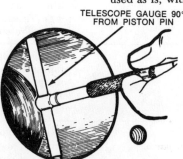

Measure the cylinder bore with a telescope gauge

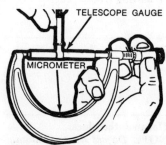

Measure the telescope gauge with a micrometer to determine the cylinder bore

Cylinder Block Reconditioning

Procedure	Method
	NOTE: *Prior to submitting the block for boring, perform the following operation(s).*
Check the cylinder block bearing alignment:	Remove the upper bearing inserts. Place a straightedge in the bearing saddles along the centerline of the crankshaft. If clearance exists between the straightedge and the center saddle, the block must be alignbored.

Check the main bearing saddle alignment

*Check the deck height:	The deck height is the distance from the crankshaft centerline to the block deck. To measure, invert the engine, and install the crankshaft, retaining it with the center main cap. Measure the distance from the crankshaft journal to the block deck, parallel to the cylinder centerline. Measure the diameter of the end (front and rear) main journals, parallel to the centerline of the cylinders, divide the diameter in half, and subtract it from the previous measurement. The results of the front and rear measurements should be identical. If the difference exceeds .005″, the deck height should be corrected. NOTE: *Block deck height and warpage should be corrected at the same time.*
Check the block deck for warpage:	Using a straightedge and feeler gauges, check the block deck for warpage in the same manner that the cylinder head is checked (see Cylinder Head Reconditioning). If warpage exceeds specifications, have the deck resurfaced. NOTE: *In certain cases a specification for total material removal (Cylinder head and block deck) is provided. This specification must not be exceeded.*
Clean and inspect the pistons and connecting rods:	Using a ring expander, remove the rings from the piston. Remove the retaining rings (if so equipped) and remove piston pin. NOTE: *If the piston pin must be pressed out, determine the proper method and use the proper tools; otherwise the piston will distort.* Clean the ring grooves using an appropriate tool, exercising care to avoid cutting too deeply. Thoroughly clean all carbon and varnish from the piston with solvent. CAUTION: *Do not use a wire brush or caustic solvent on pistons.* Inspect the pistons for scuffing, scoring, cracks, pitting, or excessive ring groove wear. If wear is evident, the piston must be replaced. Check the connecting rod length by measuring the rod from the inside of the large end to the

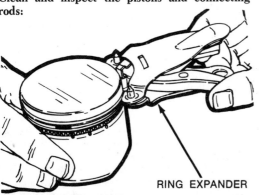

RING EXPANDER

Remove the piston rings

Cylinder Block Reconditioning

Procedure	Method

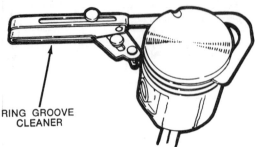

RING GROOVE
CLEANER

Clean the piston ring grooves

inside of the small end using calipers (see illustration). All connecting rods should be equal length. Replace any rod that differs from the others in the engine.

* Have the connecting rod alignment checked in an alignment fixture by a machinist. Replace any twisted or bent rods.

* Magnaflux the connecting rods to locate stress cracks. If cracks are found, replace the connecting rod.

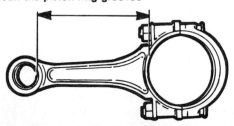

Check the connecting rod length (arrow)

Fit the pistons to the cylinders:

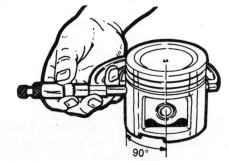

90°

Measure the piston prior to fitting

Using a telescope gauge and micrometer, or a dial gauge, measure the cylinder bore diameter perpendicular to the piston pin, 2½" below the deck. Measure the piston perpendicular to its pin on the skirt. The difference between the two measurements is the piston clearance. If the clearance is within specifications or slightly below (after boring or honing), finish honing is all that is required. If the clearance is excessive, try to obtain a slightly larger piston to bring clearance within specifications. Where this is not possible, obtain the first oversize piston, and hone (or if necessary, bore) the cylinder to size.

Assemble the pistons and connecting rods:

Install the piston pin lock-rings (if used)

Inspect piston pin, connecting rod small end bushing, and piston bore for galling, scoring, or excessive wear. If evident, replace defective part(s). Measure the I.D. of the piston boss and connecting rod small end, and the O.D. of the piston pin. If within specifications, assemble piston pin and rod.
CAUTION: *If piston pin must be pressed in, determine the proper method and use the proper tools; otherwise the piston will distort.*
    Install the lock rings; ensure that they seat properly. If the parts are not within specifications, determine the service method for the type of engine. In some cases, piston and pin are serviced as an assembly when either is defective. Others specify reaming the piston and connecting rods for an oversize pin. If the connecting rod bushing is worn, it may in many cases be replaced. Reaming the piston and replacing the rod bushing are machine shop operations.

Cylinder Block Reconditioning

Procedure	Method

Clean and inspect the camshaft:

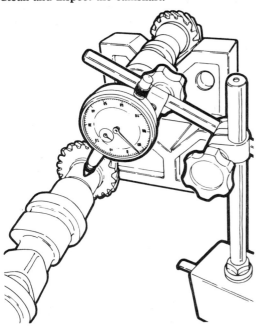

Check the camshaft for straightness

Degrease the camshaft, using solvent, and clean out all oil holes. Visually inspect cam lobes and bearing journals for excessive wear. If a lobe is questionable, check all lobes as indicated below. If a journal or lobe is worn, the camshaft must be reground or replaced.

NOTE: *If a journal is worn, there is a good chance that the bushings are worn.* If lobes and journals appear intact, place the front and rear journals in V-blocks, and rest a dial indicator on the center journal. Rotate the camshaft to check straightness. If deviation exceeds .001″, replace the camshaft.

* Check the camshaft lobes with a micrometer, by measuring the lobes from the nose to base and again at 90° (see illustration). The lift is determined by subtracting the second measurement from the first. If all exhaust lobes and all intake lobes are not identical, the camshaft must be reground or replaced.

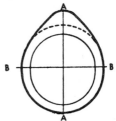

Camshaft lobe measurement

Replace the camshaft bearings (OHV engines only):

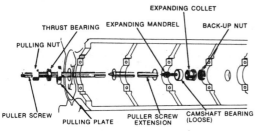

Camshaft bearing removal and installation tool (OHV engines only)

If excessive wear is indicated, or if the engine is being completely rebuilt, camshaft bearings should be replaced as follows: Drive the camshaft rear plug from the block. Assemble the removal puller with its shoulder on the bearing to be removed. Gradually tighten the puller nut until bearing is removed. Remove remaining bearings, leaving the front and rear for last. To remove front and rear bearings, reverse position of the tool, so as to pull the bearings in toward the center of the block. Leave the tool in this position, pilot the new front and rear bearings on the installer, and pull them into position: Return the tool to its original position and pull remaining bearings into position.

NOTE: *Ensure that oil holes align when installing bearings.* Replace camshaft rear plug, and stake it into position to aid retention.

Finish hone the cylinders:

Chuck a flexible drive hone into a power drill, and insert it into the cylinder. Start the hone, and move it up and down in the cylinder at a rate which will produce approximately a 60° cross-hatch pattern.

NOTE: *Do not extend the hone below the cylin-*

Cylinder Block Reconditioning

Procedure	Method

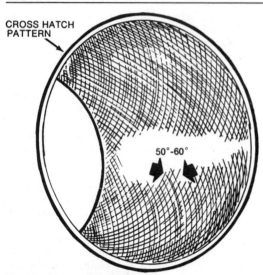

der bore. After developing the pattern, remove the hone and recheck piston fit. Wash the cylinders with a detergent and water solution to remove abrasive dust, dry, and wipe several times with a rag soaked in engine oil.

Cylinder bore after honing

Check piston ring end-gap:

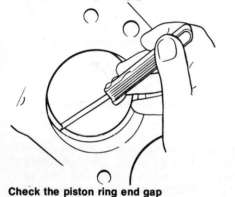

Check the piston ring end gap

Compress the piston rings to be used in a cylinder, one at a time, into that cylinder, and press them approximately 1″ below the deck with an inverted piston. Using feeler gauges, measure the ring end-gap, and compare to specifications. Pull the ring out of the cylinder and file the ends with a fine file to obtain proper clearance.
CAUTION: *If inadequate ring end-gap is utilized, ring breakage will result.*

Install the piston rings:

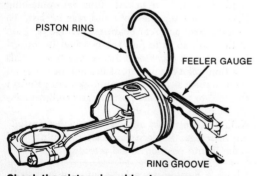

Check the piston ring side clearance

Inspect the ring grooves in the piston for excessive wear or taper. If necessary, recut the grooves(s) for use with an overwidth ring or a standard ring and spacer. If the groove is worn uniformly, overwidth rings, or standard rings and spacers may be installed without recutting. Roll the outside of the ring around the groove to check for burrs or deposits. If any are found, remove with a fine file. Hold the ring in the groove, and measure side clearance. If necessary, correct as indicated above.
NOTE: *Always install any additional spacers above the piston ring.*
   The ring groove must be deep enough to allow the ring to seat below the lands (see illustration). In many cases, a "go-no-go" depth gauge will be provided with the piston rings. Shallow grooves may be corrected by recutting, while deep grooves require some type of filler or expander behind the piston. Consult the piston ring sup-

Cylinder Block Reconditioning

Procedure	Method
	plier concerning the suggested method. Install the rings on the piston, lowest ring first, using a ring expander.
	NOTE: *Position the ring as specified by the manufacturer.* Consult the engine service procedures earlier in this chapter for details concerning specific engines.
Install the camshaft (OHV engines only):	Liberally lubricate the camshaft lobes and journals, and install the camshaft.
	CAUTION: *Exercise extreme care to avoid damaging the bearings when inserting the camshaft.*
	Install and tighten the camshaft thrust plate retaining bolts.
	See the engine service procedures earlier in this chapter for details concerning specific engines.
Check camshaft end-play (OHV engines only):	Using feeler gauges, determine whether the clearance between the camshaft boss (or gear) and backing plate is within specifications. Install shims behind the thrust plate, or reposition the camshaft gear and retest endplay. In some cases, adjustment is by replacing the thrust plate.
Check the camshaft end-play with a feeler gauge	See the engine service procedures earlier in this chapter for details concerning specific engines.
DIAL INDICATOR CAMSHAFT	*Mount a dial indicator stand so that the stem of the dial indicator rests on the nose of the camshaft, parallel to the camshaft axis. Push the camshaft as far in as possible and zero the gauge. Move the camshaft outward to determine the amount of camshaft endplay. If the endplay is not within tolerance, install shims behind the thrust plate, or reposition the camshaft gear and retest.
Check the camshaft end-play with a dial indicator	See the engine service procedures earlier in this chapter for details concerning specific engines.
Install the rear main seal:	See the engine service procedures earlier in this chapter for details concerning specific engines.
Install the crankshaft:	Thoroughly clean the main bearing saddles and caps. Place the upper halves of the bearing inserts on the saddles and press into position.
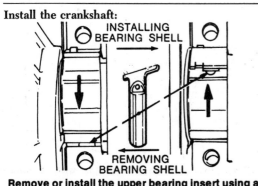	NOTE: *Ensure that the oil holes align.* Press the corresponding bearing inserts into the main bearing caps. Lubricate the upper main bearings, and lay the crankshaft in position. Place a strip of Plastigage on each of the crankshaft journals, install the main caps, and torque to specifications. Remove the main caps, and compare the Plastigage to the scale on the Plastigage envelope. If clearances are within tolerances, remove the Plastigage, turn the crankshaft 90°, wipe off all oil and retest. If all clearances are correct, re-
Remove or install the upper bearing insert using a roll-out pin	

Cylinder Block Reconditioning

Procedure	Method

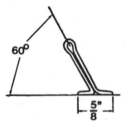

Home-made bearing roll-out pin

move all Plastigage, thoroughly lubricate the main caps and bearing journals, and install the main caps. If clearances are not within tolerance, the upper bearing inserts may be removed, without removing the crankshaft, using a bearing roll out pin (see illustration). Roll in a bearing that will provide proper clearance, and retest. Torque all main caps, excluding the thrust bearing cap, to specifications. Tighten the thrust bearing cap finger tight. To properly align the thrust bearing, pry the crankshaft the extent of its axial travel several times, the last movement held toward the front of the engine, and torque the thrust bearing cap to specifications. Determine the crankshaft end-play (see below), and bring within tolerance with thrust washers.

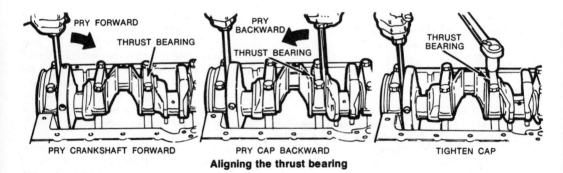

Aligning the thrust bearing

Measure crankshaft end-play:

Mount a dial indicator stand on the front of the block, with the dial indicator stem resting on the nose of the crankshaft, parallel to the crankshaft axis. Pry the crankshaft the extent of its travel rearward, and zero the indicator. Pry the crankshaft forward and record crankshaft end-play.
NOTE: *Crankshaft end-play also may be measured at the thrust bearing, using feeler gauges (see illustration).*

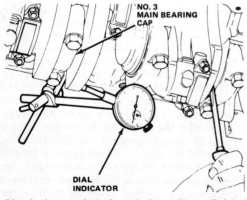

Check the crankshaft end-play with a dial indicator

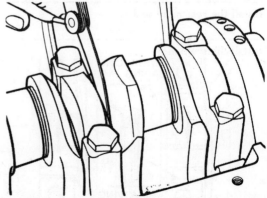

Check the crankshaft end-play with a feeler gauge

Cylinder Block Reconditioning

Procedure	Method
Install the pistons: 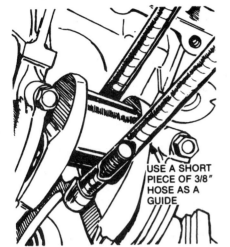 USE A SHORT PIECE OF 3/8" HOSE AS A GUIDE **Use lengths of vacuum hose or rubber tubing to protect the crankshaft journals and cylinder walls during piston installation**  RING COMPRESSOR **Install the piston using a ring compressor**	Press the upper connecting rod bearing halves into the connecting rods, and the lower halves into the connecting rod caps. Position the piston ring gaps according to specifications (see car section), and lubricate the pistons. Install a ring compresser on a piston, and press two long (8″) pieces of plastic tubing over the rod bolts. Using the tubes as a guide, press the pistons into the bores and onto the crankshaft with a wooden hammer handle. After seating the rod on the crankshaft journal, remove the tubes and install the cap finger tight. Install the remaining pistons in the same manner. Invert the engine and check the bearing clearance at two points (90° apart) on each journal with Plastigage. NOTE: *Do not turn the crankshaft with Plastigage installed.* If clearance is within tolerances, remove *all* Plastigage, thoroughly lubricate the journals, and torque the rod caps to specifications. If clearance is not within specifications, install different thickness bearing inserts and recheck. CAUTION: *Never shim or file the connecting rods or caps.* Always install plastic tube sleeves over the rod bolts when the caps are not installed, to protect the crankshaft journals.
Check connecting rod side clearance:  **Check the connecting rod side clearance with a feeler gauge**	Determine the clearance between the sides of the connecting rods and the crankshaft, using feeler gauges. If clearance is below the minimum tolerance, the rod may be machined to provide adequate clearance. If clearance is excessive, substitute an unworn rod, and recheck. If clearance is still outside specifications, the crankshaft must be welded and reground, or replaced.
Inspect the timing chain (or belt):	Visually inspect the timing chain for broken or loose links, and replace the chain if any are found. If the chain will flex sideways, it must be replaced. Install the timing chain as specified. Be sure the timing belt is not stretched, frayed or broken. NOTE: *If the original timing chain is to be reused, install it in its original position.*

Cylinder Block Reconditioning

Procedure	Method
Check timing gear backlash and runout (OHV engines):	Mount a dial indicator with its stem resting on a tooth of the camshaft gear (as illustrated). Rotate the gear until all slack is removed, and zero the indicator. Rotate the gear in the opposite direction until slack is removed, and record gear backlash. Mount the indicator with its stem resting on the edge of the camshaft gear, parallel to the axis of the camshaft. Zero the indicator, and turn the camshaft gear one full turn, recording the runout. If either backlash or runout exceed specifications, replace the worn gear(s).

Check the camshaft gear backlash

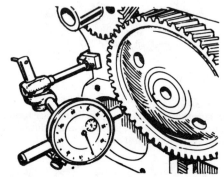

Check the camshaft gear run-out

Completing the Rebuilding Process

Following the above procedures, complete the rebuilding process as follows:

Fill the oil pump with oil, to prevent cavitating (sucking air) on initial engine start up. Install the oil pump and the pickup tube on the engine. Coat the oil pan gasket as necessary, and install the gasket and the oil pan. Mount the flywheel and the crankshaft vibration damper or pulley on the crankshaft. NOTE: *Always use new bolts when installing the flywheel.* Inspect the clutch shaft pilot bushing in the crankshaft. If the bushing is excessively worn, remove it with an expanding puller and a slide hammer, and tap a new bushing into place.

Position the engine, cylinder head side up. Lubricate the lifters, and install them into their bores. Install the cylinder head, and torque it as specified. Insert the pushrods (where applicable), and install the rocker shaft(s) (if so equipped) or position the rocker arms on the pushrods. Adjust the valves.

Install the intake and exhaust manifolds, the carburetor(s), the distributor and spark plugs. Adjust the point gap and the static ignition timing. Mount all accessories and install the engine in the car. Fill the radiator with coolant, and the crankcase with high quality engine oil.

Break-in Procedure

Start the engine, and allow it to run at low speed for a few minutes, while checking for leaks. Stop the engine, check the oil level, and fill as necessary. Restart the engine, and fill the cooling system to capacity. Check the point dwell angle and adjust the ignition timing and the valves. Run the engine at low to medium speed (800–2500 rpm) for approximately ½ hour, and retorque the cylinder head bolts. Road test the car, and check again for leaks.

Follow the manufacturer's recommended engine break-in procedure and maintenance schedule for new engines.

Emission Controls and Fuel System

Every car, regardless of other emission equipment, has been equipped with positive crankcase ventilation (PCV), the most basic component of an emission control system. This device simply captures the crankcase fumes, which on earlier cars had been dispelled through the road-draft tube, and feeds them into the carburetor. From there they are fed into the cylinders with the gasoline mixture and are ignited. The feeding of the gases into the carburetor is regulated by the PCV valve. With this information in mind, it is easy to understand why cleaning and/or replacement of the PCV valve, as well as regular carburetor servicing, are musts for the maintenance of peak performance.

Until 1968, models were still equipped with a crankcase breather cap. Post-1967 models have a closed crankcase which provides a further reduction in pollutant emissions.

Thermactor System

Beginning in 1966, some models were equipped with the Thermactor emission control system, which makes use of a belt-driven air pump to inject fresh air into the hot exhaust stream through the engine exhaust ports. The result is the extended burning of those fumes which were not completely ig-

nited in the combustion chamber and the subsequent reduction of some of the hydrocarbon and carbon monoxide content of the exhaust emissions into harmless carbon dioxide and water.

The Thermactor system is composed of the following components:
1. Air supply pump (belt-driven);
2. Air by-pass valve;
3. Check valves;
4. Air manifolds (internal or external);
5. Air supply tubes (on external manifolds only).

Air for the Thermactor system is cleaned by means of a centrifugal filter fan mounted on the air pump driveshaft. The air filter does not require any type of replaceable element.

To prevent excessive pressure, the air pump is equipped with a pressure relief valve which uses a replaceable plastic plug to control the pressure setting.

The Thermactor air pump has sealed bearings which are lubricated for the life of the unit and preset rotor vane and bearing clearances, which do not require any periodic adjustments.

The air supply from the pump is controlled by the air by-pass valve, sometimes called a dump valve. During engine deceleration, the air by-pass valve opens, momentarily diverting the air supply through a silencer and into

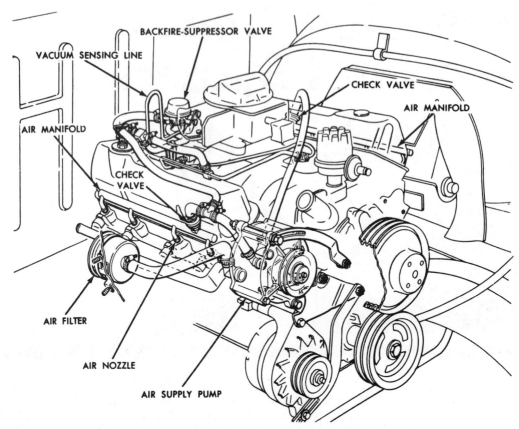

BACKFIRE-SUPPRESSOR VALVE

VACUUM SENSING LINE

CHECK VALVE

AIR MANIFOLD

AIR MANIFOLD

CHECK VALVE

AIR FILTER

AIR NOZZLE

AIR SUPPLY PUMP

Thermactor system installation—V8 engines

the atmosphere, thus preventing backfires within the exhaust system when deceleration supplies larger-than-normal amounts of unburned fuel to the exhaust ports.

A check valve is incorporated in the air inlet side of the air manifolds. Its purpose is to prevent exhaust gases from backing up into the Thermactor system. This valve is especially important in the event of drive belt failure and also during deceleration, when the air by-pass valve is dumping the air supply.

The air manifolds and air supply tubes channel the air from the Thermactor air pump into the exhaust ports of each cylinder, thus completing the cycle of the Thermactor system.

Beginning in 1968, a conspicuous decal listing all tune-up specifications which contribute to the effectiveness of the emission control equipment is located in the engine compartment.

IMCO System

The improved combustion (IMCO) emission control system was first fitted in 1968. Unlike

Thermactor, which consists of bolt-on components, the IMCO system involves both modifications to the engine itself and bolt-on equipment. As the past several years have seen increasingly rigid government-imposed emission control standards, the IMCO system has been modified in order to meet the requirements.

For the 1968 and 1969 model years, the IMCO system was used only in non-high-performance engines with automatic transmissions. Cars, with standard transmissions and all high-performance cars regardless of transmission type still used Thermactor systems. In 1970 and 1971, the IMCO system was used in all models, and certain high-performance engine options combined the Thermactor system with IMCO engine modifications. For 1972, the Thermactor system is not used.

In addition to the closed crankcase which was used beginning in 1968, the IMCO system in its original form consisted of a dual-diaphragm distributor and distributor vacuum (temperature sensing) valve, idle mixture limiter caps (on the carburetor), and a

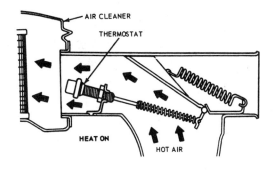

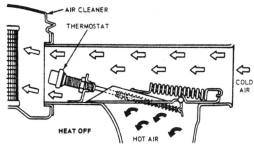

Temperature-operated duct and valve assembly

cooled, the vacuum supply is returned to its normal source—the carburetor.

The idle mixture limiter caps found on the carburetors of IMCO-equipped engines restrict the degree of richness to which the carburetor may be set. The leanness of air-fuel mixture, combined with the advance/retard characteristics of the distributor, results in more complete combustion of fuel within the engine.

The heated air-intake system improves the efficiency of cold-weather and cold-start operation of the engine. A hot-air duct, which runs from the exhaust manifold to the air cleaner, supplies air to the carburetor which has been warmed by the exhaust manifold. The result is reduced throttle-plate icing, and better performance from the lean mixtures which are necessary to successful emission control. A temperature-sensing unit is included in this system, to decrease the supply of manifold-warmed air as the engine reaches its normal operating temperatures.

heated-air-intake system. These components reduce exhaust emissions by promoting the complete and efficient combustion of fuel within the engine rather than by burning the exhaust gases in the manifold as in the Thermactor system.

The dual-diaphragm distributor consists of two diaphragms which operate independently of each other. The outer (or primary) diaphragm uses carburetor vacuum to advance the ignition timing. The inner (or secondary) diaphragm uses intake manifold vacuum to provide additional retardation of ignition timing during periods of closed throttle deceleration and idle.

The distributor vacuum control valve, or temperature-sensing valve, is in the distributor vacuum advance supply line, and is installed in the coolant outlet elbow. During prolonged periods of idle, or any other situation which causes higher-than-normal engine operating temperatures, the valve, which under normal conditions simply connects the vacuum advance diaphragm to its vacuum source within the carburetor, closes the normal source vacuum port and engages the alternate source vacuum port. This alternate source is from the intake manifold which, under idle conditions, maintains a high vacuum. This increase in vacuum supply to the distributor diaphragm advances the timing, increasing the idle speed and speeding up the fan. When the engine has sufficiently

Deceleration Valve

Beginning in the 1969 model year, some engines were equipped with a distributor vacuum advance control valve (deceleration valve) which is used with dual-diaphragm distributors to further aid in controlling ignition timing. The deceleration valve is in the vacuum line which runs from the outer (or advance) diaphragm to the carburetor—the normal source of vacuum supply for the distributor vacuum advance. During periods of deceleration, the intake manifold vacuum pressure rises causing the deceleration valve to close the carburetor vacuum source and open the intake manifold vacuum source to the distributor advance diaphragm. The increase in vacuum pressure provides maximum ignition timing advance, resulting in more complete fuel combustion within the engine, and decreasing exhaust system backfiring.

Distributor Modulator System

In 1970, the Distributor Modulator System—also known as Dist-O-Vac—was first used as a further extension of the IMCO system of emissions control. This system supersedes the distributor vacuum advance control valve, but retains the temperature-sensing valve to prevent overheating. The temperature-sensing valve—when used with

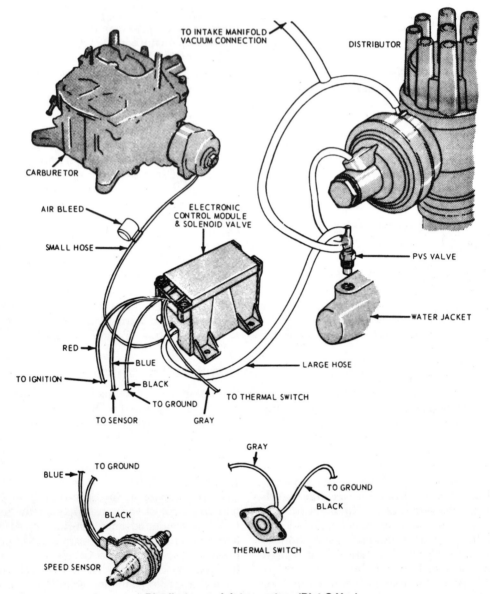

TO INTAKE MANIFOLD
VACUUM CONNECTION

DISTRIBUTOR

CARBURETOR

AIR BLEED

ELECTRONIC
CONTROL MODULE
& SOLENOID VALVE

SMALL HOSE

PVS VALVE

WATER JACKET

RED

BLUE

TO IGNITION

BLACK

LARGE HOSE

TO GROUND

TO THERMAL SWITCH

TO SENSOR

GRAY

GRAY

TO GROUND

BLUE

TO GROUND

BLACK

BLACK

THERMAL SWITCH

SPEED SENSOR

Distributor modulator system (Dist-O-Vac)

the Distributor Modulator System—is also called a Ported Vacuum Switch (PVS).

The three components of the Dist-O-Vac system are the speed sensor, the thermal switch, and the electronic control module. The electronic control module consists of two sub-assemblies; the electronic control amplifier and the three-way solenoid valve.

The speed sensor, a small unit mounted in the speedometer cable contains a rotating magnet and a stationary winding which is insulated from ground. The magnet, which rotates with the speedometer cable, generates a small amount of voltage which increases in direct proportion to speed. This voltage is generated to the electronic control amplifier.

The thermal switch consists of a bimetallic-element switch which is mounted in the right door pillar and senses the temperatures above 58°F. This switch is also closed at 58°F or lower, and open at temperatures above 58°F. This switch is also connected to the electronic control amplifier.

Within the electronic control module case, there is a printed circuit board and an electronic amplifier. As previously mentioned, the speed sensor and thermal switch are connected to this assembly. The thermal switch is the dominant circuit. When the temperature of the outside air is 58° or lower, the circuit is closed, so that regardless of speed, the electronic control amplifier will not trigger the three-way solenoid valve. At temperatures above 58°, the thermal switch circuit is open, allowing the circuit from the speed sensor to control the action of the solenoid valve.

The three-way solenoid valve is located within the electronic control module and below the printed circuit board of the amplifier. It is vented to the atmosphere at the top and connected at the bottom to the carburetor spark port (small hose) and the primary—or advance—side of the dual-diaphragm distributor (large hose) The large hose is also channeled through the temperature-sensing valve. The small hose is equipped with an air bleed to provide a positive air flow in the direction of the carburetor. The air bleed purges the hose of vacuum, thus assuring that gasoline will not be drawn through the hose and into the distributor diaphragm.

When the thermal switch is closed (outside air temperature of 58° or lower), or when it is open and the speed sensor is not sending out a strong enough voltage signal (speeds below approximately 35 mph), the amplifier will not activate the solenoid valve and the valve is in the closed position, blocking the passage of air from the small tube through the large tube. With the valve in this position, the larger hose is vented to the atmosphere through the top opening in the three-way valve assembly. Consequently, there is no vacuum being supplied to the primary diaphragm on the distributor—hence no vacuum advance.

When the outside air temperature is above 58° and/or the speed of the car is sufficient to generate the required voltage (35 mph or faster), the valve opens, blocking the vent to the atmosphere while opening the vacuum line from the carburetor spark port to the primary diaphragm of the distributor.

Spark Delay Valve

The spark delay valve is a plastic, spring-loaded, color-coded valve which is installed in the vacuum line to the distributor advance diaphragm on many 1971–73 models. Under heavy throttle applications, the valve will close, blocking normal carburetor vacuum to the distributor. After the designated period of closed time, the valve opens, restoring carburetor vacuum to the distributor.

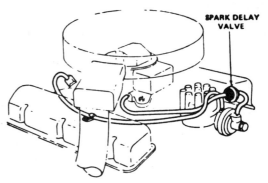

Spark delay valve installation—V8 shown

Exhaust Gas Recirculation System

All 1973 models are equipped with an exhaust gas recirculation (EGR) system to control oxides of nitrogen.

On V8 engines, exhaust gases travel through the exhaust gas crossover passage in the intake manifold. On 6 cylinder engines, an external tube carries exhaust manifold gases to a carburetor spacer. On spacer entry equipped engines, a portion of these gases are diverted into a spacer which is mounted under the carburetor. On floor entry models, a regulated portion of exhaust gases enters the intake manifold through a pair of small holes drilled in the floor of the intake manifold riser. The EGR control valve, which is attached to the rear of the spacer or intake manifold, consists of a vacuum diaphragm with an attached plunger which normally blocks off exhaust gases from entering the intake manifold.

On all models, the EGR valve is controlled by a vacuum line from the carburetor which passes through a ported vacuum switch. The EGR ported vacuum switch provides vacuum to the EGR valve at coolant temperatures above 125°F. The vacuum diaphragm then opens the EGR valve permitting exhaust gases to flow through the carburetor spacer and enter the combustion chambers. The exhaust gases are relatively oxygen-free, and tend to dilute the combustion charge. This lowers peak combustion temperature thereby reducing oxides of nitrogen.

On some models equipped with a 351C V8, an EGR subsystem, consisting of a speed sensor and control amplifier, prevents exhaust gases from entering the combustion mixture when the car is traveling 65 mph or faster.

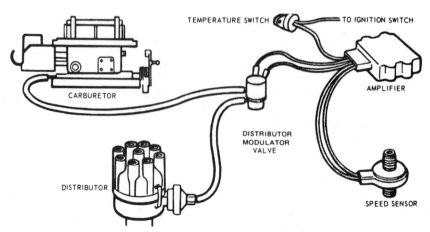

Electronic spark control system

Electronic Spark Control System

The Electronic Spark Control System is actually the old Dist-O-Vac system, with several minor modifications. The electronic control amplifier and the distributor modulator valve are two separate units instead of being enclosed within a single case as on the Dist-O-Vac system. The distributor modulator valve itself has been modified to include the internal air bleed which formerly was a separate unit in the line connecting the modulator valve to the carburetor spark port.

Transmission-Regulated Spark Control System

The Transmission-Regulated Spark Control System differs from the Dist-O-Vac and Elec-

tronic Spark Control Systems in that the speed sensor and amplifier are replaced by a valve located on the transmission. On manual transmissions, the valve is activated by a mechanical linkage which opens the switch when the transmission is shifted into high gear. On automatic transmissions, the valve is opened by fluid pressure when the vehicle is in high range or reverse. Either valve, when opened, causes the opening of the vacuum lines to the distributor, thus providing vacuum advance.

The PVS (ported vacuum switch) may be used with either spark control system. For 1972, this switch has been modified to react to coolant temperatures of 230°F rather than 220° for pre-1972 cars. Temperature sensors for 1972 feature a critical temperature range of 49–65° instead of the 50–58° range of earlier models.

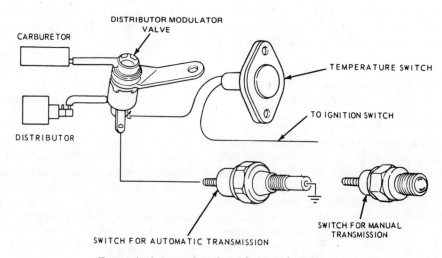

Transmission regulated spark control system

1972 Spark Control System Applications
49 States and Canada

Engine, Transmission	Type of Spark Control System
250 lv, Manual	TRS
250 1v, Automatic	none
302 2v, Manual and Automatic	none
351 C 2v, Manual and Automatic	none
351 C 4v, Manual and Automatic	none
351 C 4v, HO, Manual and Automatic	none
California Only	
250 1v, Automatic	ESC
302 2v, Automatic	ESC
351 2v, Automatic	ESC
351 4v, Manual	TRS
351 4v, Automatic	ESC
351 4v, HO, Manual	TRS

TRS—Transmission Regulated Spark Control
ESC—Electronic Spark Control System

Temperature Activated Vacuum (TAV) System

1973 models using the 250 six-cylinder engine and automatic transmission built before March 15, 1973 are equipped with a Temperature Activated Vacuum (TAV) system to control distributor spark advance. The system contains a 3-way solenoid valve, an ambient temperature switch located in the front door hinge pillar, a vacuum bleed line to the carburetor airhorn and a spark delay valve.

When the ambient temperature is above 60°F, the contacts in the temperature sensor close and complete the circuit to the 3-way solenoid. This energizes the solenoid and connects the EGR vacuum port on the carburetor to the distributor vacuum advance.

Delay Vacuum By-Pass (DVB) System

All 1973 models equipped with 351C or W engines manufactured before 3/15/73 are supplied with this system. It provides two paths by which carburetor vacuum can reach the distributor vacuum advance. When the ambient temperature is below 49°F, the temperature switch contacts are open and the vacuum solenoid is deenergized. Under these conditions, the distributor receives full vacuum. When the temperature is above 60°F, the solenoid is energized, blocking the vacuum path. Distributor vacuum now must flow through the spark delay valve. When there is too much vacuum, the valve blocks distributor vacuum for 5–30 seconds by venting it to the atmosphere in a one-way valve. After this period, the distributor gets normal vacuum.

Evaporative Emission Controls

Cars produced for sale and use in California, after 1969, were equipped with fuel system Evaporative Emission Controls. For 1971, the system was modified somewhat and used on all models.

Changes in atmospheric temperature cause fuel tanks to "breathe." Air within the tank expands and contracts according to how the outside air temperature is changing. As the temperature rises, air escapes through the tank vent tube or the vent in the tank cap. The air which escapes contains gasoline vapors. In a similar manner, the gasoline which fills the carburetor float bowl expands when the engine is stopped. Engine heat causes this expansion. The vapors escape through the carburetor and air cleaner.

The Evaporative Emission Control System provides a sealed fuel system with the capability to store and condense fuel vapors. The system has three parts: a fill control vent system; a vapor vent and storage system; a pressure and vacuum relief system (special fill cap).

The fill control vent system is a modification to the fuel tank design. It consists of an air space within the tank which is 10–12 percent of the volume of the tank, when the tank is filled to capacity. The air space is sufficient to provide for the thermal expansion of the fuel.

The in-tank vent system consists of the air space previously described, plus a vapor separator assembly. This separator assembly is mounted to the top of the fuel tank, and is secured by a cam-lock ring similar to the one which secures the fuel sending unit. Foam material fills the vapor separator assembly. The foam material serves the purpose of separating raw fuel and vapors, thus retarding the entrance of raw fuel into the vapor line.

The sealed filler cap features a pressure-vacuum relief valve. Under normal operating conditions, the filler cap operates as a check valve, allowing air to enter the tank to replace the fuel which is consumed. At the same time, it works to prevent vapors from escaping through the cap. In the event of excessive pressure within the tank, the filler cap valve will open to relieve the pressure.

Because the filler cap is sealed, fuel vapors have but one place through which they may escape—the vapor separator assembly at the top of the fuel tank. The vapors pass through the foam material and continue through a single vapor line which leads to a canister in the engine compartment. The canister is filled with activated charcoal.

Another vapor line runs from the top of the carburetor float chamber to the charcoal canister.

As the fuel vapors (hydrocarbon molecules) enter the charcoal canister, they are absorbed by the charcoal. The air in which the hydrocarbon molecules were suspended is dispelled through the open bottom of the charcoal canister, leaving the molecules trapped within the charcoal. When the engine is started, the operation of the carburetor produces a vacuum within the line which runs from the float chamber to the charcoal canister. The vacuum causes fresh air to be drawn into the canister from its open bottom. The fresh air passes through the charcoal, picking up the hydrocarbon molecules which are trapped there, feeding them into the carburetor. From the carburetor, they proceed into the intake manifold, where they are fed into the engine and burned with the fuel mixture.

Crankcase Ventilation System

TESTING

1. Replace the crankcase ventilator regulator valve with a known good valve of identical design.

2. Start the engine and compare idle conditions with the prior idle conditions. If engine idle is satisfactory (with the new valve installed) trouble exists in the old valve and it should be replaced.

3. If loping or rough idle still persists with the good regulator valve in place, the trouble is elsewhere. Check the crankcase ventilator system for restriction at the intake manifold or carburetor spacer.

4. If the system is not restricted, explore further the aspects of tune-up and the various elements of exhaust emission control.

SERVICING

Complete and detailed procedures for the servicing of the crankcase ventilation system are found in the "Maintenance" section of chapter one.

Exhaust Gas Recirculation System Service

All 1973 models are equipped with an exhaust gas recirculation (EGR) system to control oxides of nitrogen. Because the system channels exhaust gases through narrow passages into the induction system, deposits build up quickly in the system, eventually blocking the exhaust recirculation flow. Therefore, to keep the car's emission levels up to federal standards, it is necessary to service the system at the recommended intervals. EGR service consists of cleaning or replacing the EGR valve, and cleaning all of the exhaust gas channels.

Thermactor System

TESTING AND SERVICE

Prior to performing any extensive tests of the Thermactor system:

1. Be sure that a problem exists.

2. Determine that the engine, as a basic unit, is functioning properly by disconnecting the air bypass valve vacuum sensing line at the intake manifold and plugging the manifold connection to prevent leakage.

3. Normal engine diagnosis procedures can then be performed.

Air Pump Test

1. To test the air supply pump, a test gauge adaptor must be made. Make the adaptor as follows:

A. Obtain a ½ in. pipe T.

B. A 2 in. length of ½ in. galvanized pipe, threaded at one end only.

C. A ½ in. pipe plug.

D. A ½ in. reducer bushing or suitable gauge adaptor.

E. Apply sealer to the threads of the 2 in. length of pipe and screw it into one end of the T.

F. Apply sealer to the pipe plug and install it into the other end of the T.

G. Apply sealer to the threads of the ½ in. reducer bushing or adaptor for the pressure gauge and install it in the side opening of the T.

H. Drill an $^{11}/_{32}$ in. (0.3437) diameter hole through the center of the pipe plug. Clean out the chips.

I. Install a standard fuel pump or other suitable testing gauge into the side opening of the T. The gauge must be graduated in ¼ psi increments.

2. Bring the engine to operating temperature.

3. Inspect all hoses and connections for leaks. Correct if necessary.

4. Check the air pump belt tension; adjust if necessary.

5. Disconnect air supply hose(s) at air manifold check valve(s). If there are two valves, block off one hose with a tapered plug; secure the plug with a clamp to prevent blowout.

6. Insert the open pipe end of the test gauge adaptor in the other air supply hose. Clamp the hose to the adaptor to prevent blowout.

7. Position the adaptor and test gauge so that air discharge from the drilled hole in the adaptor will cause no trouble.

8. Connect the tachometer to the engine.

9. Start the engine and slowly accelerate to 1,500 rpm. Air pressure registered on the gauge should be greater than 1 psi.

10. If the air pressure does not meet or exceed the above pressures, disconnect and plug the air supply hose at the bypass valve. Clamp the plug in place and repeat the pressure test.

11. If air pump pressure still does not meet minimum requirements, install a new air pump and repeat the pump test.

12. Replace the air pump if necessary.

Check Valve Test

This test can be performed at the same time as the air pump test.

1. Run the engine until it reaches operating temperature.

2. Inspect all hoses and connections. Correct any existing leaks before testing the check valve operation.

3. Disconnect the air supply hose(s) at the check valve(s).

4. Note the position of the valve plate inside the valve body. It should be lightly positioned against the valve seat, away from the air manifold.

5. Insert a probe into the hose connection on the check valve and depress the valve plate. It should freely return to its original position against the valve seat when released. If there are two check valves, check both for freedom of operation.

6. With the hose(s) disconnected, start the engine. Slowly accelerate to 1,500 rpm and watch for exhaust leaks at the check valve(s). There should be none. The valve may flutter

or vibrate at idle. This is normal, due to exhaust pulsations in the manifold.

7. If check valve(s) does not meet recommended conditions (steps four, five, and six), replace it.

Air Bypass Valve Tests

1. Remove the hose that connects the air bypass valve to the air manifold check valve at the bypass valve side.

2. With the transmission in Neutral and the parking brake on, start the engine and operate at normal idle speed. Be sure air is flowing from the air bypass valve hose connection. Air pressure should be noted, as this is the normal delivery flow to the air manifold(s).

3. Momentarily (for about five seconds), pinch the vacuum hose to the bypass valve. This duplicates the air bypass cycle.

4. Release the pinched vacuum hose. Air flow through the air bypass valve should diminish or stop for a short period. The length of time required to resume normal flow cannot be established. Variables in engine vacuum and the length of time the vacuum line is pinched off are determining factors.

5. Check the bypass valve for diaphragm leakage by performing the following check:

A. Remove the vacuum supply hose to the air bypass valve at the bypass valve connection.

B. Insert a T-fitting into the vacuum supply hose.

C. Connect a vacuum gauge to one of the remaining hose connections on the T.

D. Connect a short length of hose (about 3 in.) to the remaining connection.

E. Insert a suitable plug in the open end of the short length of hose.

F. Start the engine and note the vacuum gauge reading.

G. Remove the plug from the short length of hose and connect the hose to the air bypass valve vacuum connection.

H. Note the vacuum gauge reading. If the indicated reading does not correspond with the previous reading after about 1 minute, replace the air bypass valve.

REPLACEMENT OR ADJUSTMENT OF BELT

1. Loosen the air pump adjusting bolt. Loosen the air pump-to-mounting bracket bolt and push the air pump toward the cylinder block. Remove the belt.

2. Install a new drive belt. With a suitable

bar, pry against the rear cover of the air pump to obtain the specified belt tension.

3. Then, retighten the pump mounting bolts.

NOTE: *It is highly advisable to use a belt tension gauge to check belt tension. When using this tool, follow the manufacturer's instructions and specifications. Any belt which has been operated for 10 minutes or more is considered to be a "used" belt, and should be adjusted accordingly.*

In the event that a belt tension gauge is not available, the thumb deflection method of belt tension adjustment may be used. This method is discussed in chapter one.

AIR BYPASS VALVE REPLACEMENT

1. Disconnect the air and vacuum hoses at the air by-pass valve body.

2. Position the air by-pass valve and connect the respective hoses.

CHECK VALVE REPLACEMENT

1. Disconnect the air supply hose at the valve. (Use a 1¼ in. crowfoot wrench; the valve has a standard, right-hand pipe thread.)

2. Clean the threads on the air manifold adaptor (air supply tube on 289 or 302 V8 engine) with a wire brush. Do not blow compressed air through the check valve in either direction.

3. Install the check valve and tighten it.

4. Connect the air suppy hose.

AIR MANIFOLD REMOVAL AND INSTALLATION (EXCEPT 289 AND 302 V8)

Removal

1. Disconnect the air supply hose at the check valve, position the hose out of the way, and remove the valve.

2. Loosen all of the air manifold-to-cylinder head tube coupling nuts (compression fittings).

Cleaning and Inspection

Inspect the air manifold for damaged threads and fittings, and for leaking connections. Repair or replace as required.

Clean the manifold and associated parts with kerosene. Do not dry with compressed air.

Installation

1. Position the air manifold(s) on the cylinder head. Be sure all of the tube coupling nuts are aligned with the cylinder head.

2. Screw each coupling nut into the cylinder head, 1–2 threads. Tighten the tube coupling nuts.

3. Install the check valve and torque it to specifications.

4. Connect the air supply hose to the check valve.

AIR SUPPLY TUBE REMOVAL AND INSTALLATION (289 V8)

Removal

1. Disconnect the air supply hose at the check valve and move the hose out of the way.

2. Remove the check valve.

3. Remove the air supply tube bolt and seal washer.

4. Carefully remove the air supply tube and seal washer from the cylinder head.

Cleaning and Inspection

Inspect the air supply tube for evidence of leaking threads or seal surfaces. Examine the attaching bolt head, seal washers, and supply tube surface for leaks. Inspect the attaching bolt and cylinder head threads for damage.

Clean the air supply tube, seal washers, and bolt with kerosene. Do not dry with compressed air.

Installation

1. Install the seal washer and air supply tube on the cylinder head. Be sure it is positioned in the same manner as before removal.

2. Install the seal washer and mounting bolt. Torque to specifications.

3. Install the check vale; torque to specifications.

4. Connect the air supply hose to the check valve.

AIR NOZZLE REPLACEMENT (EXCEPT 289 AND 302 V8)

Normally, air nozzles should be replaced during cylinder head reconditioning. A nozzle may be replaced, however, without removing the cylinder head, by removing the air manifold and using a hooked tool.

Clean the nozzles with kerosene and a stiff brush. Inspect the air nozzles for eroded tips.

AIR PUMP FILTER FAN REPLACEMENT

1. Loosen the air pump as described in earlier procedures.

2. Remove the drive pulley attaching bolts and pull the pulley off the air pump shaft.

3. Pry the outer disc loose, then remove the centrifugal filter fan. Care must be used to prevent foreign matter from entering the air intake hole, especially if the fan breaks during removal. Do not attempt to remove the metal drive hub.

4. Install the new filter fan by drawing it into position with the pulley bolts.

NOTE: *Some 1966–67 air pumps have air filters with replaceable, non-cleanable elements.*

AIR PUMP REMOVAL AND INSTALLATION

Removal

1. Disconnect the air outlet hose at the air pump.

2. Loosen the pump belt tension adjuster.

3. Disengage the drive belt.

4. Remove the mounting bolt and air pump.

Installation

1. Position the air pump on the mounting bracket and install the mounting bolt.

2. Place the drive belt in pulleys and attach the adjusting arm to the air pump.

3. Adjust the drive belt tension to specifications and tighten the adjusting arm and mounting bolts.

4. Connect the air outlet hose to the air pump.

AIR PUMP RELIEF VALVE REPLACEMENT

Do not disassemble the air pump on the car to replace the relief valve, but remove the pump from the engine.

1. Position tool T66L-9A486-D on the air pump and remove the relief valve with the aid of a slide hammer (T59L-100-B).

2. Position the relief valve on the pump housing and hold tool T66L-9A486-B in position.

3. Use a hammer to lightly tap the tool until the relief valve is seated.

RELIEF VALVE PRESSURE-SETTING PLUG REPLACEMENT

1. Compress the locking tabs inward (together) and remove the plastic pressure-setting plug.

2. Before installing the new plug, be sure that the plug is the correct one. The plugs are color-coded.

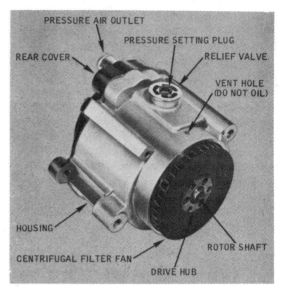

Thermactor air pump

3. Insert the plug in the relief valve hole and push in until it snaps into place.

Imco System

TESTING AND SERVICE

Other than the PCV system, the only IMCO component which requires service at a regular interval is the carbon canister within the Evaporative Emission Control system. The carbon should be replaced every two years or 24,000 miles, whichever occurs first.

Beside the carburetor idle speed and mixture adjustments—which are discussed in Chapter Two—none of the IMCO components require any adjustments.

All IMCO components may be simply replaced. No specific procedures for removal and installation are necessary.

DISTRIBUTOR MODULATOR SYSTEM TEST

1. Bypass the control module by connecting the carburetor vacuum port and the single vacuum hose (upstream of temperature-sensing vacuum control valve) to the distributor, together, at the rear of the engine.

2. Check the distributor vacuum advance operation. If it is correct, the difficulty is probably in the modulator system.

3. Return all connections to normal. Pull the hose from the carburetor vacuum port and connect a vacuum gauge in its place.

Note the vacuum reading at 1,500 rpm. Remove the gauge and replace the hose.

4. Bypass the control module as in step one. Connect the vacuum gauge to the primary (outside) distributor vacuum connection. Note the vacuum reading at 1,500 rpm.

5. Remove the control module bypass hose. Reconnect the module hoses. If the vacuum reading is zero or less than that in step three, check for blockage or leaks in the vacuum system. If the vacuum readings are about equal, proceed with step six.

6. Leave the vacuum gauge connected as in step four. With the engine idling at normal operating temperature, raise the rear wheels. Disconnect the thermal switch from the pillar post. Hold it in your hand long enough to warm it above 68°F.

7. Shift into Drive and slowly accelerate to 35 mph. Note the vacuum reading. If the gauge reads zero at all speeds, check the electrical connections, hose connections, and control module. If the vacuum cuts in between 20–30 mph, the system is operating correctly. If the vacuum cuts in at start of acceleration or before 20 mph, check the electrical connections, hose connections, control module, and speed sensor.

Speed Sensor Test

1. Unplug the sensor. Using an ohmmeter, attach one lead to each speed sensor wire connection. The reading should be 40–60 ohms at room temperature.

2. Attach one ohmmeter lead to the black wire on the speed sensor and the other to the sensor housing. The ohmmeter should read zero.

3. If the readings are not correct, replace the sensor. It is not repairable.

Thermal Switch Test

1. Unplug the switch. Connect one ohmmeter lead to the gray (or white) wire and the other to the balck.

2. Warm the switch in your hand. The ohmmeter should read zero with the switch at 58—68°F or higher.

3. Chill the switch with cold water. There should be an ohmmeter reading at 58–50°F or lower.

4. Replace the switch if the readings are not correct. It is not repairable.

Control Module Test

1. Unplug the connector for red and gray wires from the module. Reconnect the red wires with a jumper wire.

2. Connect a vacuum gauge to the carburetor vacuum port. Run the engine at fast idle and note the vacuum reading. Reconnect the vacuum hose.

3. Connect the vacuum gauge to the primary (outside) distributor vacuum connection.

4. Ground the gray (or white) wire from the control module.

5. Run the engine at fast idle and note the vacuum reading.

6. Replace the control module if the vacuum reading in step five is not the same or slightly less than that taken in step two. The module is not repairable.

DISTRIBUTOR TEMPERATURE-SENSING VACUUM CONTROL VALVE TEST

1. Check the routing and connection of all vacuum hoses.

2. Attach a tachometer to the engine.

3. Bring engine up to normal operating temperature. The engine must not be overheated.

4. Note the engine speed when the transmission is in Neutral and the throttle is in the curb idle position.

5. Disconnect the vacuum hose from the intake manifold at the temperature-sensing valve. Plug or clamp the hose.

6. Note the idle speed with the hose disconnected. If there is no change in rpm, the valve is good. If there is a drop of 100 or more rpm, the valve should be replaced. Replace the vacuum line.

7. Check to make sure that the all-season cooling mixture is to specifications and that the correct radiator cap is in place and functioning.

8. Block the radiator air flow to induce a higher-than-normal temperature condition.

9. Continue to operate until the engine temperature or heat indicator shows above normal.

If engine speed by this time has increased 100 or more rpm, the temperature-sensing valve is satisfactory. If not, it should be replaced.

DISTRIBUTOR DECELERATION VACUUM CONTROL VALVE TEST

1. Connect a tachometer to the engine and bring the engine to the normal operating temperature.

2. Check the idle speed and set it to spec-

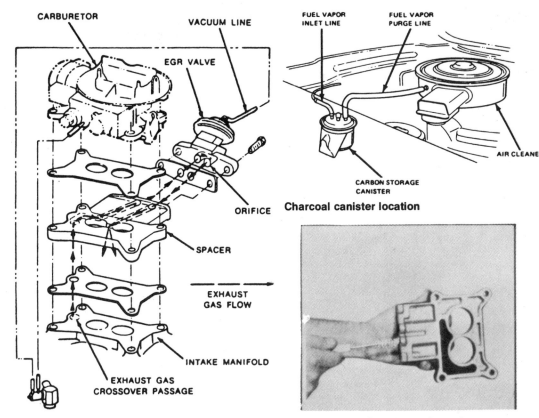

Routing of exhaust gases through spacer

Charcoal canister location

Cleaning the exhaust gas channels

ifications with the headlights on high beam if necessary.

3. Turn off the headlights and note the idle rpm.

4. Remove the plastic cover from the valve. Slowly turn the adjusting screw counterclockwise without pressing in. After five, and no more than six, turns, idle speed should suddenly increase to about 1000 rpm. If the speed does not increase after six turns, push inward on the end of valve spring retainer and release it. Speed should now increase.

5. Slowly turn the adjusting screw clockwise until the idle speed drops to the speed noted in step three. Make one more turn clockwise.

6. Increase the engine speed to 2,000 rpm, hold for five seconds, and release the throttle. The engine should return to idle speed within four seconds. If idle is not resumed in four seconds, back off the dashpot adjustment and repeat the check. If the idle is not resumed in three seconds with the dashpot backed off, turn the deceleration valve adjustment screw an additional quarter turn clockwise and again repeat check. Re-

peat quarter turn adjustments and idle return checks until the engine returns to idle within the required time.

7. If it takes more than one complete turn from step five to meet the idle return time specification, replace the valve.

DUAL-DIAPHRAGM VACUUM ADVANCE AND VACUUM RETARD FUNCTIONAL CHECK

1. To check vacuum advance, disconnect the vacuum lines from both the advance (outer) and retard (inner) diaphragms. Plug the line removed from the retard diaphragm.

Connect a tachometer and timing light to the engine. Increase idle speed by setting the screw on the first step of the fast idle cam. Note ignition timing setting, using a timing light.

Connect the carburetor vacuum line to the advance diaphragm. If the timing advances immediately, the advance unit is functioning properly. Adjust the idle speed to 550–600 rpm.

2. Check the vacuum retardation as follows: using a timing light, note the ignition timing. Remove the plug from the manifold

vacuum line and connect the line to the inner diaphragm. Timing should retard immediately.

3. If vacuum retardation is not to specifications, replace the dual-diaphragm advance unit. If the advance (vacuum) does not function properly, calibrate the unit on a distributor test stand. If the advance part of the unit cannot be calibrated, or if either diaphragm is leaking, replace the dual-diaphragm vacuum advance unit.

EVAPORATIVE EMISSION CONTROL SYSTEM CHECK

Aside from a visual check to make sure that none of the vapor lines are broken, there is no test for this equipment. To maintain its efficiency, however, the charcoal should be replaced at the proper intervals.

Electronic Spark Control
SYSTEM OPERATIONAL TEST

1. Raise the rear of the car until the wheels are clear of the ground by at least 4 in. Support the car with safety stands.

CAUTION: *The rear of the car must be firmly supported during this test. If one of the rear wheels should come in contact with the ground while it is turning, the car will move forward very rapidly and unexpectedly.*

2. Disconnect the vacuum hose from the distributor vacuum advance chamber. This is the outer hose on cars with a dual diaphragm.

3. Connect the hose to a vacuum gauge.

4. Pour hot water on the temperature sensing switch to ensure that it is above 65°. The temperature sensor is located on the right door pillar.

5. Start the engine, apply the foot brake, and put the transmission selector lever in Drive.

6. Slowly release the foot brake and allow the transmission to shift into high (third) gear.

7. Have a friend observe the vacuum gauge while you raise the speed of the engine until the speedometer reads 35 mph.

8. If the system is working properly, there should be no reading on the vacuum gauge until the speedometer reads 35 mph, at which time the vacuum gauge should show a reading.

9. If the vacuum gauge shows a reading below 35 mph, a component in the electronic spark control system is defective. If the vac-

uum gauge does not show a reading, even above 35 mph, there is either a defective component in the electronic spark control system, or there is a broken or clogged vacuum passage between the carburetor and distributor.

HEATED AIR INTAKE TEST

1. With the engine completely cold, look inside the cold air duct and make sure that the valve plate is in the up position (the plate is closing off the cold air duct).

2. Start the engine and bring it to operating temperature.

3. Turn the engine off and look inside the cold air duct again. The valve plate should be down, allowing an opening from the cold air duct into the air cleaner.

4. If the unit appears to be malfunctioning, remove it, examine it to make sure that the springs are not broken or disconnected, and replace the thermostat if all other parts appear intact and properly connected.

TRANSMISSION VALVE (TRS) TEST

1. Attach a test light to the wire which connects the transmission valve to the distributor modulator valve.

2. Jack up the vehicle so that the rear wheels are free to turn.

3. Start the engine, and engage the transmission (manual or automatic) in a low gear. Observe the test light, which should be lighted at this time.

4. On standard transmissions, engage high gear and check to see that the light goes out when high gear is engaged.

5. On automatic transmissions, place the vehicle in Drive and allow it to fully upshift. Upon the shift into high gear, the test lamp should go out.

6. If the test lamp fails to function properly, replace the transmission valve.

FUEL SYSTEM

Fuel Pump

All models have used the single-action, permanently sealed fuel pump. The size and volume flow of the unit varies with the engine application. All fuel pumps require no adjustments.

Fuel pump testing is done with a special instrument which is part vacuum gauge and part fuel pump tester. Unless the fuel pump

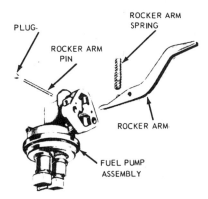

Fuel pump-V8

is leaking, it is unlikely that it is causing any trouble. The test must be performed with the fuel pump installed in the car.

REMOVAL AND INSTALLATION

1. Remove the inlet and outlet lines from the pump.

2. Remove the fuel pump retaining screws, and the pump and gasket.

3. Clean all gasket material from the pump mounting surface on the engine, and apply a coat of oil-resistant sealer to the new gasket.

4. Position the pump on the engine, install the retaining screws, tighten them, and torque them. Torque specifications for the retaining bolts on six-cylinder engines are 12–15 ft. lbs., and for V8 engines, 20–24 ft. lbs.

5. Reinstall the lines, start the engine, and check the unit for leaks.

NOTE: *If resistance is felt while positioning the fuel pump on the block, the camshaft eccentric is in the high position. To ease installation, connect a remote engine starter switch to the engine and "tap" the remote switch until resistance fades.*

Carburetor Operation

The carburetor is a seemingly mystical device which is mounted on the intake manifold and performs the following tasks; opens and closes its intake port to maintain a predetermined amount of gasoline in its reservoir; channels air into the engine through the air cleaner; atomizes measured amounts of gasoline and introduces the vapor into the incoming air stream; provides metered amounts of air-fuel mixture to the deceleration valve while it is operating, is a vacuum source for the distributor vacuum advance mechanism; and, in addition, must change the air-fuel mixture it supplies to the engine for normal warm weather driving, acceleration, maximum power, cold engine operation, and idling. However, there are many carburetor adjustments and repairs that can be performed by those who have a certain amount of mechanical aptitude. Take your time, concentrate on what you are doing, and don't let it intimidate you; remember it's only a carburetor.

FLOAT, NEEDLE VALVE AND SEAT

As previously stated, the carburetor contains a reservoir for gasoline. Two devices in the carburetor control the flow of gasoline into this reservoir: the needle valve and its seat, and the float. When fuel enters the carburetor it passes around the needle valve, through the needle valve seat, and into the reservoir. As the level of the fuel in the carburetor increases, it contacts the float, moving the float upward. A tang on the end of the float contacts the needle valve and, as the float moves upward, the tang on the float pushes the needle valve into its seat, limiting the flow of gasoline into the engine. When the float reaches a predetermined level, the float tang pushes the needle valve completely into its seat, preventing any more gasoline from entering the carburetor. As the engine uses fuel from the carburetor, the float drops down allowing more fuel to enter the carburetor. If the float is adjusted in such a way that it does not close the needle valve when the reservoir is full, or if the needle valve does not completely seal on its seat, the reservoir will overfill and dump raw gasoline into the engine. If the float is adjusted to close the needle valve too soon, the reservoir will contain an insufficient supply of gasoline, and the engine will run lean under some conditions, causing hesitation or stalling.

MAIN METERING SYSTEM

When the engine is operating at a constant speed above idle, the passage of air through the center of the carburetor (throttle bore) and into the engine draws fuel from the carburetor; the carburetor does not inject gasoline into the engine. This drawing of gas out of the carburetor is due to pressure, vacuum, and other such matters. The throttle plates control the flow of air through the carburetor. These are small discs mounted in the base of the carburetor. When the throttle plates are closed, no air can pass into the engine, so no gasoline can be drawn from the carburetor. The accelerator pedal of the car is connected to the throttle plates, so that when you push down on the pedal, you open the throttle plates. The greater the throttle-plate opening, the greater the amount of air that can flow through the carburetor and into the engine.

Gasoline, on its way from the carburetor reservoir to the throttle bore, passes through metering jets which determine the amount of gasoline that will enter the throttle bore. These jets are screwed into an internal part of the carburetor housing. They are not adjustable; the only way that fuel supply to the engine can be increased is by changing the jets.

POWER VALVE

2 and 4 Barrel Carburetors

Since the main metering jet determines the amount of fuel that can be drawn into the engine by the air passing through the carburetor throttle bore, the size of these jets must necessarily be a compromise. The smaller the jets, the greater fuel economy will be (to a certain end point) and the larger the jets are, the better performance will be. (Once again, this is only up to a certain point.) Therefore, a jet size is picked that will give the best all-around performance. However, this compromise jet size cannot supply a sufficient amount of fuel for wide-open throttle operation. Therefore, the carburetor contains a power valve to supplement the normal fuel supply to the engine during wide-open throttle. The power valve is normally closed but is allowed to open by low intake manifold vacuum. While it is open, additional fuel passes through the power valve circuit in the carburetor, bypassing the main metering jets, and then combining with the normal fuel supply to enrich the air-fuel mixture supplied to the engine. If the power valve becomes defective, it will open too soon, or remain partially open at all times, causing the air-fuel mixture to be too rich.

ACCELERATOR PUMP

When you push down quickly on the pedal to accelerate, the throttle plates open very quickly. Thus the air flow through the carburetor increases very quickly. However, for a brief moment, this rapidly increased air flow cannot draw a proportionately increased amount of gas from the carburetor. To compensate for this, the carburetor contains an accelerator pump.

The accelerator pump is a diaphragm pump mounted on the body of the carburetor and connected, by linkage, to the carburetor throttle linkage. When the throttle linkage is moved to accelerate the car, the movement produces a corresponding movement of the accelerator pump linkage. The movement of the accelerator pump linkage compresses the accelerator pump diaphragm and the compression of the diaphragm forces a stream of gasoline into the throttle bore of the carburetor. This occurs only while the accelerator pedal is being depressed to give a greater throttle plate opening. The accelerator pump is completely mechanical in operation and not dependent on the amount of air flowing through the carburetor. The purpose of the accelerator pump is to momentarily supplement the fuel flow from the carburetor during acceleration, thereby preventing a lean air-fuel mixture. If the accelerator pump system is not working properly this lean condition will cause the engine to hesitate on acceleration. Accelerator pump problems can be caused by a defective diaphragm or spring, a defective check ball, binding linkage, or clogged passages in the system. A good way to check the operation of the accelerator pump system is to look into the top of the carburetor with the air cleaner removed and the engine not running. Have a friend depress the gas pedal. A stream of gasoline should appear in the throttle bore of the carburetor, as soon as the pedal moves, and continue until the pedal is fully depressed.

CHOKE SYSTEM

During cold engine operation, the engine requires a richer air-fuel mixture. The choke system makes this richer mixture possible. The choke system consists of a choke plate which is mounted in the carburetor air intake horn, a temperature-sensitive coil spring which is contained in the choke housing on the side of the carburetor, a choke plate vacuum pull-down device, and a choke unloader tab, and a fast idle cam.

Application of the choke is controlled by the choke spring. This coil spring is connected to the choke plate. It expands when cold and contracts when hot. When the engine has not been running for a while and the ambient temperature is low, the coil spring expands and exerts pressure on the choke plate. When the accelerator pedal is depressed before starting the engine, this spring pressure forces the choke plate closed.

The fast idle cam is also attached, by linkage, to the choke plate. The fast idle cam is a stepped cam which is pulled up into its working position when the accelerator pedal is depressed before starting the engine. A fast idle speed adjusting screw, which is attached to the throttle shaft, contacts the cam and, by holding the throttle plates open, raises the idle speed of the engine to the required level.

Engine exhaust manifold heat passes through the choke coil spring housing while the engine is operating. As the engine reaches operating temperature, the increased temperature of the exhaust manifold causes the spring to contract. This removes spring pressure from the choke plate and allows the choke plate to return to the open position. This movement of the plate also disengages the fast idle cam and allows the engine idle speed to return to normal.

The choke plate vacuum pull-down device opens the choke plate slightly when the engine has started and continues to function after the choke is off. On some engines, the device consists of a piston which is contained in the choke housing. On other engines, it consists of a diaphragm and spring which are contained in an extension on the choke housing. When the engine is running, intake manifold vacuum is applied to the diaphragm or piston. The diaphragm or piston then exerts a corresponding pull on the choke plate. When the engine is cold, and the choke coil spring is exerting pressure on the choke plate, the pull of the diaphragm or piston opens the choke plate slightly. After the engine has reached normal operating temperature and the choke spring has contracted, the diaphragm or piston holds the choke plate in the full open position.

The choke unloader is a tab which is attached to the carburetor throttle shaft, opposite the fast idle adjusting screw. When the accelerator pedal is depressed to the full open position, the fast idle adjusting screw moves away from the fast idle cam and the unloader tab moves up to contact the cam. The cam, through its connecting linkage,

then partially opens the choke plate. This allows additional air to enter the engine, and serves to aid in starting a flooded engine.

Carburetor Adjustments

Nine different types of carburetors have been used. These include:
1—barrel
- Autolite 1100
- Carter YF
- Carter RBS

2—barrel
- Autolite 2100
- Motorcraft 2100D

4—barrel
- Autolite 4100
- Autolite (Motorcraft) 4300
- Holley 4150
- Holley 4150 C
- Rochester Quadrajet 4MV

AUTOLITE 1100 CARBURETOR
Choke Plate Pull-Down Clearance Adjustment

1. Determine that the fast idle speed adjustment has been properly set. Remove the air cleaner and position the fast idle adjusting screw on the highest step of the fast idle cam.

2. Insert a drill of the specified thickness between the lower edge of the choke plate and the wall of the carburetor air horn.

3. With the drill properly positioned, hold the choke plate in position and adjust the plastic nut on the choke pull-down rod until it contacts the swivel on the choke lever assembly.

Fuel Float Level Adjustment

1. Remove the carburetor air horn and gasket from the carburetor.

2. Measure the distance from the gasket surface of the air horn to the top of the float. If the measurement is not within the specified tolerance, bend the float arm tab as necessary to obtain the specified dimension. Be careful not to exert any pressure on the fuel inlet needle, as this will damage it and result in an improper fuel level within the float bowl.

3. Install the carburetor air horn to the main body of the carburetor, using a new gasket.

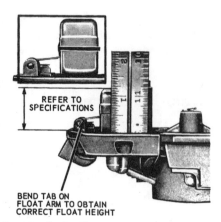

REFER TO
SPECIFICATIONS

BEND TAB ON
FLOAT ARM TO OBTAIN
CORRECT FLOAT HEIGHT

Carburetor float adjustment—Autolite 1100

CARTER YF CARBURETOR

Dechoke Clearance Adjustment

1. Remove the carburetor air cleaner.
2. Hold the throttle plate to the full open position while closing the choke plate as far as possible without forcing it. Use a drill of the proper diameter to check the clearance between the choke plate and air horn.
3. If the clearance is not within the specified limits, adjust it by bending the arm on the choke trip lever. Bending the arm down will increase the clearance—up will decrease it. Always check the clearance after making any adjustments.
4. If you have made an adjustment with the carburetor on the engine, adjust the idle

speed, fuel mixture, and dashpot (if so equipped).

Choke Pull-down Clearance Adjustment

1. Remove the carburetor air cleaner and the choke thermostatic spring housing.
2. Bend a section of 0.026 in. diameter wire gauge at a 90° angle approximately ¼ in. from one end.
3. Insert the bent end of the wire gauge between the choke piston slot and the right-hand slot in the choke housing. Rotate the choke piston lever counterclockwise until the gauge is snug in the piston slot.
4. Exert light pressure upon the choke piston lever to hold the gauge in position. Check the clearance with a drill of the diameter of the specified clearance between the lower edge of the choke plate and the carburetor bore.
5. Choke plate pull-down clearance may be adjusted by bending the choke piston lever as required to obtain the desired clearance. It is recommended that the choke piston lever be removed prior to bending, in order to prevent distortion of the piston link.
6. Install the choke thermostatic spring housing and gasket, and set the housing to the proper specification.

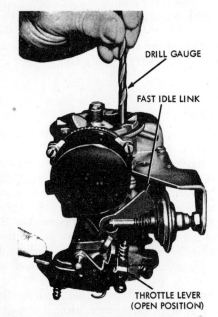

DRILL GAUGE

FAST IDLE LINK

THROTTLE LEVER
(OPEN POSITION)

Dechoke clearance adjustment—Carter YF

DRILL GAUGE

CHOKE PISTON
LEVER

.026"
WIRE
GAUGE

Choke plate pull-down clearance adjustment
Carter YF

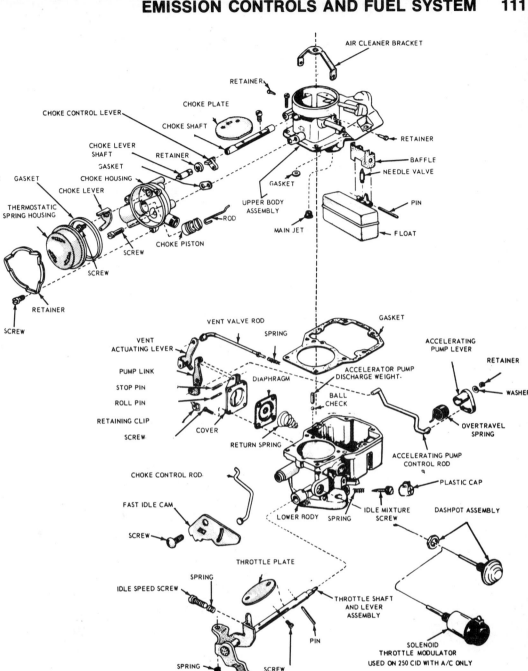

AIR CLEANER BRACKET

RETAINER

CHOKE PLATE

CHOKE CONTROL LEVER

CHOKE SHAFT

RETAINER

CHOKE LEVER SHAFT

RETAINER

GASKET

GASKET

CHOKE HOUSING

CHOKE LEVER

GASKET

RETAINER

BAFFLE

NEEDLE VALVE

THERMOSTATIC SPRING HOUSING

UPPER BODY ASSEMBLY

PIN

ROD

GASKET

MAIN JET

FLOAT

CHOKE PISTON

SCREW

SCREW

RETAINER

SCREW

VENT VALVE ROD

SPRING

GASKET

ACCELERATING PUMP LEVER

RETAINER

VENT ACTUATING LEVER

WASHER

PUMP LINK

DIAPHRAGM

ACCELERATOR PUMP DISCHARGE WEIGHT.

STOP PIN

ROLL PIN

BALL CHECK

OVERTRAVEL SPRING

RETAINING CLIP

SCREW

COVER

RETURN SPRING

ACCELERATING PUMP CONTROL ROD

CHOKE CONTROL ROD

PLASTIC CAP

FAST IDLE CAM

IDLE MIXTURE SCREW

DASHPOT ASSEMBLY

SCREW

LOWER BODY

SPRING

THROTTLE PLATE

SPRING

IDLE SPEED SCREW

THROTTLE SHAFT AND LEVER ASSEMBLY

PIN

SOLENOID THROTTLE MODULATOR

USED ON 250 CID WITH A/C ONLY

SPRING

SCREW

SCREW

Autolite 1100 carburetor

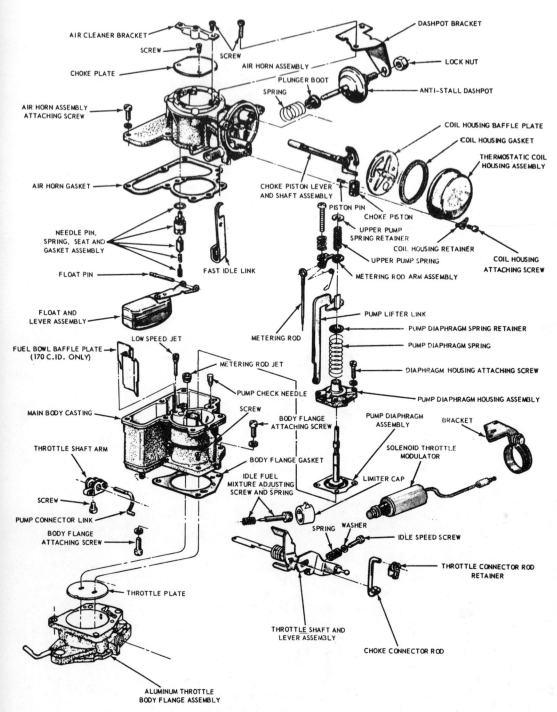

AIR CLEANER BRACKET

SCREW

CHOKE PLATE

AIR HORN ASSEMBLY
ATTACHING SCREW

AIR HORN GASKET

NEEDLE PIN,
SPRING, SEAT AND
GASKET ASSEMBLY

FLOAT PIN

FLOAT AND
LEVER ASSEMBLY

FUEL BOWL BAFFLE PLATE
(170 C.ID. ONLY)

MAIN BODY CASTING

THROTTLE SHAFT ARM

SCREW

PUMP CONNECTOR LINK

BODY FLANGE
ATTACHING SCREW

THROTTLE PLATE

ALUMINUM THROTTLE
BODY FLANGE ASSEMBLY

SCREW

AIR HORN ASSEMBLY

PLUNGER BOOT

SPRING

CHOKE PISTON LEVER
AND SHAFT ASSEMBLY

FAST IDLE LINK

LOW SPEED JET

METERING ROD JET

PUMP CHECK NEEDLE

SCREW

BODY FLANGE
ATTACHING SCREW

BODY FLANGE GASKET

IDLE FUEL
MIXTURE ADJUSTING
SCREW AND SPRING

METERING ROD

DASHPOT BRACKET

LOCK NUT

ANTI-STALL DASHPOT

COIL HOUSING BAFFLE PLATE

COIL HOUSING GASKET

THERMOSTATIC COIL
HOUSING ASSEMBLY

PISTON PIN

CHOKE PISTON

UPPER PUMP
SPRING RETAINER

COIL HOUSING RETAINER

UPPER PUMP SPRING

COIL HOUSING
ATTACHING SCREW

METERING ROD ARM ASSEMBLY

PUMP LIFTER LINK

PUMP DIAPHRAGM SPRING RETAINER

PUMP DIAPHRAGM SPRING

DIAPHRAGM HOUSING ATTACHING SCREW

PUMP DIAPHRAGM HOUSING ASSEMBLY

PUMP DIAPHRAGM
ASSEMBLY

BRACKET

SOLENOID THROTTLE
MODULATOR

LIMITER CAP

SPRING   WASHER

IDLE SPEED SCREW

THROTTLE CONNECTOR ROD
RETAINER

THROTTLE SHAFT AND
LEVER ASSEMBLY

CHOKE CONNECTOR ROD

Carter YF 1-barrel carburetor

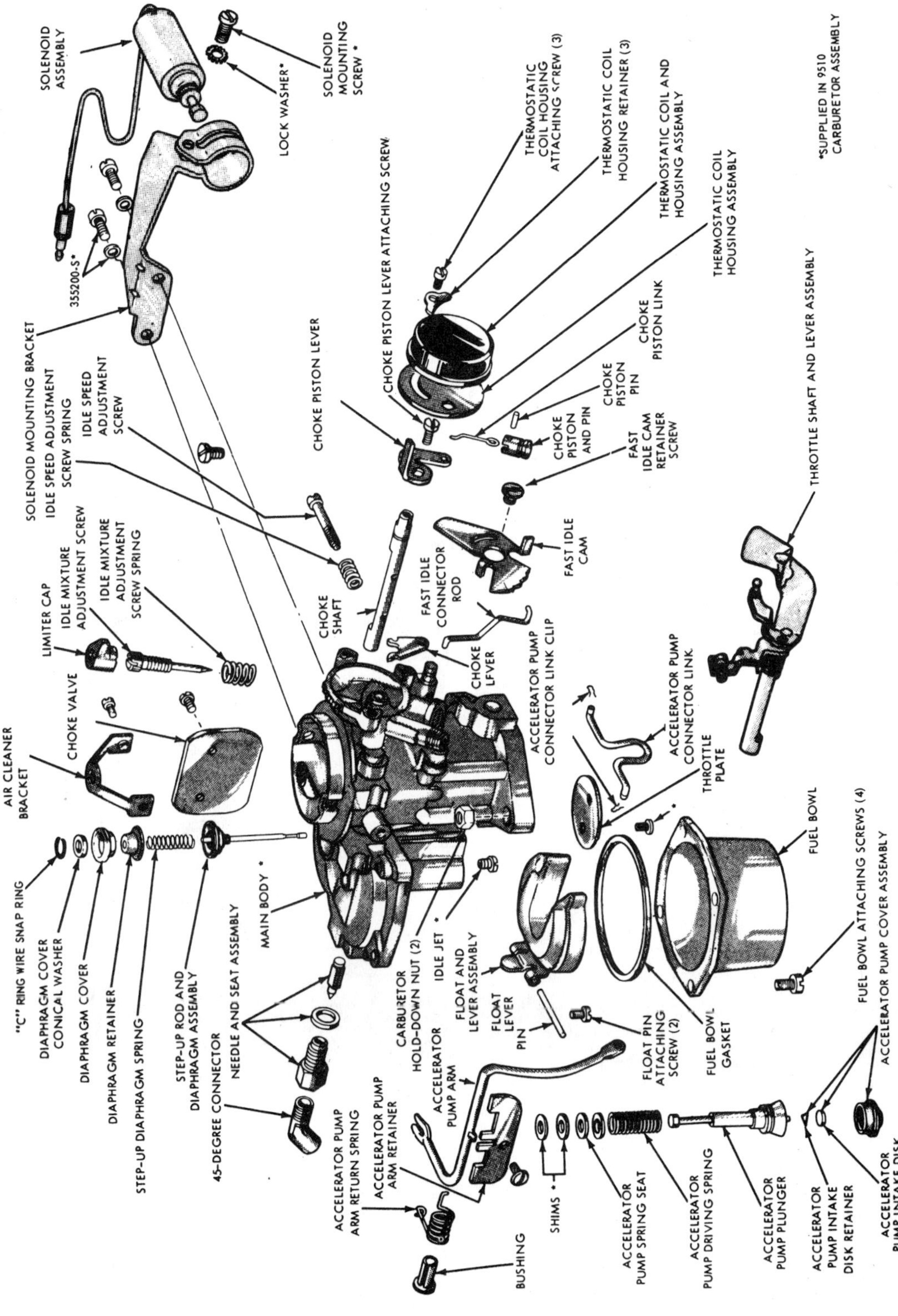

Carter RBS 1-barrel carburetor

SOLENOID ASSEMBLY

LOCK WASHER*

SOLENOID MOUNTING SCREW *

THERMOSTATIC COIL HOUSING ATTACHING SCREW (3)

THERMOSTATIC COIL HOUSING RETAINER (3)

THERMOSTATIC COIL AND HOUSING ASSEMBLY

THERMOSTATIC COIL HOUSING ASSEMBLY

*SUPPLIED IN 9510 CARBURETOR ASSEMBLY

355200-S*

SOLENOID MOUNTING BRACKET

IDLE SPEED ADJUSTMENT SCREW SPRING

IDLE SPEED ADJUSTMENT SCREW

CHOKE PISTON LEVER ATTACHING SCREW

CHOKE PISTON LEVER

CHOKE PISTON LINK

CHOKE PISTON PIN

CHOKE PISTON AND PIN

FAST IDLE CAM RETAINER SCREW

THROTTLE SHAFT AND LEVER ASSEMBLY

LIMITER CAP

IDLE MIXTURE ADJUSTMENT SCREW

IDLE MIXTURE ADJUSTMENT SCREW SPRING

CHOKE SHAFT

FAST IDLE CONNECTOR ROD

FAST IDLE CAM

CHOKE VALVE

AIR CLEANER BRACKET

CHOKE LEVER

ACCELERATOR PUMP CONNECTOR LINK CLIP

ACCELERATOR PUMP CONNECTOR LINK

THROTTLE PLATE

FUEL BOWL

"C" RING WIRE SNAP RING

DIAPHRAGM COVER CONICAL WASHER

DIAPHRAGM COVER

DIAPHRAGM RETAINER

STEP-UP DIAPHRAGM SPRING

STEP-UP ROD AND DIAPHRAGM ASSEMBLY

45-DEGREE CONNECTOR

NEEDLE AND SEAT ASSEMBLY

MAIN BODY *

IDLE JET

CARBURETOR HOLD-DOWN NUT (2)

FLOAT AND LEVER ASSEMBLY

FLOAT LEVER PIN

FLOAT PIN ATTACHING SCREW (2)

FUEL BOWL GASKET

FUEL BOWL ATTACHING SCREWS (4)

ACCELERATOR PUMP COVER ASSEMBLY

ACCELERATOR PUMP ARM RETURN SPRING

ACCELERATOR PUMP ARM RETAINER

ACCELERATOR PUMP ARM

BUSHING

SHIMS *

ACCELERATOR PUMP SPRING SEAT

ACCELERATOR PUMP DRIVING SPRING

ACCELERATOR PUMP PLUNGER

ACCELERATOR PUMP INTAKE DISK RETAINER

ACCELERATOR PUMP INTAKE DISK

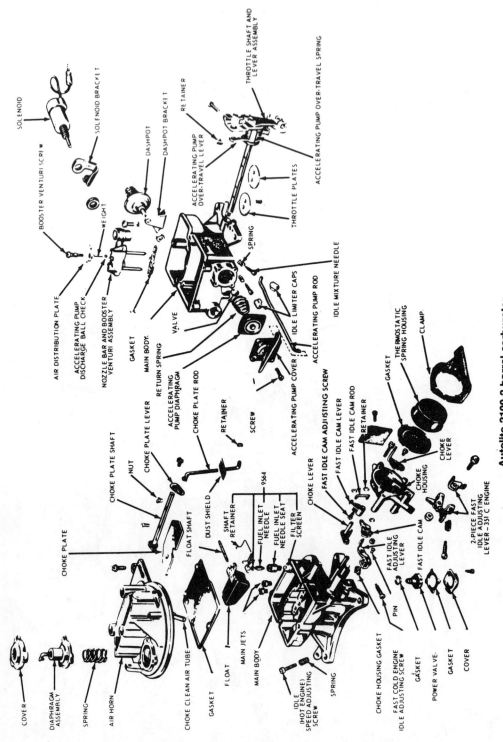

Autolite 2100 2-barrel carburetor

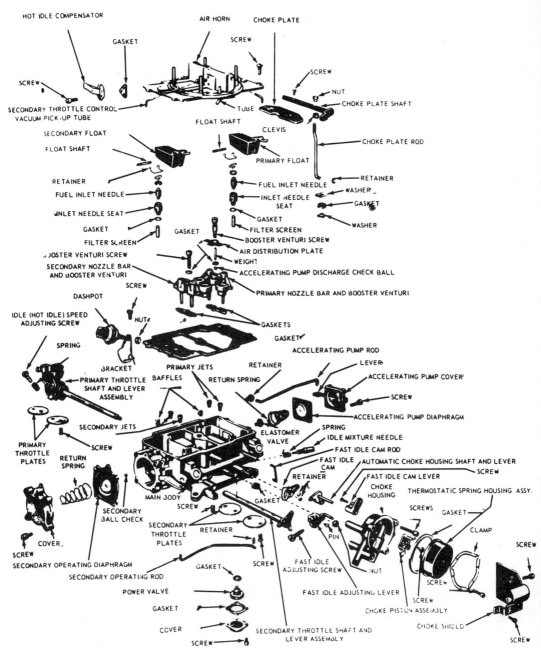

HOT IDLE COMPENSATOR

GASKET

AIR HORN

CHOKE PLATE

SCREW

SCREW

SCREW

NUT

CHOKE PLATE SHAFT

SECONDARY THROTTLE CONTROL
VACUUM PICK-UP TUBE

TUBE

FLOAT SHAFT

CLEVIS

CHOKE PLATE ROD

SECONDARY FLOAT

FLOAT SHAFT

PRIMARY FLOAT

RETAINER

RETAINER

FUEL INLET NEEDLE

WASHER

FUEL INLET NEEDLE

INLET NEEDLE
SEAT

GASKET

INLET NEEDLE SEAT

WASHER

GASKET

FILTER SCREEN

GASKET

FILTER SCREEN

BOOSTER VENTURI SCREW

BOOSTER VENTURI SCREW

AIR DISTRIBUTION PLATE

SECONDARY NOZZLE BAR
AND BOOSTER VENTURI

WEIGHT

ACCELERATING PUMP DISCHARGE CHECK BALL

SCREW

PRIMARY NOZZLE BAR AND BOOSTER VENTURI

DASHPOT

IDLE (HOT IDLE) SPEED
ADJUSTING SCREW

NUT

GASKETS

GASKET

SPRING

ACCELERATING PUMP ROD

BRACKET

PRIMARY JETS

LEVER

PRIMARY THROTTLE
SHAFT AND LEVER
ASSEMBLY

BAFFLES

RETURN SPRING

ACCELERATING PUMP COVER

SCREW

ACCELERATING PUMP DIAPHRAGM

SECONDARY JETS

SPRING

PRIMARY
THROTTLE
PLATES

RETURN
SPRING

SCREW

ELASTOMER
VALVE

IDLE MIXTURE NEEDLE

FAST IDLE CAM ROD

FAST IDLE
CAM

AUTOMATIC CHOKE HOUSING SHAFT AND LEVER

RETAINER

SCREW

FAST IDLE CAM LEVER

CHOKE
HOUSING

THERMOSTATIC SPRING HOUSING ASSY.

MAIN BODY

SCREW

GASKET

SCREWS

GASKET

SECONDARY
BALL CHECK

SECONDARY
THROTTLE
PLATES

RETAINER

CLAMP

SCREW

COVER

PIN

SCREW

SCREW

SECONDARY OPERATING DIAPHRAGM

GASKET

SCREW

FAST IDLE
ADJUSTING SCREW

NUT

SCREW

SECONDARY OPERATING ROD

POWER VALVE

FAST IDLE ADJUSTING LEVER

SCREW

GASKET

CHOKE PISTON ASSEMBLY

COVER

CHOKE SHIELD

SECONDARY THROTTLE SHAFT AND
LEVER ASSEMBLY

SCREW

SCREW

Autolite 4100 4-barrel carburetor

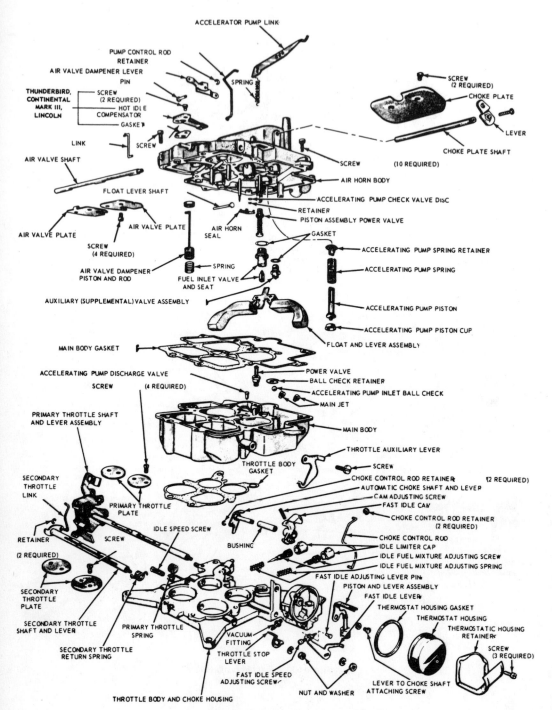

Autolite (Motorcraft) 4300 4-barrel carburetor

Holley 4150-C carburetor—also typical of Holley 4150

LOCK SCREW
GASKET
GASKET
FUEL INLET NEEDLE AND SEAT
O-RING
SCREW
GASKET
SECONDARY FUEL BOWL
FLOAT PIN SHAFT
FUEL LEVEL ADJUSTING NUT
SPRING
FLOAT
SIGHT PLUG
HINGE
GASKET
GASKET
SECONDARY METERING BODY
ACCELERATING PUMP DISCHARGE NOZZLE
ACCELERATING PUMP DISCHARGE NEEDLE
CHOKE PLATE
SCREW
GASKET
MAIN BODY
CHOKE ROD SEAL
GASKET
CHOKE HOUSING SHAFT AND LEVER
AIR CLEANER ANCHOR SCREW
SCREW
RETAINER
CHOKE ROD
RETAINER
POWER VALVE
IDLE FUEL MIXTURE NEEDLES
DIAPHRAGM LEVER ASSEMBLY
SPRING
SCREW
SHAFT BUSHINGS
SCREW
SECONDARY THROTTLE PLATES
RETAINER
WASHER
SECONDARY THROTTLE SHAFT
THROTTLE CONNECTING ROD
RETAINER
SCREW
ACCELERATING PUMP CAM
SCREW
SCREW
SPRING
SCREW
SPRING
SLEEVE NUT
RETAINER
PRIMARY THROTTLE PLATES
PRIMARY THROTTLE SHAFT ASSEMBLY
SCREW AND WASHER
COVER
DIAPHRAGM SPRING
SECONDARY DIAPHRAGM
RETAINER
SECONDARY BALL CHECK
SECONDARY HOUSING
SCREW AND WASHER
SCREWS
GASKET
NUT
LOCK WASHER
CHOKE SHAFT
LEVER
GASKETS
SCREW
GASKET
FAST IDLE CAM ASSEMBLY
RETAINER
GASKET
BAFFLE
LIMITER
MAIN JETS
FAST IDLE CAM LEVER
SCREW
THROTTLE BODY
SCREW
SCREW
ACCELERATING PUMP OPERATING LEVER
CHOKE THERMOSTAT HOUSING AND SPRING
CLAMP
SCREW
GASKET
SPACER
CHOKE THERMOSTAT LEVER LINK AND PISTON
CHOKE HOUSING
PRIMARY METERING BLOCK
DISTRIBUTOR VACUUM FITTING
LIMITER
FLOAT
HINGE
FLOAT SPRING
FLOAT PIN (SHAFT)
SCREW
PRIMARY FUEL BOWL
GASKET
FUEL INLET AND FILTER
FUEL DISTRIBUTION TUBE FITTING
FUEL DISTRIBUTION TUBE
LOCK SCREW
GASKET
FUEL LEVEL ADJUSTING NUT
GASKET
FUEL INLET NEEDLE AND SEAT
SIGHT PLUG
O-RING
GASKET
DISTRIBUTION TUBE FITTING
GASKET
SCREW
DIAPHRAGM SPRING
DIAPHRAGM ASSEMBLY
SCREW

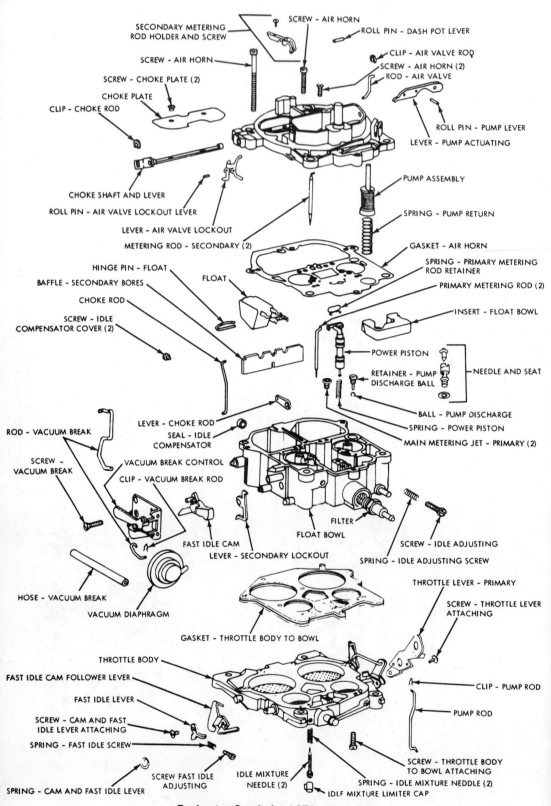

SCREW - AIR HORN

SECONDARY METERING
ROD HOLDER AND SCREW

ROLL PIN - DASH POT LEVER

SCREW - AIR HORN

CLIP - AIR VALVE ROD

SCREW - AIR HORN (2)

SCREW - CHOKE PLATE (2)

ROD - AIR VALVE

CHOKE PLATE

CLIP - CHOKE ROD

ROLL PIN - PUMP LEVER

LEVER - PUMP ACTUATING

PUMP ASSEMBLY

CHOKE SHAFT AND LEVER

ROLL PIN - AIR VALVE LOCKOUT LEVER

SPRING - PUMP RETURN

LEVER - AIR VALVE LOCKOUT

GASKET - AIR HORN

METERING ROD - SECONDARY (2)

SPRING - PRIMARY METERING
ROD RETAINER

HINGE PIN - FLOAT

FLOAT

PRIMARY METERING ROD (2)

BAFFLE - SECONDARY BORES

CHOKE ROD

INSERT - FLOAT BOWL

SCREW - IDLE
COMPENSATOR COVER (2)

POWER PISTON

NEEDLE AND SEAT

RETAINER - PUMP
DISCHARGE BALL

LEVER - CHOKE ROD

BALL - PUMP DISCHARGE

ROD - VACUUM BREAK

SEAL - IDLE
COMPENSATOR

SPRING - POWER PISTON

MAIN METERING JET - PRIMARY (2)

SCREW -
VACUUM BREAK

VACUUM BREAK CONTROL

CLIP - VACUUM BREAK ROD

FILTER

SCREW - IDLE ADJUSTING

FAST IDLE CAM

FLOAT BOWL

SPRING - IDLE ADJUSTING SCREW

LEVER - SECONDARY LOCKOUT

THROTTLE LEVER - PRIMARY

HOSE - VACUUM BREAK

SCREW - THROTTLE LEVER
ATTACHING

VACUUM DIAPHRAGM

GASKET - THROTTLE BODY TO BOWL

THROTTLE BODY

CLIP - PUMP ROD

FAST IDLE CAM FOLLOWER LEVER

PUMP ROD

FAST IDLE LEVER

SCREW - CAM AND FAST
IDLE LEVER ATTACHING

SPRING - FAST IDLE SCREW

SCREW - THROTTLE BODY
TO BOWL ATTACHING

SCREW FAST IDLE
ADJUSTING

IDLE MIXTURE
NEEDLE (2)

SPRING - IDLE MIXTURE NEEDLE (2)

SPRING - CAM AND FAST IDLE LEVER

IDLE MIXTURE LIMITER CAP

Rochester Quadrajet 4 MV carburetor

Fast Idle Cam Index Setting

1. Position the fast idle screw on the kick-down step of the fast idle cam against the shoulder of the high step.

2. Adjust by bending the choke plate connecting rod to obtain the specified clearance between the lower edge of the choke plate and the carburetor bore.

Fuel Level Float Adjustment

1. Remove the air horn and gasket from the main body of the carburetor.

2. Fabricate a float level gauge of the specified dimension. (Most kits include a prefabricated float level gauge.)

3. Invert the air horn assembly. Check the clearance from the top of the float to the bottom of the air horn, using the float level gauge. Hold the air horn assembly at eye level when checking the float level clearance. The float arm should be resting on the needle pin. Bend the float arm as necessary to obtain the specified clearance, but exert no pressure on the needle when adjusting the float level, and do not bend the tab on the end of the float arm.

4. Reinstall the air horn assembly, using a new gasket. This dry float level adjustment is the final adjustment of float level for this carburetor.

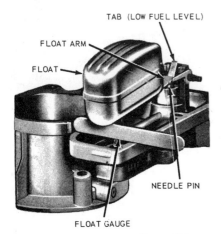

Fuel float level adjustment—Carter YF

CARTER RBS CARBURETOR

Fast Idle Cam Index Setting

This procedure is the same as that for the Carter YF carburetor.

Automatic Choke Thermostatic Spring Housing Adjustment

1. Remove the air cleaner assembly from the carburetor.

2. Loosen the thermostatic spring housing retaining screws. Set the spring housing to the specified index mark and tighten the clamp retaining screws.

3. If no other carburetor adjustments are required, install the air cleaner assembly on the carburetor.

Choke Plate Pull-down Adjustment

Follow the procedure for the Carter YF carburetor.

Dechoke Clearance Adjustment

The procedure given for the Carter YF carburetor also applies to this type, except that the adjustment is made by bending the tang on the throttle lever.

Float Level Adjustment (Carburetor Removed from Car)

1. Remove the fuel bowl and its gasket.

2. Invert the main body of the carburetor, so that the float assembly is pressing against the inlet needle and seat. Measure the vertical distance between the main body casting surface for the fuel bowl and the raised tips formed on the outer ends of the float.

3. Measure for the specified setting at both ends of the float. If it is necessary to equalize the measurement, hold the float lever securely with needle-nose pliers at the narrow portion, and twist the float as required. While holding the float lever, adjust

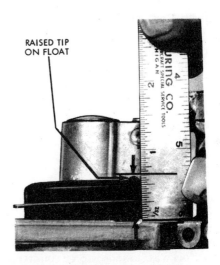

Measuring fuel float level—Carter RBS

the float to the specified setting, while holding the tab of the float lever away from the inlet needle.

4. Replace the gasket and fuel bowl. Install the carburetor if no further adjustments are required.

AUTOLITE 2100 CARBURETOR MOTORCRAFT 2100D CARBURETOR

Automatic Choke Thermostatic Spring Housing Adjustment

Refer to the procedures listed for the Carter RBS carburetor.

Choke Plate Pull-down Adjustment

1. Remove the air cleaner.
2. With the engine at its normal operating temperature, loosen the choke thermostatic spring housing retaining screws and set the housing 90° in the rich direction.
3. Disconnect and remove the choke heat tube from the choke housing.
4. Turn the fast idle adjusting screw outward one full turn.
5. Start the engine. Use a drill of the specified diameter to check the clearance between the lower edge of the choke plate and the air horn wall.
6. To adjust the clearance, turn, the diaphragm stopscrew (located on the underside of the choke diaphragm housing); clockwise will decrease the clearance, counterclockwise will increase it.
7. Connect the choke heat tube and set the choke thermostatic spring housing to the proper specification. Adjust the fast idle speed to specifications.

Fast Idle Cam Clearance

1. Loosen the choke thermostatic spring housing retaining screws and position the housing 90° in the rich direction.
2. Position the fast idle speed screw at the kick-down step of the fast idle cam. This kick-down step is identified by a small V stamped in the side of the casting.
3. Be sure that the fast idle cam is in the kick-down position while checking or adjusting the fast idle cam clearance. Check the clearance between the lower edge of the choke plate and the wall of the air horn by inserting a drill of the specified diameter between them. Adjustment may be accomplished by turning the fast idle cam adjusting screw clockwise to increase or counterclockwise to decrease the clearance.

4. Set the choke thermostatic spring housing to specifications, and adjust the antistall dashpot, idle speed, and fuel mixture.

Fuel Float Level Adjustment—Dry

This preliminary setting of the float level adjustment must be performed with the carburetor off the engine.

1. Remove the air horn and see that the float is raised and the fuel inlet needle is seated. Check the distance between the top surface of the main body (with the gasket removed) and the top surface of the float. Depress the float tab to seat the fuel inlet needle. Take a measurement near the center of the float, at a point ⅛ in. from the free end. If you are using a prefabricated float gauge, place the gauge in the corner of the enlarged end section of the fuel bowl (see illustration). The gauge should touch the float near the end, but not on the end radius.
2. If necessary, bend the tab on the end of the float to bring the setting within the specified limits.

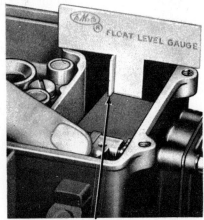

FLOAT SHOULD JUST
TOUCH AT THIS POINT

Dry fuel float level adjustment—Autolite 2100

Fuel Level Float Adjustment—Wet

1. Bring the engine to its normal operating temperature, park on as nearly level a surface as possible, and stop the engine.
2. Remove the air cleaner assembly from the carburetor.
3. Remove the air horn retaining screws and the carburetor identification tag. Leave the air horn and gasket in position on the carburetor main body. Start the engine, let it idle for several minutes, rotate the air horn out of the way, and remove the gasket to provide access to the float assembly.

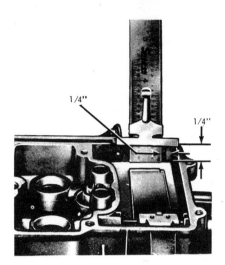

Wet fuel float level adjustment—Autolite 2100

4. With the engine idling, use a standard depth scale to measure the vertical distance from the top machined surface of the carburetor main body to the surface of the fuel in the fuel bowl. This measurement must be made at least ¼ in. away from any vertical surface in order to assure an accurate reading.

5. Stop the engine prior to making any adjustment to the float level. Adjustment is accomplished by bending the float tab (which contacts the inlet valve) up or down, as required, to raise or lower the fuel level. After making an adjustment, start the engine and allow it to idle for several minutes before repeating the fuel level check. Repeat as necessary until the proper fuel level is attained.

6. Reinstall the air horn with a new gasket and secure it with the screws. Install the identification tag in its proper location.

7. Check the idle speed, fuel mixture, and dashpot adjustments. Install the air cleaner assembly.

AUTOLITE 4100 CARBURETOR

Choke Plate Clearance and Fast Idle Cam Adjustment

1. Remove the air cleaner and the choke thermostatic spring housing.

2. Bend a wire gauge of 0.036 diameter at a 90° angle approximately ⅛ in. from one end.

3. Block the throttle about halfway open and make certain that the fast idle cam does not contact the fast idle adjusting screw. Insert the bent end of the wire gauge between the lower edge of the piston slot and the upper edge of the righthand slot in the choke housing.

4. Pull the choke piston lever counterclockwise until the gauge is snug in the piston slot. Hold the wire gauge in place by exerting light pressure on the choke piston lever. Check the clearance between the lower edge of the choke plate and the air horn wall. To obtain the proper clearance, turn the choke plate clevis adjusting nut as required (see illustration).

5. Install the gasket and thermostatic spring housing on the choke housing. Install the retainer.

6. Rotate the spring housing counterclockwise (rich direction) to align the center index mark on the choke housing with the index mark on the spring housing.

7. Rotate the spring housing an additional 90° counterclockwise and tighten the retaining screws. Check the clearance between the front of the choke plate and the air horn wall. If adjustment is required, turn the fast idle cam lever adjusting screw inward to increase the clearance, or outward to decrease it. Be certain that the adjustment is made with the fast idle screw at the index mark of the fast idle cam.

8. Position the fast idle screw on the second step of the fast idle cam.

9. Set the thermostatic choke housing to the specified index mark and tighten the retaining screws.

10. If these adjustments were performed while the carburetor was installed on the car, perform an idle speed and fuel mixture adjustment. If so equipped, adjust the antistall dashpot.

Fuel Float Level Adjustments—Wet and Dry

Refer to the procedures for this adjustment on the Autolite 2100 two-barrel carburetor.

AUTOLITE (MOTORCRAFT) 4300 4 BARREL CARBURETOR

Automatic Choke Thermostatic Spring Housing Adjustment

The procedure listed for the Carter RBS one-barrel carburetor also applies to this model.

Fast Idle Cam Clearance

The procedure for this adjustment on the Autolite 2100 carburetor also applies to this model.

Dechoke Clearance

Follow the procedure given for the adjustment of dechoke clearance for the Carter YF Carburetor. Adjustment to the Autolite 4300 is accomplished by bending the pawl on the fast idle speed lever forward to increase or backward to decrease the clearance.

Fuel Level Float and Auxiliary (Supplemental) Valve Setting

1. Refer to the illustration for details of construction of a tool for checking the parallel setting of the dual pontoons.

2. Install the gauge on the carburetor and set it to the specified height.

3. Check the clearance and alignment of the pontoons to the gauge. Both pontoons should just barely touch the gauge for the proper setting. Pontoons may be aligned if necessary by slightly twisting them.

4. To adjust the float level, bend the primary needle tab down to raise the float and up to lower it.

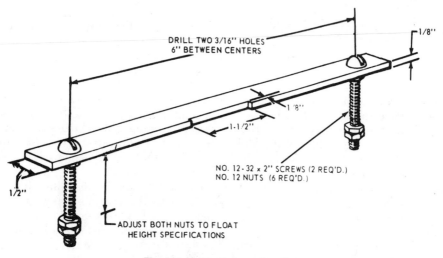

Float level gauge construction

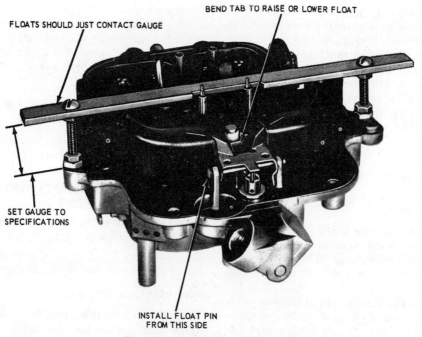

Checking float level—Autolite 4300

HOLLEY 4150 AND 4150 C CARBURETORS

Choke Plate Clearance and Fast Idle Cam Adjustment

1. Remove the choke thermostatic housing cap.

2. Place the choke plate in the fully closed position by opening the throttle lever to about ⅓ throttle, and pressing down on the front side of the choke plate. While holding the choke plate closed, release the throttle lever.

3. With the choke plate in the closed position, measure the distance between the flat of the fast idle cam and the choke housing mouting post. If adjustment is required, straighten or bend the choke rod until the desired clearance is obtained.

4. Bend a 0.036 in. gauge wire at a 90° angle at approximately ¹/₁₆–⅛ in. from one end. Insert the bent end between the lower edge of the piston slot and the upper edge of the slot in the choke housing. Open the throttle lever to approximately ⅓ throttle and rotate the choke lever counterclockwise so that the bent end of the wire is held in the housing slot by the piston slot with light pressure applied to the choke lever. Measure the distance between the air horn wall and the lower edge of the choke plate. If the clearance is not to specification, bend the adjusting tab on the choke lever to obtain the specified clearance.

5. Install the choke thermostatic housing. Be sure that the bimetallic loop is installed around the choke lever. Set the cap notch to specifications.

6. Connect a tachometer to the engine. With the engine operating and the temperature stabilized, set the fast idle screw on the kick-down or second step of the fast idle cam.

Fuel Float Level Adjustment—Dry

This preliminary adjustment—which is accomplished with the carburetor off the car—is performed simply by inverting the fuel bowl and checking to see that the center of the float is an equal distance from the top and bottom of the fuel bowl.

Fuel Float Level Adjustment—Wet

1. Position the vehicle on a level floor, be sure that the fuel pump pressure is within the specifications, and operate the engine until normal operating temperature has been reached.

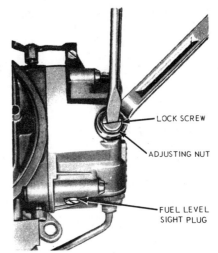

Wet fuel level adjustment—Holley 4150 and 4150 C

2. Check the fuel level in each fuel bowl separately. Place a suitable container below the fuel level sight plug to catch any spillover of fuel. Remove the fuel level sight plug and gasket, and check the fuel level. The fuel level within the bowl should be at the lower edge of the sight plug opening ¹/₁₆ in.

3. If the fuel level is satisfactory, install the sight plug. Do not install the air cleaner at this time.

4. If the fuel level is too high, stop the engine, install the sight plug, drain the fuel bowl, refill it, and check it again before altering the float setting. This will eliminate the possibility that dirt or foreign matter caused a temporary flooding condition. To drain the fuel bowl, loosen one lower retaining bolt from the fuel bowl and drain the fuel into a suitable container. Install the bolt and the fuel level sight plug and start the engine to fill the fuel bowl. After the fuel level has stabilized, stop the engine and check the fuel level.

If the fuel level is too high, it should be first lowered below specifications and then raised until it is just at the lower edge of the sight plug opening. If the level was too low, it is necessary only to raise it to the specified level. If either is necessary, refer to the procedures for either adjustment.

TO LOWER FUEL LEVEL

1. With the engine stopped, loosen the lockscrew on top of the fuel bowl just enough to allow rotation of the adjusting nut underneath. Do not loosen the lockscrew or attempt to adjust the fuel level with the sight

plug removed and the engine running because the pressure in the line will spray fuel out and present a fire hazard.

2. Turn the adjusting nut approximately ½ turn in to lower the fuel level below specifications (⅙ turn of the adjusting nut, depending on direction of rotation, will raise or lower the float assembly at the fuel level sight plug opening ³/₆₄ in.).

3. Tighten the lockscrew and reinstall the fuel level sight plug. Start the engine. After the fuel level has stabilized, stop the engine and check the fuel level at the sight plug opening. The fuel level should be below specified limits. If it is not, repeat the previous steps, turning the adjusting nut an additional amount sufficient to lower the fuel below the specified level.

4. Loosen the lockscrew and turn the adjusting nut out in increments of ⅙ turn or less until the correct fuel level is achieved. After each adjustment, tighten the lockscrew, install the fuel level sight plug, and then start the engine and stabilize the fuel level. Check the fuel level at the sight plug opening. Install the sight plug and gasket.

5. Check the idle fuel mixture and idle speed adjustments. Adjust the carburetor as required.

TO RAISE FUEL LEVEL

Perform steps one, four, and five under the procedure "To Lower Fuel Level."

ROCHESTER QUADRAJET 4MV CARBURETOR

Air Valve Dashpot Adjustment

1. Seat the vacuum break diaphragm using an outside vacuum source.

2. With the air valve completely closed and the diaphragm seated, measure the clearance between the air valve dashpot rod and the air valve lever.

3. The dimension should be as specified. If not, bend the rod at the air valve end to adjust.

Dechoke Adjustment

1. Hold the choke plate in the closed position. This can be done by attaching a rubber band or spring to the vacuum break lever and a stationary part of the carburetor.

2. Open the primary throttle plates to the wide open position.

3. Insert the specified plug gauge between the lower edge of the choke plates and inside the air horn wall. The choke rod should be in bottom of slot when checking setting.

4. To adjust, bend the tang on the fast idle lever to the rear to increase and to the front to decrease the clearance. It is advisable to recheck the unloader setting after the carburetor is installed on the engine by depressing the accelerator pedal.

Fuel Float Level Adjustment

1. Remove the air horn assembly.

2. With an adjustable T-scale, measure the distance from the top of the float bowl surface (gasket removed) to the top of the float at the toe (locate gauging point ¹/₁₆ in. back from the toe on the float surface). Do not gauge on top of part number.

When checking the adjustment, make sure the float hinge pin is firmly seated and the float arm is held down against the float needle so that it is seated.

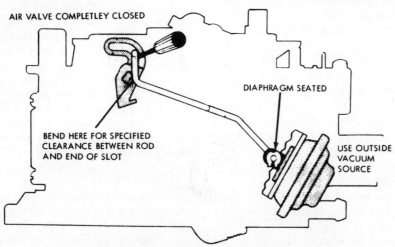

AIR VALVE COMPLETLEY CLOSED

DIAPHRAGM SEATED

BEND HERE FOR SPECIFIED CLEARANCE BETWEEN ROD AND END OF SLOT

USE OUTSIDE VACUUM SOURCE

Air valve dashpot adjustment—Rochester Quadrajet

CHILTON'S
FUEL ECONOMY
& TUNE-UP TIPS

Tune-up • Spark Plug Diagnosis • Emission Controls

Fuel System • Cooling System • Tires and Wheels

General Maintenance

CHILTON'S FUEL ECONOMY & TUNE-UP TIPS

Fuel economy is important to everyone, no matter what kind of vehicle you drive. The maintenance-minded motorist can save both money and fuel using these tips and the periodic maintenance and tune-up procedures in this Repair and Tune-Up Guide.

There are more than 130,000,000 cars and trucks registered for private use in the United States. Each travels an average of 10-12,000 miles per year, and, and in total they consume close to 70 billion gallons of fuel each year. This represents nearly ⅔ of the oil imported by the United States each year. The Federal government's goal is to reduce consumption 10% by 1985. A variety of methods are either already in use or under serious consideration, and they all affect you driving and the cars you will drive. In addition to "down-sizing", the auto industry is using or investigating the use of electronic fuel delivery, electronic engine controls and alternative engines for use in smaller and lighter vehicles, among other alternatives to meet the federally mandated Corporate Average Fuel Economy (CAFE) of 27.5 mpg by 1985. The government, for its part, is considering rationing, mandatory driving curtailments and tax increases on motor vehicle fuel in an effort to reduce consumption. The government's goal of a 10% reduction could be realized — and further government regulation avoided — if every private vehicle could use just 1 less gallon of fuel per week.

How Much Can You Save?

Tests have proven that almost anyone can make at least a 10% reduction in fuel consumption through regular maintenance and tune-ups. When a major manufacturer of spark plugs sur-

TUNE-UP

1. Check the cylinder compression to be sure the engine will really benefit from a tune-up and that it is capable of producing good fuel economy. A tune-up will be wasted on an engine in poor mechanical condition.

2. Replace spark plugs regularly. New spark plugs alone can increase fuel economy 3%.

3. Be sure the spark plugs are the correct type (heat range) for your vehicle. See the Tune-Up Specifications.

Heat range refers to the spark plug's ability to conduct heat away from the firing end. It must conduct the heat away in an even pattern to avoid becoming a source of pre-ignition, yet it must also operate hot enough to burn off conductive deposits that could cause misfiring.

The heat range is usually indicated by a number on the spark plug, part of the manufacturer's designation for each individual spark plug. The numbers in bold-face indicate the heat range in each manufacturer's identification system.

Manufacturer	Typical Designation
AC	R **45** TS
Bosch (old)	WA **145** T30
Bosch (new)	HR **8** Y
Champion	RBL **15** Y
Fram/Autolite	**4**15
Mopar	P-**62** PR
Motorcraft	BRF-**42**
NGK	BP **5** ES-15
Nippondenso	W **16** EP
Prestolite	14GR **5** 2A

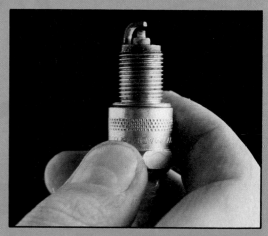

Periodically, check the spark plugs to be sure they are firing efficiently. They are excellent indicators of the internal condition of your engine.

On AC, Bosch (new), Champion, Fram/Autolite, Mopar, Motorcraft and Prestolite, a higher number indicates a hotter plug. On Bosch (old), NGK and Nippondenso, a higher number indicates a colder plug.

4. Make sure the spark plugs are properly gapped. See the Tune-Up Specifications in this book.

5. Be sure the spark plugs are firing efficiently. The illustrations on the next 2 pages show you how to "read" the firing end of the spark plug.

6. Check the ignition timing and set it to specifications. Tests show that almost all cars have incorrect ignition timing by more than 2°.

veyed over 6,000 cars nationwide, they found that a tune-up, on cars that needed one, increased fuel economy over 11%. Replacing worn plugs alone, accounted for a 3% increase. The same test also revealed that 8 out of every 10 vehicles will have some maintenance deficiency that will directly affect fuel economy, emissions or performance. Most of this mileage-robbing neglect could be prevented with regular maintenance.

Modern engines require that all of the functioning systems operate properly for maximum efficiency. A malfunction anywhere wastes fuel. You can keep your vehicle running as efficiently and economically as possible, by being aware of your vehicle's operating and performance characteristics. If your vehicle suddenly develops performance or fuel economy problems it could be due to one or more of the following:

PROBLEM	POSSIBLE CAUSE
Engine Idles Rough	Ignition timing, idle mixture, vacuum leak or something amiss in the emission control system.
Hesitates on Acceleration	Dirty carburetor or fuel filter, improper accelerator pump setting, ignition timing or fouled spark plugs.
Starts Hard or Fails to Start	Worn spark plugs, improperly set automatic choke, ice (or water) in fuel system.
Stalls Frequently	Automatic choke improperly adjusted and possible dirty air filter or fuel filter.
Performs Sluggishly	Worn spark plugs, dirty fuel or air filter, ignition timing or automatic choke out of adjustment.

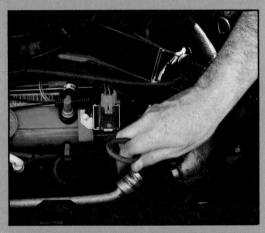

Check spark plug wires on conventional point type ignition for cracks by bending them in a loop around your finger.

Be sure that spark plug wires leading to adjacent cylinders do not run too close together. (Photo courtesy Champion Spark Plug Co.)

7. If your vehicle does not have electronic ignition, check the points, rotor and cap as specified.

8. Check the spark plug wires (used with conventional point-type ignitions) for cracks and burned or broken insulation by bending them in a loop around your finger. Cracked wires decrease fuel efficiency by failing to deliver full voltage to the spark plugs. One misfiring spark plug can cost you as much as 2 mpg.

9. Check the routing of the plug wires. Misfiring can be the result of spark plug leads to adjacent cylinders running parallel to each other and too close together. One wire tends to pick up voltage from the other causing it to fire "out of time".

10. Check all electrical and ignition circuits for voltage drop and resistance.

11. Check the distributor mechanical and/or vacuum advance mechanisms for proper functioning. The vacuum advance can be checked by twisting the distributor plate in the opposite direction of rotation. It should spring back when released.

12. Check and adjust the valve clearance on engines with mechanical lifters. The clearance should be slightly loose rather than too tight.

SPARK PLUG DIAGNOSIS

Normal

APPEARANCE: This plug is typical of one operating normally. The insulator nose varies from a light tan to grayish color with slight electrode wear. The presence of slight deposits is normal on used plugs and will have no adverse effect on engine performance. The spark plug heat range is correct for the engine and the engine is running normally.

CAUSE: Properly running engine.

RECOMMENDATION: Before reinstalling this plug, the electrodes should be cleaned and filed square. Set the gap to specifications. If the plug has been in service for more than 10-12,000 miles, the entire set should probably be replaced with a fresh set of the same heat range.

Oil Deposits

APPEARANCE: The firing end of the plug is covered with a wet, oily coating.

CAUSE: The problem is poor oil control. On high mileage engines, oil is leaking past the rings or valve guides into the combustion chamber. A common cause is also a plugged PCV valve, and a ruptured fuel pump diaphragm can also cause this condition. Oil fouled plugs such as these are often found in new or recently overhauled engines, before normal oil control is achieved, and can be cleaned and reinstalled.

RECOMMENDATION: A hotter spark plug may temporarily relieve the problem, but the engine is probably in need of work.

Incorrect Heat Range

APPEARANCE: The effects of high temperature on a spark plug are indicated by clean white, often blistered insulator. This can also be accompanied by excessive wear of the electrode, and the absence of deposits.

CAUSE: Check for the correct spark plug heat range. A plug which is too hot for the engine can result in overheating. A car operated mostly at high speeds can require a colder plug. Also check ignition timing, cooling system level, fuel mixture and leaking intake manifold.

RECOMMENDATION: If all ignition and engine adjustments are known to be correct, and no other malfunction exists, install spark plugs one heat range colder.

Photos Courtesy Fram Corporation

Carbon Deposits

APPEARANCE: Carbon fouling is easily identified by the presence of dry, soft, black, sooty deposits.

CAUSE: Changing the heat range can often lead to carbon fouling, as can prolonged slow, stop-and-start driving. If the heat range is correct, carbon fouling can be attributed to a rich fuel mixture, sticking choke, clogged air cleaner, worn breaker points, retarded timing or low compression. If only one or two plugs are carbon fouled, check for corroded or cracked wires on the affected plugs. Also look for cracks in the distributor cap between the towers of affected cylinders.

RECOMMENDATION: After the problem is corrected, these plugs can be cleaned and reinstalled if not worn severely.

MMT Fouled

APPEARANCE: Spark plugs fouled by MMT (Methycyclopentadienyl Maganese Tricarbonyl) have reddish, rusty appearance on the insulator and side electrode.

CAUSE: MMT is an anti-knock additive in gasoline used to replace lead. During the combustion process, the MMT leaves a reddish deposit on the insulator and side electrode.

RECOMMENDATION: No engine malfunction is indicated and the deposits will not affect plug performance any more than lead deposits (see Ash Deposits). MMT fouled plugs can be cleaned, regapped and reinstalled.

High Speed Glazing

APPEARANCE: Glazing appears as shiny coating on the plug, either yellow or tan in color.

CAUSE: During hard, fast acceleration, plug temperatures rise suddenly. Deposits from normal combustion have no chance to fluff-off; instead, they melt on the insulator forming an electrically conductive coating which causes misfiring.

RECOMMENDATION: Glazed plugs are not easily cleaned. They should be replaced with a fresh set of plugs of the correct heat range. If the condition recurs, using plugs with a heat range one step colder may cure the problem.

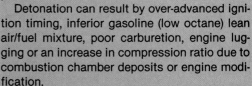

Ash (Lead) Deposits

APPEARANCE: Ash deposits are characterized by light brown or white colored deposits crusted on the side or center electrodes. In some cases it may give the plug a rusty appearance.

CAUSE: Ash deposits are normally derived from oil or fuel additives burned during normal combustion. Normally they are harmless, though excessive amounts can cause misfiring. If deposits are excessive in short mileage, the valve guides may be worn.

RECOMMENDATION: Ash-fouled plugs can be cleaned, gapped and reinstalled.

Detonation

APPEARANCE: Detonation is usually characterized by a broken plug insulator.

CAUSE: A portion of the fuel charge will begin to burn spontaneously, from the increased heat following ignition. The explosion that results applies extreme pressure to engine components, frequently damaging spark plugs and pistons.

Detonation can result by over-advanced ignition timing, inferior gasoline (low octane) lean air/fuel mixture, poor carburetion, engine lugging or an increase in compression ratio due to combustion chamber deposits or engine modification.

RECOMMENDATION: Replace the plugs after correcting the problem.

Photos Courtesy Champion Spark Plug Co.

EMISSION CONTROLS

13. Be aware of the general condition of the emission control system. It contributes to reduced pollution and should be serviced regularly to maintain efficient engine operation.

14. Check all vacuum lines for dried, cracked or brittle conditions. Something as simple as a leaking vacuum hose can cause poor performance and loss of economy.

15. Avoid tampering with the emission control system. Attempting to improve fuel econ-

FUEL SYSTEM

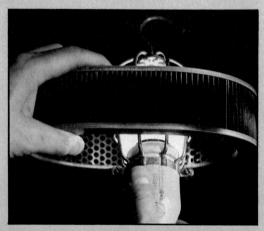

Check the air filter with a light behind it. If you can see light through the filter it can be reused.

Extremely clogged filters should be discarded and replaced with a new one.

18. Replace the air filter regularly. A dirty air filter richens the air/fuel mixture and can increase fuel consumption as much as 10%. Tests show that ⅓ of all vehicles have air filters in need of replacement.

19. Replace the fuel filter at least as often as recommended.

20. Set the idle speed and carburetor mixture to specifications.

21. Check the automatic choke. A sticking or malfunctioning choke wastes gas.

22. During the summer months, adjust the automatic choke for a leaner mixture which will produce faster engine warm-ups.

COOLING SYSTEM

29. Be sure all accessory drive belts are in good condition. Check for cracks or wear.

30. Adjust all accessory drive belts to proper tension.

31. Check all hoses for swollen areas, worn spots, or loose clamps.

32. Check coolant level in the radiator or expansion tank.

33. Be sure the thermostat is operating properly. A stuck thermostat delays engine warm-up and a cold engine uses nearly twice as much fuel as a warm engine.

34. Drain and replace the engine coolant at least as often as recommended. Rust and scale

TIRES & WHEELS

38. Check the tire pressure often with a pencil type gauge. Tests by a major tire manufacturer show that 90% of all vehicles have at least 1 tire improperly inflated. Better mileage can be achieved by over-inflating tires, but never exceed the maximum inflation pressure on the side of the tire.

39. If possible, install radial tires. Radial tires deliver as much as ½ mpg more than bias belted tires.

40. Avoid installing super-wide tires. They only create extra rolling resistance and decrease fuel mileage. Stick to the manufacturer's recommendations.

41. Have the wheels properly balanced.

omy by tampering with emission controls is more likely to worsen fuel economy than improve it. Emission control changes on modern engines are not readily reversible.

16. Clean (or replace) the EGR valve and lines as recommended.

17. Be sure that all vacuum lines and hoses are reconnected properly after working under the hood. An unconnected or misrouted vacuum line can wreak havoc with engine performance.

23. Check for fuel leaks at the carburetor, fuel pump, fuel lines and fuel tank. Be sure all lines and connections are tight.

24. Periodically check the tightness of the carburetor and intake manifold attaching nuts and bolts. These are a common place for vacuum leaks to occur.

25. Clean the carburetor periodically and lubricate the linkage.

26. The condition of the tailpipe can be an excellent indicator of proper engine combustion. After a long drive at highway speeds, the inside of the tailpipe should be a light grey in color. Black or soot on the insides indicates an overly rich mixture.

27. Check the fuel pump pressure. The fuel pump may be supplying more fuel than the engine needs.

28. Use the proper grade of gasoline for your engine. Don't try to compensate for knocking or "pinging" by advancing the ignition timing. This practice will only increase plug temperature and the chances of detonation or pre-ignition with relatively little performance gain.

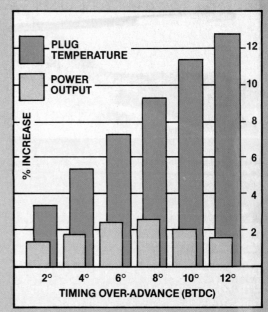

Increasing ignition timing past the specified setting results in a drastic increase in spark plug temperature with increased chance of detonation or preignition. Performance increase is considerably less. (Photo courtesy Champion Spark Plug Co.)

that form in the engine should be flushed out to allow the engine to operate at peak efficiency.

35. Clean the radiator of debris that can decrease cooling efficiency.

36. Install a flex-type or electric cooling fan, if you don't have a clutch type fan. Flex fans use curved plastic blades to push more air at low speeds when more cooling is needed; at high speeds the blades flatten out for less resistance. Electric fans only run when the engine temperature reaches a predetermined level.

37. Check the radiator cap for a worn or cracked gasket. If the cap does not seal properly, the cooling system will not function properly.

42. Be sure the front end is correctly aligned. A misaligned front end actually has wheels going in differed directions. The increased drag can reduce fuel economy by .3 mpg.

43. Correctly adjust the wheel bearings. Wheel bearings that are adjusted too tight increase rolling resistance.

Check tire pressures regularly with a reliable pocket type gauge. Be sure to check the pressure on a cold tire.

GENERAL MAINTENANCE

Check the fluid levels (particularly engine oil) on a regular basis. Be sure to check the oil for grit, water or other contamination.

A vacuum gauge is another excellent indicator of internal engine condition and can also be installed in the dash as a mileage indicator.

44. Periodically check the fluid levels in the engine, power steering pump, master cylinder, automatic transmission and drive axle.

45. Change the oil at the recommended interval and change the filter at every oil change. Dirty oil is thick and causes extra friction between moving parts, cutting efficiency and increasing wear. A worn engine requires more frequent tune-ups and gets progressively worse fuel economy. In general, use the lightest viscosity oil for the driving conditions you will encounter.

46. Use the recommended viscosity fluids in the transmission and axle.

47. Be sure the battery is fully charged for fast starts. A slow starting engine wastes fuel.

48. Be sure battery terminals are clean and tight.

49. Check the battery electrolyte level and add distilled water if necessary.

50. Check the exhaust system for crushed pipes, blockages and leaks.

51. Adjust the brakes. Dragging brakes or brakes that are not releasing create increased drag on the engine.

52. Install a vacuum gauge or miles-per-gallon gauge. These gauges visually indicate engine vacuum in the intake manifold. High vacuum = good mileage and low vacuum = poorer mileage. The gauge can also be an excellent indicator of internal engine conditions.

53. Be sure the clutch is properly adjusted. A slipping clutch wastes fuel.

54. Check and periodically lubricate the heat control valve in the exhaust manifold. A sticking or inoperative valve prevents engine warm-up and wastes gas.

55. Keep accurate records to check fuel economy over a period of time. A sudden drop in fuel economy may signal a need for tune-up or other maintenance.

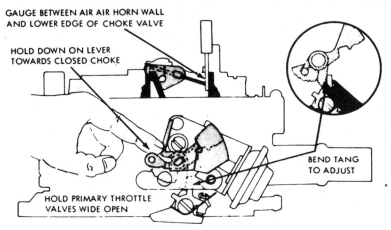

GAUGE BETWEEN AIR AIR HORN WALL AND LOWER EDGE OF CHOKE VALVE

HOLD DOWN ON LEVER TOWARDS CLOSED CHOKE

BEND TANG TO ADJUST

HOLD PRIMARY THROTTLE VALVES WIDE OPEN

Dechoke adjustment—Rochester Quadrajet

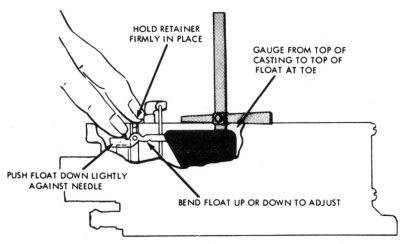

HOLD RETAINER FIRMLY IN PLACE

GAUGE FROM TOP OF CASTING TO TOP OF FLOAT AT TOE

PUSH FLOAT DOWN LIGHTLY AGAINST NEEDLE

BEND FLOAT UP OR DOWN TO ADJUST

Fuel float level adjustment

Carburetor Adjustments

	Choke Plate Pulldown Clearance Adjustment ± 0.010 in.	Fuel Float Level Adjustment ± $^{1}/_{32}$ in.	Dechoke Clearance Adjustment (Minimum)	Fast Idle Cam Index Setting	Air Valve Dashpot Adjustment ± $^{1}/_{64}$ in.
Autolite 1100	0.15 in.	$1^{3}/_{32}$ in.	$^{15}/_{64}$ in.	—	—
Carter YF	0.265 in.	$^{7}/_{32}$ in.	0.25 in.	0.035 in.	$^{7}/_{64}$ in.
Carter RBS	0.19 in.	$^{9}/_{16}$ in.	—	—	$^{7}/_{32}$ in.
Autolite 2100 Motorcraft 2100D	0.12 in.	$^{3}/_{8}$ in.	0.06 in.	0.11 in.	—
Autolite 4100	0.14 in.	pri $^{17}/_{32}$ in. sec $^{11}/_{16}$ in.	0.06 in.	0.12 in.	—
Autolite (Motorcraft) 4300	0.12 in.	$^{13}/_{16}$ in.	0.3 in.	0.09 in.	—
Holley 4150 and 4150C	—	—	—	—	—
Rochester Quadrajet	—	$^{5}/_{8}$ in.	0.3 in.	—	$^{1}/_{32}$ in.

3. To adjust, bend the float pontoon up or down at the point shown in the illustration.

4. Install a new air horn gasket on the float bowl, then install the air horn.

OVERHAUL

Carburetors are complex units whose proper performance depends upon the cleanliness of internal and external components and the proper adjustment of all parts. In addition to the usual adjustments made to external components at regular tune-up intervals, it eventually becomes advisable to remove, disassemble, clean, and overhaul the entire carburetor in order to restore its original performance. To overhaul a carburetor, one must first purchase the proper rebuilding kit. It is advisable to read the instructions and study the exploded view of the carburetor thoroughly, prior to the actual removal, disassembly, etc.

When the carburetor has been removed from the car and disassembled, the parts (except for the accelerator pump diaphragm, spark control valve, power valve, secondary operating diaphragm, antistall dashpot, and the carburetor solenoid, if so equipped) should be soaked in clean carburetor cleaning solvent, rinsed in clean kerosine to remove all traces of the cleaning solvent, and dried with compressed air to remove all traces of dirt from all passages. The use of rags should be avoided. Drills, wire brushes, and similar tools should never be used for carburetor cleaning. All traces of old gaskets should be removed from the parts prior to reassembly.

When reassembling any carburetor, all of the applicable new parts in the rebuilding kit should be used. One carburetor rebuilding kit is usually used for several different types of carburetors. There may be parts in the kit which are not applicable to your particular carburetor. Check the choke shaft for grooves, wear, and excessive looseness or binding. Inspect the choke plate for nicked edges and freedom of operation. Make sure that the automatic choke housing and piston are clean and the piston moves freely when installed in the housing. Check the throttle shafts in their bores for excessive looseness or damage and make sure that the throttle plates—when installed—close properly.

The float should be checked for leaks by immersing it in water which has been heated to just below the boiling point and watching carefully for bubbles. If bubbles appear, the float is leaking, and should be replaced. When installing the float, check for binding on its shaft. If binding occurs, check the shaft for grooves or damage, and replace it if necessary. When the float is installed, check its adjustment with the tool which is included in the carburetor rebuilding kit.

All stripped screws and nuts should be replaced, as should any distorted or broken springs.

If any gasket mating surfaces show damage, the part(s) involved should be replaced.

On carburetors equipped with an antistall dashpot, the rubber boot should be carefully checked for proper installation in the groove of the stem bushing. Check the stem movement for smooth, free operation and replace the assembly if it is damaged. Do not lubricate the stem.

CARBURETOR REMOVAL

1. Remove the air cleaner.

2. Remove the throttle cable or rod from the throttle lever. Disconnect the distributor vacuum line, the fuel line at the inline fuel filter, and the choke heat tube at the carburetor.

3. Disconnect the choke clean air line from the air horn.

4. Remove the carburetor retaining nuts. Pull the carburetor straight up to remove it from the intake manifold. If the fuel in the float bowl is to be examined for contamination, keep the carburetor in the right-side up position.

5. Remove the carburetor mounting gasket, the spacer (if so equipped), and the lower gasket from the intake manifold. Discard these old gaskets.

CARBURETOR INSTALLATION

1. Thoroughly clean the gasket surface of the carburetor, spacer, and intake manifold. Place the spacer (if so equipped) between two new gaskets and then place the spacer and gasket assembly on the intake manifold.

2. Place the carburetor onto the space (if so equipped) and gasket assembly, and install the retaining nuts. Alternately step-tighten the nuts.

3. Connect the fuel line at the inline fuel filter, throttle cable, choke heat tube, and distributor vacuum line.

4. Connect the choke clean air line to the air horn (if so equipped).

5. Perform the preliminary adjustments of idle speed and mixture settings. On car-

buretors not fitted with plastic limiter caps on the idle mixture adjusting screws, turn these screws clockwise until they lightly seat, and then turn them counterclockwise 1½ turns. Do not tighten the mixture setting screw(s) on any carburetor until they seat hard, as this will damage the tip of the screw and necessitate replacement. On carburetors with limiter caps, the mixture adjusting screw(s) should be turned to the full counterclockwise position. To adjust the idle speed adjusting screw, turn it clockwise until it barely contacts the screw stop on the throttle shaft and lever assembly, and then turn the screw clockwise another 1½ turns. Be sure that the dashpot (if so equipped) does not interfere with the operation of the throttle lever.

6. Start the engine and bring it to its full operating temperature. This may be accomplished by letting it run at high idle (approximately 1,500 rpm) for 20 minutes. When it is fully warmed, stop the engine.

7. Make sure that the ignition timing and distributor advance and retard are in proper adjustment before attempting the final carburetor adjustments.

8. On manual-shift cars, the carburetor idle adjustment should be made with the transmission in neutral. On automatics, the transmission should be in Drive for the idle adjustment. When adjusting the carburetor with the car in Drive, be sure that the wheels are adequately blocked.

9. See that the choke plate is in the full open position.

10. Attach an accurate tachometer to the engine, following the procedure recommended by the manufacturer of the instrument.

11. Remove the air cleaner, start the engine, and turn the headlights on high beam. On 1965–1969 cars, except 302 V8s with automatic transmissions and 200 cu in. six-cylinder engines, the air conditioning should be on. On all other cars, the air conditioning should be off.

12. If your car is equipped with a throttle solenoid, examine the solenoid assembly. It will consist of either an assembly held in place by a bracket with a locknut, a fixed assembly with a nut head on the end of the plunger, or an assembly which can be adjusted by turning a screw in the base of the assembly. Determine the type with which your car is equipped, and adjust it to obtain the correct idle. Bear in mind that the correct idle speed is, in this case, the higher figure of the two-figure specification. (See chapter two for idle speed specifications.) Disconnect the solenoid lead wire at the bullet connector and adjust the carburetor throttle stop adjusting screw to obtain an idle that corresponds with the lower figure in the two-figure specification. Connect the solenoid lead wire, open the throttle slightly by hand, and observe that the solenoid plunger follows the throttle lever and remains in the fully extended position while the ignition key is in the on position. Check the tachometer to be sure that the higher figure in the idle specification is obtained. Install the air cleaner, check this idle speed again, and adjust if the installation of the air cleaner affected the idle. Remember that the final idle speed must be obtained with the air cleaner installed.

13. On vehicles not equipped with a throttle solenoid, simply turn the throttle stop adjusting screw to obtain the specified idle. Install the air cleaner, check the idle, and adjust it if necessary.

14. To adjust the mixture on carburetors equipped with limiter caps, turn the adjusting screws(s) clockwise until the smoothest possible idle is obtained. On carburetors with more than one mixture adjusting screw, the screws should be turned an equal amount. Remember that you should be making this adjustment with the air cleaner installed.

15. On carburetors not equipped with limiter caps, turn the adjusting screw(s) in until the idle begins to drop slightly, and then out. As a general rule, one-barrel (1-bbl) carburetors require one-half to one full turn out, depending upon the point at which the smoothest idle is attained. Two-barrel carburetors usually require about one full turn. (In all cases adjustment is correct when the smoothest possible idle is attained.) Like those carburetors with limiter caps, this must be done with the air cleaner installed.

16. Adjust the fast idle by manually closing the choke plate, moving the fast idle cam until the fast idle adjusting screw rests on the proper step of the cam—usually indicated by an arrow on the cam—and adjusting the screw to fast idle specifications. When the adjustment has been made, allow all equipment, which you positioned for the adjustment, to return to its normal position.

17. When all other adjustments have been made and checked, the antistall dashpot

should be adjusted. First, refer to the accompanying chart to find the proper adjustment for your car. On all carburetors except the Autolite 1100, loosen the antistall dashpot locknut, hold the throttle in the closed position, and depress the plunger with a screwdriver blade. Measure the distance between the throttle lever and the plunger tip. Turn the antistall dashpot in whichever direction is necessary to attain the proper clearance between the tip of its plunger and the throttle lever. Tighten the locknut to secure the adjustment and check the adjustment to assure that it was not altered during tightening. On the Autolite 1100 carburetor, turn the dashpot adjusting screw outward until it is clear of the dashpot plunger assembly. Turn the same screw inward until it contacts the plunger assembly and then turn it in (clockwise) against the plunger assembly. On cars with manual transmissions, three turns in against the plunger assembly are required. On automatic models, two turns will suffice.

Dashpot Adjustment

| Model | Clearance (in.) | |
	Manual	Automatic
1965 2v carburetors		$5/64$
1965 4v carburetors		$5/16$
1966 2v carburetors		0.060–0.090
1966 4v carburetors		0.060–0.090
1967 289 2v with emission control		0.110–0.140
1967 390 4v with emission control		$1/8$
1968 390 2v		0.125
1968 390 4v		0.093
1968 428 4v		0.093
1969 302 2v	$1/8$	$1/8$
1969 351 2v	$7/64$	—
1969 351 4v	$3/32$	—
1969 390 4v	$1/8$	—
1969 429 4v	$3/32$	—
1970–72 302, 351		$1/8$
1970–72 429 4v		0.100

NOTE: *Many models are equipped with a solenoid instead of a dashpot.*

DASHPOT ADJUSTING SCREW

ADJUST TO CURB IDLE POSITION
BEFORE ADJUSTING DASHPOT

Antistall dashpot adjustment—Autolite 1100 1-V carburetor

FUEL TANK

REMOVAL

1. Raise the rear of the vehicle and position safety stands.
2. Remove the fuel tank drain plug and drain the fuel into a suitable container.
3. Disconnect the fuel gauge sending unit wire at the sending unit.
4. Loosen the hose clamp, slide the clamp forward, and disconnect the fuel line at the fuel gauge sending unit.

5. Disconnect the fuel tank vent hose at the tank, if so equipped.

If the fuel gauge sending unit is to be removed, turn the unit retaining ring counterclockwise and remove the sending unit retaining ring and gasket.

6. Remove the spare tire from the luggage compartment. Pull the compartment floor mat out of the way for access to the fuel tank.
7. Remove the fuel tank filler neck retaining screws.
8. Loosen the filler neck to tank hose clamps. Remove the filler neck, mounting gasket, and filler neck-to-tank hose.
9. Remove the fuel tank-to-luggage compartment floor pan retaining screws and remove the fuel tank.

NOTE: *On cars so equipped, the orifice vapor separator of the evaporative emission control system is removed and installed in the same manner as the fuel gauge sending unit.*

INSTALLATION

1. Make sure all the old sealer has been removed from the fuel tank mounting flange and mounting surface at the luggage compartment floor pan. Apply caulking cord to the fuel tank mounting surface at the luggage compartment floor pan.
2. Position the fuel tank to the luggage compartment floor pan and install the retaining screws.

3. Position the hose and filler neck assembly and gasket to the body back panel. Position the hose to the fuel tank neck.

4. Install the filler neck-to-body back panel retaining screws and tighten the hose clamps.

5. If the fuel gauge sending unit was removed, make sure all the old O-ring material has been removed from the unit mounting surface on the fuel tank. Using a new gasket, position the fuel gauge to the fuel tank and secure it with the retaining ring.

6. Position the luggage compartment floor mat and install the spare tire.

7. Connect the fuel gauge sending unit wire to the sending unit.

8. Connect the fuel line at the fuel gauge sending unit and tighten the hose clamps securely. Install the drain plug.

9. Connect the fuel tank vent hose, if so equipped.

10. Remove the safety stands and lower the vehicle.

11. Fill the tank and check all connections for leaks.

Chassis Electrical

HEATER

Factory Air Conditioned Cars

To service the heater and its components on cars equipped with factory air conditioning, it is first necessary to disconnect the refrigerant lines and purge the system. This—as discussed in chapter three—should be undertaken only by trained air conditioning servicemen. It is, therefore, advisable to refer any necessary heater/air conditioner system repairs to a reputable air conditioning mechanic.

Cars Without Air Conditioning
BLOWER MOTOR REMOVAL AND INSTALLATION

The blower motor on all models is located inside the heater assembly. To replace the blower motor, remove the heater assembly from the car following the steps in the above procedures. Once the heater assembly is removed, it is a simple operation to remove the motor attaching bolts and remove the motor. On all pre-1966 cars, the blower cage must be removed from the motor before the motor can be removed. On all post-1966 models, the motor and cage are removed as an assembly.

HEATER ASSEMBLY REMOVAL AND INSTALLATION
1965–1966

1. Partially drain the cooling system.
2. Remove the glove compartment.
3. Disconnect the three control cables.
4. Disconnect the defroster hoses at the plenum.
5. Disconnect the heater hoses at the water pump and carburetor heater and remove the hoses from the retaining clips. On V8 models remove the hoses from the choke clip.
6. Disconnect the motor wire and ground wire-to-dash panel retaining screw.
7. Remove the heater and motor assembly retaining nuts from the dash panel.
8. Disconnect the fresh-air inlet boot and pull the heater assembly from the panel.
9. Install in the reverse of above.

1967–1968

1. Disconnect the battery and drain the coolant.
2. Disconnect the heater hoses at the engine.
3. Loosen the screws at the choke housing and move the hose out of the way.
4. Remove the nuts retaining the heater to the dash.

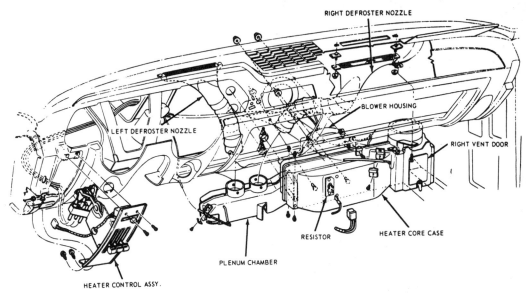

Heater assembly—typical pre-1969

5. Remove the screw retaining the ground wire at the dash and disconnect the two wires. Remove the glove box liner.

6. Disconnect the defroster hoses, temperature control cable, defroster control cable, and heat control cable.

7. Remove the screw retaining the heater to the air intake.

8. Remove the heater assembly from the vehicle pulling the hose through the dash.

9. Install in the reverse of above.

1969–1970

1. Disconnect the battery and drain the coolant.

2. Remove the instrument panel pad.

3. Remove the glove compartment liner and door.

4. Remove the air distribution duct from the heater.

5. Disconnect the control cables from the heater assembly.

6. Disconnect the wires from the blower motor resistor.

7. Remove the right courtesy light located on the underside of the instrument panel, if so equipped.

8. Remove the heater support-to-dash panel retaining screw.

9. Disconnect the vacuum hoses and remove the power air vent duct, if so equipped.

10. Remove the blower motor ground wire grounding screw.

11. Install in the reverse of above.

1971

1. Drain the coolant.

2. Disconnect both heater hoses at the dash.

3. Remove the nuts retaining the heater assembly to the dash.

4. Disconnect the temperature and defroster cables at the heater.

5. Disconnect the wires from the resistor, and disconnect the blower motor wires and clip retaining the heater assembly to the defroster nozzle.

6. Remove the glove box.

7. Remove the nuts retaining the right air duct and remove the duct assembly.

8. Remove the heater assembly.

9. Reverse the procedure for installation.

1972 and Later

1. Drain the engine coolant.

2. Disconnect the two heater hoses from the core tubes.

3. Remove the glove box for access and remove the right vent air duct assembly (one duct-to-upper cowl mounting screw and three duct-to-blower mounting nuts).

4. Disconnect the two control cables from the heater case assembly.

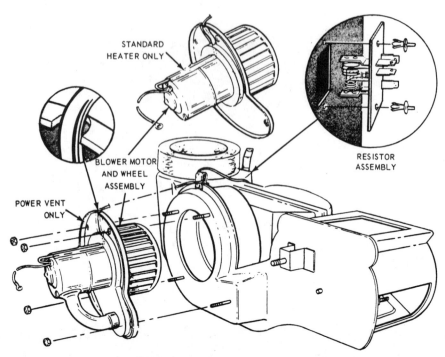

STANDARD HEATER ONLY

BLOWER MOTOR AND WHEEL ASSEMBLY

POWER VENT ONLY

RESISTOR ASSEMBLY

Heater assembly—typical 1969–72

5. Remove the defroster-to-plenum snap clip.

6. Disconnect the electrical wiring from the resistor assembly.

7. Remove the heater case assembly (four heater case-to-dash panel mounting stud nuts).

8. Install in the reverse of above.

HEATER CORE REMOVAL AND INSTALLATION

1965–1968

1. Remove the heater as above.

2. Remove the clips retaining the housing halves and separate the halves.

3. Lift the core from the housing chamber.

4. Install in the reverse of above.

1969–1970

1. Remove the heater assembly.

2. Remove the air inlet seal from the heater assembly.

3. Remove the eleven clips from the heater assembly flange and separate the heater assembly housing.

4. Remove the heater core from the heater assembly housing. Reverse the procedure for installation.

1971–1973

The heater core is located in the heater case in a diagonal position. It is serviced through an opening in the back plate. Remove the heater core cover and pad and remove the core. Reverse the procedure for installation.

RADIO

REMOVAL AND INSTALLATION

1965–1966

1. Pull the radio and control knobs off. Remove the nuts and washers retaining the radio to the instrument panel.

2. Disconnect the antenna lead at the right side of the radio.

3. Disconnect the speaker lead.

4. Disconnect the radio lead wire at the fuse panel and disconnect the pilot light wire. Remove the lead wire from the retaining clips.

5. Remove the radio right support bracket-to-radio retaining bolt. Remove the radio left support bracket-to-radio retaining nut (one bracket only on the Bendix radio).

6. Remove the radio assembly from the instrument panel.

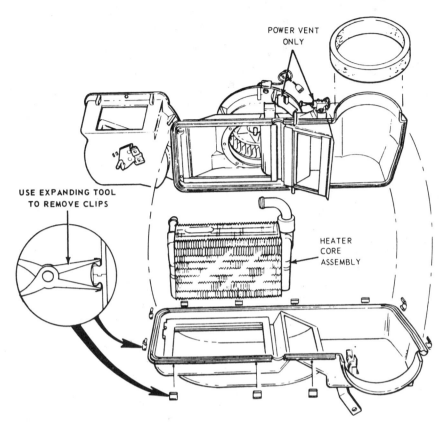

POWER VENT
ONLY

USE EXPANDING TOOL
TO REMOVE CLIPS

HEATER
CORE
ASSEMBLY

Heater core removal—typical 1969–73

7. Position the radio to the instrument panel, and install the washers and retaining nuts at the knob shafts. Be sure the radio mounting stud enters the support bracket.

8. Install the radio support bracket retaining nut and bolt. Tighten all mounting nuts to 25 in. lbs torque.

9. Connect the antenna lead to the radio.

10. Connect the radio speaker lead and the pilot light lead.

11. Connect the radio power lead and the pilot light lead.

12. Install the radio control knobs.

13. Check the radio operation and adjust the antenna trimmer.

1967–1968 without Console

1. Disconnect the battery.

2. Remove the rear support bracket attaching nut.

3. Remove the four screws that attach the bezel and receiver to the instrument panel.

4. Move the receiver rearward away from the instrument panel.

5. Disconnect the antenna, speaker and power leads, and remove the receiver from the instrument panel.

6. To install, position the radio under the instrument panel and connect the speaker, antenna, and power leads.

7. Secure the receiver to the instrument panel with attaching screws.

8. Secure the rear support bracket to the receiver with the attaching nut.

9. Connect the battery.

10. Check operation of the radio.

1967–1968 with Console

1. Disconnect the battery.

2. Remove the two screws attaching the right and left supports to the support bracket.

3. Remove the console assembly.

4. Disconnect the radio wiring and antenna lead.

5. Remove the control knobs from the radio.

6. Remove the two nuts and washers from the radio shafts and remove the radio.

7. To install, position the radio in the opening and install the nuts and washers on the control shafts.

8. Install the control knobs.

9. Connect the radio wires and antenna lead cable.

10. Install the console assembly.

11. Install the two screws attaching the right and left supports to the support bracket.

12. Connect the battery.

1969–1973

1. Disconnect the battery.

2. Pull the control knobs, discs, and sleeve from the radio control shafts.

3. Remove the radio applique from the instrument panel.

4. Remove the right and left finish panels.

5. Remove the two mounting plate attaching screws.

6. Pull the radio out of the instrument panel and disconnect the wires from the radio.

7. Remove the mounting plate and rear support from the radio.

8. Remove the radio.

9. To replace, install the mounting plate and rear support on the radio.

10. Position the radio near the opening and connect the wires to the radio.

11. Install the jumper wire to ground the radio to the instrument panel.

12. Connect the battery and check the operation of the radio.

13. Adjust the antenna trimmer.

14. Disconnect the battery and remove the jumper cable.

15. Insert the radio and wires into the panel opening. Be sure the radio rear support slips over the instrument panel reinforcement.

16. Install the mounting plate attaching screws.

17. Install the left and right finish panels.

18. Install the radio applique, sleeve, discs, and control knobs.

19. Connect the radio ground cable and set push buttons.

WINDSHIELD WIPER MOTOR

REMOVAL AND INSTALLATION
1965–1966

1. Disconnect the harness from the wiper motor.

2. Remove the three bolts retaining the

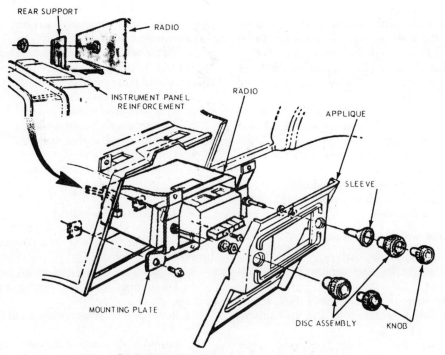

Radio installation—typical of 1969–73 cars

wiper motor and the mounting bracket assembly to the dash panel.

3. Lower the assembly and disconnect the wiper links at the motor.

4. Remove the motor and bracket assembly.

5. To install, assemble the motor and bracket assembly and connect the wiper links to the motor.

6. Install the motor and bracket assembly on the dash by installing the three retaining bolts.

7. Connect the harness connector to the wiper motor.

8. Connect the battery and check the operation of the wiper motor.

1967–1968

1. Disconnect the battery.

2. Remove the courtesy light. If the car is air-conditioned, lower the air conditioner to the floor.

3. Disconnect the wiper motor plug connector.

4. Remove the nut retaining the pivot arm and wiper arms to the motor.

5. Remove the bolts and star washers retaining the motor to the mounting bracket and remove the motor.

6. To install the motor, attach the motor to the mounting bracket with the bolts and star washers.

7. Position the pivot arm and wiper arms on the motor and install the retaining nut.

8. Connect the motor wire plug and battery.

9. Check the motor operation and install the courtesy light and air conditioner.

1969–1970

1. Remove the wiper arm and blade assemblies from the pivot shafts and disconnect the left-side washer hose at the T fitting on the cowl grille.

2. Remove the eight screws and the cowl top grille.

3. The motor is located inside the left fresh air plenum chamber. Disconnect the motor ground wire by removing one screw at the forward edge of the plenum chamber.

4. Disconnect the motor wire at the plug and push it back into the plenum chamber.

5. Disconnect the linkage drive arm from the motor output arm crank pin by removing the retaining clip.

6. Remove the three bolts that retain the motor to the mounting bracket, rotate the motor output arm 180°, and remove the motor.

7. Before installing motor, rotate the output arm 180°. Before connecting the linkage drive arm to the motor, turn the ignition to "acc" position to allow the motor to go to the park position.

1971–1973

1. Disconnect the battery and wiper motor connector.

2. Remove the cowl top left vent screen by removing the four retaining drive pins.

3. Remove the wiper link retaining clip from the wiper motor arm.

4. Remove the three wiper motor retaining bolts and the wiper motor and mounting bracket.

5. To install the motor, place the wiper motor and mounting bracket against the dash panel and install the three retaining bolts.

6. Position the wiper link on the motor drive arm and install the connecting clip. Be sure to force the clip locking flange into the locked position as shown in the figure.

7. Install the cowl top vent screen and secure it with four drive pins.

8. Check the motor operation and connect the wiring plugs.

Vacuum Headlight Doors

Vacuum is supplied by the intake manifold and is distributed, by a valve through an orange hose, to a check valve which is used in the vacuum source line to prevent vacuum from leaking from the reservoir back through the engine.

A white hose connects the check valve to the vacuum reservoir tank which stores enough vacuum to permit limited operation of the headlight covers without the car engine running.

Another white hose comes from the check valve and supplies vacuum to the center connector on the distribution valve mounted on the back of the headlight switch. When the switch is pulled out, it actuates the distribution valve and supplies vacuum through the green hose to the open side port of the vacuum motor and opens the headlight covers.

When the switch is pushed in to turn the headlights off, it actuates the distribution valve and supplies vacuum through the yellow hose to the closed side port of the vacuum motor and closes the headlight covers.

A by-pass valve is provided between the

headlight switch and the vacuum motor to vent the system and allow the covers to open when they will not automatically open.

VACUUM MOTOR
Removal and Installation

1. Remove the spring clip that connects the motor push rod to the cover actuating shaft.
   a. Push the clip tab out to release the clip and then pull the clip up and off.
2. Remove the bolts that retain the bumper lower extension and let it hang on the parking light leads.
3. Disconnect the vacuum hoses.
4. Remove the motor attaching nuts and remove the motor from under the car.
5. Position the vacuum motor and install the retaining nuts.
6. Connect the vacuum hoses.
7. Position the bumper lower extension and replace the retaining bolts.
8. Connect the motor push rod to the cover actuating shaft and install the spring clip.

VACUUM RESERVOIR
Removal and Installation

1. Remove the four bolts which retain the reservoir to the bracket behind the left headlights.
2. Disconnect the vacuum hose from the reservoir and remove the reservoir.
3. Connect the vacuum hose to the reservoir.
4. Position the reservoir to the retaining bracket and install the four retaining bolts.

HEADLIGHT COVERS WON'T OPEN

1. Turn on the headlight switch.
2. Turn the by-pass valve to the parallel position and see if the covers open.
3. If they do open, check the yellow and green hoses between the by-pass valve and the headlight switch for kinks or cracks.
4. If the hoses are in good condition, replace the headlight switch.
5. If the covers do not open when the by-pass valve is turned parallel, check the yellow and green hoses between the by-pass valve and the vacuum motor or motors for kinks or cracks.
6. If the hoses are in good condition replace the by-pass valve.

NOTE: *On models not having a by-pass valve, check for a plugged venting hole on the headlight switch.*

HEADLIGHT COVERS WON'T CLOSE

1. If the car contains a by-pass valve located between the headlight switch and the motor or motors, make sure it is in the normal position.
2. Start the engine and check for vacuum at the orange hose that connects the intake manifold to the check valve.
3. If there is no vacuum available, check the orange hose for leaks or kinks.
4. If vacuum is available, turn off the headlight switch and leak test the white hose that connects the check valve to the headlight switch. Leak test it again with the switch on.
5. Leak test the vacuum motor, headlight switch, and vacuum reservoir and replace if necessary.
6. Check the yellow and green vacuum hoses, between each component, for kinks or leaks.
7. Check for a plugged venting hole on the headlight switch.

VACUUM TEST PROBE

A vacuum probe tester cannot be obtained commercially, but can be made easily.

1. Cut a length of $3/16$ in. vacuum hose long enough to reach from the engine intake manifold to any part of the vacuum system.
2. Insert a four-way connector into the working end of the hose.
3. Attach a vacuum gauge to one of the four-way connector nipples.
4. Install a short length of $3/16$ in. hose, with an adjustable hose restrictor, onto another nipple of the four-way connector. An adjustable hose restrictor may be obtained from some automatic transmission tester kits.
5. Install a short length of hose onto the last nipple of the four-way connector. Insert a tee connector into this hose.
6. Install a short length of hose to the two open ends of the tee connector.
7. Install a $3/16$–$1/8$ in. reducer in one hose and a $3/16$ in. splice connector in the other hose.
8. By adding or removing connectors (splices) to these test probe hoses, they can be connected to any $3/16$–$1/8$ in. hose, nipple, or connector, while the other test hose is plugged; or both the $3/16$ and $1/8$ in. tester probes can be used at the same time.
9. To adjust the probe to the required 14 in. of test vacuum, plug the test probe hoses into the vacuum source at the carburetor.

10. Adjust the hose restrictor until the vacuum gauge reads 14 in.

HEADLIGHT COVER VACUUM SYSTEM LEAK TEST

1. A leak test on any part or component of the headlight cover vacuum system can be done with the use of the vacuum test probe.

2. Plug the probe into the system at the desired point.

3. The reading on the gauge should momentarily fall below the preset valve of 14 in.

4. If there are no leaks in the part being checked, the gauge reading should come back to 14 in. of vacuum and hold.

5. If there is a leak in the part being checked, the gauge reading will not come up to 14 in. of vacuum.

HEADLIGHT SWITCH LEAK TEST

1. Connect the vacuum test probe to the center (white) port of the headlight switch.

2. Cap the two outside ports of the headlight switch.

3. Move the switch selector thru the OFF-PARK-ON positions.

4. The gauge should read 14 in. of vacuum in each position.

5. If the gauge reading should fall off at any position, the switch should be replaced.

INSTRUMENT CLUSTER

REMOVAL AND INSTALLATION

1965–1966

1. Disconnect the battery cable.

2. Disconnect the speedometer cable from the speedometer head.

3. Remove the six screws retaining the instrument cluster assembly to the instrument panel and tilt the cluster forward.

4. Disconnect the wiring and the bulb sockets and remove the cluster assembly.

   NOTE: *All individual instruments may be removed and serviced at this time.*

5. Position the cluster and connect the wiring and bulb sockets.

6. Install the instrument cluster assembly to the instrument panel with the six retaining screws.

7. Connect the speedometer cable and the battery cable.

8. Check the operation of all gauges, lights, and signals.

1967–1968

1. Disconnect the battery.

2. Cover the steering column.

3. Remove the instrument panel front pad assembly retaining screws and remove the pad assembly.

4. Remove the four screws retaining the heater control assembly to the instrument panel and position the control assembly outward.

5. Reaching through the heater control opening, disconnect the speedometer cable from the speedometer.

6. Remove the three ash tray receptacle retaining screws.

7. Disconnect the cigar lighter element wiring connector and remove the ash tray receptacle.

8. Reaching through the ash tray opening, remove the nut and washer which retain the inboard end of the instrument cluster to the instrument panel.

9. Remove the seven external screws retaining the instrument cluster to the instrument panel.

10. Position the cluster assembly to outward, disconnect the two multiple connectors and remove the instrument cluster. Reverse the procedure for installation.

1969–1973

1. Disconnect the battery.

2. Remove the cluster opening finish panel from the pad assembly below the instrument cluster (two screws).

3. Remove the right and left lower end moldings for access to the pad retaining screws at the lower ends of the instrument panel.

4. Remove the three pad retaining screws from the top inner edge of the pad-to-pad support.

5. Remove the two retaining screws from the right and left lower pad end.

6. Remove the three retaining screws from the lower right pad to the instrument panel.

7. Pull the pad assembly back, disconnect the clock and courtesy light wires behind the right side of pad, and remove the pad assembly.

8. Remove the six screws retaining the cluster to the instrument panel and withdraw the cluster slightly.

9. Disconnect the multiple plug to the printed circuit and the tachometer plug, if so equipped.

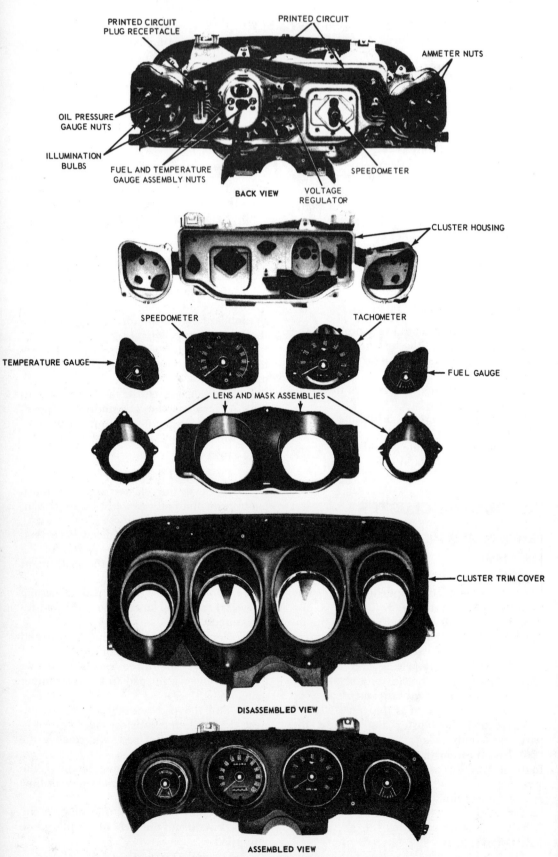

Instrument cluster—1970 shown, typical of late models

FIXED STEERING COLUMN

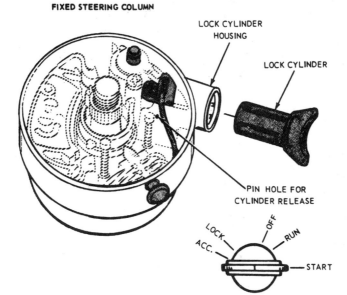

LOCK CYLINDER
HOUSING

LOCK CYLINDER

PIN HOLE FOR
CYLINDER RELEASE

LOCK CYLINDER
OPERATING PATTERN

Lock cylinder removal and installation

10. Disconnect the speedometer cable by pressing on the flat surface of the plastic connector and pulling the cable away from the speedometer.

11. Remove the cluster. Reverse the procedure for installation.

IGNITION SWITCH

LOCK CYLINDER REPLACEMENT

1965–1969

1. Insert the key and turn to "acc" position.

2. With a stiff wire in the hole, depress the lockpin and rotate the cylinder counterclockwise, then pull out the cylinder.

1970–1973

1. Disconnect the negative battery cable.

2. On cars with a fixed steering column, remove the steering wheel trim pad and the steering wheel. Insert a stiff wire into the hole located in the lock cylinder housing. On cars with a tilt steering wheel, this hole is located on the outside of the steering column near the emergency flasher button and it is not necessary to remove the steering wheel.

3. Place the gear shift lever in reverse on standard-shift cars and in Park on cars with automatic transmissions, then turn the ignition key to the "on" position.

4. Depress the wire and remove the lock cylinder and wire.

5. Insert a new cylinder into the housing and turn it to the "off" position. This will lock the cylinder into position.

6. Reinstall the steering wheel and pad.

7. Connect the negative battery cable.

IGNITION SWITCH REPLACEMENT

1965–69

1. Remove the cylinder as above.

2. Press in on the rear of the switch and rotate the switch one-eighth turn counterclockwise. Remove the bezel, switch, and spacer.

3. Remove the nut from the back of the switch. Remove the accessory and gauge feed wires from the accessory terminal. Pull the insulated plug from the rear of the switch.

4. Install in the reverse of above.

1970–1973

1. Disconnect the battery.

2. Remove the shrouding from the steering column, and detach and lower the steering column from the brake support bracket.

3. Disconnect the switch wiring at the multiple plug.

4. Remove the two nuts that retain the switch to the steering column

5. Detach the switch plunger from the switch actuator rod and remove the switch.

6. To reinstall the switch, place both the locking mechanism at the top of the column

and the switch itself in the lock position for the correct adjustment. To hold the column in the lock position, place the automatic shift lever in Park or the manual shift lever in reverse, turn to "lock," and remove the key. New switches are held in the lock by plastic shipping pins. To pin the existing switches, pull the switch plunger out as far as it will go and push it back in to the first detent. Insert a $^3/_{32}$ in. diameter wire in the locking hole in top of the switch.

RELEASE–PIN HOLE

Ignition switch removal

7. Connect the switch plunger to the switch actuator rod.

8. Position the switch on the column and install the attaching nuts. Do not tighten them.

9. Move the switch up and down to locate the middle position of rod lash, and then tighten the nuts.

10. Remove the locking pin or wire.

11. Attach the steering column-to-brake support bracket and install the shrouding.

WIRING DIAGRAMS

Wiring diagrams have been left out of this book. As cars have become more complex, and available with longer and longer option lists, wiring diagrams have grown in size and complexity also. It has become virtually impossible to provide a readable reproduction in a reasonable number of pages. Information on ordering wiring diagrams from the vehicle manufacturer can be found in the owners manual.

Turn Signal Flasher Locations

Year	Location
1965	Back of instrument panel, on the steering column brace
1966	Back of instrument panel, on the steering column brace
1967	Front side of the air duct, under instrument panel
1968	Right of the steering column, under the instrument panel
1969	Lower left edge of radio opening, under the instrument panel
1970	Under the instrument panel, to the right of the ash tray
1971	Bracket above the glove box, under the instrument panel
1972– 73	Bracket above the glove box, under the instrument panel

Light Bulb Specifications

Unit	Candela or ① Wattage	Trade Number	1965	1966	1967	1968	1969	1970	1971	1972–73
EXTERIOR										
Headlamp	40/50W	6012	X	X	X	X		X	X	X②
Hi-Low Beam	37.5/50W	4002					X			
Hi-Beam	37.5/50W	4001					X			
Fog Lamp	35W	4415	X	X	X	X	X	X	X	X
Front Turn Signal/Parking Lamp	4-32C	1157	X	X						
	4-32C	1157A			X	X				
	3-32C	1157A					X	X	X	X
Taillight/Stop/Turn Signal	4-32C	1157	X	X						
	4-32C	1157-A			X	X				
	3-32C	1157-A					X	X	X	X
License Plate Lamp	4C	1155	X	X						
	4C	97			X	X	X	X	X	X
Back-Up Lamps	21C	1142	X	X	X	X	X			
	32C	1156						X	X	X
Spotlight (4.4 in. Diameter)	30W	4405	X	X	X	X	X	X	X	X
Front Side Marker	4C	1178-A				X	X			
	4C	97-A						X		
	2C	194							X	X
Rear Side Marker	2C	194					X	X	X	X
Turn Signal Indicator (on hood)	1C	53X				X		X		
	2C	1895						X		
Hood-Mounted Turn Signals (Mach 1)	1C	53X					X			
Sport Lamps	15C	96							X	X
INTERIOR										
Luggage Compartment	6C	631	X	X	X	X	X	X	X	X
Dome Lamp	15C	1003	X	X	X	X	X			
	12C	105						X	X	
	12C	561								X
Glove Compartment	2C	1895	X	X		X			X	X
	1.5C	1445	X•	X•	X					
	2C	1891					X	X		
Map Light	6C	631	X	X	X	X				
	15C	1004						X		
	6C	212							X	X
Roof Console Map Light	6C	631					X			
Engine Compartment Lamp	6C	631			X	X	X	X	X	X
Courtesy Lamps (Under Inst. Panel)	6C	631			X	X	X	X③	X	X
Courtesy Lamps (Door-Mounted)	15C	1003	X	X						
	15C	1004			X					
	6C	631				X				
	6C	212					X	X		
Courtesy Lamp (Console)	3C	1816	X	X		X				
	2C	1895			X					
	1.5C	1445					X			
Courtesy Lamp (C-Pillar)	12C	105						X		
Portable Trunk Lamp	15C	1003					X	X	X	X
INSTRUMENTATION										
Emergency Flasher Indicator	2C	1895	X	X	X	X				
High Beam Indicator	2C	1895	X	X	X	X				
	2C	194					X	X	X	X
Parking Brake Warning Light	1.6C	256	X	X	X	X	X	X	X	X
Parking Brake Reminder	2C	158							X	X
Cigar Lighter	2C	1895			X	X			X	X
Ash Tray Lamp (Console)	1.3C	1892						X		
Ash Tray Lamp (Inst. Panel)	1.5C	1445						X		
Oil, Gen (or Alt) & Temp Warning	2C	1895	X	X	X	X				
	2C	194					X	X④	X	X
Service Brake Warning Light	2C	194					X	X	X	X
Turn Signal Indicators	2C	1895	X	X	X⑤	X				
	2C	194					X⑥	X⑥	X⑥	X⑥

Light Bulb Specifications (cont.)

Unit	Candela or ① Wattage	Trade Number	1965	1966	1967	1968	1969	1970	1971	1972–73
INSTRUMENTATION										
Clock	2C	1895	X⑦	X⑦	X⑦	X⑦	X	X		
	2C	194							X	X
Automatic Transmission Selector	2C	1895	X	X						
	1.5C	1445			X			X	X	X
Heater/AC Controls	1.9C	1893				X	X			
	2C	1895	X	X	X	X	X	X		
	1C	161							X	X
Radio Pilot Light (AM)	1.9C	1893	X	X	X	X	X	X	X	X
Radio Pilot Light (FM)	1.3C	1892					X			
AM/FM Radio Stereo Jewel	1.9C	1893						X	X	X
	1.3C	1892								X
Tachometer	2C	1895	X	X	X	X	X⑧			
Instrument Cluster	2C	1895	X	X	X	X				
	2C	194					X	X	X	X
Seat Belt Warning	2C	1895			X	X	X⑨			
	1.5C	1445						X⑨	X	X
Fog Light Switch	1C	53-X					X	X	X	X
"Headlight On" Light	1.6C	—						X		
Headlight Switch Bezel	2C	1895							X	X
Wiper/Washer Bezel	2C	1895							X	X
Open Door Warning	2C	1895							X	X
Auxiliary Instrument (Chg. Ind)	2C	1895							X	X
Rear Window Electric Defroster Indicator	Bulb and Wire Ass'y								X	X

① Candela is the New International Term for Candlepower.
② On Vehicles Built After 1-3-72, The 50-60W Bulb No. 6014 is used.
③ Models 63 & 76 Use Fuse-Type Light #562.
④ Oil & Alt Warning Light Used With Tachometer Installation Only.
⑤ Minnesota and Wisconsin Require 1895-G.
⑥ Turn Signal Indicators are also Emergency Flasher Indicators.
⑦ 3C-1816 For Rally-Pac.
⑧ Included in instrument cluster.
⑨ Convenience package uses 2C-1891.
● Console Glove Box.

Fuses and Circuit Breakers

Unit	Location	Rating Type	1965	1966	1967	1968	1969	1970	1971	1972–73
Dome Courtesy—Map Cargo	Fuse Panel	7½ SFE	X	X	X	X				
		14 SFE					X	X	X	X
Tail—Park, License, and Stop Lights, Horn, and Side Markers	Light Switch	15 C.B.	X	X	X	X	X	X	X	X
Clock	Fuse Panel	7½ SFE	X	X	X	X				
		14 SFE					X	X	X	X
Back-Up Lamp	Fuse Panel	14 SFE	X	X	X	X				
		AGC or 20 SFE					X			
		AGC or 15 SFE						X	X	X
Turn Signals		Flasher Acts as Circuit Breaker								
Radio	Fuse Panel (Acc. Socket)	14 SFE	X	X	X	X				
		AGC or 15 SFE						X	X	X

Fuses and Circuit Breakers (cont.)

	Location	Rating Type	1965	1966	1967	1968	1969	1970	1971	1972–73
Heater (Non A/C)	Fuse Panel	14 SFE	X	X	X	X	X	X	X	X
Heater (With A/C)	Fuse Panel	8 AG or AGX 30				X	X	X	X	X
Heater Dial	Fuse Panel Heater Socket	14 SFE	X	X						
Cigar Lighter	Fuse Panel	14 SFE	X	X		X		X	X	X
		AGC or 20 SFE			X		X			
Emergency Warning Flasher	Fuse Panel	20 SFE	X	X	X	X	X	X	X	X
Tachometer	Fuse Panel	7½ SFE	X	X						
		AGA 2.5			X	X				
Convertible Top	Between Starter Relay and Junction Block	Fuse Link	X	X	X	X	X			
	Attached to Starter Motor Relay	20 C.B.						X	X	X
Power Windows and Seats	On Starter Relay	20 B.C.	X	X	X	X	X	X	X	X
Motors—Windshield Wiper, Conv. Top, Power Windows and Seats	Part of Each Motor	C.B.	X	X	X	X	X	X	X	X
Power Window Relay Feed	Fuse Panel	AGC or 20 SFE					X			
Windshield Wiper (1 speed)	Wiper Switch	5 C.B.	X	X						
		6 C.B.			X	X	X	X	X	X
Windshield Washer	Fuse Panel Acc. Socket	14 SFE	X	X						
		AGC or 15 SFE						X	X	X
Instrument Panel Lights Instrument Cluster, Clock, Tachometer ②, Ash Receptacle, Auto. Trans. Quadrant, Radio Light, Wiper and Washer Controls	Fuse Panel ①	2½ AGA	X	X	X	X				
		4 SFE						X	X	X
Auto. Trans. Quadrant (Console)	Fuse Panel	14 SFE	X	X	X	X				
		AGC or 20 SFE					X			
		15 C.B.						X	X	X
Luggage Compartment Light	Fuse Panel	7½ SFE	X	X	X	X				
		14 SFE					X	X	X	X
Glove Box Light	Fuse Panel	7½ SFE	X	X	X	X				
		14 SFE					X	X	X	X
Spotlight	Inline	7½ SFE	X	X						
Headlamps	Light Switch	12 C.B.				X	X	X	X	X
		18 C.B.					X			
Air Conditioner (Integrated)	Ignition Switch	25 C.B.	X	X	X					
		SFE 30					X			
Air Conditioner (Economy)	Inline From Acc. Terminal of Ignition Switch	AGC-15	X	X	X					
Courtesy Light	Fuse Panel	7½ SFE			X	X				
		14 SFE					X	X	X	X
Door Ajar Lamps and Seat Belt Warning	Fuse Panel	7½ SFE			X	X				
		AGC or 20 SFE					X			

Fuses and Circuit Breakers (cont.)

	Location	Rating Type	1965	1966	1967	1968	1969	1970	1971	1972–73
Map Light	Fuse Panel	7½ SFE			X	X				
		14 SFE					X	X	X	X
Turn Signals	Fuse Panel	14 SFE			X	X				
		AGC or 20 SFE					X	X	X	X
Speed Control	Inline From Acc. Terminal of Ignition Switch	7½ SFE			X	X				
		AGC or 20 SFE					X			
Parking Brake Warning	Inline	7½ SFE			X	X				
		AGC or 15 SFE						X	X	X
Defogger	Inline	7½ SFE				X				
Engine Compartment Light	Fuse Panel	7½ SFE				X	X	X	X	X
Fog Lights	Fuse Panel	10 C.B.				X	X			
Swing-Tilt Steering Wheel	Inline	7½ SFE				X				
		AGC or 20 SFE					X			
Horns	Headlight Switch	15 C.B.					X	X	X	X
Emission Control And/Or Throttle Solenoid		14 SFE						X	X	X
Stop Lights	Headlight Switch	15 C.B.						X	X	X
Taillights	Headlight Switch	15 C.B.						X	X	X
Front Seat Back Latch Solenoid	Integral with Solenoid	C.B.							X	X
Intermittent Windshield Wiper		7 C.B.							X	X

① Instrument LP Socket Connected To 15 C.B. Light Switch.
② 1967–73

Clutch and Transmission

MANUAL TRANSMISSION

Five different transmissions have been offered, depending on year. These include:
• Ford-designed, light-duty, top cover, 2.77 three-speed with non-synchromesh low gear, used in 1965 and 1966 six-cylinder cars.
• Ford-designed, heavy-duty, top cover, fully synchronized 3.03 three-speed used with six-cylinder engines from 1967 to the present, and in all V8 applications.
NOTE: *The designations 2.77 and 3.03 refer to the distance in inches between the centerlines of the countershaft and the input shaft.*
• Dagenham-designed, light-duty, side cover, fully-synchronized four-speed, used on six-cylinder cars in 1965 and 1966.
• Borg-Warner T-10, heavy-duty, side cover, all-synchromesh four-speed, offered as an option in early high-performance 289 V8s.
• Ford-designed, heavy-duty, top cover, fully-synchronized four-speed transmission, used as the standard four-speed with V8s.

CLUTCH AND/OR TRANSMISSION REMOVAL

1. Disconnect and remove the starter and dust ring, if the clutch is to be removed.

2. Raise the car. Remove the boot retainer and the shift lever.
3. Disconnect the driveshaft at the rear universal joint and remove the driveshaft.
4. Disconnect the speedometer cable at the transmission extension. On cars with the Transmission-Regulated Spark, disconnect the lead wire at the connector.
5. Disconnect the gear shift rods from the transmission shift levers. If car is equipped with a four-speed, remove the bolts that secure the shift control bracket to the extension housing.
6. Remove the bolt holding the extension housing to the rear support, and remove the muffler inlet pipe bracket-to-housing bolt.
7. Remove the two rear support bracket insulator nuts from the underside of the crossmember. Remove the crossmember.
8. Place a jack (equipped with a protective piece of wood) under the rear of the engine oil pan. Raise the engine, slightly.
9. Remove transmission-to-flywheel housing bolts. On clutch removal only, thread the guide studs into the bottom attaching bolt holes.
NOTE: *On 429 cu in. engines the upper left-hand transmission attaching bolt is a seal bolt. Carefully note its position so that it may be reinstalled in its original position.*

10. Slide the transmission back and out of the car.

11. Remove the release lever retracting spring and disconnect the pedal at the equalizer bar.

12. Remove the bolts and secure the engine rear plate to the front lower part of the bellhousing.

13. Remove the bolts that attach the bell housing to the cylinder block and remove the housing and release lever as a unit.

14. Loosen the six pressure plate cover attaching bolts evenly to release spring pressure. Mark the cover and flywheel to facilitate reassembly in the same position.

15. Remove the six attaching bolts while holding the pressure plate cover. Remove the pressure plate and clutch disc.

CLUTCH AND/OR TRANSMISSION INSTALLATION

1. Wash the flywheel surface with alcohol.

2. Attach the clutch disc and pressure plate assembly to the flywheel with the bolts finger-tight.

3. Align the clutch disc with a pilot tool. Torque the cover bolts to 23–28 ft. lbs. on 1965–66 vehicles and to 12–20 ft. lbs. on 1967–73 vehicles.

4. Lightly lubricate the release lever fulcrum ends. Install the release lever in the flywheel housing and install the dust shield.

5. Apply very little lubricant on the release bearing retainer journal. Attach the release bearing and hub on the release lever.

6. Install the flywheel housing and torque the attaching bolts to 40–50 ft. lbs. on all 1965 vehicles and on the 1966–73 V8s. 1966–73 sixes to 23–33 ft. lbs. Install the dust cover and torque the bolts to 17–20 ft. lbs.

7. Connect the release rod and the retracting spring. Connect the pedal-to-equalizer rod at the equalizer bar.

8. Install the starter and dust ring.

9. Start the transmission extension housing up and over the rear support. After moving the transmission back just far enough for the pilot shaft to clear the clutch housing, move it upward and into position on the transmission guide studs.

10. Move the transmission forward and place it against the flywheel housing.

11. Remove the guide studs and attach the transmission with a torque of 37–42 ft. lbs. on all cars except 1965–66 models with six-cylinder engines and four-speed transmissions. Torque 1965–66 six-cylinder, four-speed cars to 40–45 ft. lbs.

12. Position the crossmember into the frame, and install the retaining bolts. Lower the engine onto the crossmember.

13. Install and torque the insulator-to-crossmember nuts to 25–35 ft. lbs. on all 1965–69 vehicles except 1968–69 390, 427, and 428 CJ models. Torque 1968–69 390, 427, and 428 CJ models to 30–42 ft. lbs. Torque 1970–73 models to 25–35 ft. lbs.

14. Connect the gear shift rods and the speedometer cable. Install the gearshift lever and boot retainer. On cars with TRS, connect the lead wire at the transmission.

15. Hook up the driveshaft.

16. Refill the transmission to the proper level.

LINKAGE ADJUSTMENT

3-Speed Floor and Console Shift Linkage

1. Loosen the three shift linkage adjustment nuts.

2. Install a ¼ in. diameter alignment pin through the control bracket and levers.

3. Tighten the three shift linkage adjustment nuts and remove the alignment pin.

4. Check the gear lever for smooth crossover.

4-Speed Floor and Console Shift Linkage

1. Place the hand shifter lever in the neutral position, then raise the car on a hoist.

2. Insert a ¼ in. rod into the alignment holes of the shift levers.

3. If the holes are not in exact alignment, check for bent connecting rods or loose lever locknuts at the rod ends. Make replacements or repairs, then adjust as follows.

4. Loosen the three rod-to-lever retaining locknuts and move the levers until the ¼ in. gauge rod will enter the alignment holes. Be sure that the transmission shift levers are in neutral and that the reverse shifter lever is in the neutral detent.

5. Install the shift rods and torque the locknuts to 12–15 ft. lbs. on 1965 transmission, and 18–23 ft. lbs. on 1966 and later transmissions.

6. Remove the ¼ in. gauge rod.

7. Operate the shift levers to assure correct shifting.

8. Lower the car and road-test it.

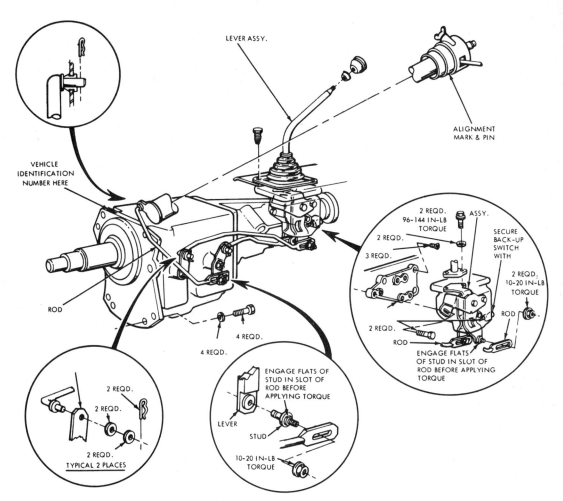

Shift linkage and lock rod adjustment—3 speed transmission

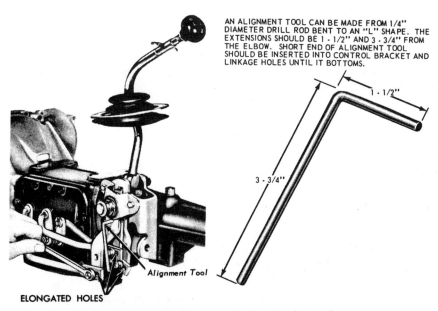

AN ALIGNMENT TOOL CAN BE MADE FROM 1/4"
DIAMETER DRILL ROD BENT TO AN "L" SHAPE. THE
EXTENSIONS SHOULD BE 1 - 1/2" AND 3 - 3/4" FROM
THE ELBOW. SHORT END OF ALIGNMENT TOOL
SHOULD BE INSERTED INTO CONTROL BRACKET AND
LINKAGE HOLES UNTIL IT BOTTOMS.

Floor-shift linkage adjustment—4 speed

TRANSMISSION LOCK ROD ADJUSTMENT

Post-1969 models with floor or console-mounted shifters and manual transmissions incorporate a transmission lock rod which prevents the shifter from being moved from the reverse position when the ignition lock is in the "off" position. The lock rod connects the shift tube in the steering column to the transmission reverse lever. The lock rod cannot be properly adjusted until the manual linkage adjustment is correct.

CLUTCH

REMOVAL AND INSTALLATION

The procedures for the removal and installation of the clutch are explained earlier in this chapter, under "Clutch and/or Transmission Removal and Installation."

CLUTCH PEDAL FREE-PLAY ADJUSTMENT

The free-travel of the clutch pedal should be checked every six months or 6,000 miles, and adjusted whenever the clutch does not engage properly or when new clutch parts are installed. Improper clutch pedal free-travel adjustment is one of the most frequent causes of clutch failure and can be a contributing factor in some transmission failures. The procedure for adjusting the pedal free-travel is as follows:

TOTAL TRAVEL   FREE TRAVEL

1965

1. Measure the total travel of the pedal. If the total travel is less than 6⅜in. or greater than 6⅝ in., move the pedal bumper and the bracket up or down until the travel is within specifications. Always check and adjust total travel before checking free-travel.

2. With the clutch pedal against its bumper (pedal released), measure the overall length of the spring. The spring should measure 10 in. If it does not, it must be replaced, as it is not adjustable.

3. With the engine at normal idle, depress the pedal just enough to take up the free-travel, and measure this distance with a tape measure. The difference between this reading and the reading taken where the pedal is released is the clutch pedal free-travel. If the free-travel is not between ⅞ in. and 1⅛ in., adjust the clutch pedal-to-equalizer rod. To increase the free-travel, loosen the rearward

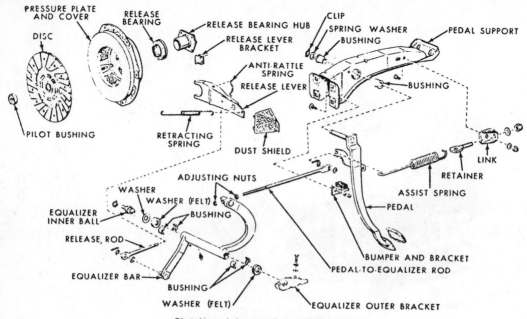

Clutch pedal mounting and linkage

adjusting nut and tighten the forward nut. To reduce the free-travel, loosen the forward nut and tighten the rearward nut. Both nuts must be tightened against the trunnion after making the adjustment.

4. As an additional check, measure the pedal free-travel with the transmission in neutral and the engine running at 3,000 rpm. If free-travel at this speed is not ½ in., readjust the clutch pedal-to-equalizer rod. Otherwise, the release fingers may contact the release bearing continuously, resulting in premature bearing failure. Free-travel must be exactly as specified.

1966–1973

1. Disconnect the clutch return spring from the release lever.

2. Loosen the release lever rod locknut and adjusting nut.

3. Move the clutch release lever rearward until the release bearing lightly contacts the pressure plate release fingers.

4. Adjust the rod adaptor length until the adaptor seats in the release lever pocket.

5. Insert the specified feeler gauge against the back face of the rod adaptor. Tighten the adjusting nut finger-tight against the gauge. The proper feeler gauge sizes are as follows:
- 1966–67 . . . 6 cylinder—0.178 in.; V8—0.128 in.
- 1968–71 . . . 390, 427, 428, 429— 0.178 in.; all others—0.136 in.
- 1972–73 . . . all—0.194 in.

6. Tighten the locknut against the adjusting nut, being careful not to disturb the adjustment. Torque the locknut to 10–15 ft. lbs. and remove the feeler gauge.

7. Install the clutch return spring.

8. Depress and release the clutch pedal a minimum of five times and recheck the free-play setting with a feeler gauge. Readjust if necessary.

9. Finally, with the engine running at 3,000 rpm and the transmission in neutral, check the pedal free-travel. Free-travel at this speed must be at least ½ in. Free-travel must be exactly to specification. Otherwise, the release fingers may contact the release bearing continuously, resulting in premature bearing and clutch failure.

AUTOMATIC TRANSMISSION

Three different automatic transmissions have been used; the C4, C6, and FMX.

The C4 is a light-duty, dual-range, three-speed unit with an aluminum case. It is used in all six-cylinder models, all V8s prior to 1967, and all V8s of less than 351 cu in. since 1967, with the exception of small block high-performance engines.

The FMX, a dual-range three-speed unit with an aluminum case, is used with all 351 V8 engines from 1969 to the present, except for the 1971 351 CJ and Boss 351, and the 1972 351 HO.

The C6 is a heavy-duty, dual-range, three-speed transmission in an aluminum case. Its applications include all V8 engines larger than 351 cu in., all GTs, and all high—performance V8 engines—regardless of size—from 1967 to the present.

BAND ADJUSTMENT
C-4 Cruisomatic
INTERMEDIATE BAND

1. Clean all the dirt from the adjusting screw and remove and discard the locknut.

2. Install a new locknut on the adjusting screw. Using the tool shown in the illustration, tighten the adjusting screw until the wrench clicks and breaks at 10 ft. lbs. torque.

3. Back off the adjusting screw *exactly* 1¾ turns.

4. Hold the adjusting screw steady and tighten the locknut to the proper torque.

Tool—T59P-77370-B or 7345

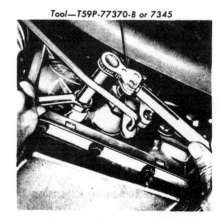

Intermediate band adjustment—C-4

LOW-REVERSE BAND

1. Clean all dirt from around the band adjusting screw, and remove and discard the locknut.

2. Install a new locknut on the adjusting screw. Using the tool shown in the illustra-

tion, tighten the adjusting screw until the wrench clicks and breaks at 10 ft. lbs. torque.

3. Back off the adjusting screw *exactly three full turns*.

4. Hold the adjusting screw steady and tighten the locknut to the proper torque.

C-6 Cruisomatic

INTERMEDIATE BAND ADJUSTMENT

1. Raise the car on a hoist or place it on jack stands.

2. Clean the threads of the intermediate band adjusting screw.

3. Loosen the adjustment screw locknut.

4. Tighten the adjusting screw to 10 ft. lbs. and back the screw off exactly 1½ turns. Tighten the adjusting screw locknut.

FMX Cruisomatic

FRONT BAND ADJUSTMENT

When it is necessary to adjust the front band of the transmission, perform the following procedure:

1. Drain the transmission fluid and remove the oil pan, fluid filter screen, and clip. The same transmission fluid may be reused if it is filtered through a 100-mesh screen before being installed. Only transmission fluid in good condition should be used.

2. Clean the pan and filter screen and remove the old gasket.

3. Loosen the front servo adjusting screw locknut. See the illustration.

NOTE: *Special band adjusting wrenches are recommended to do this operation correctly and quickly.*

4. Pull back the actuating rod and insert a ¼ in. spacer bar between the adjusting screw and the servo piston stem. Tighten the adjusting screw to 10 in. lbs torque. Remove

the spacer bar and tighten the adjusting screw an additional ¾ turn. Hold the adjusting screw fast and tighten the locknut securely (20–25 ft. lbs.).

5. Install the transmission fluid filter screen and clip. Install the pan with a new pan gasket.

6. Refill the transmission to the "full" mark on the dipstick. Start the engine, run for a few minutes, shift the selector lever through all positions, and place it in Park. Recheck the fluid level again and add fluid to proper level if necessary.

REAR BAND ADJUSTMENT

The rear band of the FMX transmission may be adjusted by any of the methods given below. On most cars, the basic external band adjustment is satisfactory. The internal band adjustment procedure may be done when the external adjustment procedure cannot be done correctly. On certain cars with a console floor shift, the entire console, shift lever and linkage will have to be removed to gain access to the rear band external adjusting screw.

REAR BAND EXTERNAL ADJUSTMENT

The procedure for adjusting the rear band externally is as follows:

1. Locate the external rear band adjusting screw on the transmission case, clean all dirt from the threads, and coat the threads with light oil.

NOTE: *The adjusting screw is located on the upper right side of the transmission case. Access is often through a hole in the front floor to the right of center under the carpet.*

2. Loosen the locknut on the rear band external adjusting screw.

3. Using the special preset torque wrench

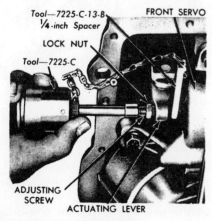

Front band adjustment—FMX

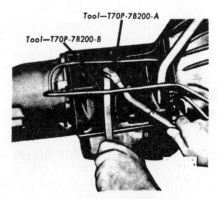

External rear band adjustment—C-8

shown, tighten the adjusting screw until the handle clicks at 10 ft. lbs. torque. If the adjusting screw is tighter than 10 ft. lbs. torque, loosen the adjusting screw and retighten to the proper torque.

4. Back off the adjusting screw 1½ turns. Hold the adjusting screw steady while tightening the locknut to the proper torque (35–40 ft. lbs.). *Severe damage may result if the adjusting screw is not backed off exactly 1½ turns.*

REAR BAND INTERNAL ADJUSTMENT

The rear band is adjusted internally as follows:

1. Drain the transmission fluid. If it is to be reused, pour the fluid through a 100-mesh screen as it drains from the transmission. Reuse the transmission fluid only if it is in good condition.

2. Remove and clean the pan, fluid filter, and clip.

3. Loosen the rear servo adjusting locknut.

4. Pull the adjusting screw end of the actuating lever away from the servo body and insert the spacer tool (see illustration) between the servo accumulator piston and the adjusting screw. *Be sure the flat surfaces of the tool are placed squarely between the adjusting screw and the accumulator piston. The tool must not touch the servo piston and the handle must not touch the servo piston spring retainer.*

5. Using a torque wrench with an allen-head socket, tighten the adjusting screw to 24 in. lbs torque.

6. Back off the adjusting screw exactly 1½

turns. Hold the adjusting screw steady and tighten the locknut securely. Remove the spacer tool.

7. Install the fluid filter, clip, and pan with a new gasket.

8. Fill the transmission with the correct amount of fluid.

NEUTRAL START SWITCH ADJUSTMENT

1965–1967

1. With the manual linkage properly adjusted, try to engage the starter in each position on the quadrant. The starter should engage only in neutral or Park.

2. Remove the handle from the shift lever and the chrome trim panel from the top of the console.

3. Place the lever in neutral, remove the quadrant retaining screws and indicator light, and lift the quadrant from the console.

4. Loosen the switch attaching screws and move the shift lever back and forth until the gauge pin (no. 43 drill) can be inserted into the gauge pin holes.

5. Place the shift lever in neutral and slide the switch back and forward until the switch actuating lever contacts the shift lever.

6. Reassemble the shift quadrant in the console.

7. Check the starter engagement as in step one.

1968–1973

1. With the manual linkage properly adjusted, try to engage the starter at each posi-

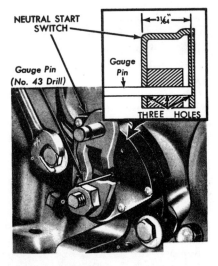

Internal rear band adjustment—C-6

Neutral start switch

tion on the quadrant. The starter should engage only in neutral and Park.

2. Remove the shift handle from the shift lever, and the console from the vehicle.

3. Loosen the switch attaching screws and move the shift lever back and forward until the gauge pin (no. 43 drill) can be inserted fully.

4. Place the shift lever firmly against the neutral detent stop and slide the switch back and forward until the switch lever contacts the shift lever.

5. Tighten the switch attaching screws and check the starter engagement as in step one.

6. Reinstall the console and shift linkage.

CHANGING TRANSMISSION FLUID, PAN REMOVAL

C-4, C-6, FMX Cruisomatic

Normal maintenance and lubrication requirements do not include periodic changes of transmission fluid. Only when it is necessary to remove the pan for major repairs or adjustments will it be necessary to replace the transmission fluid. At this time the converter, oil cooler core, and cooler lines should be thoroughly flushed out to remove any dirt or deposits that might clog these units later.

When filling a completely dry (no fluid) transmission and converter, install five quarts of transmission fluid and then start the engine. Shift the selector lever through all positions briefly and set at Park position. Check the fluid level and add enough fluid to raise the level to between the "add" and "full" marks on the dipstick. *Do not overfill the transmission.*

The procedure for a partial drain and refill of the transmission fluid is as follows:

1. Raise the car on a hoist or jack stands.

2. Place a drain pan under the transmission pan.

NOTE: *On some models of the C-4 transmission, the fluid is drained by disconnecting the filler tube from the transmission fluid pan.*

3. Loosen the pan attaching bolts to allow the fluid to drain.

4. When the fluid has stopped draining to level of the pan flange, remove the pan bolts starting at the rear and along both sides of the pan, allowing the pan to drop and drain gradually.

5. Remove the eight 10-24 x 1-⅜-inch screws that attach the oil screen to the body and remove the screen and gasket. Be careful not to lose the throttle pressure limit valve and spring when separating the oil screen from the valve body.

6. After completing the transmission repairs or adjustments, install the fluid filter screen, a new pan gasket, and the pan on the transmission. Tighten the pan attaching bolts on C-4 and C-6 to (12–16 ft. lbs.). On FMX transmissions, tighten the pan attaching bolts to 10–13 ft. lbs.

NOTE: *Be sure to use Type "F" transmission fluid. The use of any other type of fluid such as Type "A" suffix "A," or DEXRON will materially affect the service life of the transmission.*

7. Install three quarts of transmission fluid through the filler tube. If the filler tube was removed to drain the transmission, install the filler tube using a new O-ring.

8. Start and run the engine for a few minutes at a low idle speed and then at the fast idle speed (about 1200 rpm) until the normal operating temperature is reached. *Do not race the engine.*

9. Move the selector lever through all positions and place it at the Park position. Check the fluid level and add fluid until the level is between the "add" and "full" marks on the dipstick. *Do not overfill the transmission.*

MANUAL LINKAGE ADJUSTMENT

Floor or Console Shift

1. Place the transmission shift lever in D, (large dot) on most 1966 cars and D on some 1966 and all 1967 and later cars.

2. Raise the vehicle and loosen the manual lever shift rod retaining nut. Move the transmission lever to D_1 or D position. On most 1966 transmissions, D_1 is the fifth detent from the rear. On 1966 GTs with select shift, and on all 1967 and later cars, D is the fourth detent from the rear.

3. With the transmission shift lever and the transmission manual lever in position, tighten the nut at point A to 10–20 ft. lbs.

4. Check the transmission operation for all selector lever detent positions.

NOTE: *Since 1970, all models with a floor or console-mounted selector lever have incorporated a transmission lock out rod to prevent the transmission selector from being moved out of the Park position when the ignition lock is in the "off" position.*

The lock rod connects the shift tube in the steering column to the transmission manual lever. The lock rod cannot be properly adjusted until the manual linkage adjustment is correct.

LOCK ROD ADJUSTMENT

1970–1973

1. With the transmission selector lever in the Drive position, loosen the lock rod adjustment nut on the transmission manual lever.

2. Insert a 0.180 in. diameter rod (no. 15 drill bit) in the gauge pin hole in the steering column socket casting, it is located at the six o'clock position directly below the ignition lock.

3. Manipulate the pin so that the casting will not move when the pin is fully inserted.

4. Torque the lock rod adjustment nut to 10–20 ft. lbs.

5. Remove the pin and check the linkage operation.

THROTTLE LINKAGE ADJUSTMENT

C-4 Cruisomatic

INITIAL ADJUSTMENTS

1. Apply the parking brake and place the selector lever at N.

2. Run the engine at the normal idle speed. If the engine is cold, run the engine at fast idle speed (about 1200 rpm) until it reaches the normal operating temperature. When the engine is warm, slow it down to the normal idle speed.

3. Connect the tachometer to the engine.

4. Adjust the engine idle speed to the specified rpm with the transmission selector lever at D, D_1 or D_2.

5. The carburetor throttle lever must be against the hot idle speed adjusting screw at the specified idle speed in D, D_1, or D_2.

FINAL ADJUSTMENT—1965–1966

1. With the engine stopped and the accelerator pedal in the normal idle position, check the pedal for a height of 3⅞ in. Be sure the fast idle cam is not contacting the fast idle screw of the carburetor.

2. To check for free pedal travel, depress the accelerator pedal to the full throttle position (carburetor throttle lever against full throttle stop). Release the pedal and recheck the pedal height.

3. If necessary, adjust the pedal height. On six-cylinder engines, disconnect the carburetor return spring and carburetor rod. Adjust the length of the rod to bring the pedal height within the specifications. Connect the carburetor rod, tighten the jam nut, and install the return spring. On V8 engines, disconnect the carburetor return springs and the carburetor rod where it connects to the accelerator shaft. Adjust the length of rod to

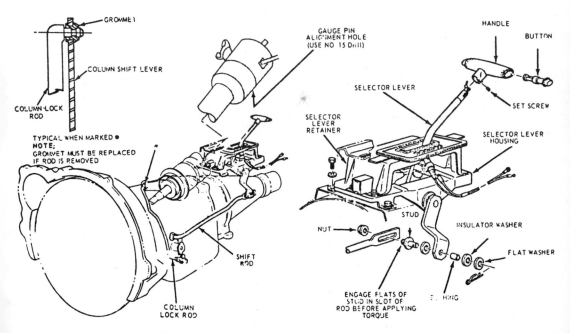

Shift linkage and lock rod—automatic transmission

bring pedal height within specifications. Connect the carburetor rod and return spring.

4. On six-cylinder engines, disconnect the downshift cable return spring at the transmission, carburetor return spring at the manifold and downshift cable where it connects to the accelerator shaft.

5. Position the down shift lever in the downshift position (carburetor wide open).

6. Hold the downshift lever on the transmission against the stop in a counterclockwise direction (downshift position).

7. Adjust the trunnion on the downshift cable where it connects to the accelerator shaft so that it aligns with the hole in the downshift lever, then install the attaching clip.

8. Install the return springs.

9. On V8 engines, disconnect the downshift return spring at the bellcrank, carburetor return spring, and down shift lever at the bellcrank.

10. Hold the carburetor rod in the wide open position. The step in the rod should place the bellcrank in the downshift position.

11. Hold the downshift lever rod in the downward position. This places the transmission lever in the downshift position.

12. Adjust the downshift lever trunnion at the bellcrank so that it aligns with the hole in the bellcrank. Install the trunnion and retaining clip.

13. Release the levers and install the carburetor rod and bellcrank.

FINAL ADJUSTMENT—1967–1969 6 CYLINDER, 1967–1968 V8

1. With the engine off, check the accelerator pedal for a height of 4½ in. measured from the top of the pedal at the pivot point to the floor pan. To obtain the correct pedal height, adjust the accelerator connecting link at point A in the figure.

2. With the engine off, disconnect the downshift control cable at point B from the accelerator shaft lever.

3. With the carburetor choke off, depress the accelerator to the floor. Block the pedal to hold it in the wide open position.

4. Rotate the down shift lever C counterclockwise to place it against the internal stop.

5. With the lever held in this position, and all slack removed from the cable, adjust the trunnion so that it will slide into the accelerator shaft lever. Turn one additional turn clockwise, then secure it to the lever with a retaining clip.

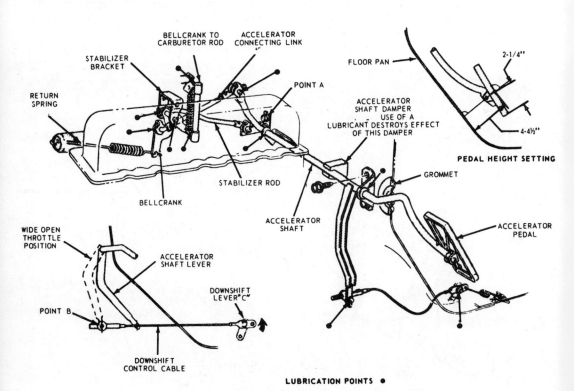

C-4 Throttle linkage adjustment—1967-1969 cylinder

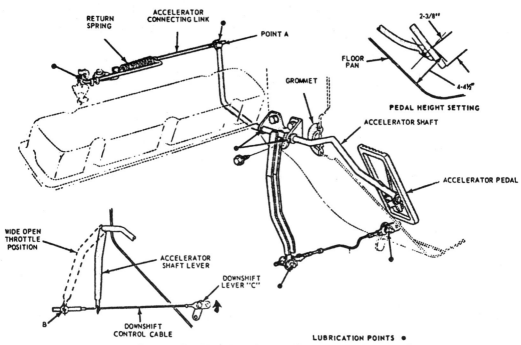

C-4 and C-6 Throttle linkage adjustment—1967–68 V8

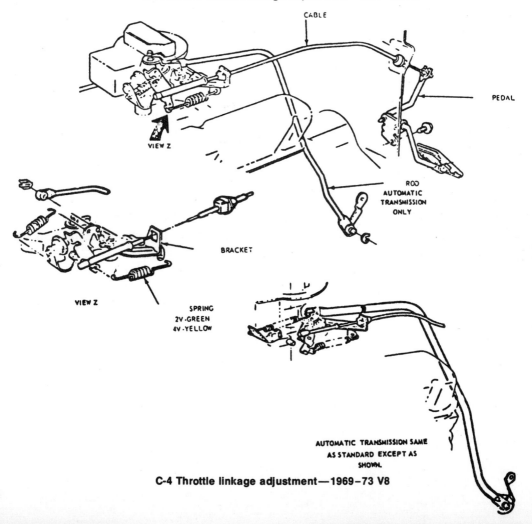

C-4 Throttle linkage adjustment—1969–73 V8

6. Remove the block to release the carburetor linkage.

FINAL ADJUSTMENT—1970 6 CYLINDER

1. Disconnect the throttle return spring and remove the trunnion and cable at the bellcrank.
2. Hold transmission in the full downshift against the stop.
3. Hold the carburetor throttle lever wide open against the stop.
4. Adjust the trunnion at the bellcrank until the ball stud on the shaft and the ball stud receiver on the cable align. Turn the trunnion one full additional turn to increase the length.
5. Release the transmission and carburetor to the normal free position.
6. Install the throttle return spring.

FINAL ADJUSTMENT—1969–1973 V8 ENGINES, 1971–1973 6 CYLINDER

1. Disconnect the throttle and downshift return springs.
2. Hold the carburetor throttle lever in the wide open position against the stop.
3. Hold the transmission in the full downshift position against the internal stop.
4. Turn the adjustment screw on the carburetor downshift lever to within 0.040–0.080 in. of contacting the pick-up surface of the carburetor throttle lever.
5. Release the transmission and carburetor to the normal free positions.
6. Install the throttle and downshift return springs.

FMX Cruisomatic

INITIAL ADJUSTMENT

See C-4 Cruisomatic "Initial Adjustment" procedure.

FINAL ADJUSTMENT—1969

See "Final Adjustment" procedure for 1967–69 C-4 Cruisomatic.

FINAL ADJUSTMENT—1970–1973

See "Final Adjustment" procedure for 1970 C-4 Cruisomatic (V8 engines).

C-6 Cruisomatic

INITIAL ADJUSTMENT

See C-4 Cruisomatic "Initial Adjustment" procedure.

FINAL ADJUSTMENT—1967–1968

1. With the engine off, check the accelerator pedal for a height of 4½ in. measured from the top of the pedal at the pivot point to the floor pan. To obtain the correct pedal height, adjust the accelerator connecting link at point A.
2. With the engine off, disconnect the downshift control cable at point B and from the accelerator shaft lever.
3. With the carburetor choke in "off" position, depress the accelerator pedal to the floor. Block the pedal to hold it in the wide open position.
4. Rotate the downshift lever C counterclockwise to place it against the internal stop.
5. With the lever held in this position, and with all slack removed from the cable, adjust the trunnion so that it will slide into the accelerator shaft lever. Turn it one turn clockwise, then secure it to the lever with the retaining clip.
6. Remove the block to release the accelerator linkage.

FINAL ADJUSTMENT—1969–1973

See the 1970–1973 V8 procedures under the C-4 Cruisomatic section.

Drive Train

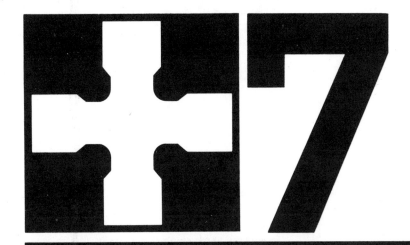

DRIVESHAFT AND UNIVERSAL JOINTS

The driveshaft is the means by which the power from the engine and transmission (in the front of the car) is transferred to the differential and rear axles, and finally to the rear wheels.

The driveshaft assembly incorporates two universal joints (one at each end) and a slip yoke at the front, which fits into the back of the transmission.

All driveshafts are balanced when installed in a car. It is therefore important to cover the driveshaft and universal joint assembly completely before applying undercoating to the chassis. A layer of undercoat on one side of a driveshaft will cause imbalance and vibration.

DRIVESHAFT REMOVAL

1. Mark the relationship of the rear driveshaft yoke to the drive pinion flange of the axle. If the original yellow alignment marks are visible, there is no need for new marks. The purpose of this marking is to replace the assembly in its original position, maintaining proper balance.

2. Remove the four bolts which hold the rear universal joint to the pinion flange (see illustration). Wrap tape around the loose bearing caps in order to prevent them from falling off the spider.

3. Pull the driveshaft toward the rear until the slip yoke clears the transmission housing and the seal. Plug the hole at the rear of the transmission housing or place a container under the opening to catch any fluid which might leak.

UNIVERSAL JOINT OVERHAUL

1. Position the driveshaft assembly in a vise.

2. Remove the snap-rings which retain the bearings in the slip yoke (front only) and in the driveshaft (front and rear).

3. Using a large punch or an arbor press, drive one of the bearings in toward the center of the universal joint, forcing the opposite bearing out.

4. As each bearing is pressed or punched far enough out of the universal joint assembly, grip it with a pair of pliers, and pull it from the driveshaft yoke. Drive or press the spider in the opposite direction to make the opposite bearing accessible, and pull it free. Remove all bearings from both universal joints.

5. After removing the bearings, lift the spider from the yoke.

6. Thoroughly clean all dirt and foreign

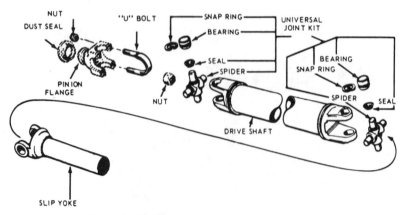

Driveshaft and universal joints—disassembled

matter from the yoke area on both ends of the driveshaft.

NOTE: *When installing new bearings within the yokes, it is advisable to use an arbor press. However, if this tool is not available, the bearings should be driven into position with extreme care, as a heavy jolt on the needle bearings can easily damage or misalign them.*

7. Start a new bearing into the yoke at the rear of the driveshaft.

8. Position a new spider in the rear yoke and press (or drive) the new bearing ¼ in. below the outer surface of the yoke.

9. With the bearing in position, install a new snap-ring.

10. Start a new bearing into the opposite side of the yoke.

11. Press (or drive) the bearing until the opposite bearing—which you have just installed—contacts the inner surface of the snap-ring.

12. Install a new snap-ring on the second bearing. It may be necessary to grind the surface of this second snap-ring to ease installation.

13. Reposition the driveshaft in the vise, to work on the front universal joint.

14. Install the new bearings, new spider, and new snap-rings in the same manner as for the rear universal joint.

15. Position the slip yoke on the spider. Install new bearings, nylon thrust bearings (1967–1971 cars only), and snap-rings.

16. Check both reassembled joints for freedom of movement. If misalignment of any part is causing a bind, a sharp rap on the side of the yoke with a brass hammer should seat the bearing needles, and provide freedom of movement. Care should be used to

firmly support the shaft end during this operation, as well as to prevent blows to the bearings themselves. Under no circumstances should a driveshaft be installed if there is any bind in the universal joints.

DRIVESHAFT INSTALLATION

1. Carefully inspect the rubber seal on the output shaft and the seal in end of the transmission extension housing. Replace them if they are damaged.

2. Examine the lugs on the axle pinion flange and replace the flange if the lugs are shaved or distorted.

3. Coat the yoke spline with special-purpose lubricant. (The Ford part number for this lubricant is B8A-19589-A.)

4. Remove the plug inserted into the rear of the transmission housing.

5. Insert the yoke into the transmission housing and onto the transmission output shaft. Use care to make sure that the yoke assembly does not bottom on the output shaft with excessive force.

6. Locate the marks made on the rear driveshaft yoke and the pinion flange prior to removal of the driveshaft assembly. Install the driveshaft assembly with the marks properly aligned.

7. Install the U-bolts and nuts that attach the universal joint to the pinion flange. Torque the U-bolt nuts to 8–15 ft. lbs.

DRIVE AXLE

Two basic types of rear axle assembly are used. These are the integral carrier type and the removable carrier type. Service procedures will vary somewhat, depending upon the type.

The integral carrier type of rear axle assembly is exclusive to six-cylinder cars. Although this type features an inspection plate which provides working access to the differential components, it is recommended that the entire integral carrier assembly be removed from the car for purposes of performing differential work.

The removable carrier assembly, which is used in all V8 models, may be removed from the car without removing the axle housings.

Procedures for removing the axle shafts and their bearings are the same for both integral and removable carrier rear axle assemblies. In order to remove the axles, their housings need not be removed from the car.

AXLE SHAFT SEAL REPLACEMENT

1. Remove the axle shaft.

2. Using a two-fingered seal puller (slide hammer), remove the seal from the axle housing.

3. Thoroughly clean the recess in the rear axle housing from which the seal was removed.

4. Position a new seal on the housing and drive it into place with a seal installation tool. If this tool is not available, a wood block of the appropriate size may be substituted.

NOTE: *Although the right and left-hand seals are identical, there are many different types of seals which have been used. It is advisable to have one of the old seals when you purchase new ones, in order to visually identify the proper seal.*

5. When the seal is properly installed, install the axle shaft.

AXLE SHAFT AND/OR BEARING REPLACEMENT

NOTE: *Bearings must be pressed on and off of the shaft with an arbor press. Unless you have access to one, it is inadvisable to attempt to perform any repair work on the axle shaft and bearing assemblies.*

1. Remove the wheel, tire, and brake drum.

2. Remove the nuts holding the retainer plate to the backing plate. Disconnect the brake line.

3. Remove the retainer and install nuts, finger-tight, to prevent the brake backing plate from being dislodged.

4. Pull out the axle shaft and bearing assembly, using a slide hammer.

NOTE: *If end-play is found to be excessive, the bearing should be replaced. Shimming the bearing is not recommended as this ignores end-play of the bearing itself and could result in improper seating of the bearing.*

5. Using a chisel, nick the bearing retainer

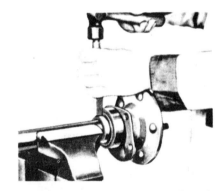

Removing rear wheel bearing retainer ring

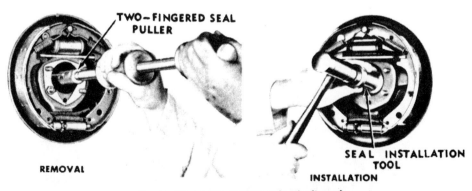

TWO-FINGERED SEAL PULLER

REMOVAL

SEAL INSTALLATION TOOL

INSTALLATION

Removing and installing axle shaft seal

in three or four places. The retainer does not have to be cut, merely collapsed sufficiently, to allow the bearing retainer to be slid from the shaft.

6. Press off the bearing and install the new one by pressing it into position.

7. Press on the new retainer.

NOTE: *Do not attempt to press the bearing and the retainer on at the same time.*

8. Assemble the shaft and bearing in the housing, being sure that the bearing is seated properly in the housing.

9. Install the retainer, drum, wheel and tire. Bleed the brakes.

Suspension and Steering

The Mustang/Cougar have always featured the same basic suspension configuration: the spring-on-upper-arm front suspension and the semi-elliptic leaf spring suspension in the rear. The front shock absorbers have in all cases been placed within the coil springs.

In recent years, certain large-engined, high-performance models have been equipped with a staggered rear shock absorber configuration, designed for better traction and directional stability during full-throttle starts. In this arrangement, the left shock absorber is relocated to the rear of the axle, while the right shock absorber retains its standard placement in front of the axle. This arrangement gives effective control of spring wind-up, wheel hop, and pitching motion.

REAR SUSPENSION

Leaf Springs

REMOVAL

1. Raise the vehicle on a hoist and place supports beneath the underbody and under the axle.
2. Disconnect the lower end of the shock absorber from the spring clip plate and move it out of the way. Remove the supports from under the axle.

3. Remove the spring plate nuts from the U-bolts and remove the clip plate. Raise the rear axle just enough to remove the weight of the housing from the spring.
4. Remove the two rear shackle attaching nuts, the shackle bar and two inner bushings.
5. Remove the rear shackle assembly and two outer bushings.
6. Remove the nut from the spring mounting bolt and tap the bolt out of the bushing at the front hanger. Lift out the spring assembly.
7. If the front hanger bushing is to be replaced, it may be necessary to take the spring assembly to a machine shop and have the old bushing pressed out and a new one pressed in.

INSPECTION

Inspect the rear shackle and hanger assembly, bushings, and studs for wear, damage, cracks, or distortion. Check for broken spring leaves. Inspect the leaves for missing anti-squeak inserts. Inspect the spring clips for worn or damaged threads. Check the spring clip plate and insulator retainers for distortion. If the spring center tie bolt requires replacement, clamp the spring in a vise to keep the spring compressed during bolt removal and replacement. Replace all parts found to be defective.

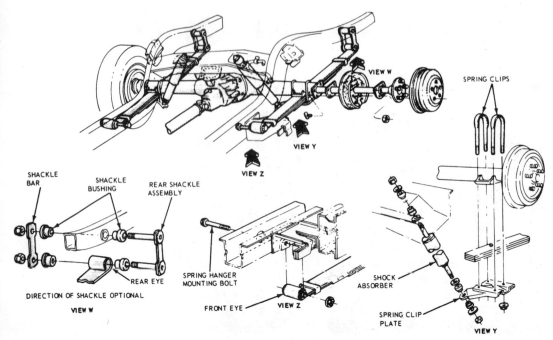

SPRING CLIPS

VIEW W

VIEW Y

VIEW Z

SHACKLE BAR

SHACKLE BUSHING

REAR SHACKLE ASSEMBLY

REAR EYE

DIRECTION OF SHACKLE OPTIONAL

VIEW W

SPRING HANGER MOUNTING BOLT

FRONT EYE

VIEW Z

SHOCK ABSORBER

SPRING CLIP PLATE

VIEW Y

Standard rear suspension

INSTALLATION

NOTE: *All used attaching components (nuts, bolts, etc.) must be discarded and replaced with new ones prior to reassembly. This is due to extreme stresses and weather which weaken the attaching hardware under normal service. If a used component is reinstalled, it may break.*

1. Position the leaf spring under the axle housing and insert the shackle assembly into the rear hanger bracket and the rear eye of the spring.

2. Install the shackle inner bushings, shackle plate, and locknuts. Hand-tighten the locknuts.

3. Position the spring front eye in the front hanger, slip the washer on the front hanger bolt, and, from the inboard side, insert the bolt through the hanger and eye. Install the locknut on the hanger bolt and tighten finger-tight.

4. Lower the rear axle housing so that it rests on the spring. Place the spring plate on the U-bolts. Install the U-bolt nuts and torque to 30–45 ft. lbs. on 1968 and earlier models and 35–50 ft. lbs. on 1969–1973 models.

5. Attach the lower end of the shock absorber to the spring plate using a new nut.

6. Place safety stands under the axle housing, lower the vehicle until the spring is in the approximate curb load position, and then torque the front hanger stud locknut to specification. On pre-1970 models torque the locknut to 35–55 ft. lbs.; 1970 models, 70–100 ft. lbs.; 1971 models, 100–300 ft. lbs.; 1972 models, 90–110 ft. lbs.; 1973 models, 100–140 ft. lbs.

7. Torque the locknuts on the rear shackle to 15–22 ft. lbs. on pre 1970 and 1973 models, and 18–29 ft. lbs. on 1970–1972 models. Close the hole in the inner rail with a body plug.

8. Remove the safety stands and lower the vehicle.

Shock Absorbers

1. Disconnect the shock absorber from the spring plate.

2. Remove the shock absorber access plate from the luggage compartment. On convertible models, remove the rear seat and seat back in order to reach the access covers.

3. Remove the shock absorber upper attaching nut.

4. Compress the shock absorber and remove it from the vehicle.

5. Place the bushing and inner washer on the top stud of a new shock absorber.

6. Connect the upper stud to its mounting, and install the bushing, the outer washer, and a new nut on the stud. Torque the nut to 15–25 ft. lbs. Install the shock

absorber access cover. On convertibles, reinstall the rear seat if it was removed for access.

7. Connect the lower stud to the spring plate, and install the bushing, outer washer, and a new nut on the stud. Examine the spring plate for burrs. Tighten the nut and torque to 14–26 ft. lbs.

FRONT SUSPENSION

The front coil springs are mounted on top of the upper control arm to a tower in the sheet metal of the body. This type of mounting provides good stability. The lower arm and stabilizing strut substitute for the conventional A frame and serve to guide the lower part of the spindle through its cycle of up-and-down movement. The rod type stabilizing strut is mounted between two rubber buffer pads at the front end to cushion fore and aft thrust of the suspension. The effective length of this rod is variable and must be considered in maintenance. Ball joints are of the usual steel construction.

Coil Spring

REMOVAL

1965

1. Raise the front of the car and remove the wheel and tire assembly.

NOTE: *The jacks must be placed beneath the lower control arms.*

2. Remove the suspension bumper and bracket assembly.

3. Remove the shock absorber and mounting bracket assembly. Then install one bolt to hold the spring upper seat to the spring housing while the spring is being compressed.

4. Compress the spring with a suitable spring compressor.

5. Remove the bolt holding the spring upper seat and allow the control arm to drop down slightly to gain clearance.

6. Remove the spring and compressor from the car as a unit.

1966–1973

1. Raise the hood and remove the shock absorber upper mounting bracket bolts.

2. Raise the front of vehicle and place safety stands under the inboard ends of the lower control arms.

3. Remove the shock absorber lower attaching nuts, washers, and insulators.

4. Lift the shock absorber and upper bracket from the spring tower.

5. Remove the wheel cover or hub cap.

6. Remove the grease cap, cotter pin, nut lock, adjusting nut, and outer bearing.

7. Pull the wheel, tire, and hub and drum off the spindle as an assembly.

8. Install the spring compressor.

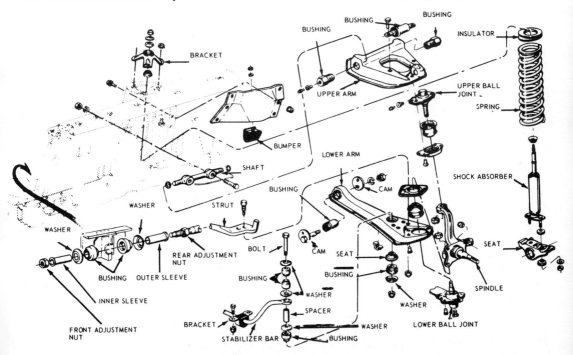

Front suspension assembly

9. Compress the spring until all tension is removed from the control arms.

10. Remove the two upper control arm attaching nuts and swing the control arm out board.

11. Release the spring compressor and remove it.

12. Remove the spring.

INSTALLATION
1965

1. Position the spring and compressor tool assembly in the spring housing with the end of the bottom coil bearing making contact with the punched end of the recess in the spring lower seat. Secure the spring upper seat to the top of the spring housing with two bolts and washers. Release the spring pressure.

2. Remove the two bolts and washers securing the spring upper seat to the spring housing. Remove the spring compressor. Install the spring mounting retainer over the bottom coil of the spring so that the retainer holes align with the shock absorber lower retaining bolt holes in the spring lower seat.

3. Place the shock absorber and upper mounting bracket assembly in the car. The lower retaining bolts of the shock absorber fit through the holes in the small retaining plate and the spring lower seat.

4. Install the shock absorber lower retaining nuts. Position the bracket-to-dash panel brace to the wide leg of the shock absorber mounting bracket, then install the upper mounting bracket retaining bolts and washers. Install the suspension bumper and bracket assembly with the retaining bolts and washers, and torque to 10–15 ft. lbs. Torque the upper mounting bracket retaining bolts to 36–46 ft. lbs.

5. Install the wheel and tire assembly, and lower the vehicle.

1966–1973

1. Place the upper spring insulator on the spring and secure it in place with tape.

2. Position the spring in the spring tower and compress it with a spring compressor.

3. Swing the upper control arm in board and install the attaching nuts. Torque the nuts to 75–100 ft. lbs.

4. Release the spring pressure and guide the spring into the upper arm spring seat. The end of the spring must not be more than ½ in. from the tab on the spring seat.

5. Remove the spring compressor and position the wheel, tire, and hub and drum on the spindle.

6. Install the bearing, washer, and adjusting nut.

7. On cars with disc brakes, loosen the adjusting nut three turns and rock the wheel hub and rotor assembly in and out to push the disc brakes, loosen the adjusting nut three turns and rock the wheel hub and rotor assembly in and out to push the disc brake pads away from the rotor.

8. While rotating the wheel, hub, and drum assembly, torque the adjusting nut to 17–25 ft. lbs. to seat the bearing.

9. With a 1⅛ in. box wrench, back off the adjusting nut ½ turn and tighten the nut to 10–15 in. lbs. or finger-tight.

10. Position the lock on the adjusting nut and install the new cotter pin. Bend the ends of the pin around the castellated flange of the nut lock.

11. Check the front wheel rotation and install the grease cap and hub cap.

12. Install the shock absorber and upper bracket assembly, making sure the shock absorber lower studs have insulators and are in the pivot plate holes.

13. Install the nuts and washers on the lower studs and torque them to 8–12 ft. lbs. on 1970 and later models and 12–17 ft. lbs. on 1966–1969 models.

14. Install the nuts on the shock absorber bracket and torque them to 20–28 ft. lbs.

15. Remove the safety stands and lower the vehicle.

Upper Control Arm
REMOVAL AND REPLACEMENT

1. Remove the shock absorber and upper mounting bracket from the car as an assembly.

2. Raise the vehicle and remove the wheel and tire as an assembly.

3. Install the spring compressor tool.

4. Place a safety stand under the lower arm.

5. Remove the cotter pin from the upper ball joint stud and loosen the nut.

6. Using a suitable tool, loosen the ball joint in the spindle, then remove the nut and lift the stud from the spindle.

7. Remove the upper arm attaching nuts from the engine compartment and remove the upper arm.

8. To install the arm, position it on the

mounting bracket and install the attaching nuts on the inner shaft attaching bolts.

NOTE: *The original equipment keystone type lockwashers must be used with the inner shaft attaching nuts and bolts.*

9. Install the upper ball joint stud in the spindle and tighten the nut to 55 ft. lbs. Install a new cotter pin.

10. Remove the spring compressor and position the spring on the upper arm. Install the wheel and check front end alignment.

Lower Ball Joint and Control Arm
INSPECTION

The lower ball joint is an integral part of the lower control arm. If the lower ball joint is defective, the entire lower control arm must be replaced.

1. Raise the vehicle on a hoist or floor jack so that the front wheel falls to the full down position.

2. Have an assistant grasp the bottom of the tire and move the wheel in and out.

3. As the wheel is being moved, observe the lower control arm where the spindle attaches to it.

4. Any movement between the lower part of the spindle and the lower control arm indicates a bad control arm which must be replaced.

NOTE: *During this check, the upper ball joint will be unloaded and may move; this is normal and not an indication of a bad ball joint. Also, do not mistake a loose wheel bearing for a worn ball joint.*

REMOVAL AND REPLACEMENT

1. Position an upper control arm support between the upper arm and side rail as shown in the illustration.

2. Raise the vehicle, position jack stands, and remove the wheel and tire.

3. Remove the stabilizer bar-to-link attaching nut and disconnect the bar from the link.

4. Remove the link bolt from the lower arm.

5. Remove the strut bar-to-lower attaching nuts and bolts.

6. Remove the lower ball joint cotter pin and back off the nut. Using a suitable tool, loosen the ball joint stud in the spindle.

7. Remove the nut from the arm and lower arm.

8. Remove the lower arm-to-underbody cam attaching parts and remove the arm.

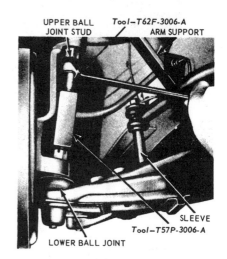

Loosening ball joint studs in spindle

9. To install, position the lower arm in the underbody and install the ball joint and cam attaching parts loosely.

10. Install the stabilizer and strut, and torque the attaching parts to specifications.

11. Torque the lower arm pivot and ball joint stud to specifications.

12. Lower the car and remove the upper arm support.

13. Front end alignment must be rechecked.

Upper Ball Joint
INSPECTION

1. Raise the vehicle on a hoist or floor jack so that the front wheels hang in the full down position.

2. Have an assistant grasp the wheel top and bottom and apply alternate in and out pressure to the top and bottom of the wheel.

3. Radial play of ¼ in. is acceptable measured at the inside of the wheel adjacent to the upper arm.

NOTE: *This radial play measurement is multiplied at the outer circumference of the tire and should not be measured here. Measure only at the inside of the wheel.*

REMOVAL AND REPLACEMENT

1. Position the support between the upper arm and frame rail as shown in the illustration.

2. Raise the vehicle and remove the tire and wheel.

3. Remove the upper ball joint cotter pin and loosen the nut.

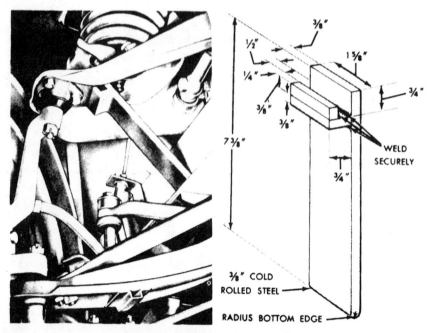

Front suspension upper arm support

4. Using a suitable tool, loosen the ball joint in the spindle.

5. Remove the three ball joint retaining rivets using a large chisel.

6. Remove the nut from the ball joint stud and remove the ball joint.

7. Clean and remove all burrs from the ball joint mounting area of the control arm before installing a new ball joint.

8. Install the ball joint in the upper arm using the service part nuts and bolts. Do not attempt to rivet a new ball joint to the arm.

9. Install and torque the ball joint stud nut and install the cotter pin.

10. Lubricate the new joint with a hand type grease gun only, using an air pressure gun may loosen the ball joint seal.

11. Install the wheel, lower the vehicle, and remove the upper arm support.

12. Check front end alignment.

Shock Absorbers

REMOVAL AND INSTALLATION

1. Raise the hood. Remove the three shock absorber upper mounting bracket-to-spring tower attaching nuts.

2. Raise the front of the vehicle. Place safety stands under the lower arms.

3. Remove the two shock absorber lower attaching nuts and washers.

4. Lift the shock absorber and upper bracket from the spring tower (see illustration) and remove the bracket from the shock absorber.

5. Install the upper mounting bracket on a new shock absorber and secure the attaching bolts.

6. Position the shock absorber and upper mounting bracket in the spring tower, making sure that the shock absorber lower studs are properly positioned within the pivot plate holes.

7. Install the washers and attaching nuts on the shock absorber lower studs, and torque them to 8–12 ft. lbs.

8. Install the three shock absorber upper mounting bracket-to-spring tower attaching bolts, and torque them to 20–30 ft. lbs.

Wheel Alignment

Front wheel alignment is the position of the front wheels relative to each other and to the vehicle. It is determined and must be maintained to provide safe, accurate steering with minimum tire wear. Many factors are involved in wheel alignment and adjustments are provided to return those that might change due to normal wear to their original value. The factors which determine wheel alignment are dependent on one another; therefore, when one of the factors is adjusted, the others must be adjusted to compensate.

NOTE: *The procedure for checking and adjusting front wheel alignment requires specialized equipment and professional skills. The following descriptions are for general reference only.*

Descriptions of these factors and their affects on the car are provided below.

NOTE: *Do not attempt to check and adjust the front wheel alignment without first making a thorough inspection of the front suspension components.*

CAMBER

Camber angle is the number of degrees that the centerline of the wheel is inclined from the vertical. Camber reduces loading of the outer wheel bearing and improves the tire contact patch while cornering.

CASTER

Caster angle is the number of degrees that a line drawn through the steering knuckle pivots is inclined from the vertical toward the front or rear of the car. Caster improves directional stability and decreases susceptibility to crosswinds or road surface deviations.

STEERING AXIS INCLINATION

Steering axis inclination is the number of degrees that a line drawn through the steering knuckle pivots is inclined to the vertical, when viewed from the front of the car. This, in combination with caster, is responsible for directional stability and self-centering of the steering. As the steering knuckle swings from lock to lock, the spindle generates an arc, the high point being the straight-ahead position of the wheel. Due to this arc, as the wheel turns, the front of the car is raised. The weight of the car acts against this lift, and attempts to return the spindle to the high point of the arc, resulting in self-centering when the steering wheel is released, and straight-line stability.

TOE-IN

Toe-in is the difference of the distance between the center and rear of the front wheels. It is most commonly measured in inches, but is occasionally referred to as an angle between the wheels. Toe-in is necessary to compensate for the tendency of the

Wheel Alignment Specifications

Year	Model	Caster Range (deg)	Caster Pref Setting (deg)	Camber Range (deg)	Camber Pref Setting (deg)	Toe-in (in.)	Steering Axis Inlcin.	Wheel Pivot Ratio (deg) Inner Wheel	Wheel Pivot Ratio (deg) Outer Wheel
1965	6 Cyl.	¾P to 1¾P	1¼P	0 to 1P	½P	¼ to ⁵/₁₆	7	20	19
	V8	¼N to ¾P	¼P	0 to 1P	½P	¼ to ⁵/₁₆	7	20	18¾
1966	6 Cyl.	0 to 2 P	1P	¼N to 1¼P	½P	⅛ to ⅜	7	20	18⅞ ①
	V8	1N to 1P	0	¼N to 1¼P	½P	⅛ to ⅜	6⅞	20	19⅛ ①
1967	All	¼N to ¾P	¼P	½P to 1½P	1P	⅛ to ¼	6¾	20	18¾
1968	All	¾N to 1¼P	¼P	¼P to 1¾P	1P	³/₁₆ to ⁵/₁₆	6¾	20	18¾
1969	All	¾N to 1¼P	¼P	¼P to 1¾P	¾P	⅛ to ¼	6¾	20	18¾
1970–71 All		1N to 1P	0	0 to 1½P ②	1P	¹/₁₆ to ⁵/₁₆	6¾	20	18⅔
1972–73 All		2N to 2P	0	½N to 1½P	½P	¹/₁₆ to ⅜	6¾	20	17¾

① V8 power steering—18¾°; 6 cyl. power steering—20⅛°
② 1970 models—¼P to 1¾P
N Negative
P Positive

wheels to deflect rearward while in motion. Due to this tendency, the wheels of a vehicle with properly adjusted toe-in are traveling straight forward when the vehicle itself is traveling straight forward, resulting in directional stability and mininimum tire wear.

Steering wheel spoke misalignment is often an indication of incorrect front end alignment. Care should be exercised when aligning the front end to maintain steering wheel spoke position. When adjusting the tie-rod ends, adjust each an equal amount (in the opposite direction) to increase or decrease toe-in. If, following the toe-in adjustment, further adjustments are necessary to center the steering wheel spokes, adjust the tie-rod ends an equal amount in the same direction.

ADJUSTMENT OF CASTER, CAMBER, AND TOE-IN

On 1965–66 cars, caster and camber are controlled by shims between the frame bracket and the upper suspension arm pivot shaft. Caster is adjusted by removing shims from the front bolt and placing them at the rear bolt, or vice versa. Camber is varied by adding or removing the same number of shims from both front and rear bolts.

From 1967 to 1973, any caster adjustment is accomplished by lengthening or shortening the struts at the frame cross-member. In order to adjust, both nuts should be turned an equal number of turns in the same direction, and the adjustment for one side should be within ¼° of the adjustment for the opposite side. Caster adjustment on these cars is accomplished by loosening the lower control arm pivot bolt and rotating the eccentrics.

Toe-in on all models is adjusted by loosening the clamps on the sleeves at the outer ends of the tie rod and turning the sleeves equal amounts in the opposite direction, in order that the steering wheel spoke alignment is maintained during the adjustment of

STEERING

The manual steering gear is of the worm and recirculating ball type. The sector shaft is straddle-mounted in the cover above the gear and a housing-mounted roller bearing is below the gear. The steering linkage consists of a pitman arm, a steering (pitman) arm-to-idler arm rod, an idler arm, and tie rods.

Power steering is available as an option. On 1965–1970 models, the power steering system is not integral, meaning that the pump provides assist to the steering linkage and hydraulically assisted worm and recirculating ball steering gear. In 1971–73, an integral type power steering unit is used. On this type of steering, hydraulic assist is directly applied to the steering gear, eliminating all hoses and hardware previously mounted under the chassis. The integral power steering unit used is the Saginaw type. This Rotary Valve Safety power steering gear operates by displacing fluid in order to provide hydraulic fluid pressure assits only when turning. The entire gear assembly is always filled with fluid. Consequently, all internal components of the gear assembly are immersed in fluid, making periodic lubrication of the steering gear unnecessary. Furthermore, the fluid acts as a cushion to absorb road shocks that may be transmitted through the steering assembly to the driver. With the exception of the pressure and return hoses, all fluid passages are contained internally within the unit.

Steering Wheel
REMOVAL AND INSTALLATION

1. Open the hood and disconnect the negative cable from the battery.
2. On 1968 and later models equipped with safety crash pads, remove the crash pad attaching screws from the underside of the steering wheel spoke and remove the pad. Remove the horn button or ring by pressing down evenly and turning it counterclockwise approximately 20° and then lifting it from the steering wheel. Disconnect the horn wires.
3. Remove the nut at the end of the shaft. Mark the steering shaft and hub prior to removal. Install a steering wheel puller on the end of the shaft and remove the wheel.

CAUTION: *The use of a knock-off type steering wheel puller or the use of a hammer on the steering shaft will damage the column bearing and, on collapsible columns, the column itself may be damaged.*

4. Lubricate the horn switch brush plate and the upper surface of the steering shaft upper brushing with Lubriplate or a similar product. Transfer all serviceable parts to the new steering wheel.
5. Position the steering wheel on the shaft so that the alignment marks made prior to removal line up. Install a new locknut and

torque it to 20–30 ft. lbs. Connect the horn wires.

6. Install the horn button or ring by turning it clockwise and install the crash pad on post-1967 models.

TURN SIGNAL SWITCH REPLACEMENT

1. Open the hood and disconnect the negative battery cable.

2. On post-1968 models, remove the retaining screw from the underside of each steering wheel spoke and remove the crash pad and horn switch cover as an assembly.

3. Remove the steering wheel retaining nut. Remove the steering wheel as outlined in the "Steering Wheel Removal and Installation" section.

4. Remove the turn signal handle from the side of the column. Remove the emergency flasher retainer and knob, if so equipped.

5. On pre-1968 models, disconnect the two wire connector blocks at the dash panel above the steering column. On post-1967 models, remove the wire assembly cover and disconnect the wire connector plugs. Record the location and color code of each wire then tape the wires together. Make sure that the horn wires are disconnected. Remove the plastic cover from the wiring harness. Attach a piece of heavy cord to the switch wires to pull them through the column during installation.

6. Remove the retaining clips and attaching screws from the turn signal switch and lift the switch and wire assembly from the top of the column.

7. Tape the ends of the new switch wires together and transfer the pull cord to these wires.

8. Pull the wires down through the column with the cord and attach the new switch to the column hub.

9. Connect the wiring plugs to their mating plugs at the lower end of the column and install the plastic cover at the harness.

10. Install all retaining clips and wire assembly covers that were removed and install the turn signal handle. Install the emergency flasher retainer and knob, if so equipped.

11. Install the steering wheel and retaining nut as outlined in the "Steering Wheel Removal and Installation" section.

12. Install the horn ring or button. On post-1968 models, install the crash pad with the retaining screws at the underside of each steering wheel spoke.

13. Connect the negative battery cable and test the operation of the turn signals, horn, and emergency flashers, if so equipped.

STEERING GEAR INSPECTION

Before any steering gear adjustments are made, it is recommended that the front end of the car be raised and a thorough inspection be made for stiffness or lost motion in the steering gear, steering linkage and front suspension. Worn or damaged parts should be replaced, since a satisfactory adjustment of the steering gear cannot be obtained if bent or badly worn parts exist.

It is also very important that the steering gear be properly aligned in the car. Misalignment of the gear places a stress on the steering worm shaft, therefore, a proper adjustment is impossible. To align the steering gear, loosen the mounting bolts to permit the gear to align itself. Check the steering gear mounting seat and, if there is a gap at any of the mounting bolts, proper alignment may be obtained by placing shims where excessive gap appears. Tighten the steering gear bolts. Alignment of the gear in the car is very important and should be done carefully so that a satisfactory, trouble-free gear adjustment may be obtained.

Manual Steering Gear

STEERING WORM AND SECTOR GEAR ADJUSTMENTS

The ball nut assembly and the sector gear must be adjusted properly to maintain a minimum amount of steering shaft end-play and a minimum amount of backlash between the sector gear and the ball nut. There are only two adjustments that may be done on this steering gear and they should be done as given below:

1. Disconnect the pitman arm from the steering pitman-to-idler arm rod.

2. Loosen the locknut on the sector shaft adjustment screw and turn the adjusting screw counterclockwise.

3. Measure the worm bearing preload by attaching an in. lbs. torque wrench to the steering wheel nut. With the steering wheel off center, note the reading required to rotate the input shaft about 1½ turns either side of center. If the torque reading is not about 4–5 in. lbs., adjust the gear as given in the next step.

4. Loosen the steering shaft bearing adjus-

Steering gear adjustments

ter locknut and tighten or back off the bearing adjusting screw until the preload is within the specified limits.

4. Loosen the steering shaft bearing adjuster locknut and tighten or back off the bearing adjusting screw until the preload is within the specified limits.

5. Tighten the steering shaft bearing adjuster locknut and recheck the preload torque.

6. Turn the steering wheel slowly to either stop. Turn *gently* against the stop to avoid possible damage to the ball return guides. Then rotate the wheel 2¾ turns to center the ball nut.

7. Turn the sector adjusting screw clockwise until the proper torque (9–10 in. lbs.) is obtained that is necessary to rotate the worm gear past its center (high spot).

8. While holding the sector adjusting screw, tighten the sector screw adjusting locknut to 32–40 ft. lbs. and recheck the backlash adjustment.

9. Connect the pitman arm to the steering arm-to-idler arm rod.

STEERING GEAR REMOVAL AND INSTALLATION

1. Remove the bolt(s) that holds the flex coupling to the steering shaft.

2. Remove the nut and lockwasher that secures the pitman arm to the sector shaft using a suitable gear puller or Tool T64P-3590-F.

CAUTION: *Do not hammer on the end of the puller as this can damage the steering gear.*

3. To gain enough clearance on some cars

with standard transmissions, it may be necessary to disconnect the clutch linkage. On some cars with V8 engines, it may be necessary to lower the exhaust system.

4. Remove the steering gear-to-side rail bolts and remove the steering gear.

5. To install the steering gear, position the steering gear and flex coupling in place, and install and torque the steering gear-to-side rail bolts to 50–65 ft. lbs.

6. If the clutch linkage has been disconnected, reposition and adjust it. If the exhaust system has been lowered, reinstall it to its proper position.

7. Position the pitman arm and the sector shaft and install the attaching nut and lockwasher. Tighten the nut to 150–225 ft. lbs.

8. Install the flex coupling attaching nut(s) and tighten them to specification (tilt steering column, one bolt—20–37 ft. lbs.; fixed-column, two bolts—10–22 ft. lbs.).

Power Steering System Inspection

LUBRICATION

Proper lubrication of the steering linkage and the front suspension is very important for the proper operation of the power steering systems. Check the steering gear box for sufficient lubricant by removing the filler plug and checking the level. Add enough fluid gear oil S.A.E. 90 to bring the oil level to the filler plug hole if necessary.

CAUTION: *Do not use a pressure gun to add fluid gear oil since the pressure will force the oil out of the steering gear box.*

AIR BLEEDING

Air bubbles in the power steering system must be removed from the fluid. Be sure the reservoir is filled to the proper level and the fluid is warmed up to the operating temperature. Turn the steering wheel through its full travel three or four times until all the air bubbles are removed. *Do not hold the steering wheel against its stops.* Recheck the fluid level.

FLUID LEVEL CHECK

1. Run the engine until the fluid is at the normal operating temperature. Then, turn the steering wheel through its full travel three or four times and turn off the engine.

2. Check the fluid level in the steering reservoir. On cars built before 1968, the fluid level is checked by removing the reservoir

cap and looking in the filler tube for the fluid level. On 1968 and later cars, a dipstick is provided in the filler tube that shows the proper fluid level. If the fluid level is low, add enough fluid to raise the level to the Full mark on the dipstick or filler tube. Use automatic transmission fluid, type A.

PUMP BELT CHECK

1. Inspect the pump belt for cracks, glazing, or worn places. Using a belt tension gauge, check the belt adjustment. The amount of tension varies with the make of car and the condition of the belt. New belts (those belts used less than 15 minutes) require a higher figure. The belt deflection method of adjustment may be used only if a belt tension gauge is not available. The belt should be adjusted for a deflection of ⅜–½ in.

FLUID LEAKS

Check all possible leakage points (hoses, power steering pump, or steering gear) for loss of fluid. Start the engine and rotate the steering wheel from lock to lock several times. Tighten all loose fittings and replace any defective lines or valve seats.

TURNING EFFORT

Check the effort required to turn the steering wheel after aligning the front wheels and inflating the tires to the proper pressure.

1. With the vehicle on dry pavement and the front wheels straight ahead, set the parking brake and turn the engine on.

2. After a short warm-up period, turn the steering wheel back and forth several times to warm the steering fluid.

3. Attach a spring scale to the steering wheel rim and measure the pull required to turn the steering wheel one complete revolution in each direction. The effort needed to turn the steering wheel should not exceed the limits given in the specifications.

NOTE: *This test may be done with a torque wrench on the steering wheel nut. See the section on manual steering for a discussion of this test.*

POWER STEERING HOSE INSPECTION

1. Inspect both the input and output hoses of the power steering pump for worn spots, cracks, or signs of leakage. Replace the hose if it is defective, being sure to reconnect the replacement hose properly. Many power steering hoses are identified as to where they are to be connected by special means, such as fittings that will only fit on the correct pump fitting, or hoses of special lengths.

CHECKING THE OIL FLOW AND PRESSURE RELIEF VALVE IN THE PUMP ASSEMBLY

When the wheels are turned hard right or hard left, against the stops, the oil flow and pressure relief valves come into action. If these valves are working, there should be a slight buzzing noise. Do not hold the wheels in the extreme position for over three or four seconds because, if the pressure relief valve is not working, the pressure could get high enough to damage the system.

TEST-DRIVING CAR TO CHECK THE POWER STEERING

When test-driving to check the power steering, drive at a speed between 15 and 20 mph. Make several turns in each direction. When a turn is completed, the front wheels should return to the straight-ahead position with very little help from the driver.

If the front wheels fail to return as they should and yet the steering linkage is free and properly adjusted, the trouble is probably due to misalignment of the power cylinder or improper adjustment of the spool valve.

1. Lubricate the sector shaft journal and install the sector shaft and cover. With the cover moved to one side, fill the gear with steering gear lubricant (0.90 lb.). Push the cover and the sector shaft into place and install the two top housing bolts. Do not tighten the bolts until checking to see that there is some lash between the ball nut and the sector gear teeth. Hold or push the cover away from the ball nut and tighten the bolts to 30–40 ft. lbs.

2. Loosely install the sector shaft adjusting screw locknut and adjust the sector shaft mesh load as given earlier. Tighten the adjusting screw locknut.

Non-integral Linkage Type Power Steering System

The Ford non-integral linkage type power steering system is a hydraulically controlled system composed of an integral pump and fluid reservoir, a control valve, a power cylinder, connecting fluid lines, and the steering linkage. The hydraulic pump, which is driven by a belt turned by the engine, draws

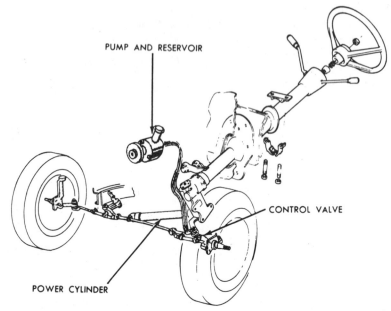

PUMP AND RESERVOIR

CONTROL VALVE

POWER CYLINDER

Power steering system

fluid from the reservoir and provides fluid pressure through hoses to the control valve and the power cylinder. There is a pressure relief valve to limit the pressures within the steering system to a safe level. After the fluid has passed from the pump to the control valve and the power cylinder, it returns to the reservoir.

IN-CAR ADJUSTMENT
Control Valve Centering Spring Adjustment

1. Raise the car and remove the spring cap attaching screws and the spring cap.

CAUTION: *Be very careful not to position the hoist adaptors of two-post hoists under the suspension and/or steering components. Place the hoist adaptors under the front suspension lower arms.*

2. Tighten the adjusting nut snugly (about 90–100 in. lbs.); then loosen the nut ¼ turn (90°). Do not tighten the adjusting nut too tightly.

3. Place the spring cap on the valve housing. Lubricate and install the attaching screws and washers. Tighten the screws to 72–100 in. lbs.

4. Lower the car and start the engine. Check the steering effort using a spring scale attached to the steering wheel rim for a torque of no more than 12 lbs.

Integral Type Power Steering System

The rotary type power steering gear is designed with all components in one housing.

The power cylinder is an integral part of the gear housing. A double-acting piston allows oil pressure to be applied to either side of the piston. The one-piece piston and power rack is meshed to the sector shaft.

The hydraulic control valve is composed of a sleeve and valve spool. The spool is held in the neutral position by the torsion bar and spool actuator. Twisting of the torsion bar moves the valve spool, allowing oil pressure to be directed to either side of the power piston, depending on the directional rotation of the steering wheel, to give power assist.

ROLLER PUMP REMOVAL AND INSTALLATION
Removal

Remove the reservoir cover and use a suction gun to empty the reservoir. Disconnect the hoses from the pump and tie them in a raised position to prevent oil spillage. Loosen pump adjusting screw and remove the pump belt, then take out the retaining bolts and remove the pump and reservoir.

NOTE: *On cars equipped with air conditioning, the pump is removed from underneath the vehicle.*

Installation

Position the pump assembly and install the retaining bolts. Be sure there is clearance between the pump bracket and the engine front support bracket. Install the hoses and place the pump belt on the pulley. Adjust the belt to ½ in. deflection, then tighten the adjusting screw.

Connect the hoses to the pump assembly.

Fill the reservoir to within ½ in. of the top with automatic transmission fluid type A.

Start the engine and rotate the steering wheel several times to the right and left to expel air from the system, then recheck the oil level and install the reservoir cover.

POWER STEERING UNIT
Fluid Used

This unit uses automatic transmission fluid type A.

Bleeding the System

Fill the pump reservoir to within ½ in. of the top. Start and run the engine to attain normal operating temperatures. Now, turn the steering wheel through its entire travel three or four times to expel air from the system, then recheck the fluid level.

Checking Steering Effort

Run the engine to attain normal operating temperatures. With the wheels on a dry floor, hook a pull scale to the spoke of the steering wheel at the outer edge. The effort required to turn the steering wheel should be 3½–5 lbs. If the pull is not within these limits, check the hydraulic pressure.

Pressure Test

To check the hydraulic pressure, disconnect the pressure hose from the gear. Now connect the pressure gauge between the pressure hose from the pump and the steering gear housing. Run the engine to attain normal operating temperatures, then turn the wheel to a full right and a full left turn to the wheel stops.

Hold the wheel in this position only long enough to obtain an accurate reading.

The pressure gauge reading should be within the limits specified. If the pressure reading is less than the minimum pressure needed for proper operation, close the valve at the gauge and see if the reading increases. If the pressure is still low, the pump is defective and needs repair. If the pressure reading is at or near the minimum reading, the pump is normal and needs only an adjustment of the power steering gear or power assist control valve.

Worm Bearing Preload and Sector Mesh Adjustments

Disconnect the pitman arm from the sector shaft, then back off on the sector shaft adjusting screw on the sector shaft cover.

Center the steering on the high point, then attach a pull scale to the spoke of the steering wheel at the outer edge. The pull required to keep the wheel moving for one complete turn should be ½–⅔ lbs.

If the pull is not within these limits, loosen the thrust bearing locknut and tighten or back off on the valve sleeve adjuster locknut to bring the preload within limits. Tighten the thrust bearing locknut and recheck the preload.

Slowly rotate the steering wheel several times, then center the steering on the high point. Now, turn the sector shaft adjusting screw until a steering wheel pull of 1–1½ lbs. is required to move the worm through the center point. Tighten the sector shaft adjusting screw locknut and recheck the sector mesh adjustment.

Install the pitman arm and draw the arm into position with the nut.

Brakes

HYDRAULIC SYSTEM

When the brake pedal is depressed, the master cylinder piston or pistons move forward, displacing the brake fluid. Due to the fact that the fluid volume is constant, the displacement results in increased hydraulic pressure. This pressure is exerted upon the wheel cylinders and/or caliper pistons thus forcing the brake shoes or friction pads against the drums or discs.

Hydraulic pressure is exerted in proportion to the effort applied to the brake pedal. All disc front/drum rear applications since 1965 utilize a proportioning valve which maintains a predetermined front/rear hydraulic pressure ratio, thereby reducing the possibility of premature rear wheel lock-up. All 1972 and later models are equipped with a metering valve which delays pressure buildup to the front discs upon application. The metering valve extends disc pad life by preventing the front discs from carrying the majority of the braking load at low operating line pressures.

When the brake pedal is released, hydraulic pressure drops. On drum brakes, the brake return springs, and on disc brakes, the piston seals return the shoes or disc pads to their retracted positions and force the displaced fluid back into the master cylinder.

The hydraulic brake lines and brake linings are to be inspected at the recommended intervals in the maintenance schedule. Follow the steel tubing from the master cylinder to the flexible hose fitting at each wheel. If a section of the tubing is found to be damaged, replace the entire section with tubing of the same type (steel, not copper), size, shape, and length. When installing a new section of brake tubing, flush clean brake fluid or denatured alcohol through to remove any dirt or foreign material from the line. Be sure to flare both ends to provide sound, leakproof connections. When bending the tubing to fit the underbody contours, be careful not to kink or crack the line. Torque all hydraulic connections to 10–15 ft. lbs.

Check the flexible brake hoses that connect the steel tubing to each wheel cylinder. Replace the hose if it shows any signs of softening, cracking, or other damage. When installing a new front brake hose, position the hose to avoid contact with other chassis parts. Place a new copper gasket over the hose fitting and thread the hose assembly into the front wheel cylinder. A new rear brake hose must be positioned clear of the exhaust pipe or shock absorber. Thread the hose into the rear brake tube connector. When installing either a new front or rear brake hose, engage the opposite end of the hose to the bracket

on the frame. Install the horseshoe-type retaining clip and connect the tube to the hose
with the tube fitting nut.

Always bleed the system after hose or line
replacement. Before bleeding, make sure
that the master cylinder is topped up with
high-temperature, extra-heavy-duty fluid of
at least SAE 70R3 quality.

NOTE: *Never reuse brake fluid that has
been bled from the system as it contains
microscopic air bubbles. On vehicles with
dual brake systems, centralize the pressure
differential valve after bleeding the system.
Top up the master cylinder to the specified
level.*

Power Brake Unit

REMOVAL

1. Working inside the car, below the instrument panel, disconnect the booster valve
operating rod from the brake pedal assembly.

2. Open the hood and disconnect the
wires from the stop light switch at the brake
master cylinder.

3. Disconnect the brake line at the master
cylinder outlet fitting.

4. Disconnect the manifold vacuum hose
from the booster unit.

5. Remove the four bracket-to-dash panel
attaching bolts.

6. Remove the booster and bracket assembly from the dash panel, sliding the valve operating rod out from the engine side of the
dash panel.

INSTALLATION

1. Mount the booster and bracket assembly to the dash panel by sliding the valve operating rod in through the hole in the dash
panel, and installing the attaching bolts.

2. Connect the manifold vacuum hose to
the booster.

3. Connect the brake line to the master
cylinder outlet fitting.

4. Connect the stop light switch wires.

5. Working inside the car, below the instrument panel, install the rubber boot on
the valve-operating rod at the passenger side
of the dash panel.

6. Connect the valve-operating rod to the
brake pedal with the bushings, eccentric
shoulder bolt, and nut.

Master Cylinder

On 1965 and 1966 models, single master cylinders are used. These units consist of a single cylinder and reservoir, mounted on the
engine side of the firewall. On post-1966
models, a dual or tandem type master cylinder is used. This system divides the brake
hydraulic system into two independent and
hydraulically separated halves, with the front
of the cylinder operating the rear brakes and
the rear of the cylinder operating the front
brakes. A failure in one system will still allow
braking in the other. Whenever the hydraulic pressure is unequal in one of the systems, a pressure differential valve activates a
warning light on the dashboard to warn the
driver.

REMOVAL AND INSTALLATION

1965–1966

STANDARD BRAKES

1. Disconnect the rubber boot from the
rear of the master cylinder in the passenger
compartment.

2. Disconnect the brake line from the
master cylinder.

3. Remove the master cylinder retaining
bolts from the firewall and lift the cylinder
away from the pushrod and boot.

4. To reinstall the master cylinder, guide
it carefully onto the pushrod and replace the
mounting bolts.

5. Connect the brake line to the master
cylinder, but leave the brake line fitting
loose.

6. Fill the master cylinder and, with the
brake line loose, slowly bleed the air from
the cylinder using the foot pedal.

7. Tighten the line at the master cylinder
and refill to within ¼ in. of the top.

POWER BRAKES

1. Disconnect the brake line from the
master cylinder.

2. Remove the two nuts and lockwashers
that attach the master cylinder to the brake
booster.

3. Remove the master cylinder from the
booster.

4. Reverse the above procedure to reinstall.

5. Fill the master cylinder and bleed the
entire brake system.

6. Refill the master cylinder.

1967–1973

STANDARD BRAKES

1. Working under the dash, disconnect
the master cylinder pushrod from the brake

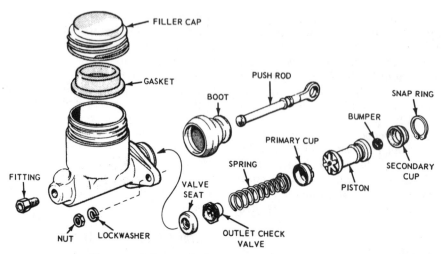

Master cylinder used with standard brake system

pedal. The pushrod cannot be removed from the master cylinder.

2. Disconnect the stoplight switch wires and remove the switch from the brake pedal, using care not to damage the switch.

3. Disconnect the brake lines from the master cylinder.

4. Remove the attaching screws from the firewall and remove the master cylinder from the car.

5. Reinstall in the reverse of above order, leaving the brake line fittings loose at the master cylinder.

6. Fill the master cylinder and, with the

brake lines loose, slowly bleed the air from the master cylinder uing the foot pedal.

POWER BRAKES

The procedure for removing and installing the tandem type master cylinder with power brakes is the same as the procedure for the 1965–1966 single master cylinder with power brakes.

OVERHAUL

The following procedure applies to both single and dual master cylinders. On single type

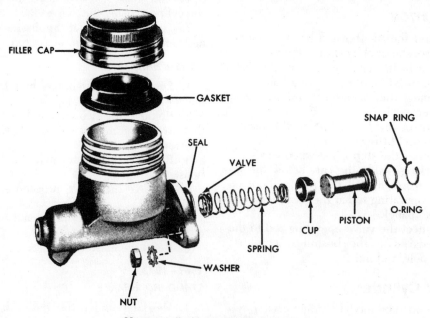

Master cylinder used with booster

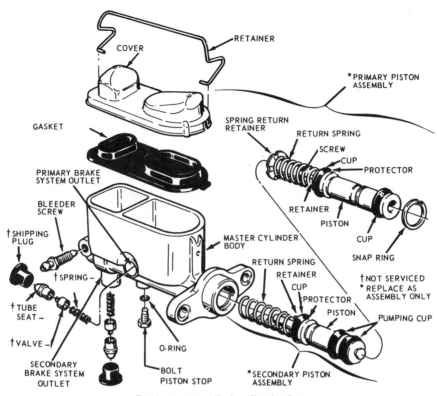

Dual master cylinder-disc brakes

master cylinders, there is no stop-screw and only one piston assembly.

1. Remove the cylinder from the car and drain the brake fluid.

2. Mount the cylinder in a vise so that the outlets are up and remove the seal from the hub.

3. Remove the stopscrew from the bottom of the front reservoir.

4. Remove the snap-ring from the front of the bore and remove the rear piston assembly.

5. Remove the front piston assembly, using compressed air. Cover the bore opening with a cloth to prevent damage to the piston.

6. Clean the metal parts in brake fluid and discard the rubber parts.

7. Inspect the bore for damage or wear, and check the pistons for damage and the proper clearance in the bore.

8. If the bore is only slightly scored or pitted, it may be honed. Always use hones that are in good condition and completely clean the cylinder with brake fluid when the honing is completed. If any evidence of contamination exists in the master cylinder, the entire hydraulic system should be flushed

and refilled with clean brake fluid. Blow out the passages with compressed air.

9. Install new secondary seals in the two grooves in the flat end of the front piston. The lips of the seals will be facing away from each other.

10. Install a new primary seal and the seal protector on the opposite end of the front piston with the lips of the seal facing outward.

11. Coat the seals with brake fluid. Install the spring on the front piston with the spring retainer in the primary seal.

12. Insert the piston assembly—spring end first—into the bore and use a wooden rod to seat it.

13. Coat the rear piston seals with brake fluid and install them into the piston grooves with the lips facing the spring end.

14. Assemble the spring onto the piston and install the assembly into the bore spring first. Install the snap-ring.

15. Hold the piston train at the bottom of the bore and install the stopscrew. Install a new seal on the hub. Bench-bleed the cylinder or install and bleed the cylinder on the car.

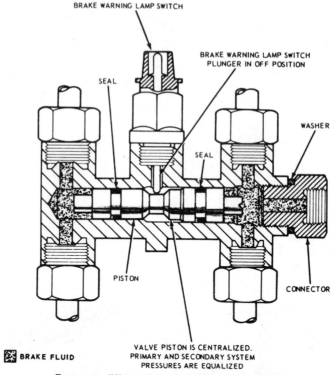

BRAKE WARNING LAMP SWITCH

BRAKE WARNING LAMP SWITCH
PLUNGER IN OFF POSITION

SEAL

SEAL

WASHER

PISTON

CONNECTOR

BRAKE FLUID

VALVE PISTON IS CENTRALIZED.
PRIMARY AND SECONDARY SYSTEM
PRESSURES ARE EQUALIZED

Pressure differential warning valve-sectional

Pressure Differential Warning Valve

Since the introduction of dual master cylinders to the hydraulic brake system, a pressure differential warning signal has been added. This signal consists of a warning light on the dashboard activated by a differential pressure switch located below the master cylinder. The signal indicates a hydraulic pressure differential between the front and rear brakes of 80–150 psi and should warn the driver that a hydraulic failure has occurred.

After repairing and bleeding any part of the hydraulic system, the warning light may remain on due to the pressure differential valve remaining in the off-center position. To centralize the valve a pressure difference must be created in the opposite branch of the hydraulic system that was repaired or bled last.

NOTE: *Front wheel balancing of cars equipped with disc brakes may also cause a pressure differential in the front branch of the system.*

1967–1969

To centralize the valve:

1. Switch the ignition on. Have an assistant apply pressure to the brake pedal.

2. Loosen the bleeder screw at the opposite side of the brake system that was affected or repaired last.

3. Press the brake pedal slowly until the valve is centralized and the light goes out. Retighten the wheel cylinder bleeder screw.

4. Check the brake fluid level and brake pedal height and firmness. Road-test the car.

1970–1973

To centralize the valve:

1. Turn the ignition to "acc" or "on."

2. Check the fluid level in the master cylinder reservoirs. Fill up to within ¼ in. of the top.

3. Depress the brake pedal firmly and the valve will centralize itself causing the brake warning light to go out.

4. Turn the ignition off.

5. Prior to driving the vehicle, check the operation of the brakes and obtain a firm pedal.

Proportioning Valve

On vehicles equipped with front disc and rear drum brakes, a proportioning valve is an important part of the system. It is installed in the hydraulic line to the rear brakes. Its function is to maintain the correct proportion be-

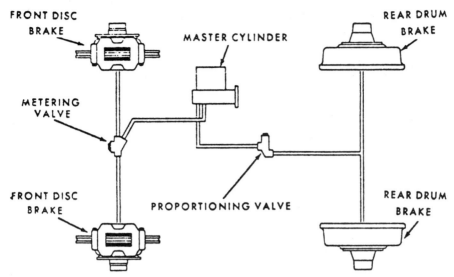

FRONT DISC BRAKE

MASTER CYLINDER

REAR DRUM BRAKE

METERING VALVE

FRONT DISC BRAKE

PROPORTIONING VALVE

REAR DRUM BRAKE

Disc brake hydraulic system

tween line pressures to the front and rear brakes. *No attempt at adjustment of this valve should be made, as adjustment is preset and tampering will result in uneven braking action.*

To assure correct installation when replacing the valve, the outlet to the rear brakes is stamped with the letter "R."

Metering Valve

On some vehicles equipped with front disc brakes, a metering valve is used. This valve is installed in the hydraulic line to the front brakes, and functions to delay pressure buildup to the front brakes on application. Its purpose is to reduce the front brake pressure until the rear brake pressure builds up adequately to overcome the rear brake shoe return springs. In this way, disc brake pad life is extended because it prevents the front disc brakes from carrying all or most of the braking load at low operating line pressures.

The metering valve can be checked very simply. With the car stopped, gently apply the brakes. At about 1 in. of travel, a very small change in pedal effort (like a small bump) will be felt if the valve is operating properly. Metering valves are not serviceable and must be replaced if defective.

Wheel Cylinders and Calipers

Since repair or replacement of these components requires the removal of the brake shoes, the procedures are included in the brake shoe replacement section of this chapter. Wheel cylinder procedures can be found

under "Drum Brakes and Calipers" under "Disc Brakes."

Hydraulic System Bleeding

The purpose of bleeding the brakes is to expel air trapped in the hydraulic system; there are two methods of accomplishing this. The quickest and easiest of the two is pressure-bleeding, but special pressure equipment is needed to externally pressurize the hydraulic system. The other, more commonly used, method is gravity bleeding.

Master cylinders equipped with bleed screws may be bled independently. When bleeding the Bendix type dual master cylinder, it is necessary to solidly cap one reservoir section while bleeding the other to prevent pressure loss through the cap vent hole.

Disc brakes may be bled in the same manner as drum brakes, except that:

1. Brakes should be bled in this order: right rear, left rear, right front, left front.

2. It usually requires a longer time to bleed a disc brake thoroughly.

3. The disc should be rotated to make sure that the piston has returned to the unapplied position when bleeding is completed and the bleed screw closed.

Pressure-bleeding disc brakes will close the metering valve; the front brakes will not bleed. For this reason it is necessary to manually hold the metering valve open during pressure-bleeding. Never use a block or clamp to hold the valve open and never force the valve stem beyond its normal position. Two different types of valves are used. The most common type requires the valve stem to be held in while bleeding the brakes, while the second type requires the valve stem to be held out (0.060 in. minimum travel). Determine the type by visual inspection.

NOTE: *Since the front and rear hydraulic systems are independent, if it is known that only one system contains air, only that system has to be bled.*

1. Fill the master cylinder with brake fluid.

2. Install a ⅜ in. box-end wrench on the bleeder screw on the right rear wheel.

3. Push a piece of small diameter rubber tubing over the bleeder screw until it is flush against the wrench. Submerge the other end of the rubber tubing in a glass jar partially filled with clean brake fluid. Make sure the rubber tube fits on the bleeder screw snugly.

4. Have a friend apply pressure to the brake pedal. Open the bleeder screw and observe the bottle of brake fluid. If bubbles appear in the glass jar, it means there is air in the system. When your friend has pushed the pedal to the floor, immediately close the bleeder screw before he releases the pedal.

5. Repeat this procedure until no bubbles appear in the jar. Refill the master cylinder.

6. Repeat this procedure on the left rear, right front, and left front wheels, in that order. Periodically refill the master cylinder so it does not run dry.

7. On 1970–1973 cars, if the brake warning light is on, depress the brake pedal firmly. If there is no air in the system, the light will go out.

BRAKE SYSTEMS

Three types of brakes have been used. Drum brakes, the first type, have always been Bendix-designed duo-servo self-adjusting brakes, and have been the standard equipment offered. Federal regulations have required the use of a dual master cylinder since 1967.

Front disc brakes, offered as an option since 1965, have been of two types. Pre-1968 models were four-piston, fixed-caliper discs. Since 1968, single-piston, floating-caliper discs have been used.

Drum Brakes

All drum brakes employ single-anchor, internal expanding, self-adjusting brake assemblies. The automatic adjuster continuously maintains correct operating clearance between the linings and the drums by adjusting the brake in small increments in direct proportion to lining wear. The linings tend to follow the rotating drum counterclockwise, thus forcing the upper end of the primary shoe against the anchor pin. The wheel cylinder pushes the upper end of the secondary shoe and cable guide outward simultaneously, away from the anchor pin. This movement of the secondary shoe causes the cable to pull the adjusting lever upward against the end of the tooth on the adjusting screw star wheel. As lining wear increases, the upward travel of the adjusting lever also increases. When the linings have worn sufficiently to allow the lever to move upward far enough, it passes over the end of the tooth and engages it. When the brakes are released, the adjusting spring pulls the adjuster lever downward, turning the star wheel and expanding the brakes.

INSPECTION

1. Raise the front or rear of the car and support the car with safety stands. Make sure the parking brake is not on.

2. If you are going to check the rear brakes, remove the tires and wheels from the car. Using a pair of pliers, remove the tinnerman nuts from the wheel studs. Pull the brake drum off the axle shaft. If the brakes are adjusted too tightly to remove the drum, see step four.

3. If you are going to check the front brakes, the front tire, wheel, and brake drum can be removed as an assembly. Remove the hub cap, then either pry the dust cover off the spindle with a screcriver or pull it off with a pair of channel-lock pliers. Remove the cotter pin from the spindle. Slide the nut lock off the adjusting nut, then loosen the adjusting nut until it reaches the end of the spindle. Do not remove the adjusting nut yet. Grab the tire and pull it out toward yourself, then push it back into position. This will free the outer wheel bearing from the drum hub. If the brakes are adjusted too tightly to allow the drum to be pulled off, go to step four and loosen the brakes, then return to this step. Remove the adjusting nut, washer, and outer bearing from the spindle. Pull the tire, wheel, and brake drum off the spindle.

4. If the brakes are too tight to remove the drum, get under the car (make sure you have safety stands under the car to support it) and

remove the rubber plug from the bottom of the brake backing plate. Shine a flashlight into the slot in the plate. You will see the top of the adjusting screw star wheel and the adjusting lever for the automatic brake adjusting mechanism. To back off on the adjusting screw, you must first insert a small, thin screw-driver or a piece of firm wire (coat hanger wire) into the adjusting slot and push the adjusting lever away from the adjusting screw. Insert a brake adjusting spoon into the slot and engage the top of the star wheel. Lift up on the bottom of the adjusting spoon to force the adjusting screw star wheel downward. Repeat this operation until the brake drum is free of the brake shoes and can be pulled off.

5. Clean the brake shoes and the inside of the brake drum. There must be at least $^{1}/_{16}$ in. of brake lining above the heads of the brake shoe attaching rivets. The lining should not be cracked or contaminated with grease or brake fluid. If there is grease or brake fluid on the lining it must be replaced and the source of the leak must be found and corrected. Brake fluid on the lining means leaking wheel cylinders. Grease on the brake lining means a leaking grease retainer (front wheels) or axle seal (rear brakes). If the lining is slightly glazed but otherwise in good condition, it can be cleaned up with medium sandpaper. Lift up the bottom of the wheel cylinder boots and inspect the ends of the wheel cylinders. A small amount of fluid in the end of the cylinders should be considered normal. If fluid runs out of the cylinder when the boots are lifted, however, the wheel cylinder must be rebuilt or replaced. Examine the inside of the brake drum. It should have a smooth, dull finish. If excessive brake shoe wear caused grooves to wear in the drum, it must be machined or replaced. If the inside of the drum is slightly glazed, but otherwise good, it can be cleaned up with medium sandpaper.

6. If no repairs are required, install the drum and wheel. If the brake adjustment was changed to remove the drum, adjust the brakes until the drum will just fit over the brakes. After the wheel is installed it will be necessary to complete the adjustment. See "Brake Adjustment. See "Brake Adjustment" later in this chapter. If a front wheel was removed, tighten the wheel bearing adjusting nut to 17–25 ft. lbs. while spinning the wheel. This will seat the bearing. Loosen the

adjusting nut ½ turn, then retighten it to 10–15 in. lbs.

BRAKE SHOE REMOVAL

NOTE: *If you are not thoroughly familiar with the procedures involved in brake replacement, only disassemble and assemble one side at a time, leaving the other wheel intact as a reference.*

1. Remove the brake drum. See the "Inspection" procedure above.

2. Place the hollow end of a brake spring service tool (available at auto parts stores) on the brake shoe anchor pin and twist it to disengage one of the brake retracting springs. Repeat this operation to remove the other spring.

CAUTION: *Be careful the springs do not slip off the tool during removal, as they could cause personal injury.*

3. Reach behind the brake backing plate and place a finger on the end of one of the brake hold-down spring mounting pins. Using a pair of pliers, grasp the washer on the top of the hold-down spring that corresponds to the pin that you are holding. Push down on the pliers and turn them 90° to align the slot in the washer with the head on the spring mounting pin. Remove the spring and washer and repeat this operation on the hold-down spring on the other brake shoe.

4. Place the tip of a screwdriver on the top of the brake adjusting screw and move the screwdriver upward to lift up on the brake adjusting lever. When there is enough slack in the automatic adjuster cable, disconnect the loop on the top of the cable from the anchor. Grasp the top of each brake shoe and move it outward to disengage it from the wheel cylinder (and parking brake link on rear wheels). When the brake shoes are clear, lift them from the backing plate. Twist the shoes slightly and the automatic adjuster assembly will disassemble itself.

5. If you are working on rear brakes, grasp the end of the brake cable spring with a pair of pliers and, using the brake lever as a fulcrum, pull the end of the spring away from the lever. Disengage the cable from the brake lever.

WHEEL CYLINDER OVERHAUL

Since the travel of the pistons in the wheel cylinder changes when new brake shoes are installed, it is possible for previously good wheel cylinders to start leaking after new

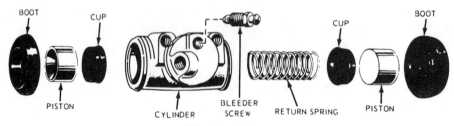

Wheel cylinder

brakes are installed. Therefore, to save your-self the expense of having to replace new brakes that become saturated with brake fluid and the aggravation of having to take everything apart again, it is strongly recommended that wheel cylinders be rebuilt every time new brake shoes are installed. This is especially true for cars with high mileage.

1. Remove the brakes.

2. Place a bucket or old newspapers under the brake backing plate to catch the brake fluid that will run out of the wheel cylinder.

3. Remove the boots from the ends of the wheel cylinders.

4. Push one piston toward the center of the cylinder to force the opposite piston and cup out the other end of the cylinder. Reach into the open end of the cylinder and push the spring, cup and piston out of the cylinder.

5. Remove the bleeder screw from the rear of the cylinder, on the back of the backing plate.

6. Inspect the inside of the wheel cylinder. If it is scored in any way, the cylinder must be honed with a wheel cylinder hone or fine emery paper, and finished with crocus cloth if emery paper is used. If the inside of the cylinder is excessively worn, the cylinder will have to be replaced, as only 0.003 in. of material can be removed from the cylinder walls. When honing or cleaning wheel cylinders, keep a small amount of brake fluid in the cylinder to serve as a lubricant.

7. Clean any foreign matter from the pistons. The sides of the pistons must be smooth for the wheel cylinders to operate properly.

8. Clean the cylinder bore with alcohol and a lint-free rag. Pull the rag through the bore several times to remove all foreign matter and dry the cylinder.

9. Install the bleeder screw and the return spring in the cylinder.

10. Coat new cylinder cups with new

brake fluid and install them in the cylinder. Make sure they are square in the bore or they will leak.

11. Install the pistons in the cylinder after coating them with new brake fluid.

12. Coat the insides of the boots with new brake fluid and install them on the cylinder. Install the brakes.

WHEEL CYLINDER REPLACEMENT

1. Remove the brake shoes.

2. On rear brakes, loosen the brake line on the rear of the cylinder, but do not pull the line away from the cylinder or it may bend.

3. On front brakes, disconnect the metal brake line from the rubber brake hose where they join in the wheel well. Pull off the horseshoe clip that attaches the rubber brake hose to the underbody of the car. Loosen the hose at the cylinder, then turn the whole brake hose to remove it from the wheel cylinder.

4. Remove the bolts and lockwashers that attach the wheel cylinder to the backing plate and remove the cylinder.

5. Position the new wheel cylinder on the backing plate and install the cylinder attaching bolts and lockwashers.

6. Attach the metal brake line or rubber hose by reversing the procedure given in step two or three.

7. Install the brakes.

BRAKE SHOE INSTALLATION

1. On rear brakes, the brake cable must be connected to the secondary brake shoe before the shoe is installed on the backing plate. To do this, first transfer the parking brake lever from the old secondary shoe to the new one. This is done by spreading the bottom of the horseshoe clip and disengaging the lever. Position the lever on the new secondary shoe and install the spring washer and the horseshoe clip. Close the bottom of the clip after installing it. Grasp the metal tip of

the parking brake cable with a pair of pliers. Position a pair of side-cutter pliers on the end of the cable coil spring and, using the pliers as a fulcrum, pull the coil spring back. Position the cable in the parking brake lever.

2. Apply a light coating of high-temperature grease to the brake shoe contact points on the backing plate. Position the primary brake shoe on the front of the backing plate and install the hold-down spring and washer over the mounting pin. Install the secondary shoe on the rear of the backing plate.

3. If working on rear brakes, install the parking brake link between the notch in the primary brake shoe and the notch in the parking brake lever.

4. Install the automatic adjuster cable loop end on the anchor pin. Make sure the crimped side of the loop faces the backing plate.

5. Install the return spring in the primary brake shoe and, using the tapered end of a brake spring service tool, slide the top of the spring onto the anchor pin.

CAUTION: *Be careful the spring does not slip off the tool during installation, as it could cause personal injury.*

6. Install the automatic adjuster cable guide in the secondary brake shoe, making sure the flared hole in the cable guide is inside the hole in the brake shoe. Fit the cable into the groove in the top of the cable guide.

7. Install the secondary shoe return spring through the hole in the cable guide and the brake shoe. Using the brake spring tool, slide the top of the spring onto the anchor pin.

8. Clean the threads on the adjusting screw and apply a light coating of high-temperature grease to the threads. Screw the adjuster closed, then open it one-half turn.

9. Install the adjusting screw between the brake shoes with the star wheel nearest to the secondary shoe. Make sure the star wheel is in a position that is accessible from the adjusting slot in the backing plate.

10. Install the short, hooked end of the automatic adjuster spring in the proper hole in the primary brake shoe.

11. Connect the hooked end of the automatic adjuster cable and the free end of the automatic adjuster spring in the slot in the top of the automatic adjuster lever.

12. Pull the automatic adjuster lever (the lever will pull the cable and spring with it) downward and to the left and engage the pivot hook of the lever in the hole in the secondary brake shoe.

13. Check the entire brake assembly to make sure everything is installed properly. Make sure the shoes engage the wheel cylinder properly and are flush on the anchor pin. Make sure the automatic adjuster cable is flush on the anchor pin and in the slot on the back on cable guide. Make sure the adjusting lever rests on the adjusting screw star wheel. Pull upward on the adjusting cable until the adjusting lever is free of the star wheel, then release the cable. The adjusting lever should snap back into place on the adjusting screw star wheel and turn the wheel one tooth.

14. Expand the brake adjusting screw until the brake drum will just fit over the brake shoes.

15. Install the wheel and drum and adjust the brakes. See "Brake Adjustment."

BRAKE ADJUSTMENT

It will be necessary to manually adjust the self-adjusting brakes after they have been disassembled for any reason. The following procedure may be used after reinstalling the drums.

1. Raise the car and support it with safety stands.

2. Remove the rubber plug from the adjusting slot on the backing plate.

3. Insert a brake adjusting spoon into the slot and engage the lowest tooth possible on the star wheel. Move the end of the brake spoon downward to move the star wheel upward and expand the adjusting screw. Repeat this operation until the brakes lock the wheel.

4. Insert a small screwdriver or piece of firm wire (coat hanger wire) into the adjusting slot and push the automatic adjuster lever out and free of the star wheel on the adjusting screw.

5. Holding the adjusting lever out of the way, engage the topmost tooth possible on the star wheel with a brake adjusting spoon. Move the end of the adjusting spoon upward to move the star wheel downward and contract the adjusting screw. Back the adjuster off (usually 10–15 notches) until the wheel spins freely with a minimum of drag. Keep track of the number of notches the adjuster is backed off.

6. Repeat this operation on the other side of the car of the set (front or rear) of brakes that you are adjusting. When backing off the

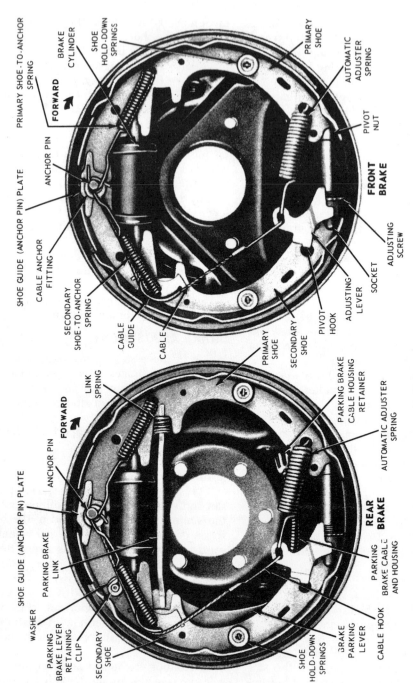

PRIMARY SHOE-TO-ANCHOR SPRING

BRAKE CYLINDER

SHOE HOLD-DOWN SPRINGS

FORWARD

PRIMARY SHOE

AUTOMATIC ADJUSTER SPRING

PIVOT NUT

SHOE GUIDE (ANCHOR PIN) PLATE

ANCHOR PIN

CABLE ANCHOR FITTING

SECONDARY SHOE-TO-ANCHOR SPRING

CABLE GUIDE

CABLE

PRIMARY SHOE

SECONDARY SHOE

PIVOT HOOK

ADJUSTING LEVER

SOCKET

ADJUSTING SCREW

FRONT BRAKE

LINK SPRING

FORWARD

ANCHOR PIN

SHOE GUIDE (ANCHOR PIN) PLATE

WASHER

PARKING BRAKE LEVER RETAINING CLIP

PARKING BRAKE LINK

SECONDARY SHOE

SHOE HOLD-DOWN SPRINGS

BRAKE PARKING LEVER

CABLE HOOK

PARKING BRAKE CABLE AND HOUSING

PARKING BRAKE CABLE HOUSING RETAINER

AUTOMATIC ADJUSTER SPRING

REAR BRAKE

Self-adjusting drum brakes

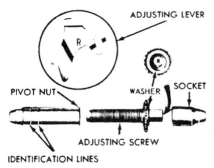

Adjusting screw and lever

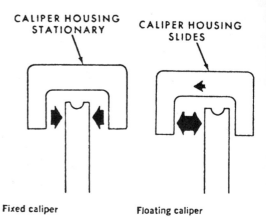

Fixed caliper   Floating caliper

Disc brake operation

brakes on the other side, the adjusting lever must be backed off same number of turns to prevent side-to-side brake pull.

7. Repeat this operation on the other set of brakes (front or rear).

8. When all four brakes are adjusted, check brake pedal travel and then make several stops while backing the car to equalize all the wheels.

NOTE: *A minimum of 50 lbs pressure for non-power brakes, and 25 lbs pressure for power brakes must be applied when making the reverse stops to adjust the brakes. After each stop the car must be moved forward.*

9. Road-test the car.

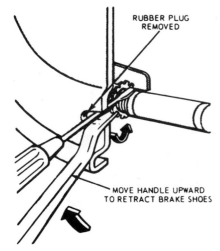

Backing off brake adjustment

Disc Brakes

Instead of the traditional, expanding brakes that press outward against a circular drum, disc brake systems utilize a cast iron disc (rotor) with brake pads on either side. Braking effect is achieved in a manner similar to the way that you would squeeze a spinning phonograph record between your fingers. The disc or rotor is a one-piece casting with cooling fins between the two braking surfaces. This design enables air to circulate between the braking surfaces thus making them less sensitive to heat buildup and fade. Dirt and water do not affect braking action since such contaminants are thrown off by the centrifugal action of the rotor, or are scraped off by the pads. Also, the equal clamping action of the brake pads tends to ensure uniform, straight-line stops. All disc brakes are inherently self-adjusting.

Kelsey-Hayes four-piston fixed-caliper brakes are used on 1965–1967 models These brakes are called fixed-caliper because the complete caliper assembly is rigidly bolted to the wheel spindle. The caliper assembly consists of two caliper halves bolted together, each half housing a pair of pistons. Braking effect is achieved by hydraulically pushing both pads against the disc sides.

Kelsey-Hayes single-piston floating-caliper brakes are used on 1968–1973 models. These differ from the fixed caliper units in that the one-piece caliper is free to move inboard and outboard parallel to the axle spindle, as the brakes are applied and released. The caliper is located atop the rotor by a single stabilizer bar bolted to the anchor plate on the spindle. A single piston is located in the caliper assembly. Braking effect is achieved by hydraulically pushing the inboard shoe into contact with the rotor, while the reaction force thus generated is used to allow the caliper to move slightly along the axle centerline and pull the outboard shoe into frictional contact with the rotor.

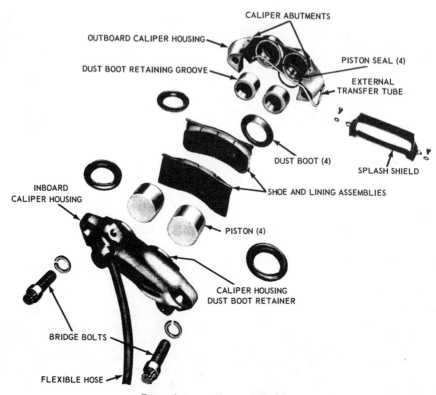

Four-piston caliper assembly

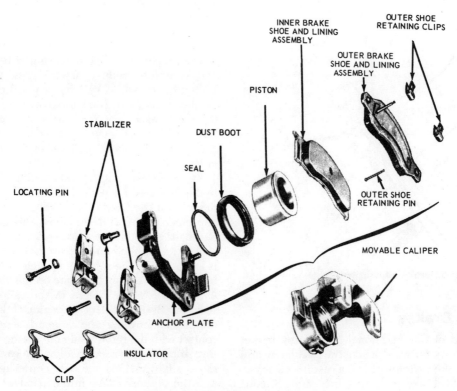

Single-piston caliper assembly

DISC BRAKE INSPECTION

1. Raise the vehicle until the wheel and tire clear the floor. Place safety stands under the vehicle.

2. Remove the wheel cover. Remove the wheel and tire from the hub and rotor.

3. Visually inspect the shoe and lining assemblies. If the lining material has worn to a thickness of 0.030 in. or less, or if the lining is contaminated with brake fluid, replace all shoe and lining assemblies on both front wheels. Make all thickness measurements across the thinnest section of the shoe and lining assembly. A slightly tapered condition on a used lining should be considered normal.

4. To check rotor run-out, tighten the wheel bearing adjusting nut to eliminate end-play. Check to see that the rotor can still be rotated.

5. Hand-spin the rotor and visually check for run-out. If the rotor appears out of round or wobbles, it must be machined or replaced. When the run-out check is finished, loosen the wheel bearing adjusting nut and re-tighten it to specifications, in order to prevent bearing damage.

6. Visually check the rotor for scoring. Minor scores can be removed with a fine emery cloth. If it is excessively scored, the rotor must be machined or replaced.

7. The caliper should be visually checked. If excess leakage is evident, the caliper should be replaced.

8. Install the wheel and hub assembly.

Hub and Rotor Assembly

REMOVAL

1. Raise the vehicle on a hoist and remove the wheel.

2. Remove the caliper mounting bolts. Slide the caliper assembly away from the rotor and suspend it using a wire loop. It is not necessary to disconnect the brake line. Insert a clean cardboard spacer between the linings to prevent the piston(s) from coming out of the cylinder bores while the caliper is removed.

3. Remove the grease cap from the hub. Remove the cotter pin, nut lock, adjusting nut, and flat washer from the spindle.

4. Remove the outer wheel bearing cone and roller assembly from the hub.

5. Remove the outer wheel bearing cone and roller assembly from the hub.

5. Remove the hub and rotor assembly from the spindle.

INSTALLATION

NOTE: *If a new rotor is being installed, remove the protective coating with carburetor degreaser. If the original rotor is being installed, make sure that the grease in the hub is clean and adequate, that the inner bearing and grease retainer are lubricated and in good condition, and that the rotor braking surfaces are clean.*

1. Install the hub and rotor assembly on the spindle.

2. Lubricate the outer bearing and install the thrust washer and adjusting nut.

3. Adjust the wheel bearing as outlined in the "Wheel Bearing Adjustment" section.

4. Install the nut lock, cotter pin, and grease cap.

5. Install the caliper assembly with the attaching bolts finger-tight. Torque first the upper, then the lower bolt to 45–60 ft. lbs. Safety-wire both bolts, making sure that any sharp wire ends are turned away from the brake hose.

6. Install the wheel and tire assembly and torque the nuts to 75–110 ft. lbs.

7. Lower the vehicle and road-test it.

Four-Piston Fixed-Caliper Disc Brakes

PAD REPLACEMENT

1. Remove and discard approximately ⅔ of the brake fluid from the rear master cylinder reservoir.

2. Raise the car and remove the front wheels.

3. Remove the retainer bolts and retainer(s).

4. Using two pairs of pliers, grasp the outer ends of one of the pads and pull straight out. Push the two pistons into their bores using a flat metal bar and install a new disc pad. Repeat for the second pad.

5. Install the retainer(s) and bolts.

6. Replace the wheels, check the brake fluid level, check the brake pedal travel, and road-test the car.

CALIPER ASSEMBLY OVERHAUL

1. Remove and discard approximately ⅔ of the brake fluid from the rear master cylinder reservoir.

2. Raise the vehicle on a hoist and remove the front wheels. Remove the dust

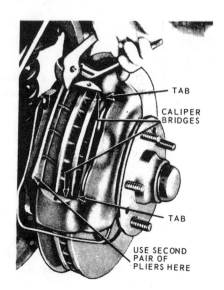

TAB

CALIPER
BRIDGES

TAB

USE SECOND
PAIR OF
PLIERS HERE

Removing brake shoe and lining assembly

shield or antirattle clips and shoe and lining assemblies.

3. Working on one side at a time, disconnect the flexible brake hose from the brake tube at the bracket on the frame. Plug the end to prevent loss of fluid.

4. Remove the two caliper retaining bolts and slide the caliper off the disc. Place the caliper assembly in a padded jaw vise, clamping on the caliper mounting lugs.

5. Remove the hydraulic crossover line and bleeder screw.

6. Remove the bridge bolts holding the caliper halves together and separate the assemblies.

7. Remove each of the four dust boots. Raise the inner diameter of the boot out of the piston groove and slide it back on the piston. Remove the outer diameter of the boot from the cylinder groove after the piston has been removed.

8. Remove the pistons being careful not to burr, scratch, or otherwise damage the outside diameter or boot groove of the piston.

9. Using a small, pointed, plastic implement, remove the piston seals from the grooves in the cylinder bores. Be careful not to scratch the cylinder bores.

10. Discard all old rubber boots and seals. Clean all parts with brake fluid and wipe them dry with a clean, lint-free cloth. Blow out the drilled passages and bores with an air hose.

11. Check the cylinder bores in both caliper housing castings for scoring or pitting.

Light scratches or corrosion in the bores may be removed only with crocus cloth. Avoid using extreme pressure with the cloth. Check the dust boot retaining rings on the caliper housing for damage.

NOTE: *Black stains in the bore are caused by the rubber piston seals and are considered normal.*

12. Inspect each piston and replace if it is scored, pitted, or if the chrome plating is wearing off.

13. Dip the new piston seals in brake fluid of at least SAE 70R3 quality and install them in the cylinder grooves. Position the seal at one area in the groove and gently work around the cylinder bore with a finger until properly seated. Be careful not to twist or roll the seals. If it is necessary to replace the dust boot retaining rings, thoroughly clean the contact area on the housing, and apply Loctite Sealant Grade H or its equivalent to the retaining rings and the seating surfaces, and install the retaining rings.

14. Coat the outside diameter of the pistons with brake fluid and install them, hollow end out, in the bores.

15. Position the piston squarely within the bore and apply slow, steady pressure until the piston bottoms within its bore. Use no tools to accomplish this seating. If the piston fails to move freely, remove it and check to make sure that the seal is properly seated. Install the new dust boots in position over the caliper retaining rings and in the piston grooves. Make certain that the dust boots are properly seated.

16. Upon installation of all four pistons, with seals and boots, into their respective caliper castings, install the outer caliper casting and bridge bolts. Torque to 75–105 ft. lbs.

NOTE: *Bridge bolts are special high tensile steel. Use only factory replacement bolts, if replacement is necessary.*

17. Install the hydraulic crossover line and tighten securely. Install the bleeder screw finger-tight.

18. Prior to installing the caliper assembly over the rotor, hand-spin the rotor, and visually check for wobbling or lateral run-out. Make sure that the wheel bearing is adjusted to zero end-play during this check. Readjust the wheel bearing as outlined in the "Wheel Bearing Adjustment" section.

19. Place the caliper assembly over the rotor and install the mounting bolts. Torque to 45–60 ft. lbs. Check to make sure that the

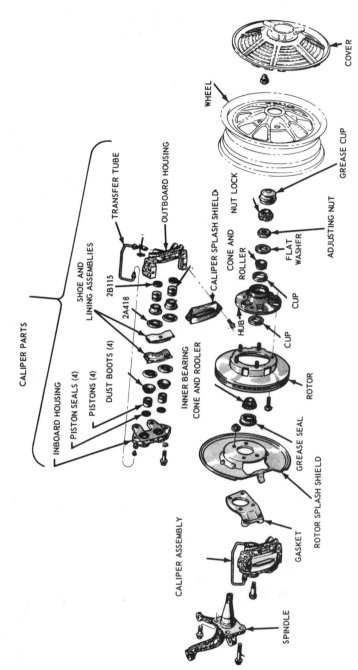

CALIPER PARTS

INBOARD HOUSING
PISTON SEALS (4)
PISTONS (4)
DUST BOOTS (4)
SHOE AND
LINING ASSEMBLIES
2B115
2A418
TRANSFER TUBE
OUTBOARD HOUSING
CALIPER SPLASH SHIELD
INNER BEARING
CONE AND ROOLER

COVER
WHEEL
GREASE CUP
NUT LOCK
ADJUSTING NUT
FLAT WASHER
CONE AND ROLLER
CUP
HUB
CUP
ROTOR
GREASE SEAL
ROTOR SPLASH SHIELD
GASKET
CALIPER ASSEMBLY
SPINDLE

Disc brake disassembled-4-piston type

rotor runs squarely and centerally between the two halves of the caliper. There should be approximately 0.090–0.120 in. clearance between the outside diameter of the braking rotor and the caliper. There should be a minimum of 0.050 in. from either rotor face to the machined groove in the outboard caliper.

20. Install the shoe and lining assemblies on each side between the caliper and the braking rotor.

21. Position the caliper splash shield or antirattle clips on the caliper and install the attaching bolts. Make sure that the splash shield opening is centered over the rotor. Torque the bolts to 9–14 ft. lbs.

22. Open the bleed screw and completely bleed the system. Allow the caliper to fill with brake fluid. After all air bubbles have escaped, close the bleeder screw. Top up the master cylinder.

23. Depress the brake pedal several times to actuate the piston seals and seat the shoe and lining assemblies.

24. Check all hydraulic connections for leaks.

25. Install the wheel and tire assembly and torque the nuts to 75–110 ft. lbs. Install the wheel cover.

26. Lower and road-test the vehicle.

CAUTION: *The vehicle may pull to one side upon the first brake application after service.*

Single-Piston Floating-Caliper Disc Brakes

PAD REPLACEMENT

1. Raise the vehicle on a hoist and remove the front wheels.

2. Remove the lockwires from the two mounting bolts and lift the caliper away from the rotor.

3. Remove the retaining clips with a screwdriver and slide the outboard pad and retaining pins out of the caliper. Remove the inboard pad.

4. Slide the new inboard pad into the caliper so that the tabs are between the retaining clips and anchor plate and the backing plate lies flush against the piston.

5. Insert the outboard pad retaining pins into the outboard pad and position them in the caliper.

NOTE: *Stabilizer, insulators, pad clips, and pins should always be replaced when the disc pads are replaced.*

6. Hold the retaining pins in place (one at a time) with a short drift pin or dowel and install the retaining clips.

7. Slide the caliper assembly over the disc and align the mounting bolt holes.

8. Install the lower bolt finger-tight. Install the upper bolt and torque to specification. Torque the lower bolt to specification. Safety-wire both bolts.

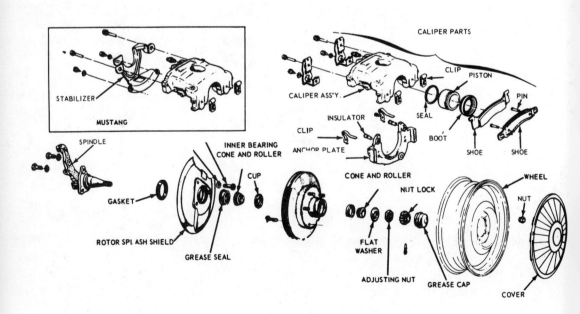

Disc brake disassembled-single-piston type

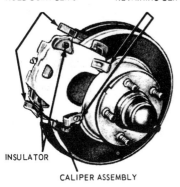

INNER BRAKE SHOE HOLD DOWN CLIPS   OUTER BRAKE SHOE RETAINING CLIPS

INSULATOR

CALIPER ASSEMBLY

Floating caliper disc brake assembly

CAUTION: *Do not deviate from this procedure. The alignment of the anchor plate depends on the proper sequence of bolt installation.*

9. Check the brake fluid level and pump the brake pedal to seat the linings against the disc. Replace the wheels and road-test the car.

CALIPER ASSEMBLY OVERHAUL

1. Raise the vehicle on a hoist and remove the front wheels.

2. Disconnect and plug the brake line.

3. Remove the lockwires from the two caliper mounting bolts and remove the bolt. Lift the caliper off the disc.

4. Remove and discard the locating pin insulators. Replace all rubber parts at reassembly.

5. Remove the retaining clips with a screwdriver and slide the outboard pad and retaining pins out of the caliper. Remove the inboard pad. Loosen the bleed screw and drain the brake fluid.

6. Remove the two small bolts and caliper stabilizers.

7. Remove the inboard pad retaining clips and bolts.

8. Clean and inspect all parts, and reinstall them on the anchor plate. Do not tighten the stabilizer bolts at this time.

9. Remove the piston by applying compressed air to the fluid inlet hole. Use care to prevent the piston from popping out of control.

CAUTION: *Do not attempt to catch the piston with the hand. Use folded towels to cushion it.*

10. Remove the piston boot. Inspect the piston for scoring, pitting, or corrosion. The piston must be replaced if there is any visible damage or wear.

11. Remove the piston seal from the cylinder bore. *Do not use any metal tools for this operation.*

12. Clean the caliper with fresh brake fluid. Inspect the cylinder bore for damage or wear. Light defects can be moved by rotating crocus cloth around the bore. (Do not use any other type of abrasive.)

13. Lubricate all new rubber parts in brake fluid. Install the piston seal in the cylinder groove. Install the boot into its piston groove.

14. Install the piston, open end out, into the bore while working the boot around the outside of the piston. Make sure the boot lip is seated in the piston groove.

15. Slide the anchor plate assembly onto the caliper housing and reinstall the locating pins. Tighten the pins to specification. Tighten the stabilizer anchor plate bolts.

16. Slide the inboard pad into the caliper so that the tabs are between the retaining clips and anchor plate and the backing plate lies flush against the piston.

17. Insert the outboard pad retaining pins into the outboard pad and position them in the caliper.

18. Hold the retaining pins in place (one at a time) with a short drift pin or dowel and install the retaining clips.

19. Slide the caliper assembly over the disc and align the mounting bolt holes.

20. Install the lower bolt finger-tight. Install the upper bolt and torque to specification. Torque the lower bolt to specification. Safety-wire both bolts.

CAUTION: *Do not deviate from this procedure. The alignment of the anchor plate depends on the proper sequence of bolt installation.*

21. Connect the brake line and bleed the brakes (see "Brake Bleeding").

22. Install the front wheels, recheck the brake fluid level, and road-test the car.

FRONT WHEEL BEARINGS

The front wheel bearings should be adjusted whenever the wheel is loose on the spindle, or if the wheel does not rotate freely with proper brake shoe-to-drum clearance. A slight drag is characteristic of disc brakes. At the proper intervals as given in the maintenance schedule, the front wheel bearings should be inspected, cleaned, and repacked.

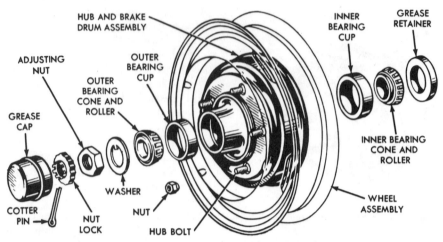

Front wheel assembly with drum brakes

CLEANING, REPACKING, AND ADJUSTING

Drum Brakes

The procedure for cleaning, repacking, and adjusting front wheel bearings on vehicles equipped with self-adjusting drum brakes is as follows:

1. Taking proper safety precautions, raise the car until the wheel and tire clear the floor.

2. Remove the wheel cover. Remove the grease cap from the hub. Then remove the cotter pin, nut lock, adjusting nut, and flat washer from the spindle. Remove the outer bearing cone and roller assembly.

3. Pull the wheel, hub, and drum assembly off the spindle. When encountering a brake drum that will not come off, disengage the adjusting lever from the adjusting screw by inserting a narrow screwdriver through the adjusting hole in the carrier plate. While the lever is disengaged, back off the adjusting screw star wheel with a brake adjusting tool. The self-adjusting mechanism will not function properly if the adjusting screw is burred, chipped, or otherwise damaged in the process, so be careful.

4. Remove the grease retainer, inner bearing cone, and roller assembly from the hub.

5. Clean all grease off the inner and outer bearing cups with solvent. Inspect the cups for pits, scratches, or excessive wear. If the cups are damaged, remove them with a drift.

6. Clean the inner and outer cone and roller assemblies with solvent and shake them dry. If the cone and roller assemblies show excessive wear or damage, replace them with the bearing cups as a unit.

7. If the new grease retainer is leather, soak it in light engine oil for 30 minutes, prior to installation. Wipe any excess from the metal portion of the retainer. Clean the spindle and the inside of the hub with solvent to thoroughly remove all old grease.

8. Covering the spindle with a clean cloth, brush all loose dirt and dust from the brake assembly. Remove the cloth carefully to keep dirt from the spindle.

9. If the inner and/or outer bearing cups were removed, install the replacement cups on the hub. Be sure that the cups seat properly in the hub.

10. It is imperative that all old grease be removed from the bearings and surrounding surfaces before repacking. The new lithium-base grease is not compatible with the sodium-base grease used in the past.

11. Pack the inside of the hub with wheel bearing grease. Add grease to the hub until it is flush with the inside diameter of both bearing cups. Work as much grease as possible between the rollers and cages in the cone and roller assemblies. Lubricate the cone surfaces with grease.

12. Position the inner bearing cone and roller assembly in the inner cup. If the leather grease retainer has soaked for 30 minutes, wipe all excess from the metal portion of the retainer and install it. Other types of grease retainers require a light film of grease on the lips before installation. Make sure that the retainer is properly seated.

13. Install the wheel, hub, and drum assembly on the wheel spindle. To prevent

damage to the grease retainer and spindle threads, keep the hub centered on the spindle.

14. Install the outer bearing cone, roller assembly, and flat washer on the spindle. Install the adjusting nut.

15. Adjust the wheel bearings by tightening the adjusting nut to 17–25 ft. lbs. with the wheel rotating. Then back off the adjusting nut ½ turn. Retighten the adjusting nut to 10–15 ft. lbs. Install the locknut so that the castellations are aligned with the cotter pin hole. Install the cotter pin. Bend the ends of the cotter pin around the castellations of the locknut to prevent interference with the radio static collector in the grease cap. Install the grease cap.

16. Remove the adjusting hole cover from the carrier plate. From the carrier plate side, turn the adjusting screw star wheel upward with a brake adjusting tool. Expand the brake shoes until a slight drag is felt with the drum rotating. Replace the adjusting hole cover.

17. Install the wheel cover.

Disc Brakes

The procedure for cleaning, repacking, and adjusting front wheel bearings on vehicles equipped with disc brakes is as follows:

1. Taking proper safety precautions, raise the car until the wheel and tire clear the floor.

2. Remove the wheel cover. Remove the wheel and tire from the hub.

3. On vehicles equipped with four-piston fixed-caliper brakes, remove the two bolts attaching the caliper to the spindle. Remove the caliper to the spindle. Remove the caliper from the rotor and wire it to the underbody to prevent damage to the brake hose. On cars with floating-caliper brakes follow steps two and three under "Caliper Assembly Overhaul."

4. Remove the grease cap from the hub, and the cotter pin, nut lock, adjusting nut, and flat washer from the spindle. Remove the outer bearing cone and roller assembly.

5. Pull the hub and rotor assembly off the wheel spindle.

6. Remove and discard the old grease retainer. Remove the inner bearing cone and roller assembly from the hub.

7. Clean all grease off the inner and outer bearing cups with solvent. Inspect for excessive wear or damage and remove with a drift if necessary.

8. If the new grease retainer is leather, soak it in light engine oil for 30 minutes prior to installation. Wipe any excess from the metal portion of the retainer.

9. Clean the inner and outer cone and roller assemblies with solvent and shake them dry. If the cone and roller assemblies show excessive wear or damage, replace them with the bearing cups as a unit.

10. Clean the spindle and the inside of the hub with solvent to thoroughly remove all old grease. Covering the spindle with a clean cloth, brush all loose dirt and dust from the brake assembly. Remove the cloth carefully so as to not get dirt on the spindle.

11. If the inner and/or outer bearing cups were removed, install the replacement cups on the hub. Be sure that the cups seat properly in the hub.

12. It is imperative that all old grease be removed from the bearings and surrounding surfaces before repacking. Sodium-based grease is not compatible with the new lithium-based grease.

13. Pack the inside of the hub with wheel bearing grease. Add grease to the hub until it is flush with the inside diameter of both bearing cups. Work as much grease as possible between the rollers and cages in the cone and roller assemblies. Lubricate the cone surfaces with grease.

14. Position the inner bearing cone and roller assembly in the inner cup. If a leather grease retainer has soaked for 30 minutes, wipe all excess from the metal portion of the retainer and install. Other types of grease retainers require a light film of grease applied to the lips prior to installation. Make sure that the retainer is properly seated.

15. Install the hub and rotor on the wheel spindle. To prevent damage to the grease retainer and spindle threads, keep the hub centered on the spindle.

16. Install the outer bearing cone and roller assembly and the flat washer on the spindle. Install the adjusting nut.

17. Adjust the wheel bearings by torqueing the adjusting nut to 17–25 ft. lbs. with the wheel rotating. Then back off the adjusting nut ½ turn. Retighten the adjusting nut to 10–15 ft. lbs. Install the locknut so that the castellations are aligned with the cotter pin hole. Install the cotter pin. Bend the ends of the cotter pin around the castellations of the locknut to prevent interference with the radio static collector in the grease cap. Install the grease cap.

18. On vehicles equipped with four-piston

fixed-caliper brakes, install the caliper to the spindle and torque attaching bolts to specifications.

NOTE: *New bolts must be used when servicing. The upper bolt must be tightened first. On cars with floating-caliper brakes, follow steps 19, 20, and 21 under "Caliper Assembly Overhaul."*

19. Install the wheel and tire on the hub.

20. Install the wheel cover.

PARKING BRAKE

The parking brake should be checked for proper operation every 12 months or 12,000 miles and adjusted whenever there is slack in the cables. A cable with too much slack will not hold the vehicle on an incline and presents a serious safety hazard. Usually, a rear brake adjustment will restore parking brake efficiency, but if the cables have stretched, adjust as necessary.

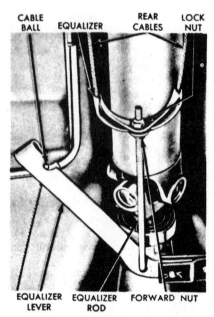

Parking brake linkage

1965

The procedure for adjusting the parking brake on all handle-actuated systems is as follows:

1. Fully release the brake handle.

2. Pull up the handle until the third notch is engaged.

3. Taking proper safety precautions, raise the car. Place the transmission in neutral.

4. Loosen the locknut on the equalizer rod and then turn the nut in front of the equalizer several turns forward.

5. Turn the locknut forward against the equalizer until the cables are just tight enough to stop forward rotation of the wheels.

6. When the cables are properly adjusted, tighten both nuts against the equalizer.

7. Release the parking brake, making sure that the brake shoes return to the fully released position.

1966–1973

The procedure for adjusting the parking brake on all pedal-actuated systems is as follows:

1. Fully release parking brake.

2. Depress the parking brake pedal one notch from its normal released position. On vacuum release brakes, the first notch is approximately 2 in. of travel.

3. Taking proper safety precautions, raise the car and place the transmission in neutral.

4. Loosen the equalizer locknut and turn the adjusting nut forward against the equalizer until moderate drag is felt when turning the rear wheels. Tighten the locknut.

5. Release the parking brake, making sure that the brake shoes return to the fully released position.

6. Lower the car and apply the parking brake. The third notch will hold the car if the brake is adjusted properly.

Brake Specifications

(All Measurements in Inches)

Year	Model	Master Cylinder		Wheel Cylinder			Brake Diameter		
				Front			Front		
		Disc	Drum	Disc	Drum	Rear	Disc	Drum	Rear
1965	All	1.0	1.0	1.13	1⅛	²⁹/₃₂	10.0	10.0	10.0
1966	8 Cyl.	0.8750 ①	1.0	—	1⅛	²⁹/₃₂	11.3	10.0	10.0
	6 Cyl.	—	1.0	—	1⅛	²⁹/₃₂	—	9.0	9.0
1967–68	6 Cyl.	1.0	1.0	2.38	1¹/₁₆	²⁷/₃₂	—	10.0	10.0
	8 Cyl.	1.0	1.0	2.38	1⅛	⅞	11.3	10.0	10.0
1969	6 Cyl.	—	1.0	—	1¹/₁₆	²⁷/₃₂	—	9.0	9.0
	V8 302	0.9375 ①	1.0	2.38	1⅛	⅞	11.3	10.0	10.0
	All 8 Cyl. exc. 302	0.9375 ①	1.0	2.38	1³/₃₂	⅞	11.3	10.0	10.0
1970	6 Cyl.	—	1.0	—	1¹/₁₆	²⁷/₃₂	—	9.0	9.0
	8 Cyl.	1.0	1.0	2.38	1⅛	⅞ ②	11.3	10.0	10.0
1971	6 Cyl.	—	1.0	—	1⅛	²⁹/₃₂	—	9.0	10.0
	8 Cyl.	1.0	1.0	2.38	1⅛	⅞	11.3	10.0	10.0
1972–73	All	1.0 ④	1.0	2.38	1⅛	⅞ ③	11.3	10.0	10.0

① Also applies to all power brakes
② 10" brakes equipped for 1972 250 1-V cars equipped with optional D70-14 or DR78-14 tires
③ ²⁹/₃₂" on all 1972 V8 equipped cars;
   ²⁷/₃₂" on all 1973 models
④ 0.9375 in 1973

Troubleshooting

10

This section is designed to aid in the quick, accurate diagnosis of automotive problems. While automotive repairs can be made by many people, accurate troubleshooting is a rare skill for the amateur and professional alike.

In its simplest state, troubleshooting is an exercise in logic. It is essential to realize that an automobile is really composed of a series of systems. Some of these systems are interrelated; others are not. Automobiles operate within a framework of logical rules and physical laws, and the key to troubleshooting is a good understanding of all the automotive systems.

This section breaks the car or truck down into its component systems, allowing the problem to be isolated. The charts and diagnostic road maps list the most common problems and the most probable causes of trouble. Obviously it would be impossible to list every possible problem that could happen along with every possible cause, but it will locate MOST problems and eliminate a lot of unnecessary guesswork. The systematic format will locate problems within a given system, but, because many automotive systems are interrelated, the solution to your particular problem may be found in a number of systems on the car or truck.

USING THE TROUBLESHOOTING CHARTS

This book contains all of the specific information that the average do-it-yourself mechanic needs to repair and maintain his or her car or truck. The troubleshooting charts are designed to be used in conjunction with the specific procedures and information in the text. For instance, troubleshooting a point-type ignition system is fairly standard for all models, but you may be directed to the text to find procedures for troubleshooting an individual type of electronic ignition. You will also have to refer to the specification charts throughout the book for specifications applicable to your car or truck.

TOOLS AND EQUIPMENT

The tools illustrated in Chapter 1 (plus two more diagnostic pieces) will be adequate to troubleshoot most problems. The two other tools needed are a voltmeter and an ohmmeter. These can be purchased separately or in combination, known as a VOM meter.

In the event that other tools are required, they will be noted in the procedures.

Troubleshooting Engine Problems

See Chapters 2, 3, 4 for more information and service procedures.

Index to Systems

System	To Test	Group
Battery	Engine need not be running	1
Starting system	Engine need not be running	2
Primary electrical system	Engine need not be running	3
Secondary electrical system	Engine need not be running	4
Fuel system	Engine need not be running	5
Engine compression	Engine need not be running	6
Engine vacuum	Engine must be running	7
Secondary electrical system	Engine must be running	8
Valve train	Engine must be running	9
Exhaust system	Engine must be running	10
Cooling system	Engine must be running	11
Engine lubrication	Engine must be running	12

Index to Problems

Problem: Symptom	Begin at Specific Diagnosis, Number ____
Engine Won't Start:	
Starter doesn't turn	1.1, 2.1
Starter turns, engine doesn't	2.1
Starter turns engine very slowly	1.1, 2.4
Starter turns engine normally	3.1, 4.1
Starter turns engine very quickly	6.1
Engine fires intermittently	4.1
Engine fires consistently	5.1, 6.1
Engine Runs Poorly:	
Hard starting	3.1, 4.1, 5.1, 8.1
Rough idle	4.1, 5.1, 8.1
Stalling	3.1, 4.1, 5.1, 8.1
Engine dies at high speeds	4.1, 5.1
Hesitation (on acceleration from standing stop)	5.1, 8.1
Poor pickup	4.1, 5.1, 8.1
Lack of power	3.1, 4.1, 5.1, 8.1
Backfire through the carburetor	4.1, 8.1, 9.1
Backfire through the exhaust	4.1, 8.1, 9.1
Blue exhaust gases	6.1, 7.1
Black exhaust gases	5.1
Running on (after the ignition is shut off)	3.1, 8.1
Susceptible to moisture	4.1
Engine misfires under load	4.1, 7.1, 8.4, 9.1
Engine misfires at speed	4.1, 8.4
Engine misfires at idle	3.1, 4.1, 5.1, 7.1, 8.4

Sample Section

Test and Procedure	Results and Indications	Proceed to
4.1—Check for spark: Hold each spark plug wire approximately ¼" from ground with gloves or a heavy, dry rag. Crank the engine and observe the spark.	→ If no spark is evident:	→4.2
	→ If spark is good in some cases:	→4.3
	→ If spark is good in all cases:	→4.6

Specific Diagnosis

This section is arranged so that following each test, instructions are given to proceed to another, until a problem is diagnosed.

Section 1—Battery

Test and Procedure	Results and Indications	Proceed to
1.1—Inspect the battery visually for case condition (corrosion, cracks) and water level.	If case is cracked, replace battery:	**1.4**
	If the case is intact, remove corrosion with a solution of baking soda and water (**CAU-TION:** *do not get the solution into the bat-tery*), and fill with water:	**1.2**

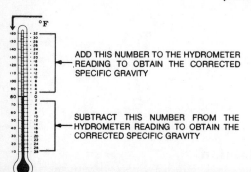

DIRT ON TOP OF BATTERY PLUGGED VENT CORROSION LOOSE CABLE OR POSTS CRACKS LOW WATER LEVEL

Inspect the battery case

1.2—Check the battery cable connections: Insert a screwdriver between the battery post and the cable clamp. Turn the headlights on high beam, and observe them as the screwdriver is gently twisted to ensure good metal to metal contact.	If the lights brighten, remove and clean the clamp and post; coat the post with petroleum jelly, install and tighten the clamp:	**1.4**
	If no improvement is noted:	**1.3**

TESTING BATTERY CABLE CONNECTIONS USING A SCREWDRIVER

1.3—Test the state of charge of the battery using an individual cell tester or hydrometer.	If indicated, charge the battery. **NOTE:** *If no obvious reason exists for the low state of charge (i.e., battery age, prolonged storage), proceed to:*	**1.4**

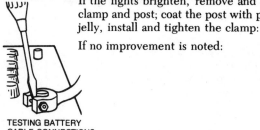

°F

ADD THIS NUMBER TO THE HYDROMETER READING TO OBTAIN THE CORRECTED SPECIFIC GRAVITY

SUBTRACT THIS NUMBER FROM THE HYDROMETER READING TO OBTAIN THE CORRECTED SPECIFIC GRAVITY

Specific Gravity (@ 80° F.)

Minimum	*Battery Charge*
1.260	100% Charged
1.230	75% Charged
1.200	50% Charged
1.170	25% Charged
1.140	Very Little Power Left
1.110	Completely Discharged

The effects of temperature on battery specific gravity (left) and amount of battery charge in relation to specific gravity (right)

1.4—Visually inspect battery cables for cracking, bad connection to ground, or bad connection to starter.	If necessary, tighten connections or replace the cables:	**2.1**

Section 2—Starting System
See Chapter 3 for service procedures

Test and Procedure	Results and Indications	Proceed to

Note: Tests in Group 2 are performed with coil high tension lead disconnected to prevent accidental starting.

Test and Procedure	Results and Indications	Proceed to
2.1—Test the starter motor and solenoid: Connect a jumper from the battery post of the solenoid (or relay) to the starter post of the solenoid (or relay).	If starter turns the engine normally:	2.2
	If the starter buzzes, or turns the engine very slowly:	2.4
	If no response, replace the solenoid (or relay).	3.1
	If the starter turns, but the engine doesn't, ensure that the flywheel ring gear is intact. If the gear is undamaged, replace the starter drive.	3.1
2.2—Determine whether ignition override switches are functioning properly (clutch start switch, neutral safety switch), by connecting a jumper across the switch(es), and turning the ignition switch to "start".	If starter operates, adjust or replace switch:	3.1
	If the starter doesn't operate:	2.3
2.3—Check the ignition switch "start" position: Connect a 12V test lamp or voltmeter between the starter post of the solenoid (or relay) and ground. Turn the ignition switch to the "start" position, and jiggle the key.	If the lamp doesn't light or the meter needle doesn't move when the switch is turned, check the ignition switch for loose connections, cracked insulation, or broken wires. Repair or replace as necessary:	3.1
	If the lamp flickers or needle moves when the key is jiggled, replace the ignition switch.	3.3

Checking the ignition switch "start" position

STARTER RELAY (IF EQUIPPED)

Test and Procedure	Results and Indications	Proceed to
2.4—Remove and bench test the starter, according to specifications in the engine electrical section.	If the starter does not meet specifications, repair or replace as needed:	3.1
	If the starter is operating properly:	2.5
2.5—Determine whether the engine can turn freely: Remove the spark plugs, and check for water in the cylinders. Check for water on the dipstick, or oil in the radiator. Attempt to turn the engine using an 18" flex drive and socket on the crankshaft pulley nut or bolt.	If the engine will turn freely only with the spark plugs out, and hydrostatic lock (water in the cylinders) is ruled out, check valve timing:	9.2
	If engine will not turn freely, and it is known that the clutch and transmission are free, the engine must be disassembled for further evaluation:	Chapter 3

Section 3—Primary Electrical System

Test and Procedure	Results and Indications	Proceed to
3.1—Check the ignition switch "on" position: Connect a jumper wire between the distributor side of the coil and ground, and a 12V test lamp between the switch side of the coil and ground. Remove the high tension lead from the coil. Turn the ignition switch on and jiggle the key.	If the lamp lights:	**3.2**
	If the lamp flickers when the key is jiggled, replace the ignition switch:	**3.3**
	If the lamp doesn't light, check for loose or open connections. If none are found, remove the ignition switch and check for continuity. If the switch is faulty, replace it:	**3.3**

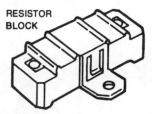

Checking the ignition switch "on" position

Test and Procedure	Results and Indications	Proceed to
3.2—Check the ballast resistor or resistance wire for an open circuit, using an ohmmeter. See Chapter 3 for specific tests.	Replace the resistor or resistance wire if the resistance is zero. **NOTE:** *Some ignition systems have no ballast resistor.*	**3.3**

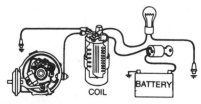

RESISTOR BLOCK

CALIBRATED RESISTANCE LEAD

Two types of resistors

Test and Procedure	Results and Indications	Proceed to
3.3—On point-type ignition systems, visually inspect the breaker points for burning, pitting or excessive wear. Gray coloring of the point contact surfaces is normal. Rotate the crankshaft until the contact heel rests on a high point of the distributor cam and adjust the point gap to specifications. On electronic ignition models, remove the distributor cap and visually inspect the armature. Ensure that the armature pin is in place, and that the armature is on tight and rotates when the engine is cranked. Make sure there are no cracks, chips or rounded edges on the armature.	If the breaker points are intact, clean the contact surfaces with fine emery cloth, and adjust the point gap to specifications. If the points are worn, replace them. On electronic systems, replace any parts which appear defective. If condition persists:	**3.4**

Test and Procedure	Results and Indications	Proceed to
3.4—On point-type ignition systems, connect a dwell-meter between the distributor primary lead and ground. Crank the engine and observe the point dwell angle. On electronic ignition systems, conduct a stator (magnetic pickup assembly) test. See Chapter 3.	On point-type systems, adjust the dwell angle if necessary. **NOTE:** *Increasing the point gap decreases the dwell angle and vice-versa.*	**3.6**
	If the dwell meter shows little or no reading;	**3.5**
	On electronic ignition systems, if the stator is bad, replace the stator. If the stator is good, proceed to the other tests in Chapter 3.	

Dwell is a function of point gap

3.5—On the point-type ignition systems, check the condenser for short: connect an ohmeter across the condenser body and the pigtail lead.	If any reading other than infinite is noted, replace the condenser	**3.6**

Checking the condenser for short

3.6—Test the coil primary resistance: On point-type ignition systems, connect an ohmmeter across the coil primary terminals, and read the resistance on the low scale. Note whether an external ballast resistor or resistance wire is used. On electronic ignition systems, test the coil primary resistance as in Chapter 3.	Point-type ignition coils utilizing ballast resistors or resistance wires should have approximately 1.0 ohms resistance. Coils with internal resistors should have approximately 4.0 ohms resistance. If values far from the above are noted, replace the coil.	**4.1**

Check the coil primary resistance

Section 4—Secondary Electrical System
See Chapters 2–3 for service procedures

Test and Procedure	Results and Indications	Proceed to
4.1—Check for spark: Hold each spark plug wire approximately ¼″ from ground with gloves or a heavy, dry rag. Crank the engine, and observe the spark.	If no spark is evident:	**4.2**
	If spark is good in some cylinders:	**4.3**
	If spark is good in all cylinders:	**4.6**

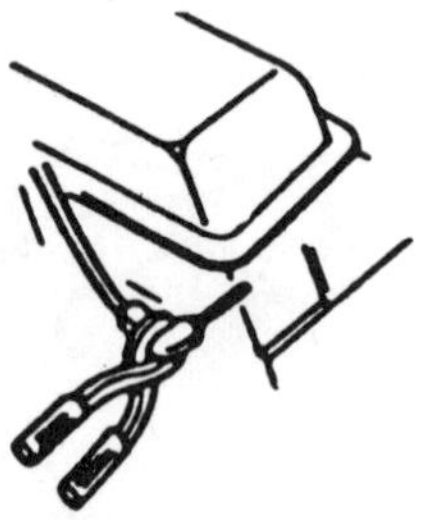

Check for spark at the plugs

4.2—Check for spark at the coil high tension lead: Remove the coil high tension lead from the distributor and position it approximately ¼″ from ground. Crank the engine and observe spark. **CAUTION:** *This test should not be performed on engines equipped with electronic ignition.*	If the spark is good and consistent:	**4.3**
	If the spark is good but intermittent, test the primary electrical system starting at 3.3:	**3.3**
	If the spark is weak or non-existent, replace the coil high tension lead, clean and tighten all connections and retest. If no improvement is noted:	**4.4**
4.3—Visually inspect the distributor cap and rotor for burned or corroded contacts, cracks, carbon tracks, or moisture. Also check the fit of the rotor on the distributor shaft (where applicable).	If moisture is present, dry thoroughly, and retest per 4.1:	**4.1**
	If burned or excessively corroded contacts, cracks, or carbon tracks are noted, replace the defective part(s) and retest per 4.1:	**4.1**
	If the rotor and cap appear intact, or are only slightly corroded, clean the contacts thoroughly (including the cap towers and spark plug wire ends) and retest per 4.1:	
	If the spark is good in all cases:	**4.6**
	If the spark is poor in all cases:	**4.5**

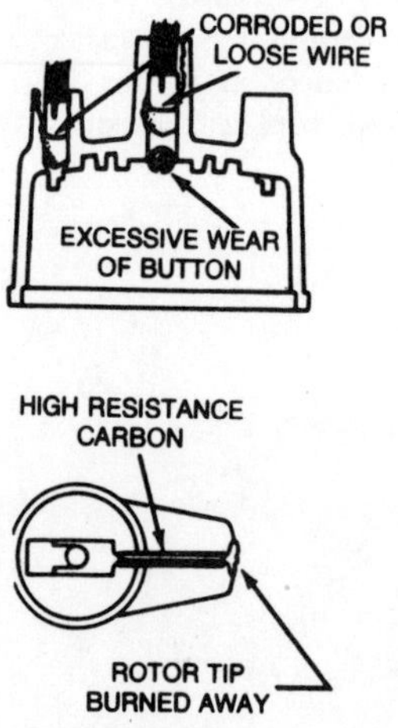

CORRODED OR LOOSE WIRE

EXCESSIVE WEAR OF BUTTON

HIGH RESISTANCE CARBON

ROTOR TIP BURNED AWAY

Inspect the distributor cap and rotor

Test and Procedure	Results and Indications	Proceed to
4.4—Check the coil secondary resistance: On point-type systems connect an ohmmeter across the distributor side of the coil and the coil tower. Read the resistance on the high scale of the ohmmeter. On electronic ignition systems, see Chapter 3 for specific tests.	The resistance of a satisfactory coil should be between 4,000 and 10,000 ohms. If resistance is considerably higher (i.e., 40,000 ohms) replace the coil and retest per 4.1. **NOTE:** *This does not apply to high performance coils.*	

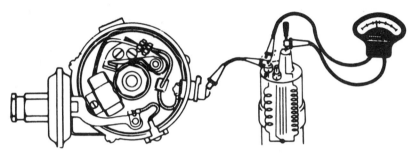

Testing the coil secondary resistance

4.5—Visually inspect the spark plug wires for cracking or brittleness. Ensure that no two wires are positioned so as to cause induction firing (adjacent and parallel). Remove each wire, one by one, and check resistance with an ohmmeter.	Replace any cracked or brittle wires. If any of the wires are defective, replace the entire set. Replace any wires with excessive resistance (over $8000\,\Omega$ per foot for suppression wire), and separate any wires that might cause induction firing.	4.6

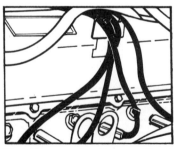

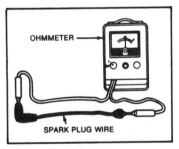

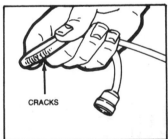

Misfiring can be the result of spark plug leads to adjacent, consecutively firing cylinders running parallel and too close together

On point-type ignition systems, check the spark plug wires as shown. On electronic ignitions, do not remove the wire from the distributor cap terminal; instead, test through the cap

Spark plug wires can be checked visually by bending them in a loop over your finger. This will reveal any cracks, burned or broken insulation. Any wire with cracked insulation should be replaced

4.6—Remove the spark plugs, noting the cylinders from which they were removed, and evaluate according to the color photos in the middle of this book.	See following.	**See following.**

Test and Procedure	Results and Indications	Proceed to
4.7—Examine the location of all the plugs.	The following diagrams illustrate some of the conditions that the location of plugs will reveal.	4.8

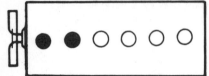

Two adjacent plugs are fouled in a 6-cylinder engine, 4-cylinder engine or either bank of a V-8. This is probably due to a blown head gasket between the two cylinders

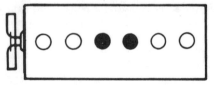

The two center plugs in a 6-cylinder engine are fouled. Raw fuel may be "boiled" out of the carburetor into the intake manifold after the engine is shut-off. Stop-start driving can also foul the center plugs, due to overly rich mixture. Proper float level, a new float needle and seat or use of an insulating spacer may help this problem

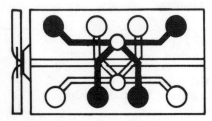

An unbalanced carburetor is indicated. Following the fuel flow on this particular design shows that the cylinders fed by the right-hand barrel are fouled from overly rich mixture, while the cylinders fed by the left-hand barrel are normal

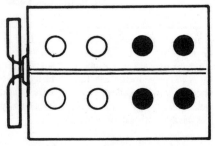

If the four rear plugs are overheated, a cooling system problem is suggested. A thorough cleaning of the cooling system may restore coolant circulation and cure the problem

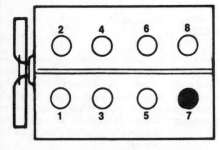

Finding one plug overheated may indicate an intake manifold leak near the affected cylinder. If the overheated plug is the second of two adjacent, consecutively firing plugs, it could be the result of ignition cross-firing. Separating the leads to these two plugs will eliminate cross-fire

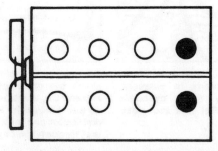

Occasionally, the two rear plugs in large, lightly used V-8's will become oil fouled. High oil consumption and smoky exhaust may also be noticed. It is probably due to plugged oil drain holes in the rear of the cylinder head, causing oil to be sucked in around the valve stems. This usually occurs in the rear cylinders first, because the engine slants that way

CHILTON'S
AUTO BODY REPAIR TIPS

Tools and Materials • Step-by-Step Illustrated Procedures
How To Repair Dents, Scratches and Rust Holes
Spray Painting and Refinishing Tips

With a little practice, basic body repair procedures can be mastered by any do-it-yourself mechanic. The step-by-step repairs shown here can be applied to almost any type of auto body repair.

TOOLS & MATERIALS

You may already have basic tools, such as hammers and electric drills. Other tools unique to body repair — body hammers, grinding attachments, sanding blocks, dent puller, half-round plastic file and plastic spreaders — are relatively inexpensive and can be obtained wherever auto parts or auto body repair parts are sold. Portable air compressors and paint spray guns can be purchased or rented.

Auto Body Repair Kits

The best and most often used products are available to the do-it-yourselfer in kit form, from major manufacturers of auto body repair products. The same manufacturers also merchandise the individual products for use by pros.

Kits are available to make a wide variety of repairs, including holes, dents and scratches and fiberglass, and offer the advantage of buying the materials you'll need for the job. There is little waste or chance of materials going bad from not being used. Many kits may also contain basic body-working tools such as body files, sanding blocks and spreaders. Check the contents of the kit before buying your tools.

BODY REPAIR TIPS

Safety

Many of the products associated with auto body repair and refinishing contain toxic chemicals. Read all labels before opening containers and store them in a safe place and manner.

• Wear eye protection (safety goggles) when using power tools or when performing any operation that involves the removal of any type of material.

• Wear lung protection (disposable mask or respirator) when grinding, sanding or painting.

Sanding

1 Sand off paint before using a dent puller. When using a non-adhesive sanding disc, cover the back of the disc with an overlapping layer or two of masking tape and trim the edges. The disc will last considerably longer.

2 Use the circular motion of the sanding disc to grind *into* the edge of the repair. Grinding or sanding away from the jagged edge will only tear the sandpaper.

3 Use the palm of your hand flat on the panel to detect high and low spots. Do not use your fingertips. Slide your hand slowly back and forth.

WORKING WITH BODY FILLER

Mixing The Filler

Cleanliness and proper mixing and application are extremely important. Use a clean piece of plastic or glass or a disposable artist's palette to mix body filler.

1 Allow plenty of time and follow directions. No useful purpose will be served by adding more hardener to make it cure (set-up) faster. Less hardener means more curing time, but the mixture dries harder; more hardener means less curing time but a softer mixture.

2 Both the hardener and the filler should be thoroughly kneaded or stirred before mixing. Hardener should be a solid paste and dispense like thin toothpaste. Body filler should be smooth, and free of lumps or thick spots.

Getting the proper amount of hardener in the filler is the trickiest part of preparing the filler. Use the same amount of hardener in cold or warm weather. For contour filler (thick coats), a bead of hardener twice the diameter of the filler is about right. There's about a 15% margin on either side, but, if in doubt use less hardener.

3 Mix the body filler and hardener by wiping across the mixing surface, picking the mixture up and wiping it again. Colder weather requires longer mixing times. Do not mix in a circular motion; this will trap air bubbles which will become holes in the cured filler.

Applying The Filler

1 For best results, filler should not be applied over ¼" thick.

Apply the filler in several coats. Build it up to above the level of the repair surface so that it can be sanded or grated down.

The first coat of filler must be pressed on with a firm wiping motion.

Apply the filler in one direction only. Working the filler back and forth will either pull it off the metal or trap air bubbles.

REPAIRING DENTS

Before you start, take a few minutes to study the damaged area. Try to visualize the shape of the panel before it was damaged. If the damage is on the left fender, look at the right fender and use it as a guide. If there is access to the panel from behind, you can reshape it with a body hammer. If not, you'll have to use a dent puller. Go slowly and work the metal a little at a time. Get the panel as straight as possible before applying filler.

1 This dent is typical of one that can be pulled out or hammered out from behind. Remove the headlight cover, headlight assembly and turn signal housing.

2 Drill a series of holes ½ the size of the end of the dent puller along the stress line. Make some trial pulls and assess the results. If necessary, drill more holes and try again. Do not hurry.

3 If possible, use a body hammer and block to shape the metal back to its original contours. Get the metal back as close to its original shape as possible. Don't depend on body filler to fill dents.

4 Using an 80-grit grinding disc on an electric drill, grind the paint from the surrounding area down to bare metal. Use a new grinding pad to prevent heat buildup that will warp metal.

5 The area should look like this when you're finished grinding. Knock the drill holes in and tape over small openings to keep plastic filler out.

6 Mix the body filler (see Body Repair Tips). Spread the body filler evenly over the entire area (see Body Repair Tips). Be sure to cover the area completely.

7 Let the body filler dry until the surface can just be scratched with your fingernail. Knock the high spots from the body filler with a body file ("Cheesegrater"). Check frequently with the palm of your hand for high and low spots.

8 Check to be sure that trim pieces that will be installed later will fit exactly. Sand the area with 40-grit paper.

9 If you wind up with low spots, you may have to apply another layer of filler.

10 Knock the high spots off with 40-grit paper. When you are satisfied with the contours of the repair, apply a thin coat of filler to cover pin holes and scratches.

11 Block sand the area with 40-grit paper to a smooth finish. Pay particular attention to body lines and ridges that must be well-defined.

12 Sand the area with 400 paper and then finish with a scuff pad. The finished repair is ready for priming and painting (see Painting Tips).

Materials and photos courtesy of Ritt Jones Auto Body, Prospect Park, PA.

REPAIRING RUST HOLES

There are many ways to repair rust holes. The fiberglass cloth kit shown here is one of the most cost efficient for the owner because it provides a strong repair that resists cracking and moisture and is relatively easy to use. It can be used on large and small holes (with or without backing) and can be applied over contoured areas. Remember, however, that short of replacing an entire panel, no repair is a guarantee that the rust will not return.

1 Remove any trim that will be in the way. Clean away all loose debris. Cut away all the rusted metal. But be sure to leave enough metal to retain the contour or body shape.

2 Grind away all traces of rust with a 24-grit grinding disc. Be sure to grind back 3-4 inches from the edge of the hole down to bare metal and be sure all traces of paint, primer and rust are removed.

3 Block sand the area with 80 or 100 grit sandpaper to get a clear, shiny surface and feathered paint edge. Tap the edges of the hole inward with a ball peen hammer.

4 If you are going to use release film, cut a piece about 2-3″ larger than the area you have sanded. Place the film over the repair and mark the sanded area on the film. Avoid any unnecessary wrinkling of the film.

5 Cut 2 pieces of fiberglass matte to match the shape of the repair. One piece should be about 1″ smaller than the sanded area and the second piece should be 1″ smaller than the first. Mix enough filler and hardener to saturate the fiberglass material (see Body Repair Tips).

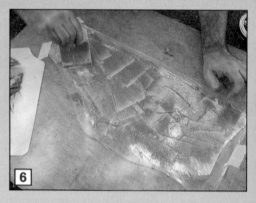

6 Lay the release sheet on a flat surface and spread an even layer of filler, large enough to cover the repair. Lay the smaller piece of fiberglass cloth in the center of the sheet and spread another layer of filler over the fiberglass cloth. Repeat the operation for the larger piece of cloth.

7 Place the repair material over the repair area, with the release film facing outward. Use a spreader and work from the center outward to smooth the material, following the body contours. Be sure to remove all air bubbles.

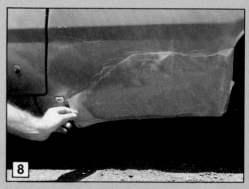

8 Wait until the repair has dried tack-free and peel off the release sheet. The ideal working temperature is 60°-90° F. Cooler or warmer temperatures or high humidity may require additional curing time. Wait longer, if in doubt.

9 Sand and feather-edge the entire area. The initial sanding can be done with a sanding disc on an electric drill if care is used. Finish the sanding with a block sander. Low spots can be filled with body filler; this may require several applications.

10 When the filler can just be scratched with a fingernail, knock the high spots down with a body file and smooth the entire area with 80-grit. Feather the filled areas into the surrounding areas.

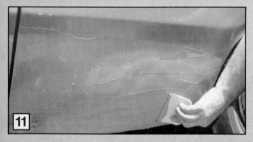

11 When the area is sanded smooth, mix some topcoat and hardener and apply it directly with a spreader. This will give a smooth finish and prevent the glass matte from showing through the paint.

12 Block sand the topcoat smooth with finishing sandpaper (200 grit), and 400 grit. The repair is ready for masking, priming and painting (see Painting Tips).

Materials and photos courtesy Marson Corporation, Chelsea, Massachusetts

PAINTING TIPS

Preparation

1 SANDING — Use a 400 or 600 grit wet or dry sandpaper. Wet-sand the area with a 1/4 sheet of sandpaper soaked in clean water. Keep the paper wet while sanding. Sand the area until the repaired area tapers into the original finish.

2 CLEANING — Wash the area to be painted thoroughly with water and a clean rag. Rinse it thoroughly and wipe the surface dry until you're sure it's completely free of dirt, dust, fingerprints, wax, detergent or other foreign matter.

3 MASKING — Protect any areas you don't want to overspray by covering them with masking tape and newspaper. Be careful not get fingerprints on the area to be painted.

4 PRIMING — All exposed metal should be primed before painting. Primer protects the metal and provides an excellent surface for paint adhesion. When the primer is dry, wet-sand the area again with 600 grit wet-sandpaper. Clean the area again after sanding.

Painting Techniques

P aint applied from either a spray gun or a spray can (for small areas) will provide good results. Experiment on an old piece of metal to get the right combination before you begin painting.

SPRAYING VISCOSITY (SPRAY GUN ONLY) — Paint should be thinned to spraying viscosity according to the directions on the can. Use only the recommended thinner or reducer and the same amount of reduction regardless of temperature.

AIR PRESSURE (SPRAY GUN ONLY) — This is extremely important. Be sure you are using the proper recommended pressure.

TEMPERATURE — The surface to be painted should be approximately the same temperature as the surrounding air. Applying warm paint to a cold surface, or vice versa, will completely upset the paint characteristics.

THICKNESS — Spray with smooth strokes. In general, the thicker the coat of paint, the longer the drying time. Apply several thin coats about 30 seconds apart. The paint should remain wet long enough to flow out and no longer; heavier coats will only produce sags or wrinkles. Spray a light (fog) coat, followed by heavier color coats.

DISTANCE — The ideal spraying distance is 8″-12″ from the gun or can to the surface. Shorter distances will produce ripples, while greater distances will result in orange peel, dry film and poor color match and loss of material due to overspray.

OVERLAPPING — The gun or can should be kept at right angles to the surface at all times. Work to a wet edge at an even speed, using a 50% overlap and direct the center of the spray at the lower or nearest edge of the previous stroke.

RUBBING OUT (BLENDING) FRESH PAINT — Let the paint dry thoroughly. Runs or imperfections can be sanded out, primed and repainted.

Don't be in too big a hurry to remove the masking. This only produces paint ridges. When the finish has dried for at least a week, apply a small amount of fine grade rubbing compound with a clean, wet cloth. Use lots of water and blend the new paint with the surrounding area.

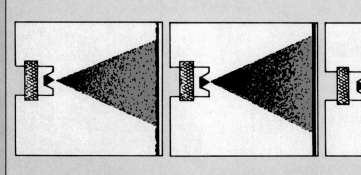

WRONG	CORRECT	WRONG
Thin coat. Stroke too fast, not enough overlap, gun too far away.	Medium coat. Proper distance, good stroke, proper overlap.	Heavy coat. Stroke too slow, too much overlap, gun too close.

Test and Procedure	Results and Indications	Proceed to
4.8—Determine the static ignition timing. Using the crankshaft pulley timing marks as a guide, locate top dead center on the compression stroke of the number one cylinder.	The rotor should be pointing toward the No. 1 tower in the distributor cap, and, on electronic ignitions, the armature spoke for that cylinder should be lined up with the stator.	**4.8**
4.9—Check coil polarity: Connect a voltmeter negative lead to the coil high tension lead, and the positive lead to ground (**NOTE:** *Reverse the hook-up for positive ground systems*). Crank the engine momentarily.	If the voltmeter reads up-scale, the polarity is correct: If the voltmeter reads down-scale, reverse the coil polarity (switch the primary leads):	**5.1** **5.1**

Checking coil polarity

Section 5—Fuel System
See Chapter 4 for service procedures

Test and Procedure	Results and Indications	Proceed to
5.1—Determine that the air filter is functioning efficiently: Hold paper elements up to a strong light, and attempt to see light through the filter.	Clean permanent air filters in solvent (or manufacturer's recommendation), and allow to dry. Replace paper elements through which light cannot be seen:	**5.2**
5.2—Determine whether a flooding condition exists: Flooding is identified by a strong gasoline odor, and excessive gasoline present in the throttle bore(s) of the carburetor.	If flooding is not evident: If flooding is evident, permit the gasoline to dry for a few moments and restart. If flooding doesn't recur: If flooding is persistent:	**5.3** **5.7** **5.5**

If the engine floods repeatedly, check the choke butterfly flap

5.3—Check that fuel is reaching the carburetor: Detach the fuel line at the carburetor inlet. Hold the end of the line in a cup (not styrofoam), and crank the engine.	If fuel flows smoothly: If fuel doesn't flow (**NOTE:** *Make sure that there is fuel in the tank*), or flows erratically:	**5.7** **5.4**

Check the fuel pump by disconnecting the output line (fuel pump-to-carburetor) at the carburetor and operating the starter briefly

Test and Procedure	Results and Indications	Proceed to
5.4—Test the fuel pump: Disconnect all fuel lines from the fuel pump. Hold a finger over the input fitting, crank the engine (with electric pump, turn the ignition or pump on); and feel for suction.	If suction is evident, blow out the fuel line to the tank with low pressure compressed air until bubbling is heard from the fuel filler neck. Also blow out the carburetor fuel line (both ends disconnected):	5.7
	If no suction is evident, replace or repair the fuel pump:	5.7
	NOTE: *Repeated oil fouling of the spark plugs, or a no-start condition, could be the result of a ruptured vacuum booster pump diaphragm, through which oil or gasoline is being drawn into the intake manifold (where applicable).*	
5.5—Occasionally, small specks of dirt will clog the small jets and orifices in the carburetor. With the engine cold, hold a flat piece of wood or similar material over the carburetor, where possible, and crank the engine.	If the engine starts, but runs roughly the engine is probably not run enough.	
	If the engine won't start:	5.9
5.6—Check the needle and seat: Tap the carburetor in the area of the needle and seat.	If flooding stops, a gasoline additive (e.g., Gumout) will often cure the problem:	5.7
	If flooding continues, check the fuel pump for excessive pressure at the carburetor (according to specifications). If the pressure is normal, the needle and seat must be removed and checked, and/or the float level adjusted:	5.7
5.7—Test the accelerator pump by looking into the throttle bores while operating the throttle. **Check for gas at the carburetor by looking down the carburetor throat while someone moves the accelerator**	If the accelerator pump appears to be operating normally:	5.8
	If the accelerator pump is not operating, the pump must be reconditioned. Where possible, service the pump with the carburetor(s) installed on the engine. If necessary, remove the carburetor. Prior to removal:	5.8
5.8—Determine whether the carburetor main fuel system is functioning: Spray a commercial starting fluid into the carburetor while attempting to start the engine.	If the engine starts, runs for a few seconds, and dies:	5.9
	If the engine doesn't start:	6.1

Test and Procedure	Results and Indications	Proceed to
5.9—Uncommon fuel system malfunctions: See below:	If the problem is solved: If the problem remains, remove and recondition the carburetor.	6.1

Condition	Indication	Test	Prevailing Weather Conditions	Remedy
Vapor lock	Engine will not restart shortly after running.	Cool the components of the fuel system until the engine starts. Vapor lock can be cured faster by draping a wet cloth over a mechanical fuel pump.	Hot to very hot	Ensure that the exhaust manifold heat control valve is operating. Check with the vehicle manufacturer for the recommended solution to vapor lock on the model in question.
Carburetor icing	Engine will not idle, stalls at low speeds.	Visually inspect the throttle plate area of the throttle bores for frost.	High humidity, 32–40° F.	Ensure that the exhaust manifold heat control valve is operating, and that the intake manifold heat riser is not blocked.
Water in the fuel	Engine sputters and stalls; may not start.	Pump a small amount of fuel into a glass jar. Allow to stand, and inspect for droplets or a layer of water.	High humidity, extreme temperature changes.	For droplets, use one or two cans of commercial gas line anti-freeze. For a layer of water, the tank must be drained, and the fuel lines blown out with compressed air.

Section 6—Engine Compression
See Chapter 3 for service procedures

6.1—Test engine compression: Remove all spark plugs. Block the throttle wide open. Insert a compression gauge into a spark plug port, crank the engine to obtain the maximum reading, and record.	If compression is within limits on all cylinders:	7.1
	If gauge reading is extremely low on all cylinders:	6.2
	If gauge reading is low on one or two cylinders: (If gauge readings are identical and low on two or more adjacent cylinders, the head gasket must be replaced.)	6.2

Checking compression

6.2—Test engine compression (wet): Squirt approximately 30 cc. of engine oil into each cylinder, and retest per 6.1.	If the readings improve, worn or cracked rings or broken pistons are indicated:	See Chapter 3
	If the readings do not improve, burned or excessively carboned valves or a jumped timing chain are indicated: **NOTE:** *A jumped timing chain is often indicated by difficult cranking.*	7.1

Section 7—Engine Vacuum
See Chapter 3 for service procedures

Test and Procedure	Results and Indications	Proceed to
7.1—Attach a vacuum gauge to the intake manifold beyond the throttle plate. Start the engine, and observe the action of the needle over the range of engine speeds.	See below.	**See below**

INDICATION: normal engine in good condition

Proceed to: 8.1

Normal engine
Gauge reading: steady, from 17–22 in./Hg.

INDICATION: sticking valves or ignition miss

Proceed to: 9.1, 8.3

Sticking valves
Gauge reading: intermittent fluctuation at idle

INDICATION: late ignition or valve timing, low compression, stuck throttle valve, leaking carburetor or manifold gasket

Proceed to: 6.1

Incorrect valve timing
Gauge reading: low (10–15 in./Hg) but steady

INDICATION: improper carburetor adjustment or minor intake leak.

Proceed to: 7.2

Carburetor requires adjustment
Gauge reading: drifting needle

INDICATION: ignition miss, blown cylinder head gasket, leaking valve or weak valve spring

Proceed to: 8.3, 6.1

Blown head gasket
Gauge reading: needle fluctuates as engine speed increases

INDICATION: burnt valve or faulty valve clearance. Needle will fall when defective valve operates

Proceed to: 9.1

Burnt or leaking valves
Gauge reading: steady needle, but drops regularly

INDICATION: choked muffler, excessive back pressure in system

Proceed to: 10.1

Clogged exhaust system
Gauge reading: gradual drop in reading at idle

INDICATION: worn valve guides

Proceed to: 9.1

Worn valve guides
Gauge reading: needle vibrates excessively at idle, but steadies as engine speed increases

White pointer = steady gauge hand   Black pointer = fluctuating gauge hand

Test and Procedure	Results and Indications	Proceed to
7.2—Attach a vacuum gauge per 7.1, and test for an intake manifold leak. Squirt a small amount of oil around the intake manifold gaskets, carburetor gaskets, plugs and fittings. Observe the action of the vacuum gauge.	If the reading improves, replace the indicated gasket, or seal the indicated fitting or plug: If the reading remains low:	**8.1** **7.3**
7.3—Test all vacuum hoses and accessories for leaks as described in 7.2. Also check the carburetor body (dashpots, automatic choke mechanism, throttle shafts) for leaks in the same manner.	If the reading improves, service or replace the offending part(s): If the reading remains low:	**8.1** **6.1**

Section 8—Secondary Electrical System
See Chapter 2 for service procedures

Test and Procedure	Results and Indications	Proceed to
8.1—Remove the distributor cap and check to make sure that the rotor turns when the engine is cranked. Visually inspect the distributor components.	Clean, tighten or replace any components which appear defective.	**8.2**
8.2—Connect a timing light (per manufacturer's recommendation) and check the dynamic ignition timing. Disconnect and plug the vacuum hose(s) to the distributor if specified, start the engine, and observe the timing marks at the specified engine speed.	If the timing is not correct, adjust to specifications by rotating the distributor in the engine: (Advance timing by rotating distributor opposite normal direction of rotor rotation, retard timing by rotating distributor in same direction as rotor rotation.)	**8.3**
8.3—Check the operation of the distributor advance mechanism(s): To test the mechanical advance, disconnect the vacuum lines from the distributor advance unit and observe the timing marks with a timing light as the engine speed is increased from idle. If the mark moves smoothly, without hesitation, it may be assumed that the mechanical advance is functioning properly. To test vacuum advance and/or retard systems, alternately crimp and release the vacuum line, and observe the timing mark for movement. If movement is noted, the system is operating.	If the systems are functioning: If the systems are not functioning, remove the distributor, and test on a distributor tester:	**8.4** **8.4**
8.4—Locate an ignition miss: With the engine running, remove each spark plug wire, one at a time, until one is found that doesn't cause the engine to roughen and slow down.	When the missing cylinder is identified:	**4.1**

Section 9—Valve Train
See Chapter 3 for service procedures

Test and Procedure	Results and Indications	Proceed to
9.1—Evaluate the valve train: Remove the valve cover, and ensure that the valves are adjusted to specifications. A mechanic's stethoscope may be used to aid in the diagnosis of the valve train. By pushing the probe on or near push rods or rockers, valve noise often can be isolated. A timing light also may be used to diagnose valve problems. Connect the light according to manufacturer's recommendations, and start the engine. Vary the firing moment of the light by increasing the engine speed (and therefore the ignition advance), and moving the trigger from cylinder to cylinder. Observe the movement of each valve.	Sticking valves or erratic valve train motion can be observed with the timing light. The cylinder head must be disassembled for repairs.	**See Chapter 3**
9.2—Check the valve timing: Locate top dead center of the No. 1 piston, and install a degree wheel or tape on the crankshaft pulley or damper with zero corresponding to an index mark on the engine. Rotate the crankshaft in its direction of rotation, and observe the opening of the No. 1 cylinder intake valve. The opening should correspond with the correct mark on the degree wheel according to specifications.	If the timing is not correct, the timing cover must be removed for further investigation.	**See Chapter 3**

Section 10—Exhaust System

Test and Procedure	Results and Indications	Proceed to
10.1—Determine whether the exhaust manifold heat control valve is operating: Operate the valve by hand to determine whether it is free to move. If the valve is free, run the engine to operating temperature and observe the action of the valve, to ensure that it is opening.	If the valve sticks, spray it with a suitable solvent, open and close the valve to free it, and retest. If the valve functions properly: If the valve does not free, or does not operate, replace the valve:	10.2 10.2
10.2—Ensure that there are no exhaust restrictions: Visually inspect the exhaust system for kinks, dents, or crushing. Also note that gases are flowing freely from the tailpipe at all engine speeds, indicating no restriction in the muffler or resonator.	Replace any damaged portion of the system:	11.1

Section 11—Cooling System
See Chapter 3 for service procedures

Test and Procedure	Results and Indications	Proceed to
11.1—Visually inspect the fan belt for glazing, cracks, and fraying, and replace if necessary. Tighten the belt so that the longest span has approximately ½″ play at its midpoint under thumb pressure (see Chapter 1).	Replace or tighten the fan belt as necessary:	**11.2**

Checking belt tension

11.2—Check the fluid level of the cooling system.	If full or slightly low, fill as necessary:	**11.5**
	If extremely low:	**11.3**
11.3—Visually inspect the external portions of the cooling system (radiator, radiator hoses, thermostat elbow, water pump seals, heater hoses, etc.) for leaks. If none are found, pressurize the cooling system to 14–15 psi.	If cooling system holds the pressure:	**11.5**
	If cooling system loses pressure rapidly, reinspect external parts of the system for leaks under pressure. If none are found, check dipstick for coolant in crankcase. If no coolant is present, but pressure loss continues:	**11.4**
	If coolant is evident in crankcase, remove cylinder head(s), and check gasket(s). If gaskets are intact, block and cylinder head(s) should be checked for cracks or holes.	
	If the gasket(s) is blown, replace, and purge the crankcase of coolant: NOTE: *Occasionally, due to atmospheric and driving conditions, condensation of water can occur in the crankcase. This causes the oil to appear milky white. To remedy, run the engine until hot, and change the oil and oil filter.*	**12.6**
11.4—Check for combustion leaks into the cooling system: Pressurize the cooling system as above. Start the engine, and observe the pressure gauge. If the needle fluctuates, remove each spark plug wire, one at a time, noting which cylinder(s) reduce or eliminate the fluctuation.	Cylinders which reduce or eliminate the fluctuation, when the spark plug wire is removed, are leaking into the cooling system. Replace the head gasket on the affected cylinder bank(s).	

Pressurizing the cooling system

Test and Procedure	Results and Indications	Proceed to
11.5—Check the radiator pressure cap: Attach a radiator pressure tester to the radiator cap (wet the seal prior to installation). Quickly pump up the pressure, noting the point at which the cap releases.	If the cap releases within ± 1 psi of the specified rating, it is operating properly:	**11.6**
	If the cap releases at more than ± 1 psi of the specified rating, it should be replaced:	**11.6**

Checking radiator pressure cap

Test and Procedure	Results and Indications	Proceed to
11.6—Test the thermostat: Start the engine cold, remove the radiator cap, and insert a thermometer into the radiator. Allow the engine to idle. After a short while, there will be a sudden, rapid increase in coolant temperature. The temperature at which this sharp rise stops is the thermostat opening temperature.	If the thermostat opens at or about the specified temperature:	**11.7**
	If the temperature doesn't increase: (If the temperature increases slowly and gradually, replace the thermostat.)	**11.7**
11.7—Check the water pump: Remove the thermostat elbow and the thermostat, disconnect the coil high tension lead (to prevent starting), and crank the engine momentarily.	If coolant flows, replace the thermostat and retest per 11.6:	**11.6**
	If coolant doesn't flow, reverse flush the cooling system to alleviate any blockage that might exist. If system is not blocked, and coolant will not flow, replace the water pump.	

Section 12—Lubrication
See Chapter 3 for service procedures

Test and Procedure	Results and Indications	Proceed to
12.1—Check the oil pressure gauge or warning light: If the gauge shows low pressure, or the light is on for no obvious reason, remove the oil pressure sender. Install an accurate oil pressure gauge and run the engine momentarily.	If oil pressure builds normally, run engine for a few moments to determine that it is functioning normally, and replace the sender.	—
	If the pressure remains low:	**12.2**
	If the pressure surges:	**12.3**
	If the oil pressure is zero:	**12.3**
12.2—Visually inspect the oil: If the oil is watery or very thin, milky, or foamy, replace the oil and oil filter.	If the oil is normal:	**12.3**
	If after replacing oil the pressure remains low:	**12.3**
	If after replacing oil the pressure becomes normal:	—

Test and Procedure	Results and Indications	Proceed to
12.3—Inspect the oil pressure relief valve and spring, to ensure that it is not sticking or stuck. Remove and thoroughly clean the valve, spring, and the valve body.	If the oil pressure improves: If no improvement is noted:	— **12.4**
12.4—Check to ensure that the oil pump is not cavitating (sucking air instead of oil): See that the crankcase is neither over nor underfull, and that the pickup in the sump is in the proper position and free from sludge.	Fill or drain the crankcase to the proper capacity, and clean the pickup screen in solvent if necessary. If no improvement is noted:	**12.5**
12.5—Inspect the oil pump drive and the oil pump:	If the pump drive or the oil pump appear to be defective, service as necessary and retest per 12.1: If the pump drive and pump appear to be operating normally, the engine should be disassembled to determine where blockage exists:	**12.1** **See Chapter 3**
12.6—Purge the engine of ethylene glycol coolant: Completely drain the crankcase and the oil filter. Obtain a commercial butyl cellosolve base solvent, designated for this purpose, and follow the instructions precisely. Following this, install a new oil filter and refill the crankcase with the proper weight oil. The next oil and filter change should follow shortly thereafter (1000 miles).		

TROUBLESHOOTING EMISSION CONTROL SYSTEMS

See Chapter 4 for procedures applicable to individual emission control systems used on specific combinations of engine/transmission/model.

TROUBLESHOOTING THE CARBURETOR
See Chapter 4 for service procedures

Carburetor problems cannot be effectively isolated unless all other engine systems (particularly ignition and emission) are functioning properly and the engine is properly tuned.

Condition	Possible Cause
Engine cranks, but does not start	1. Improper starting procedure 2. No fuel in tank 3. Clogged fuel line or filter 4. Defective fuel pump 5. Choke valve not closing properly 6. Engine flooded 7. Choke valve not unloading 8. Throttle linkage not making full travel 9. Stuck needle or float 10. Leaking float needle or seat 11. Improper float adjustment
Engine stalls	1. Improperly adjusted idle speed or mixture **Engine hot** 2. Improperly adjusted dashpot 3. Defective or improperly adjusted solenoid 4. Incorrect fuel level in fuel bowl 5. Fuel pump pressure too high 6. Leaking float needle seat 7. Secondary throttle valve stuck open 8. Air or fuel leaks 9. Idle air bleeds plugged or missing 10. Idle passages plugged **Engine Cold** 11. Incorrectly adjusted choke 12. Improperly adjusted fast idle speed 13. Air leaks 14. Plugged idle or idle air passages 15. Stuck choke valve or binding linkage 16. Stuck secondary throttle valves 17. Engine flooding—high fuel level 18. Leaking or misaligned float
Engine hesitates on acceleration	1. Clogged fuel filter 2. Leaking fuel pump diaphragm 3. Low fuel pump pressure 4. Secondary throttle valves stuck, bent or misadjusted 5. Sticking or binding air valve 6. Defective accelerator pump 7. Vacuum leaks 8. Clogged air filter 9. Incorrect choke adjustment (engine cold)
Engine feels sluggish or flat on acceleration	1. Improperly adjusted idle speed or mixture 2. Clogged fuel filter 3. Defective accelerator pump 4. Dirty, plugged or incorrect main metering jets 5. Bent or sticking main metering rods 6. Sticking throttle valves 7. Stuck heat riser 8. Binding or stuck air valve 9. Dirty, plugged or incorrect secondary jets 10. Bent or sticking secondary metering rods. 11. Throttle body or manifold heat passages plugged 12. Improperly adjusted choke or choke vacuum break.
Carburetor floods	1. Defective fuel pump. Pressure too high. 2. Stuck choke valve 3. Dirty, worn or damaged float or needle valve/seat 4. Incorrect float/fuel level 5. Leaking float bowl

Condition	Possible Cause
Engine idles roughly and stalls	1. Incorrect idle speed 2. Clogged fuel filter 3. Dirt in fuel system or carburetor 4. Loose carburetor screws or attaching bolts 5. Broken carburetor gaskets 6. Air leaks 7. Dirty carburetor 8. Worn idle mixture needles 9. Throttle valves stuck open 10. Incorrectly adjusted float or fuel level 11. Clogged air filter
Engine runs unevenly or surges	1. Defective fuel pump 2. Dirty or clogged fuel filter 3. Plugged, loose or incorrect main metering jets or rods 4. Air leaks 5. Bent or sticking main metering rods 6. Stuck power piston 7. Incorrect float adjustment 8. Incorrect idle speed or mixture 9. Dirty or plugged idle system passages 10. Hard, brittle or broken gaskets 11. Loose attaching or mounting screws 12. Stuck or misaligned secondary throttle valves
Poor fuel economy	1. Poor driving habits 2. Stuck choke valve 3. Binding choke linkage 4. Stuck heat riser 5. Incorrect idle mixture 6. Defective accelerator pump 7. Air leaks 8. Plugged, loose or incorrect main metering jets 9. Improperly adjusted float or fuel level 10. Bent, misaligned or fuel-clogged float 11. Leaking float needle seat 12. Fuel leak 13. Accelerator pump discharge ball not seating properly 14. Incorrect main jets
Engine lacks high speed performance or power	1. Incorrect throttle linkage adjustment 2. Stuck or binding power piston 3. Defective accelerator pump 4. Air leaks 5. Incorrect float setting or fuel level 6. Dirty, plugged, worn or incorrect main metering jets or rods 7. Binding or sticking air valve 8. Brittle or cracked gaskets 9. Bent, incorrect or improperly adjusted secondary metering rods 10. Clogged fuel filter 11. Clogged air filter 12. Defective fuel pump

TROUBLESHOOTING FUEL INJECTION PROBLEMS

Each fuel injection system has its own unique components and test procedures, for which it is impossible to generalize. Refer to Chapter 4 of this Repair & Tune-Up Guide for specific test and repair procedures, if the vehicle is equipped with fuel injection.

TROUBLESHOOTING ELECTRICAL PROBLEMS

See Chapter 5 for service procedures

For any electrical system to operate, it must make a complete circuit. This simply means that the power flow from the battery must make a complete circle. When an electrical component is operating, power flows from the battery to the component, passes through the component causing it to perform its function (lighting a light bulb), and then returns to the battery through the ground of the circuit. This ground is usually (but not always) the metal part of the car or truck on which the electrical component is mounted.

Perhaps the easiest way to visualize this is to think of connecting a light bulb with two wires attached to it to the battery. If one of the two wires attached to the light bulb were attached to the negative post of the battery and the other were attached to the positive post of the battery, you would have a complete circuit. Current from the battery would flow to the light bulb, causing it to light, and return to the negative post of the battery.

The normal automotive circuit differs from this simple example in two ways. First, instead of having a return wire from the bulb to the battery, the light bulb returns the current to the battery through the chassis of the vehicle. Since the negative battery cable is attached to the chassis and the chassis is made of electrically conductive metal, the chassis of the vehicle can serve as a ground wire to complete the circuit. Secondly, most automotive circuits contain switches to turn components on and off as required.

Every complete circuit from a power source must include a component which is using the power from the power source. If you were to disconnect the light bulb from the wires and touch the two wires together (don't do this) the power supply wire to the component would be grounded before the normal ground connection for the circuit.

Because grounding a wire from a power source makes a complete circuit—less the required component to use the power—this phenomenon is called a short circuit. Common causes are: broken insulation (exposing the metal wire to a metal part of the car or truck), or a shorted switch.

Some electrical components which require a large amount of current to operate also have a relay in their circuit. Since these circuits carry a large amount of current, the thickness of the wire in the circuit (gauge size) is also greater. If this large wire were connected from the component to the control switch on the instrument panel, and then back to the component, a voltage drop would occur in the circuit. To prevent this potential drop in voltage, an electromagnetic switch (relay) is used. The large wires in the circuit are connected from the battery to one side of the relay, and from the opposite side of the relay to the component. The relay is normally open, preventing current from passing through the circuit. An additional, smaller, wire is connected from the relay to the control switch for the circuit. When the control switch is turned on, it grounds the smaller wire from the relay and completes the circuit. This closes the relay and allows current to flow from the battery to the component. The horn, headlight, and starter circuits are three which use relays.

It is possible for larger surges of current to pass through the electrical system of your car or truck. If this surge of current were to reach an electrical component, it could burn it out. To prevent this, fuses, circuit breakers or fusible links are connected into the current supply wires of most of the major electrical systems. When an electrical current of excessive power passes through the component's fuse, the fuse blows out and breaks the circuit, saving the component from destruction.

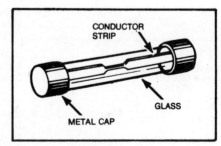

Typical automotive fuse

A circuit breaker is basically a self-repairing fuse. The circuit breaker opens the circuit the same way a fuse does. However, when either the short is removed from the circuit or the surge subsides, the circuit breaker resets itself and does not have to be replaced as a fuse does.

A fuse link is a wire that acts as a fuse. It is normally connected between the starter relay and the main wiring harness. This connection is usually under the hood. The fuse link (if installed) protects all the

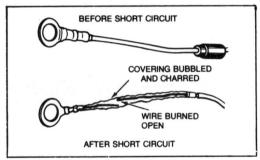

Most fusible links show a charred, melted insulation when they burn out

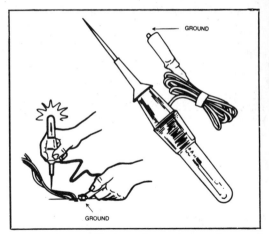

The test light will show the presence of current when touched to a hot wire and grounded at the other end

chassis electrical components, and is the probable cause of trouble when none of the electrical components function, unless the battery is disconnected or dead.

Electrical problems generally fall into one of three areas:

1. The component that is not functioning is not receiving current.

2. The component itself is not functioning.

3. The component is not properly grounded.

The electrical system can be checked with a test light and a jumper wire. A test light is a device that looks like a pointed screwdriver with a wire attached to it and has a light bulb in its handle. A jumper wire is a piece of insulated wire with an alligator clip attached to each end.

If a component is not working, you must follow a systematic plan to determine which of the three causes is the villain.

1. Turn on the switch that controls the inoperable component.

2. Disconnect the power supply wire from the component.

3. Attach the ground wire on the test light to a good metal ground.

4. Touch the probe end of the test light to the end of the power supply wire that was disconnected from the component. If the component is receiving current, the test light will go on.

NOTE: *Some components work only when the ignition switch is turned on.*

If the test light does not go on, then the problem is in the circuit between the battery and the component. This includes all the switches, fuses, and relays in the system. Follow the wire that runs back to the battery. The problem is an open circuit between the battery and the component. If the fuse is blown and, when replaced, immediately blows again, there is a short circuit in the system which must be located and repaired. If there is a switch in the system, bypass it with a jumper wire. This is done by connecting one end of the jumper wire to the power supply wire into the switch and the other end of the jumper wire to the wire coming out of the switch. If the test light lights with the jumper wire installed, the switch or whatever was bypassed is defective.

NOTE: *Never substitute the jumper wire for the component, since it is required to use the power from the power source.*

5. If the bulb in the test light goes on, then the current is getting to the component that is not working. This eliminates the first of the three possible causes. Connect the power supply wire and connect a jumper wire from the component to a good metal ground. Do this with the switch which controls the component turned on, and also the ignition switch turned on if it is required for the component to work. If the component works with the jumper wire installed, then it has a bad ground. This is usually caused by the metal area on which the component mounts to the chassis being coated with some type of foreign matter.

6. If neither test located the source of the trouble, then the component itself is defective. Remember that for any electrical system to work, all connections must be clean and tight.

Troubleshooting Basic Turn Signal and Flasher Problems
See Chapter 5 for service procedures

Most problems in the turn signals or flasher system can be reduced to defective flashers or bulbs, which are easily replaced. Occasionally, the turn signal switch will prove defective.

F = Front   R = Rear   ● = Lights off   O = Lights on

Condition		Possible Cause
Turn signals light, but do not flash	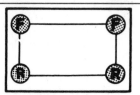	Defective flasher
No turn signals light on either side	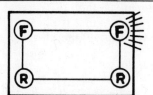	Blown fuse. Replace if defective. Defective flasher. Check by substitution. Open circuit, short circuit or poor ground.
Both turn signals on one side don't work	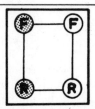	Bad bulbs. Bad ground in both (or either) housings.
One turn signal light on one side doesn't work	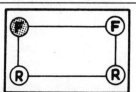	Defective bulb. Corrosion in socket. Clean contacts. Poor ground at socket.
Turn signal flashes too fast or too slowly	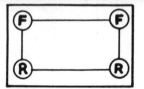	Check any bulb on the side flashing too fast. A heavy-duty bulb is probably installed in place of a regular bulb. Check the bulb flashing too slowly. A standard bulb was probably installed in place of a heavy-duty bulb. Loose connections or corrosion at the bulb socket.
Indicator lights don't work in either direction		Check if the turn signals are working. Check the dash indicator lights. Check the flasher by substitution.
One indicator light doesn't light		On systems with one dash indicator: See if the lights work on the same side. Often the filaments have been reversed in systems combining stoplights with taillights and turn signals. Check the flasher by substitution. On systems with two indicators: Check the bulbs on the same side. Check the indicator light bulb. Check the flasher by substitution.

Troubleshooting Lighting Problems
See Chapter 5 for service procedures

Condition	Possible Cause
One or more lights don't work, but others do	1. Defective bulb(s) 2. Blown fuse(s) 3. Dirty fuse clips or light sockets 4. Poor ground circuit
Lights burn out quickly	1. Incorrect voltage regulator setting or defective regulator 2. Poor battery/alternator connections
Lights go dim	1. Low/discharged battery 2. Alternator not charging 3. Corroded sockets or connections 4. Low voltage output
Lights flicker	1. Loose connection 2. Poor ground. (Run ground wire from light housing to frame) 3. Circuit breaker operating (short circuit)
Lights "flare"—Some flare is normal on acceleration—If excessive, see "Lights Burn Out Quickly"	High voltage setting
Lights glare—approaching drivers are blinded	1. Lights adjusted too high 2. Rear springs or shocks sagging 3. Rear tires soft

Troubleshooting Dash Gauge Problems
Most problems can be traced to a defective sending unit or faulty wiring. Occasionally, the gauge itself is at fault. See Chapter 5 for service procedures.

Condition	Possible Cause
COOLANT TEMPERATURE GAUGE	
Gauge reads erratically or not at all	1. Loose or dirty connections 2. Defective sending unit. 3. Defective gauge. To test a bi-metal gauge, remove the wire from the sending unit. Ground the wire for an instant. If the gauge registers, replace the sending unit. To test a magnetic gauge, disconnect the wire at the sending unit. With ignition ON gauge should register COLD. Ground the wire; gauge should register HOT.
AMMETER GAUGE—TURN HEADLIGHTS ON (DO NOT START ENGINE). NOTE REACTION	
Ammeter shows charge Ammeter shows discharge Ammeter does not move	1. Connections reversed on gauge 2. Ammeter is OK 3. Loose connections or faulty wiring 4. Defective gauge

Condition	Possible Cause

OIL PRESSURE GAUGE

Gauge does not register or is inaccurate	1. On mechanical gauge, Bourdon tube may be bent or kinked. 2. Low oil pressure. Remove sending unit. Idle the engine briefly. If no oil flows from sending unit hole, problem is in engine. 3. Defective gauge. Remove the wire from the sending unit and ground it for an instant with the ignition ON. A good gauge will go to the top of the scale. 4. Defective wiring. Check the wiring to the gauge. If it's OK and the gauge doesn't register when grounded, replace the gauge. 5. Defective sending unit.

ALL GAUGES

All gauges do not operate All gauges read low or erratically All gauges pegged	1. Blown fuse 2. Defective instrument regulator 3. Defective or dirty instrument voltage regulator 4. Loss of ground between instrument voltage regulator and frame 5. Defective instrument regulator

WARNING LIGHTS

Light(s) do not come on when ignition is ON, but engine is not started Light comes on with engine running	1. Defective bulb 2. Defective wire 3. Defective sending unit. Disconnect the wire from the sending unit and ground it. Replace the sending unit if the light comes on with the ignition ON. 4. Problem in individual system 5. Defective sending unit

Troubleshooting Clutch Problems

It is false economy to replace individual clutch components. The pressure plate, clutch plate and throwout bearing should be replaced as a set, and the flywheel face inspected, whenever the clutch is overhauled. See Chapter 6 for service procedures.

Condition	Possible Cause
Clutch chatter	1. Grease on driven plate (disc) facing 2. Binding clutch linkage or cable 3. Loose, damaged facings on driven plate (disc) 4. Engine mounts loose 5. Incorrect height adjustment of pressure plate release levers 6. Clutch housing or housing to transmission adapter misalignment 7. Loose driven plate hub
Clutch grabbing	1. Oil, grease on driven plate (disc) facing 2. Broken pressure plate 3. Warped or binding driven plate. Driven plate binding on clutch shaft
Clutch slips	1. Lack of lubrication in clutch linkage or cable (linkage or cable binds, causes incomplete engagement) 2. Incorrect pedal, or linkage adjustment 3. Broken pressure plate springs 4. Weak pressure plate springs 5. Grease on driven plate facings (disc)

Troubleshooting Clutch Problems (cont.)

Condition	Possible Cause
Incomplete clutch release	1. Incorrect pedal or linkage adjustment or linkage or cable binding 2. Incorrect height adjustment on pressure plate release levers 3. Loose, broken facings on driven plate (disc) 4. Bent, dished, warped driven plate caused by overheating
Grinding, whirring grating noise when pedal is depressed	1. Worn or defective throwout bearing 2. Starter drive teeth contacting flywheel ring gear teeth. Look for milled or polished teeth on ring gear.
Squeal, howl, trumpeting noise when pedal is being released (occurs during first inch to inch and one-half of pedal travel)	Pilot bushing worn or lack of lubricant. If bushing appears OK, polish bushing with emery cloth, soak lube wick in oil, lube bushing with oil, apply film of chassis grease to clutch shaft pilot hub, reassemble. NOTE: Bushing wear may be due to misalignment of clutch housing or housing to transmission adapter
Vibration or clutch pedal pulsation with clutch disengaged (pedal fully depressed)	1. Worn or defective engine transmission mounts 2. Flywheel run out. (Flywheel run out at face not to exceed 0.005″) 3. Damaged or defective clutch components

Troubleshooting Manual Transmission Problems
See Chapter 6 for service procedures

Condition	Possible Cause
Transmission jumps out of gear	1. Misalignment of transmission case or clutch housing. 2. Worn pilot bearing in crankshaft. 3. Bent transmission shaft. 4. Worn high speed sliding gear. 5. Worn teeth or end-play in clutch shaft. 6. Insufficient spring tension on shifter rail plunger. 7. Bent or loose shifter fork. 8. Gears not engaging completely. 9. Loose or worn bearings on clutch shaft or mainshaft. 10. Worn gear teeth. 11. Worn or damaged detent balls.
Transmission sticks in gear	1. Clutch not releasing fully. 2. Burred or battered teeth on clutch shaft, or sliding sleeve. 3. Burred or battered transmission mainshaft. 4. Frozen synchronizing clutch. 5. Stuck shifter rail plunger. 6. Gearshift lever twisting and binding shifter rail. 7. Battered teeth on high speed sliding gear or on sleeve. 8. Improper lubrication, or lack of lubrication. 9. Corroded transmission parts. 10. Defective mainshaft pilot bearing. 11. Locked gear bearings will give same effect as stuck in gear.
Transmission gears will not synchronize	1. Binding pilot bearing on mainshaft, will synchronize in high gear only. 2. Clutch not releasing fully. 3. Detent spring weak or broken. 4. Weak or broken springs under balls in sliding gear sleeve. 5. Binding bearing on clutch shaft, or binding countershaft. 6. Binding pilot bearing in crankshaft. 7. Badly worn gear teeth. 8. Improper lubrication. 9. Constant mesh gear not turning freely on transmission mainshaft. Will synchronize in that gear only.

Condition	Possible Cause
Gears spinning when shifting into gear from neutral	1. Clutch not releasing fully. 2. In some cases an extremely light lubricant in transmission will cause gears to continue to spin for a short time after clutch is released. 3. Binding pilot bearing in crankshaft.
Transmission noisy in all gears	1. Insufficient lubricant, or improper lubricant. 2. Worn countergear bearings. 3. Worn or damaged main drive gear or countergear. 4. Damaged main drive gear or mainshaft bearings. 5. Worn or damaged countergear anti-lash plate.
Transmission noisy in neutral only	1. Damaged main drive gear bearing. 2. Damaged or loose mainshaft pilot bearing. 3. Worn or damaged countergear anti-lash plate. 4. Worn countergear bearings.
Transmission noisy in one gear only	1. Damaged or worn constant mesh gears. 2. Worn or damaged countergear bearings. 3. Damaged or worn synchronizer.
Transmission noisy in reverse only	1. Worn or damaged reverse idler gear or idler bushing. 2. Worn or damaged mainshaft reverse gear. 3. Worn or damaged reverse countergear. 4. Damaged shift mechanism.

TROUBLESHOOTING AUTOMATIC TRANSMISSION PROBLEMS

Keeping alert to changes in the operating characteristics of the transmission (changing shift points, noises, etc.) can prevent small problems from becoming large ones. If the problem cannot be traced to loose bolts, fluid level, misadjusted linkage, clogged filters or similar problems, you should probably seek professional service.

Transmission Fluid Indications

The appearance and odor of the transmission fluid can give valuable clues to the overall condition of the transmission. Always note the appearance of the fluid when you check the fluid level or change the fluid. Rub a small amount of fluid between your fingers to feel for grit and smell the fluid on the dipstick.

If the fluid appears:	It indicates:
Clear and red colored	Normal operation
Discolored (extremely dark red or brownish) or smells burned	Band or clutch pack failure, usually caused by an overheated transmission. Hauling very heavy loads with insufficient power or failure to change the fluid often result in overheating. Do not confuse this appearance with newer fluids that have a darker red color and a strong odor (though not a burned odor).
Foamy or aerated (light in color and full of bubbles)	1. The level is too high (gear train is churning oil) 2. An internal air leak (air is mixing with the fluid). Have the transmission checked professionally.
Solid residue in the fluid	Defective bands, clutch pack or bearings. Bits of band material or metal abrasives are clinging to the dipstick. Have the transmission checked professionally.
Varnish coating on the dipstick	The transmission fluid is overheating

TROUBLESHOOTING DRIVE AXLE PROBLEMS

First, determine when the noise is most noticeable.

Drive Noise: Produced under vehicle acceleration.

Coast Noise: Produced while coasting with a closed throttle.

Float Noise: Occurs while maintaining constant speed (just enough to keep speed constant) on a level road.

External Noise Elimination

It is advisable to make a thorough road test to determine whether the noise originates in the rear axle or whether it originates from the tires, engine, transmission, wheel bearings or road surface. Noise originating from other places cannot be corrected by servicing the rear axle.

ROAD NOISE

Brick or rough surfaced concrete roads produce noises that seem to come from the rear axle. Road noise is usually identical in Drive or Coast and driving on a different type of road will tell whether the road is the problem.

TIRE NOISE

Tire noise can be mistaken as rear axle noise, even though the tires on the front are at fault. Snow tread and mud tread tires or tires worn unevenly will frequently cause vibrations which seem to originate elsewhere; *temporarily, and for test purposes only,* inflate the tires to 40–50 lbs. This will significantly alter the noise produced by the tires, but will not alter noise from the rear axle. Noises from the rear axle will normally cease at speeds below 30 mph on coast, while tire noise will continue at lower tone as speed is decreased. The rear axle noise will usually change from drive conditions to coast conditions, while tire noise will not. Do not forget to lower the tire pressure to normal after the test is complete.

ENGINE/TRANSMISSION NOISE

Determine at what speed the noise is most pronounced, then stop in a quiet place. With the transmission in Neutral, run the engine through speeds corresponding to road speeds where the noise was noticed. Noises produced with the vehicle standing still are coming from the engine or transmission.

FRONT WHEEL BEARINGS

Front wheel bearing noises, sometimes confused with rear axle noises, will not change when comparing drive and coast conditions. While holding the speed steady, lightly apply the footbrake. This will often cause wheel bearing noise to lessen, as some of the weight is taken off the bearing. Front wheel bearings are easily checked by jacking up the wheels and spinning the wheels. Shaking the wheels will also determine if the wheel bearings are excessively loose.

REAR AXLE NOISES

Eliminating other possible sources can narrow the cause to the rear axle, which normally produces noise from worn gears or bearings. Gear noises tend to peak in a narrow speed range, while bearing noises will usually vary in pitch with engine speeds.

Noise Diagnosis

The Noise Is:	Most Probably Produced By:
1. Identical under Drive or Coast	Road surface, tires or front wheel bearings
2. Different depending on road surface	Road surface or tires
3. Lower as speed is lowered	Tires
4. Similar when standing or moving	Engine or transmission
5. A vibration	Unbalanced tires, rear wheel bearing, unbalanced driveshaft or worn U-joint
6. A knock or click about every two tire revolutions	Rear wheel bearing
7. Most pronounced on turns	Damaged differential gears
8. A steady low-pitched whirring or scraping, starting at low speeds	Damaged or worn pinion bearing
9. A chattering vibration on turns	Wrong differential lubricant or worn clutch plates (limited slip rear axle)
10. Noticed only in Drive, Coast or Float conditions	Worn ring gear and/or pinion gear

Troubleshooting Steering & Suspension Problems

Condition	Possible Cause
Hard steering (wheel is hard to turn)	1. Improper tire pressure 2. Loose or glazed pump drive belt 3. Low or incorrect fluid 4. Loose, bent or poorly lubricated front end parts 5. Improper front end alignment (excessive caster) 6. Bind in steering column or linkage 7. Kinked hydraulic hose 8. Air in hydraulic system 9. Low pump output or leaks in system 10. Obstruction in lines 11. Pump valves sticking or out of adjustment 12. Incorrect wheel alignment
Loose steering (too much play in steering wheel)	1. Loose wheel bearings 2. Faulty shocks 3. Worn linkage or suspension components 4. Loose steering gear mounting or linkage points 5. Steering mechanism worn or improperly adjusted 6. Valve spool improperly adjusted 7. Worn ball joints, tie-rod ends, etc.
Veers or wanders (pulls to one side with hands off steering wheel)	1. Improper tire pressure 2. Improper front end alignment 3. Dragging or improperly adjusted brakes 4. Bent frame 5. Improper rear end alignment 6. Faulty shocks or springs 7. Loose or bent front end components 8. Play in Pitman arm 9. Steering gear mountings loose 10. Loose wheel bearings 11. Binding Pitman arm 12. Spool valve sticking or improperly adjusted 13. Worn ball joints
Wheel oscillation or vibration transmitted through steering wheel	1. Low or uneven tire pressure 2. Loose wheel bearings 3. Improper front end alignment 4. Bent spindle 5. Worn, bent or broken front end components 6. Tires out of round or out of balance 7. Excessive lateral runout in disc brake rotor 8. Loose or bent shock absorber or strut
Noises (see also "Troubleshooting Drive Axle Problems")	1. Loose belts 2. Low fluid, air in system 3. Foreign matter in system 4. Improper lubrication 5. Interference or chafing in linkage 6. Steering gear mountings loose 7. Incorrect adjustment or wear in gear box 8. Faulty valves or wear in pump 9. Kinked hydraulic lines 10. Worn wheel bearings
Poor return of steering	1. Over-inflated tires 2. Improperly aligned front end (excessive caster) 3. Binding in steering column 4. No lubrication in front end 5. Steering gear adjusted too tight
Uneven tire wear (see "How To Read Tire Wear")	1. Incorrect tire pressure 2. Improperly aligned front end 3. Tires out-of-balance 4. Bent or worn suspension parts

HOW TO READ TIRE WEAR

The way your tires wear is a good indicator of other parts of the suspension. Abnormal wear patterns are often caused by the need for simple tire maintenance, or for front end alignment.

Excessive wear at the center of the tread indicates that the air pressure in the tire is consistently too high. The tire is riding on the center of the tread and wearing it prematurely. Occasionally, this wear pattern can result from outrageously wide tires on narrow rims. The cure for this is to replace either the tires or the wheels.

This type of wear usually results from consistent under-inflation. When a tire is under-inflated, there is too much contact with the road by the outer treads, which wear prematurely. When this type of wear occurs, and the tire pressure is known to be consistently correct, a bent or worn steering component or the need for wheel alignment could be indicated.

Feathering is a condition when the edge of each tread rib develops a slightly rounded edge on one side and a sharp edge on the other. By running your hand over the tire, you can usually feel the sharper edges before you'll be able to see them. The most common causes of feathering are incorrect toe-in setting or deteriorated bushings in the front suspension.

When an inner or outer rib wears faster than the rest of the tire, the need for wheel alignment is indicated. There is excessive camber in the front suspension, causing the wheel to lean too much putting excessive load on one side of the tire. Misalignment could also be due to sagging springs, worn ball joints, or worn control arm bushings. Be sure the vehicle is loaded the way it's normally driven when you have the wheels aligned.

Cups or scalloped dips appearing around the edge of the tread almost always indicate worn (sometimes bent) suspension parts. Adjustment of wheel alignment alone will seldom cure the problem. Any worn component that connects the wheel to the suspension can cause this type of wear. Occasionally, wheels that are out of balance will wear like this, but wheel imbalance usually shows up as bald spots between the outside edges and center of the tread.

Second-rib wear is usually found only in radial tires, and appears where the steel belts end in relation to the tread. It can be kept to a minimum by paying careful attention to tire pressure and frequently rotating the tires. This is often considered normal wear but excessive amounts indicate that the tires are too wide for the wheels.

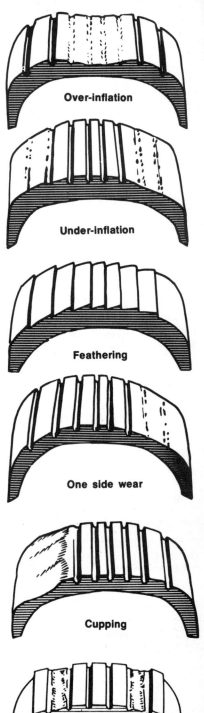

Over-inflation

Under-inflation

Feathering

One side wear

Cupping

Second-rib wear

Troubleshooting Disc Brake Problems

Condition	Possible Cause
Noise—groan—brake noise emanating when slowly releasing brakes (creep-groan)	Not detrimental to function of disc brakes—no corrective action required. (This noise may be eliminated by slightly increasing or decreasing brake pedal efforts.)
Rattle—brake noise or rattle emanating at low speeds on rough roads, (front wheels only).	1. Shoe anti-rattle spring missing or not properly positioned. 2. Excessive clearance between shoe and caliper. 3. Soft or broken caliper seals. 4. Deformed or misaligned disc. 5. Loose caliper.
Scraping	1. Mounting bolts too long. 2. Loose wheel bearings. 3. Bent, loose, or misaligned splash shield.
Front brakes heat up during driving and fail to release	1. Operator riding brake pedal. 2. Stop light switch improperly adjusted. 3. Sticking pedal linkage. 4. Frozen or seized piston. 5. Residual pressure valve in master cylinder. 6. Power brake malfunction. 7. Proportioning valve malfunction.
Leaky brake caliper	1. Damaged or worn caliper piston seal. 2. Scores or corrosion on surface of cylinder bore.
Grabbing or uneven brake action— Brakes pull to one side	1. Causes listed under "Brakes Pull". 2. Power brake malfunction. 3. Low fluid level in master cylinder. 4. Air in hydraulic system. 5. Brake fluid, oil or grease on linings. 6. Unmatched linings. 7. Distorted brake pads. 8. Frozen or seized pistons. 9. Incorrect tire pressure. 10. Front end out of alignment. 11. Broken rear spring. 12. Brake caliper pistons sticking. 13. Restricted hose or line. 14. Caliper not in proper alignment to braking disc. 15. Stuck or malfunctioning metering valve. 16. Soft or broken caliper seals. 17. Loose caliper.
Brake pedal can be depressed without braking effect	1. Air in hydraulic system or improper bleeding procedure. 2. Leak past primary cup in master cylinder. 3. Leak in system. 4. Rear brakes out of adjustment. 5. Bleeder screw open.
Excessive pedal travel	1. Air, leak, or insufficient fluid in system or caliper. 2. Warped or excessively tapered shoe and lining assembly. 3. Excessive disc runout. 4. Rear brake adjustment required. 5. Loose wheel bearing adjustment. 6. Damaged caliper piston seal. 7. Improper brake fluid (boil). 8. Power brake malfunction. 9. Weak or soft hoses.

Troubleshooting Disc Brake Problems (cont.)

Condition	Possible Cause
Brake roughness or chatter (pedal pumping)	1. Excessive thickness variation of braking disc. 2. Excessive lateral runout of braking disc. 3. Rear brake drums out-of-round. 4. Excessive front bearing clearance.
Excessive pedal effort	1. Brake fluid, oil or grease on linings. 2. Incorrect lining. 3. Frozen or seized pistons. 4. Power brake malfunction. 5. Kinked or collapsed hose or line. 6. Stuck metering valve. 7. Scored caliper or master cylinder bore. 8. Seized caliper pistons.
Brake pedal fades (pedal travel increases with foot on brake)	1. Rough master cylinder or caliper bore. 2. Loose or broken hydraulic lines/connections. 3. Air in hydraulic system. 4. Fluid level low. 5. Weak or soft hoses. 6. Inferior quality brake shoes or fluid. 7. Worn master cylinder piston cups or seals.

Troubleshooting Drum Brakes

Condition	Possible Cause
Pedal goes to floor	1. Fluid low in reservoir. 2. Air in hydraulic system. 3. Improperly adjusted brake. 4. Leaking wheel cylinders. 5. Loose or broken brake lines. 6. Leaking or worn master cylinder. 7. Excessively worn brake lining.
Spongy brake pedal	1. Air in hydraulic system. 2. Improper brake fluid (low boiling point). 3. Excessively worn or cracked brake drums. 4. Broken pedal pivot bushing.
Brakes pulling	1. Contaminated lining. 2. Front end out of alignment. 3. Incorrect brake adjustment. 4. Unmatched brake lining. 5. Brake drums out of round. 6. Brake shoes distorted. 7. Restricted brake hose or line. 8. Broken rear spring. 9. Worn brake linings. 10. Uneven lining wear. 11. Glazed brake lining. 12. Excessive brake lining dust. 13. Heat spotted brake drums. 14. Weak brake return springs. 15. Faulty automatic adjusters. 16. Low or incorrect tire pressure.

Condition	Possible Cause
Squealing brakes	1. Glazed brake lining. 2. Saturated brake lining. 3. Weak or broken brake shoe retaining spring. 4. Broken or weak brake shoe return spring. 5. Incorrect brake lining. 6. Distorted brake shoes. 7. Bent support plate. 8. Dust in brakes or scored brake drums. 9. Linings worn below limit. 10. Uneven brake lining wear. 11. Heat spotted brake drums.
Chirping brakes	1. Out of round drum or eccentric axle flange pilot.
Dragging brakes	1. Incorrect wheel or parking brake adjustment. 2. Parking brakes engaged or improperly adjusted. 3. Weak or broken brake shoe return spring. 4. Brake pedal binding. 5. Master cylinder cup sticking. 6. Obstructed master cylinder relief port. 7. Saturated brake lining. 8. Bent or out of round brake drum. 9. Contaminated or improper brake fluid. 10. Sticking wheel cylinder pistons. 11. Driver riding brake pedal. 12. Defective proportioning valve. 13. Insufficient brake shoe lubricant.
Hard pedal	1. Brake booster inoperative. 2. Incorrect brake lining. 3. Restricted brake line or hose. 4. Frozen brake pedal linkage. 5. Stuck wheel cylinder. 6. Binding pedal linkage. 7. Faulty proportioning valve.
Wheel locks	1. Contaminated brake lining. 2. Loose or torn brake lining. 3. Wheel cylinder cups sticking. 4. Incorrect wheel bearing adjustment. 5. Faulty proportioning valve.
Brakes fade (high speed)	1. Incorrect lining. 2. Overheated brake drums. 3. Incorrect brake fluid (low boiling temperature). 4. Saturated brake lining. 5. Leak in hydraulic system. 6. Faulty automatic adjusters.
Pedal pulsates	1. Bent or out of round brake drum.
Brake chatter and shoe knock	1. Out of round brake drum. 2. Loose support plate. 3. Bent support plate. 4. Distorted brake shoes. 5. Machine grooves in contact face of brake drum (Shoe Knock). 6. Contaminated brake lining. 7. Missing or loose components. 8. Incorrect lining material. 9. Out-of-round brake drums. 10. Heat spotted or scored brake drums. 11. Out-of-balance wheels.

Troubleshooting Drum Brakes (cont.)

Condition	Possible Cause
Brakes do not self adjust	1. Adjuster screw frozen in thread. 2. Adjuster screw corroded at thrust washer. 3. Adjuster lever does not engage star wheel. 4. Adjuster installed on wrong wheel.
Brake light glows	1. Leak in the hydraulic system. 2. Air in the system. 3. Improperly adjusted master cylinder pushrod. 4. Uneven lining wear. 5. Failure to center combination valve or proportioning valve.

Mechanic's Data

General Conversion Table

Multiply By	To Convert	To	
LENGTH			
2.54	Inches	Centimeters	.3937
25.4	Inches	Millimeters	.03937
30.48	Feet	Centimeters	.0328
.304	Feet	Meters	3.28
.914	Yards	Meters	1.094
1.609	Miles	Kilometers	.621
VOLUME			
.473	Pints	Liters	2.11
.946	Quarts	Liters	1.06
3.785	Gallons	Liters	.264
.016	Cubic inches	Liters	61.02
16.39	Cubic inches	Cubic cms.	.061
28.3	Cubic feet	Liters	.0353
MASS (Weight)			
28.35	Ounces	Grams	.035
.4536	Pounds	Kilograms	2.20
—	To obtain	From	Multiply by

Multiply By	To Convert	To	
AREA			
.645	Square inches	Square cms.	.155
.836	Square yds.	Square meters	1.196
FORCE			
4.448	Pounds	Newtons	.225
.138	Ft./lbs.	Kilogram/meters	7.23
1.36	Ft./lbs.	Newton-meters	.737
.112	In./lbs.	Newton-meters	8.844
PRESSURE			
.068	Psi	Atmospheres	14.7
6.89	Psi	Kilopascals	.145
OTHER			
1.104	Horsepower (DIN)	Horsepower (SAE)	.9861
.746	Horsepower (SAE)	Kilowatts (KW)	1.34
1.60	Mph	Km/h	.625
.425	Mpg	Km/1	2.35
—	To obtain	From	Multiply by

Tap Drill Sizes

National Coarse or U.S.S.

Screw & Tap Size	Threads Per Inch	Use Drill Number
No. 5	40	.39
No. 6	32	.36
No. 8	32	.29
No. 10	24	.25
No. 12	24	.17
1/4	20	8
5/16	18	.F
3/8	16	5/16
7/16	14	.U
1/2	13	27/64
9/16	12	31/64
5/8	11	17/32
3/4	10	21/32
7/8	9	49/64

National Coarse or U.S.S.

Screw & Tap Size	Threads Per Inch	Use Drill Number
1	8	7/8
1 1/8	7	63/64
1 1/4	7	1 7/64
1 1/2	6	1 11/32

National Fine or S.A.E.

Screw & Tap Size	Threads Per Inch	Use Drill Number
No. 5	44	.37
No. 6	40	.33
No. 8	36	.29
No. 10	32	.21

National Fine or S.A.E.

Screw & Tap Size	Threads Per Inch	Use Drill Number
No. 12	28	.15
1/4	28	3
6/16	24	1
3/8	24	.Q
7/16	20	.W
1/2	20	29/64
9/16	18	33/64
5/8	18	37/64
3/4	16	11/16
7/8	14	13/16
1 1/8	12	1 3/64
1 1/4	12	1 11/64
1 1/2	12	1 27/64

Drill Sizes In Decimal Equivalents

Inch	Decimal	Wire	mm
1/64	.0156		.39
	.0157		.4
	.0160	78	
	.0165		.42
	.0173		.44
	.0177		.45
	.0180	77	
	.0181		.46
	.0189		.48
	.0197		.5
	.0200	76	
	.0210	75	
	.0217		.55
	.0225	74	
	.0236		.6
	.0240	73	
	.0250	72	
	.0256		.65
	.0260	71	
	.0276		.7
	.0280	70	
	.0292	69	
	.0295		.75
	.0310	68	
1/32	.0312		.79
	.0315		.8
	.0320	67	
	.0330	66	
	.0335		.85
	.0350	65	
	.0354		.9
	.0360	64	
	.0370	63	
	.0374		.95
	.0380	62	
	.0390	61	
	.0394		1.0
	.0400	60	
	.0410	59	
	.0413		1.05
	.0420	58	
	.0430	57	
	.0433		1.1
	.0453		1.15
3/64	.0465	56	
	.0469		1.19
	.0472		1.2
	.0492		1.25
	.0512		1.3
	.0520	55	
	.0531		1.35
	.0550	54	
	.0551		1.4
	.0571		1.45
	.0591		1.5
	.0595	53	
	.0610		1.55
1/16	.0625		1.59
	.0630		1.6
	.0635	52	
	.0650		1.65
	.0669		1.7
	.0670	51	
	.0689		1.75
	.0700	50	
	.0709		1.8
	.0728		1.85

Inch	Decimal	Wire	mm
	.0730	49	
	.0748		1.9
	.0760	48	
	.0768		1.95
5/64	.0781		1.98
	.0785	47	
	.0787		2.0
	.0807		2.05
	.0810	46	
	.0820	45	
	.0827		2.1
	.0846		2.15
	.0860	44	
	.0866		2.2
	.0886		2.25
	.0890	43	
	.0906		2.3
	.0925		2.35
	.0935	42	
3/32	.0938		2.38
	.0945		2.4
	.0960	41	
	.0965		2.45
	.0980	40	
	.0981		2.5
	.0995	39	
	.1015	38	
	.1024		2.6
	.1040	37	
	.1063		2.7
	.1065	36	
	.1083		2.75
7/64	.1094		2.77
	.1100	35	
	.1102		2.8
	.1110	34	
	.1130	33	
	.1142		2.9
	.1160	32	
	.1181		3.0
	.1200	31	
	.1220		3.1
1/8	.1250		3.17
	.1260		3.2
	.1280		3.25
	.1285	30	
	.1299		3.3
	.1339		3.4
	.1360	29	
	.1378		3.5
	.1405	28	
9/64	.1406		3.57
	.1417		3.6
	.1440	27	
	.1457		3.7
	.1470	26	
	.1476		3.75
	.1495	25	
	.1496		3.8
	.1520	24	
	.1535		3.9
	.1540	23	
5/32	.1562		3.96
	.1570	22	
	.1575		4.0
	.1590	21	
	.1610	20	

Inch	Decimal	Wire & Letter	mm
	.1614		4.1
	.1654		4.2
	.1660	19	
	.1673		4.25
	.1693		4.3
	.1695	18	
11/64	.1719		4.36
	.1730	17	
	.1732		4.4
	.1770	16	
	.1772		4.5
	.1800	15	
	.1811		4.6
	.1820	14	
	.1850	13	
	.1850		4.7
	.1870		4.75
3/16	.1875		4.76
	.1890		4.8
	.1890	12	
	.1910	11	
	.1929		4.9
	.1935	10	
	.1960	9	
	.1969		5.0
	.1990	8	
	.2008		5.1
	.2010	7	
13/64	.2031		5.16
	.2040	6	
	.2047		5.2
	.2055	5	
	.2067		5.25
	.2087		5.3
	.2090	4	
	.2126		5.4
	.2130	3	
	.2165		5.5
7/32	.2188		5.55
	.2205		5.6
	.2210	2	
	.2244		5.7
	.2264		5.75
	.2280	1	
	.2283		5.8
	.2323		5.9
	.2340	A	
15/64	.2344		5.95
	.2362		6.0
	.2380	B	
	.2402		6.1
	.2420	C	
	.2441		6.2
	.2460	D	
	.2461		6.25
	.2480		6.3
1/4	.2500	E	6.35
	.2520		6.
	.2559		6.5
	.2570	F	
	.2598		6.6
	.2610	G	
	.2638		6.7
17/64	.2656		6.74
	.2657		6.75
	.2660	H	
	.2677		6.8

Inch	Decimal	Letter	mm
	.2717		6.9
	.2720	I	
	.2756		7.0
	.2770	J	
	.2795		7.1
	.2810	K	
9/32	.2812		7.14
	.2835		7.2
	.2854		7.25
	.2874		7.3
	.2900	L	
	.2913		7.4
	.2950	M	
	.2953		7.5
19/64	.2969		7.54
	.2992		7.6
	.3020	N	
	.3031		7.7
	.3051		7.75
	.3071		7.8
	.3110		7.9
5/16	.3125		7.93
	.3150		8.0
	.3160	O	
	.3189		8.1
	.3228		8.2
	.3230	P	
	.3248		8.25
	.3268		8.3
21/64	.3281		8.33
	.3307		8.4
	.3320	Q	
	.3346		8.5
	.3386		8.6
	.3390	R	
	.3425		8.7
11/32	.3438		8.73
	.3445		8.75
	.3465		8.8
	.3480	S	
	.3504		8.9
	.3543		9.0
	.3580	T	
	.3583		9.1
23/64	.3594		9.12
	.3622		9.2
	.3642		9.25
	.3661		9.3
	.3680	U	
	.3701		9.4
	.3740		9.5
3/8	.3750		9.52
	.3770	V	
	.3780		9.6
	.3819		9.7
	.3839		9.75
	.3858		9.8
	.3860	W	
	.3898		9.9
25/64	.3906		9.92
	.3937		10.0
	.3970	X	
	.4040	Y	
13/32	.4062		10.31
	.4130	Z	
	.4134		10.5
27/64	.4219		10.71

Inch	Decimal	mm
7/16	.4331	11.0
	.4375	11.11
	.4528	11.5
29/64	.4531	11.51
15/32	.4688	11.90
	.4724	12.0
31/64	.4844	12.30
	.4921	12.5
1/2	.5000	12.70
	.5118	13.0
33/64	.5156	13.09
17/32	.5312	13.49
	.5315	13.5
35/64	.5469	13.89
	.5512	14.0
9/16	.5625	14.28
	.5709	14.5
37/64	.5781	14.68
	.5906	15.0
19/32	.5938	15.08
39/64	.6094	15.47
	.6102	15.5
5/8	.6250	15.87
	.6299	16.0
41/64	.6406	16.27
	.6496	16.5
21/32	.6562	16.66
	.6693	17.0
43/64	.6719	17.06
11/16	.6875	17.46
	.6890	17.5
45/64	.7031	17.85
	.7087	18.0
23/32	.7188	18.25
	.7283	18.5
47/64	.7344	18.65
	.7480	19.0
3/4	.7500	19.05
49/64	.7656	19.44
	.7677	19.5
25/32	.7812	19.84
	.7874	20.0
51/64	.7969	20.24
	.8071	20.5
13/16	.8125	20.63
	.8268	21.0
53/64	.8281	21.03
27/32	.8438	21.43
	.8465	21.5
55/64	.8594	21.82
	.8661	22.0
7/8	.8750	22.22
	.8858	22.5
57/64	.8906	22.62
	.9055	23.0
29/32	.9062	23.01
59/64	.9219	23.41
	.9252	23.5
15/16	.9375	23.81
	.9449	24.0
61/64	.9531	24.2
	.9646	24.4
31/32	.9688	24.6
	.9843	25.0
63/64	.9844	25.0
1	1.0000	25.4

Index

Chilton's Repair & Tune-Up Guides

The Complete line covers domestic cars, imports, trucks, vans, RV's and 4-wheel drive vehicles.

RTUG Title	Part No.
AMC 1975-82	7199
Covers all U.S. and Canadian models	
Aspen/Volare 1976-80	6637
Covers all U.S. and Canadian models	
Audi 1970-73	5902
Covers all U.S. and Canadian models.	
Audi 4000/5000 1978-81	7028
Covers all U.S. and Canadian models including turbocharged and diesel engines	
Barracuda/Challenger 1965-72	5807
Covers all U.S. and Canadian models	
Blazer/Jimmy 1969-82	6931
Covers all U.S. and Canadian 2- and 4-wheel drive models, including diesel engines	
BMW 1970-82	6844
Covers U.S. and Canadian models	
Buick/Olds/Pontiac 1975-85	7308
Covers all U.S. and Canadian full size rear wheel drive models	
Cadillac 1967-84	7462
Covers all U.S. and Canadian rear wheel drive models	
Camaro 1967-81	6735
Covers all U.S. and Canadian models	
Camaro 1982-85	7317
Covers all U.S. and Canadian models	
Capri 1970-77	6695
Covers all U.S. and Canadian models	
Caravan/Voyager 1984-85	7482
Covers all U.S. and Canadian models	
Century/Regal 1975-85	7307
Covers all U.S. and Canadian rear wheel drive models, including turbocharged engines	
Champ/Arrow/Sapporo 1978-83	7041
Covers all U.S. and Canadian models	
Chevette/1000 1976-86	6836
Covers all U.S. and Canadian models	
Chevrolet 1968-85	7135
Covers all U.S. and Canadian models	
Chevrolet 1968-79 Spanish	7082
Chevrolet/GMC Pick-Ups 1970-82 Spanish	7468
Chevrolet/GMC Pick-Ups and Suburban 1970-86	6936
Covers all U.S. and Canadian $^1/_2$, $^3/_4$ and 1 ton models, including 4-wheel drive and diesel engines	
Chevrolet LUV 1972-81	6815
Covers all U.S. and Canadian models	
Chevrolet Mid-Size 1964-86	6840
Covers all U.S. and Canadian models of 1964-77 Chevelle, Malibu and Malibu SS; 1974-77 Laguna; 1978-85 Malibu; 1970-86 Monte Carlo; 1964-84 El Camino, including diesel engines	
Chevrolet Nova 1986	7658
Covers all U.S. and Canadian models	
Chevy/GMC Vans 1967-84	6930
Covers all U.S. and Canadian models of $^1/_2$, $^3/_4$, and 1 ton vans, cutaways, and motor home chassis, including diesel engines	
Chevy S-10 Blazer/GMC S-15 Jimmy 1982-85	7383
Covers all U.S. and Canadian models	
Chevy S-10/GMC S-15 Pick-Ups 1982-85	7310
Covers all U.S. and Canadian models	
Chevy II/Nova 1962-79	6841
Covers all U.S. and Canadian models	
Chrysler K- and E-Car 1981-85	7163
Covers all U.S. and Canadian front wheel drive models	
Colt/Challenger/Vista/Conquest 1971-85	7037
Covers all U.S. and Canadian models	
Corolla/Carina/Tercel/Starlet 1970-85	7036
Covers all U.S. and Canadian models	
Corona/Cressida/Crown/Mk.II/Camry/Van 1970-84	7044
Covers all U.S. and Canadian models	

RTUG Title	Part No.
Corvair 1960-69	6691
Covers all U.S. and Canadian models	
Corvette 1953-62	6576
Covers all U.S. and Canadian models	
Corvette 1963-84	6843
Covers all U.S. and Canadian models	
Cutlass 1970-85	6933
Covers all U.S. and Canadian models	
Dart/Demon 1968-76	6324
Covers all U.S. and Canadian models	
Datsun 1961-72	5790
Covers all U.S. and Canadian models of Nissan Patrol; 1500, 1600 and 2000 sports cars; Pick-Ups; 410, 411, 510, 1200 and 240Z	
Datsun 1973-80 Spanish	7083
Datsun/Nissan F-10, 310, Stanza, Pulsar 1977-86	7196
Covers all U.S. and Canadian models	
Datsun/Nissan Pick-Ups 1970-84	6816
Covers all U.S and Canadian models	
Datsun/Nissan Z & ZX 1970-86	6932
Covers all U.S. and Canadian models	
Datsun/Nissan 1200, 210, Sentra 1973-86	7197
Covers all U.S. and Canadian models	
Datsun/Nissan 200SX, 510, 610, 710, 810, Maxima 1973-84	7170
Covers all U.S. and Canadian models	
Dodge 1968-77	6554
Covers all U.S. and Canadian models	
Dodge Charger 1967-70	6486
Covers all U.S. and Canadian models	
Dodge/Plymouth Trucks 1967-84	7459
Covers all $^1/_2$, $^3/_4$, and 1 ton 2- and 4-wheel drive U.S. and Canadian models, including diesel engines	
Dodge/Plymouth Vans 1967-84	6934
Covers all $^1/_2$, $^3/_4$, and 1 ton U.S. and Canadian models of vans, cutaways and motor home chassis	
D-50/Arrow Pick-Up 1979-81	7032
Covers all U.S. and Canadian models	
Fairlane/Torino 1962-75	6320
Covers all U.S. and Canadian models	
Fairmont/Zephyr 1978-83	6965
Covers all U.S. and Canadian models	
Fiat 1969-81	7042
Covers all U.S. and Canadian models	
Fiesta 1978-80	6846
Covers all U.S. and Canadian models	
Firebird 1967-81	5996
Covers all U.S. and Canadian models	
Firebird 1982-85	7345
Covers all U.S. and Canadian models	
Ford 1968-79 Spanish	7084
Ford Bronco 1966-83	7140
Covers all U.S. and Canadian models	
Ford Bronco II 1984	7408
Covers all U.S. and Canadian models	
Ford Courier 1972-82	6983
Covers all U.S. and Canadian models	
Ford/Mercury Front Wheel Drive 1981-85	7055
Covers all U.S. and Canadian models Escort, EXP, Tempo, Lynx, LN-7 and Topaz	
Ford/Mercury/Lincoln 1968-85	6842
Covers all U.S. and Canadian models of FORD Country Sedan, Country Squire, Crown Victoria, Custom, Custom 500, Galaxie 500, LTD through 1982, Ranch Wagon, and XL; MERCURY Colony Park, Commuter, Marquis through 1982, Gran Marquis, Monterey and Park Lane; LINCOLN Continental and Towne Car	
Ford/Mercury/Lincoln Mid-Size 1971-85	6696
Covers all U.S. and Canadian models of FORD Elite, 1983-85 LTD, 1977-79 LTD II, Ranchero, Torino, Gran Torino, 1977-85 Thunderbird; MERCURY 1972-85 Cougar,	

continued on next page

RTUG Title	Part No.
1983-85 Marquis, Montego, 1980-85 XR-7; LINCOLN 1982-85 Continental, 1984-85 Mark VII, 1978-80 Versailles	
Ford Pick-Ups 1965-86 Covers all ¹/₂, ³/₄ and 1 ton, 2- and 4-wheel drive U.S. and Canadian pick-up, chassis cab and camper models, including diesel engines	6913
Ford Pick-Ups 1965-82 Spanish	7469
Ford Ranger 1983-84 Covers all U.S. and Canadian models	7338
Ford Vans 1961-86 Covers all U.S. and Canadian ¹/₂, ³/₄ and 1 ton van and cutaway chassis models, including diesel engines	6849
GM A-Body 1982-85 Covers all front wheel drive U.S. and Canadian models of BUICK Century, CHEVROLET Celebrity, OLDSMOBILE Cutlass Ciera and PONTIAC 6000	7309
GM C-Body 1985 Covers all front wheel drive U.S. and Canadian models of BUICK Electra Park Avenue and Electra T-Type, CADILLAC Fleetwood and deVille, OLDSMOBILE 98 Regency and Regency Brougham	7587
GM J-Car 1982-85 Covers all U.S. and Canadian models of BUICK Skyhawk, CHEVROLET Cavalier, CADILLAC Cimarron, OLDSMOBILE Firenza and PONTIAC 2000 and Sunbird	7059
GM N-Body 1985-86 Covers all U.S. and Canadian models of front wheel drive BUICK Somerset and Skylark, OLDSMOBILE Calais, and PONTIAC Grand Am	7657
GM X-Body 1980-85 Covers all U.S. and Canadian models of BUICK Skylark, CHEVROLET Citation, OLDSMOBILE Omega and PONTIAC Phoenix	7049
GM Subcompact 1971-80 Covers all U.S. and Canadian models of BUICK Skyhawk (1975-80), CHEVROLET Vega and Monza, OLDSMOBILE Starfire, and PONTIAC Astre and 1975-80 Sunbird	6935
Granada/Monarch 1975-82 Covers all U.S. and Canadian models	6937
Honda 1973-84 Covers all U.S. and Canadian models	6980
International Scout 1967-73 Covers all U.S. and Canadian models	5912
Jeep 1945-87 Covers all U.S. and Canadian CJ-2A, CJ-3A, CJ-3B, CJ-5, CJ-6, CJ-7, Scrambler and Wrangler models	6817
Jeep Wagoneer, Commando, Cherokee, Truck 1957-86 Covers all U.S. and Canadian models of Wagoneer, Cherokee, Grand Wagoneer, Jeepster, Jeepster Commando, J-100, J-200, J-300, J-10, J20, FC-150 and FC-170	6739
Laser/Daytona 1984-85 Covers all U.S. and Canadian models	7563
Maverick/Comet 1970-77 Covers all U.S. and Canadian models	6634
Mazda 1971-84 Covers all U.S. and Canadian models of RX-2, RX-3, RX-4, 808, 1300, 1600, Cosmo, GLC and 626	6981
Mazda Pick-Ups 1972-86 Covers all U.S. and Canadian models	7659
Mercedes-Benz 1959-70 Covers all U.S. and Canadian models	6065
Mercedes-Benz 1968-73 Covers all U.S. and Canadian models	5907

RTUG Title	Part No.
Mercedes-Benz 1974-84 Covers all U.S. and Canadian models	6809
Mitsubishi, Cordia, Tredia, Starion, Galant 1983-85 Covers all U.S. and Canadian models	7583
MG 1961-81 Covers all U.S. and Canadian models	6780
Mustang/Capri/Merkur 1979-85 Covers all U.S. and Canadian models	6963
Mustang/Cougar 1965-73 Covers all U.S. and Canadian models	6542
Mustang II 1974-78 Covers all U.S. and Canadian models	6812
Omni/Horizon/Rampage 1978-84 Covers all U.S. and Canadian models of DODGE omni, Miser, 024, Charger 2.2; PLYMOUTH Horizon, Miser, TC3, TC3 Tourismo; Rampage	6845
Opel 1971-75 Covers all U.S. and Canadian models	6575
Peugeot 1970-74 Covers all U.S. and Canadian models	5982
Pinto/Bobcat 1971-80 Covers all U.S. and Canadian models	7027
Plymouth 1968-76 Covers all U.S. and Canadian models	6552
Pontiac Fiero 1984-85 Covers all U.S. and Canadian models	7571
Pontiac Mid-Size 1974-83 Covers all U.S. and Canadian models of Ventura, Grand Am, LeMans, Grand LeMans, GTO, Phoenix, and Grand Prix	7346
Porsche 924/928 1976-81 Covers all U.S. and Canadian models	7048
Renault 1975-85 Covers all U.S. and Canadian models	7165
Roadrunner/Satellite/Belvedere/GTX 1968-73 Covers all U.S. and Canadian models	5821
RX-7 1979-81 Covers all U.S. and Canadian models	7031
SAAB 99 1969-75 Covers all U.S. and Canadian models	5988
SAAB 900 1979-85 Covers all U.S. and Canadian models	7572
Snowmobiles 1976-80 Covers Arctic Cat, John Deere, Kawasaki, Polaris, Ski-Doo and Yamaha	6978
Subaru 1970-84 Covers all U.S. and Canadian models	6982
Tempest/GTO/LeMans 1968-73 Covers all U.S. and Canadian models	5905
Toyota 1966-70 Covers all U.S. and Canadian models of Corona, MkII, Corolla, Crown, Land Cruiser, Stout and Hi-Lux	5795
Toyota 1970-79 Spanish	7467
Toyota Celica/Supra 1971-85 Covers all U.S. and Canadian models	7043
Toyota Trucks 1970-85 Covers all U.S. and Canadian models of pickups, Land Cruiser and 4Runner	7035
Valiant/Duster 1968-76 Covers all U.S. and Canadian models	6326
Volvo 1956-69 Covers all U.S. and Canadian models	6529
Volvo 1970-83 Covers all U.S. and Canadian models	7040
VW Front Wheel Drive 1974-85 Covers all U.S. and Canadian models	6962
VW 1949-71 Covers all U.S. and Canadian models	5796
VW 1970-79 Spanish	7081
VW 1970-81 Covers all U.S. and Canadian Beetles, Karmann Ghia, Fastback, Squareback, Vans, 411 and 412	6837

Chilton's Repair Manuals are available at your local retailer or by mailing a check or money order for **$15.95** per book plus **$3.50** for 1st book and **$.50** for each additional book to cover postage and handling to:

**Chilton Book Company
Dept. DM
Radnor, PA 19089**

NOTE: When ordering be sure to include your name & address, book part No. & title.